MW01253453

The Directors—
Take Two

The Directors—
Take Two
In Their Own Words

Robert J. Emery

New York

Copyright © 2000 by Media Entertainment, Inc.

All rights reserved. No part of this book may be reproduced in any form or by any means without permission in writing from the publishers, except by a reviewer who may quote brief passages in a review.

Library of Congress Cataloging-in-Publication Data

Emery, Robert J.
   The directors—take two : in their own words / [compiled by] Robert J. Emery.
      p. cm.
   Includes filmographies and indexes.
   ISBN 1-57500-129-2 (pbk.)
   1. Motion picture producers and directors—United States—Biography. I. Title.
PN1998.2.E49 1999
791.43'0233'092278—dc21
   [B]   99-043359
                                                                  CIP

Emmy® is a registered trademark of the National Academy of Television Arts and Sciences. Academy Awards® and Oscar® are registered trademarks and servicemarks of the Academy of Motion Picture Arts and Sciences.

Photos provided courtesy of Media Entertainment and the directors interviewed.

The publisher has made every effort to secure permission to reproduce copyrighted material and would like to apologize should there have been any errors or omissions.

TV Books, L.L.C.
1619 Broadway, Ninth Floor
New York, NY 10019
www.tvbooks.com

Interior design by Rachel Reiss.
Printed in Canada.

Contents

For Sue, Kevin, and Kelly

Note from the Author

The interviews contained in this book were conducted for the television series "The Directors" (Encore Movie Channel). A total of twenty-six episodes were produced, with thirteen additional shows presently in production as this book goes to press. Each one-hour episode features a single director along with guests and the extensive use of film clips from the director's movies. However, only about twenty-five minutes of each director's interview actually made it into the completed hour. It occurred to me that film enthusiasts, filmgoers as well as film students, should not be deprived of the opportunity to read and learn from what each of these outstanding directors had to say in his or her entire interview. This book, *The Directors— Take Two,* represents the second group of thirteen directors. The first volume, *The Directors—Take One,* has already been released.

As I stated in the first book, movies are magic and the directors who make them are magical. They bring to each of their films a vision that they want to share with their audience. It is a rare gift because not all directors are created equal. Some make one or two films and are never heard from again. Others, like those presented here, are members of an exclusive club. Their talent never seems to wane. They may stumble from time to time, but their overall bodies of work stand as tribute to their abilities to tell amazing stories on film. Lucky for us.

As I did in *Take One,* I wish to again thank my dear friend Milt Felsen who was so instrumental in helping get the original television project off the ground. The ongoing support of the American Film Institute is also very much appreciated, as is the effort of everyone on my staff, who worked tirelessly on the project. There are at least four dozen Hollywood agents, public relations professionals, and personal assistants who came to our aid in procuring guests and for that I am grateful.

Needless to say, without the kind cooperation of the directors interviewed there would not have been a series to begin with. I sincerely thank all of the wonderfully talented directors who participated and gave of their valuable time and shared with us many of their secrets of success.

In transcribing the on-camera interviews into this book some editing was necessary. However, I have retained as much of the original interviews as possible.

Robert J. Emery

The Directors—
Take Two

The Films of Rob Reiner

Born in New York, the son of actor/writer/director Carl Reiner, Rob Reiner comes from an entertainment-oriented family. He spent two years at the University of California, during which time he formed, along with Richard Dreyfuss, an improvisational company called The Session.

At the age of twenty-one he joined Steve Martin on the writing team of the television show *The Smothers Brothers Comedy Hour.* Other appearances of note made early on in his career include small roles in programs such as *Batman* and *The Odd Couple,* and his involvement in another improvisation group, The Committee, where he met his first wife, Penny Marshall.

In 1971 he joined the cast of *All in the Family* as Mike "Meathead" Stivic, a role for which he received two Emmy awards. In the 1980s he began to concentrate on directing. During the filming of *When Harry Met Sally* he met and married his current wife, Michele Singer.

Rob Reiner's movies have one thing in common. They are not only good movies but they make money. Lots of money. He possesses an uncanny understanding of popular tastes, and for this reason has managed to outdistance his colleagues and critics to emerge as one of the most respected directors working in Hollywood.

> *The thing about Rob is that he comes in knowing exactly what it is that he wants with the day's work. And he is very clear to everyone who is there about what needs to get done in the course of a day. So by the time everyone comes in, it's like, bam, bam, bam. Let's work. Let's get done. And he's just very, very skilled in that way.*
>
> *Kevin Bacon—Actor*

The Conversation

I was born in the Bronx in New York. We moved to New Rochelle when I was about eight years old and we lived there for about five and half years. Then we moved to California when I was about twelve and a half so I kind of had three different kinds of growing up experiences. It was very normal in my mind. Because, you know, growing up as a kid you don't think that your household is any different from anybody else's household. You just assume that this is the way everybody lives.

My father went to work every day, came home at night. The fact that his work was in front of millions of people on Saturday night made it a little different but I mean basically he was a regular guy. He came home every day from work. We had summer vacations together because he had a wonderful schedule. He would work thirty-nine weeks and he'd have thirteen weeks off. And in those thirteen weeks, which coincided with school summer vacation, we'd go off to Fire Island or wherever we'd have our vacation. So we had a very normal upbringing.

But the people that visited my house were Mel Brooks and Sid Caesar and Neil Simon and Norman Lear and Larry Gelbart. I just figured that that was normal. I didn't realize until I started visiting other people's houses that it wasn't quite as funny in other people's houses as it was in mine. But I just thought it was a typical childhood.

I liked to play sports when I was a kid growing up but I never felt comfortable around the jock mentality. There was a dullness to their way of thinking. And it wasn't until, and this may sound strange because my father was in show business, but I didn't really get drawn into theater or into acting until I was seventeen years old.

I became interested in my senior year in high school when I auditioned for the school play. There was a drama class that I was taking and then I auditioned for the school play and all of a sudden I felt comfortable around a group of people. There was a group of people speaking my language, people that sounded very familiar to me in the way they approached life and based on what I had experienced at home growing up. So that's what made me think this is something that I want to do for a living.

There's no question that I learned from my father. I learned from my father, I learned from Sid Caesar, and I learned from Norman Lear and Mel Brooks, the people that I was exposed to. You can't help but take in some of that if you're interested, and I was interested, so I was able to take this all in by osmosis.

My first acting job was in school. I played a policeman, a very small part in the school production of *Carousel*. I had about five lines in the show. I had a little scene with Albert Brooks who played the owner of the mill that all the girls in *Carousel* were working at. And he said, "Good evening, Timoney." And I said, "Good evening, Mister Baskum." And he said, "Nice night." I went, "'Deed it is." And then I said, "Say, Mister Baskum, is that one of your girls?" It wasn't very complicated. That was my first performance.

Then professionally, I did summer theater. I did summer theater two years in a row. One was the summer of 1964. I was an apprentice. I built scenery and painted scenery, and built sets, and basically, I didn't get to act, but then the second year, in Plymouth, Massachusetts, in 1965, I was a member of a resident company and then I got to act in a number of plays. And the first play I think I did was *Mary, Mary*. I played Bob. The guy's about forty years old. I was eighteen at the time. You know, with the corn-starch in the hair and the lines in the forehead and all that. And I did about five or six plays that year in summer theater.

One of the plays I did was *Enter Laughing*, which was a play based on my father's book that had been made into a Broadway show that Alan Arkin had starred in. I played the part that was essentially a semi-autobiographical character that my father had written about himself. I did the part and got very good reviews. My father came to see it. He wasn't very impressed. I kind of sensed that he didn't love it, but he never really let me know and I didn't find out until later in life that he thought I basically stunk, but I somehow pursued it anyway and I'm here today.

How He Snagged the Role in *All in the Family*

The part of Michael Stivic is interesting because Norman Lear did three pilots. Two of them were for ABC, and they made those shows with two other sets of Mike and Glorias. It wasn't Sally Struthers and myself. Neither of those pilots sold. ABC dropped the show and CBS picked it up and then they were recasting it a third time. And as I recall, I actually auditioned for it during one of the ABC pilots and I didn't get the part.

Then I auditioned again for CBS and I eventually got the part. I had been writing for a show called *The Headmaster,* which was an Andy Griffith show. I wrote five or six episodes and in one of the shows I played a young English teacher who falls in love with one of the students. I showed Norman this little show that I had done and he was kind of impressed with it. Of course he knew me from the time I was eight or nine years old. I used to play with his daughter on Fire Island. We used to play jacks together. And he reminds me of a story which even I don't remember. Apparently I was playing jacks and I was very funny. I had funny ways of cheating at jacks or something and he told my father that he thought I was really funny. My father said, "What are you talking about? This kid is sullen, he's brooding, and he's not funny. He sits in a corner by himself, he doesn't talk." My father couldn't see it. Sometimes other people can see you more clearly than your parents. But at any rate, Norman had me audition again for *All in the Family* and I got the part the third time.

People still refer to me as Meathead, but there's nothing I can do about it even if it did bother me. It will follow me for the rest of my life. I've often joked that if I win the Nobel Prize the headlines will say, "Meathead Wins Nobel." It won't matter what I do or what I accomplish. People still remember that show. It made such an impression on people. They loved the character. The odd thing that I've always found about being stuck with that name was that it branded my character as an ignorant person. It's an ignorant guy calling me Meathead and yet the public accepts that that was the truth. They never questioned the source of the nomenclature. They just said, okay, well, we just accept he's a meathead.

I'd been interested in directing since I was about nineteen. I directed my own improvisational theater group that I also acted in. Richard Dreyfuss was a part of it as well as my friend, Larry Bishop, who I went to high school and college with. And I also directed some local theater in Los Angeles. I did a production of *No Exit.* I ran acting classes when I was nineteen, twenty years old. So this was something I was always interested in even before *All in the Family.* When I got *All in the Family,* I thought it would never last because it was too hard-hitting. It'll go off after thirteen weeks and I'll go back to doing what I'm most interested in doing, which was writing and directing.

Well, eight years later, I'm still on the show and it kind of pushed back the start of my directing career a little bit, but I don't regret it because it was a tremendous learning experience for me. The fact that we were doing a live show in front of an audience every week, and I got a sense of what played for an audience, what didn't play; the structure of scenes, the structure of a show. Because it was like a little two-act play that we put on every week. It was a tremendous learning experience for me and I was allowed tremendous creative freedom.

Because I thought like a writer and director, I had tremendous input on the scripts. When we found ourselves in trouble and couldn't figure out how to stage a scene, they often would listen to me in terms of staging a particular scene or a joke. I wanted to be a director all during that period because as an actor, the main thing you're supposed to be doing is concentrating on your part and relating to the people you're in the scene with. Well, when I was acting, I'm not only doing my part; I'm watching all the other actors on the stage. I'm aware of what the audience is doing, I'm also aware of what the camera is doing. These are not particularly good qualities for an actor, but they're very good for a director.

After I finished *All in the Family* I made a decision to go in that direction. It was difficult for me. Nowadays you see everybody making the transition from television to movies. Everybody who's in television who's made a name for themselves can make an easy transition to movies. But when I was finishing *All in the Family,* if you were thought of as a television actor, a sitcom actor, you were a pariah as far as movies were concerned. That's the way it was in those days. So for me to make that transition was very difficult. People were throwing a lot of money at me to do a spin-off with Mike and Gloria. At the time I actually needed the money. I was going through a divorce and I didn't have a lot of money. But I thought, "If I do this, I'm never going to become a film director."

This Is Spinal Tap (1984)
Rob Reiner; Kimberly Stringer; Chazz Domingueza; Shari Hall; R.J. Parnell; David Kaff; Tony Hendra; Michael McKean; Christopher Guest; Harry Shearer; Bruno Kirby; Jean Cromie; Patrick Maher; Ed Begley Jr.; Danny Kortchmar.

I got involved with some of my friends who I had worked with in the past and we put together the idea for *Spinal Tap.* We made a short film, which was about twenty minutes long, kind of a demonstration film to show what the movie was going to be about. It took me about four years from the time we started creating the idea to get it into the movie theaters. It was quite a process for me. Even with my name and all that, it was very, very difficult to get the project off the ground.

My first day on *Spinal Tap* as a director I was a nervous wreck because not only had I never done this before but we didn't have a script. *Spinal Tap* was done as a mock documentary. There was no script ever. We had a basic story outline about eight pages long of what the film was going to be but we never really worked out the scenes and what was going to happen in the scenes. So it was a little bit intimidating and overwhelming. But I had studied improvisational theater and that was my background so basically I said, "Let's just dive in and let's see what happens."

We knew what we wanted to occur in any particular scene. Based on what I saw developing I would make decisions of what we would cut and what things we could move around. Then we'd do it again. I basically reinvented the wheel because what you do when you make a traditional film is you get your master and then you get your coverage, whatever pieces you want to cover in a scene, and then you edit it all together. With this, since there was no script, I would just let them go. I'd restructure the scene and then I'd shoot it again, then I'd shoot it a third and fourth time. There's no continuity like in a normal film. There's people jumping all over the set and the continuity is all over the place. But it didn't seem to matter because the whole flavor of the film was documentary.

The nature of *Spinal Tap* dictated that we do it documentary style. We were sending up rock 'n' roll documentaries. We were making fun of *Let It Be* and all those documentaries we had viewed in preparation for making our film. If we scripted *Spinal Tap* it wouldn't feel like a documentary.

We had such a small budget that one day we had six hundred extras. And those six hundred extras were going to be used to create five different rock 'n' roll venues. We were going to change the costumes, we were going to change the scenery, we were going to move the people around—and we had one day to do all that. And those five venues were going to be spread throughout the film. It took us eighteen hours to shoot all that. So we literally had an eighteen-hour shooting day. It was more than that. It was twenty-one hours. I went until three the next morning. And then I went home and went to sleep. I got up four hours later. I woke up and I sat on the side of my bed and I started crying. I was so tired and so exhausted. At that time I was going through a lot of emotional things in my life and I just started crying. I said, "I can't do this anymore."

This woman that was my assistant on this picture, she just sat down next to me. I'll never forget it and I'll never forget her help and I thank her to this day. She put her arm around me and she said, "You can do it. You can do it. Just get up and put one foot in front of the other. You can do it." And I went out and we shot the scene at Magic Mountain where they get billing underneath the puppet show. I remember that specifically. Plus, we laughed our asses off. We just laughed all the time making the show. It was great.

His whole working style is to create an atmosphere in which actors can work and thrive. And he wants them to take chances. He just basically will do anything to get you to where he wants you to be.

John Cusack—Actor

The Sure Thing (1985)

John Cusack; Daphne Zuniga; Anthony Edwards; Boyd Gaines; Tim Robbins; Lisa Jane Persky; Viveca Lindfors; Nicolette Sheridan; Marcia Christie; Robert Anthony Marcucci; Sarah Buxton; Lorrie Lightle; Joshua Cadman; Krystal Richards; John Putch.

A lot of people have said *The Sure Thing* was like a teenage version of *It Happened One Night*. It's hard to believe but at that point I'd never seen that movie. I've subsequently seen it and the only thing that's comparable to me is that it's on the road and the two people who don't particularly like each other fall in love.

The only thing that I ever shoot for is to try to be as good as I can be at the time. You may look back on something you've done ten, twelve years ago and say, "Well, that's not as good as I can do now." And it's really irrelevant. The only thing you can go by is whether this as good as you can do at the time you're doing it. And I felt when I finished *The Sure Thing*, it was as good as I could do at that time.

Being an actor makes it a little easier to direct actors because you do have an understanding of what they're going through and the problems that they have. I always act the scenes out for myself as I'm writing them, so that when we get into rehearsal or shooting, I'm never asking an actor to do something that I can't do. I'm never asking him to make a transition that I can't make in a scene. But if they're struggling with a transition or with a moment, I can act it out for them. I can show them what needs to happen.

There's music to every scene. And I have a sense of orchestrating a scene when something's supposed to go up or come down. Especially with comedy, which is all very rhythmic, and you have to have the right emphasis and you have to have the right rhythms to make the jokes work. I have a sense for that. So I can give them that. I can show them that. And then they make up their own.

If you look at *The Sure Thing*, there's a scene where John Cusack is trying to defuse this truck driver who's picked up Daphne Zuniga because he gets the sense that he may be picking her up for nefarious reasons. He jumps in the truck and defuses the situation by acting crazy. And I said to him, "You've got to really go full bore on this. It doesn't work unless the guy is so petrified of you doing something to him that he's willing to let Daphne go." The first few times he did it in a very subtle way and I said, "No, this is what I want," and I acted it out for him. I did it for him. And then he did it. But he did it his own way.

A lot of directors can't act so they don't have that tool to show an actor what they want them to do. I have that tool. Some actors don't like to hear it because they don't want to get your sound in their head. Some ask you to not give them a line read. But I find that most actors don't mind because they're going to find a way to make it their own. It's just a tool. I'm not telling them they have to do it a certain way, but I show them the essence of what I want from them. I showed it to John, and he did it.

Stand by Me (1986)

Wil Wheaton; River Phoenix; Corey Feldman; Jerry O'Connell; Kiefer Sutherland; Casey Siemaszko; Gary Riley; Bradley Gregg; Jason Oliver; Marshall Bell; Lee McCain; Bruce Kirby; William Bronder; Scott Beach; Richard Dreyfuss.

Well, *Stand by Me,* and I've said this in many interviews before, is the most important film I've made in my life. At the time I took on the project it was being developed by a couple of friends of mine for Adrian Lyne to direct. He had just finished making a movie called *9½ Weeks,* and I think he wanted to take about six months off and he didn't want to direct. So they were now looking for someone else and they gave me the script and said, "There's something missing in this film and we can't figure out what it is." They didn't give it to me to direct; they gave it to me as a friend in the hope that I could figure out how to make the film work. And I thought, boy, it's very literate. The characters were very well drawn, but it lacked focus. I said to them, "This is something that appeals to me. The tone of this thing is completely in sync with my tone and the way I look at life and the way I feel about theater, which is there's a humor and a drama to everything." It had the right kind of blend of those two things. I told them I'd be interested in taking it on.

At the time I didn't know what the focus of the film was going to be. I made a deal to do it and I still didn't know what the film was going to be about. It wasn't until I figured out the character of Gordie that I said, "Okay, it's going to be about Gordie's character and he's going to be the main focus of this film and I can push my own personality and my own feelings and thoughts through Gordie and make it his rite of passage," and it became my rite of passage. Even though I was in my thirties at the time I felt that I was taking the first step in breaking away from my father in a very significant way. *Spinal Tap,* even though it might not have been a film that my father would make, was satire. And my father was steeped in satire. I was raised in it with *Your Show of Shows.* My father did a thing called "The Three Hair Cuts," which was a take-off of a rock 'n' roll group back in the fifties. So there was a connection there for me. *The Sure Thing* was a romantic comedy. My father had made a number of romantic comedies.

The fact is that the tone of *Stand by Me* was so different from anything my father would have done and was so connected to my own personality and what I felt was the kind of film that I wanted to do. It was the seminal film for me that allowed me to differentiate myself from my father.

The stars of *Stand by Me* are four twelve-year-old boys. We went through a very extensive process of auditioning and wound up with the four that we did. Interestingly enough, Corey Feldman, who played Teddy, had the anger and the rage at an early age that he was able to project. He's had some difficulties in his life. He's overcome those difficulties, but at the time he was struggling with a lot of problems and those things came out in his performance.

River Phoenix was just a natural. He came in there and just blew us away and knocked us out. He was like another James Dean, a natural, gifted actor. It's kind of ironic that he was the peacemaker in the film. In life he was a very gentle soul. It's ironic that at the end of the film, the character that he plays, Chris Chambers, walks off at the end and he disappears out of the frame. He goes away. It's kind of strange and sad.

The reason we picked the name "Castle Rock" as the name of our production company was not because it was the name of the town in *Stand by Me* and in other Stephen King books, but because the film had such a resonance for me and was so important to me in my life. Plus we liked the name. It's a strong name.

The Princess Bride (1987)
Cary Elwes; Mandy Patinkin; Chris Sarandon; Christopher Guest;
Wallace Shawn; André the Giant; Fred Savage; Robin Wright; Peter Falk;
Peter Cook; Mel Smith; Carol Kane; Billy Crystal; Anne Dyson; Margery Mason.

The Princess Bride is based on a book by William Goldman. I read virtually every book he had ever written, from *Temple of Gold* to *Boys and Girls Together* to *Marathon Man.*

The Princess Bride was originally sent to my father. My father directed a play on Broadway called *Something Different.* Bill Goldman wrote a book about one season on Broadway and called it *The Season.* In it he talked about all the plays that opened that particular year on Broadway. He interviewed my dad about *Something Different,* and they kind of struck up a relationship. When Bill finished *The Princess Bride* he sent it to my father as somebody who might be interested in making it into a film.

My father, knowing I was a huge fan of Goldman's, sent it to *me* as somebody who might be interested in making it into a film. I was completely floored by it. It was funny; it was satirical; it's a great, wonderful adventure story. This was written for me, I thought.

Now ten, twelve years go by. I've made a couple of pictures and I'm sitting around thinking that people make movies out of books. What can I make a movie out of? What's my favorite book of all time? *The Princess Bride!* I hadn't read it in years. I read it and I was still thrilled by it. Andy Scheinman read it and thought it was sensational. And then, like a naive idiot, I thought I could call William Goldman up and maybe he'd let me direct the film.

I called William Goldman's agent and asked if Goldman would be willing to meet with me to talk about it. Goldman said he wanted to screen *Spinal Tap* since it was now out. So he took a look at that. I had just finished *The Sure Thing.* It was not yet in the theaters and it was a rough-cut. It wasn't even finished being scored or mixed or anything but I sent him that, too. He looked at those films and then agreed to meet with us.

Basically, I had to audition for him. I went with Andy Scheinman to Goldman's apartment on East 71st street in New York. We walked into his house and the first thing he met us with at the door was, "*The Princess Bride* is the favorite thing I've ever written in my life. It's my baby. I want it on my tomb-stone. What are you going to do with it?" It was like, oh, god! I mean, it was basically, oh, my god, I don't want to destroy his baby! There had been scripts written and I had read the latest version, which was about a hundred and fifty pages and deviated considerably from the book. My thought was to be more faithful to the book and that's what I told him. I wasn't doing it just to sell him.

After a while he got up and went to the kitchen to get something to drink. I just sat there with Andy not knowing what Goldman was really thinking about all of this. Then he comes back from the kitchen and he says, in a high voice like actor Andy Devine, "Well, I think it's just going great. I'm just so thrilled." And then for the next couple of hours we took notes for changes he was going to make.

When Andy and I left the apartment we were walking down Park Avenue ten feet off the ground. We were just flying. We couldn't believe it. This man, my idol and a guy I had admired so much, was allowing me to make *The Princess Bride!*

Norman Lear agreed to let us do it. We struggled to get the financing together but we finally got sixteen million bucks together and we went to England and made the picture.

Oddly enough, the greatest appeal that it ever had in all the early screenings was for the teenagers. But, for whatever reason, we could never get one teenager to come to the movie theater when it came out. Maybe the title was too soft and sounded like some kind of soft, girly fairy tale. But when we prescreened it, the biggest response was from teenagers. It's out on videotape, of course, and people have caught onto it because of that. But it's like I've always said, you never meet anybody who voted for Richard Nixon and you can't meet anybody who doesn't think *Spinal Tap* is great, even though we got crucified by the critics when it came out. But, somebody voted for Nixon. He got elected. And some-body didn't come to the theater because we didn't make money on *Spinal Tap.* It's the same case with *The Princess Bride.* There's a cult following and as the years go by people just pick up on it. It's a film you can watch with your kid and not be bored. If you went by yourself and didn't bring your kid, you'd still have a great time.

I'm going to tell you a great story about Inigo Montoya's famous line, "My name is Inigo Montoya. You killed my father. Prepare to die."

I went to dinner one night many years ago with Nora Ephron, who wrote *When Harry Met Sally,* and Nick Pellegi, who wrote *Goodfellas.* They took me to this restaurant that was frequented by John Gotti. Gotti supposedly came to this restaurant every Thursday night. Sure enough, at eight o'clock in walks John Gotti with a bunch of wiseguys and they sit down at a nearby table. Now, we finish the meal, and I walk outside and there's John Gotti's limo and this guy that looks like Luca Brasi from *The Godfather* is standing there. He looks at me and he goes, "Prepare to die." Oh, god! I almost went in my pants. He says, "I seen the *Princess Bride*. Great movie, great movie!" He was quoting a line from *The Princess Bride*. I thought he was going to kill me. That line is thrown at me quite a bit.

A Self-Assessment

Where I am as a filmmaker is for the world to assess. I'm just doing the kinds of things that appeal to me. They're certainly an eclectic group of films. You could put *Spinal Tap* and *Princess Bride* together because they're both satirical. But then you've got a pure romantic comedy in *The Sure Thing* and then you've got rite-of-passage kind of drama in *Stand by Me,* which is very different from the earlier two. *When Harry Met Sally* is a grown-up version of *The Sure Thing*. It's taking characters and making them more adult, with more adult themes and the discussions being more adult and it being more a true extension of my own personal experiences. But still, it's a romantic comedy. The genre is something that I've dealt with in my life. Then you got *Misery*. I took a big turn there. People ask me why I chose that film *Misery*—it seemed so uncharacteristic of me. And I tell people that the genre is uncharacteristic, but the theme of it is something that I connect with very deeply as an artist. I knew what that character in *Misery* felt like, how an artist is able to grow and what difficulties he faces in growing. I'm trying to break away from a stereotypical perception of me by the audience. That happened to me with *All in the Family* and it was very hard for me to make the break and become a filmmaker.

When Harry Met Sally (1989)

Billy Crystal; Meg Ryan; Carrie Fisher; Bruno Kirby; Steven Ford;
Lisa Jane Persky; Michelle Nicastro; Gretchen Palmer; Robert Alan Beuth;
David Burdick; Joe Viviani; Harley Jane Kozak; Joseph Hunt; Kevin Rooney; Franc Luz.

When Harry Met Sally was basically an extension of my personal experiences. I had met with Nora Ephron about another project that she wasn't so interested in. Then I told her that I had been trying to put to-gether a different project about someone who had been married, then is thrown back into the dating world and has trouble relating to the op-posite sex. It's something that I'd been going through for years and mak-ing a mess out of.

I certainly was not ready to get deeply involved with a woman. But at the same time you are a man and you have needs and you want contact with women. But the question is, can you be friends and not have sex? Did sex always have to come into the equation, and if it did could you still remain friends and not be totally committed? These were all questions that I had. I was totally confused. I thought this was all good fodder for a film. There had to be a lot of people like me going through this.

That's what I started with. Then I would sit with Nora and I'd tell her my experiences and we'd put those thoughts into the script. I knew that I had to work with a woman because I could only guess what women's experiences were, but I certainly couldn't know for sure. Andy Shein-man was a producer on the project but he helped us write it too. And then when Billy Crystal came on he added a lot to the script. It was re-ally a big collaboration. Just a big soup, throwing in ideas about men and women.

For instance, I would tell Nora things like the scene in the airplane where Billy explains to Meg what a man feels like after having sex. He's done. He's ready to go. He's finished. A woman, on the other hand, wants to spend all night, but a man is ready to go immediately. Men feel that way until they find the woman that they love and want to stay with them. We needed the equivalent of that kind of exposure and revelation and that kind of personal experience. But we needed that from a woman's point of view. Then Nora brought up the idea of women faking orgasms. The vast major-ity of women have faked orgasms at one point or another in their lives. And I said, "No, that's not possible because it never happened with me. I would know." And Nora said, "You don't know when it happens." I didn't believe it and I actually did my little survey around the Castle Rock office. And sure enough, there was well over 50 percent of the women who said that at one point or another they had faked an orgasm. So we put that into the film. And if you remember, it gave my mother the best line in the movie when she says, "I'll have what she's having."

The part called for an older Jewish woman. My mother had been doing little bits of acting jobs and I thought she'd be perfect. She's an older Jewish lady and she looks right, so I cast her. I didn't think at the time that I would be directing a scene and showing an actress, in this case Meg Ryan, how to have an orgasm.

By the way, when it came time to shoot Meg was very nervous about doing the scene, but she's the one that said she could do it in the first place. And she's the one that suggested we do it in an incongruous place like a deli. That was her idea. But the first couple of times we did it she was a little hesitant because it was embarrassing. She was exposing the sounds that she makes. She didn't want people to know about that. So she did it a little hesitantly the first couple of times. I said, "No, it's got to be this way," and I acted it out for her. Then I realized my mother was sitting there while I was doing this. It was unbelievably embarrassing.

A Bit of Hitchcock

I have a little game that I play with myself. I put something from one of my previous films in every new film that I do. In *The Sure Thing*, in John Cusack's dorm room there's a *Spinal Tap* poster in the background. In *Stand by Me* the character Chris Chambers thanks some guys for the ride and he says, "sure thing." Then, in *The Princess Bride*, I've got the cap that I wore in *Spinal Tap* hanging from the lamp in the little boy's room. In *When Harry Met Sally* I have Billy reading *Misery*, which I knew I was going to do next. In *Misery*, the Sheriff goes into this little general store and walks past a rack of videos and there's a video of *When Harry Met Sally*. In *A Few Good Men* I took some of the books that Paul Sheldon wrote in *Misery* and stuck them in Tom Cruise's apartment. Then in *North*. [*Pauses.*] I can't remember that one. In *The American President* I put the book *North* in the little girl's room in the White House. In *Ghosts of Mississippi* I have a couple of things from *The American President*, but I cut the scene out. Anyway, it's my version of Hitchcock. I don't appear in the films, but artifacts from other films do.

> *He doesn't put himself in a slot. He's able to branch out and direct all kinds of movies. He's a rare, rare director, actually. He doesn't go for the same stereotypical thing.*
>
> Lauren Bacall—Actress

Misery (1990)

James Caan; Kathy Bates; Richard Farnsworth; Frances Sternhagen; Lauren Bacall; Graham Jarvis; Jerry Potter; Thomas Brunelle; June Christopher; Julie Payne; Archie Hahn III; Gregory Snegoff; Wendy Bowers.

What attracted me to *Misery* was the theme of it—an artist trying to break out of a creative rut that he had fallen into as a result of his success. He wanted to grow and break away but couldn't because his fans demanded he keep doing the thing they loved. The personification of those fans was Annie Wilkes.

I worked so hard on *Misery* to plug all the plot holes and to make sure that it was seamless. It's because of what Hitchcock used to refer to as re-frigerator logic. He would talk about making a thriller or a movie that might have had some holes in it but the audience wouldn't detect them until three o'clock in the morning when they got up to get something to eat. Standing by the refrigerator they would think, "Hey, wait a minute, how could that guy have . . ." and it hits you at that point. But by then they've already left the theater and they've already enjoyed the film. But Hitchcock didn't have to withstand the scrutiny of videotape and television. So I was vigilant in trying to plug up all the plot holes.

And at one point Warren Beatty, who was considering doing the film, worked with me for a couple of months on the script and he kept press-ing me on plot points. I told him that the audience wouldn't notice but he kept pressing me to plug up the holes. And I did. So whatever you want to think about the film, whether you like it or you don't like it, there's nothing wrong with it. There's nothing where you can say, hey, that's not possible, that couldn't have happened. If you look at Hitch-cock's films, as great as they are, there are big, big plot holes in virtually every film he made.

A perfect example is in *Psycho*. Here's this woman who's just stolen forty thousand dollars from this institution. She gets in the car to go meet the love of her life, John Gavin. It gets dark and it starts to rain. She drives off the highway and pulls into the Bates Motel. Anthony Perkins asks where she's headed. She tells him the name of the town and he tells her it's only thirteen miles up the road. If you're Janet Leigh, you say thank you and you get back in your car and you drive the thirteen miles. Now, all Perkins had to do was say it was a hundred eighty miles up the road. So then you can say all right, she's tired, it's night, it's raining. She just wants to get a night's sleep. But you can't make that argument for thirteen miles.

So if she drives those thirteen miles you don't have [*makes stabbing motion and hums music from the picture*], but she didn't drive the thirteen miles and you do have [*stabbing noise*] and one of the classic thrillers of all time. But the audience didn't question it. I'm sorry to ruin it for you.

Now, back to *Misery*. Kathy Bates was my first choice for the character of Annie Wilkes. As a matter of fact, Bill Goldman suggested her. Nobody knew who she was, but *I* knew who she was. I'd seen her on stage a number of times and I knew she was perfect for the part. James Caan, to be totally honest, was not the first person I thought of. I went for Harrison Ford, Michael Douglas, Kevin Kline, Richard Dreyfuss, and William Hurt, and got turned down by all of them. William Hurt turned me down twice.

Then somebody suggested James Caan. At that time Jimmy had a lot of problems with substance abuse and he had gotten a reputation of being difficult to work with. But a lot of people told me that he had cleaned up his act and had gotten himself together. I thought, he's a great actor and it would be really interesting to have someone as physical as James Caan restricted to that bed and how frustrating that would be for him, that it would come through in his performance. So he became Paul Sheldon and I can't imagine anybody else playing that part. The fact that Jimmy is a physical guy became an asset to us because he was so frustrated being in that bed. Every day on the set I would say to him, "Okay, Jimmy, in today's scene I want you to get into bed." It got to be a daily joke.

It's difficult to work in a confined space. We were very aware of the possibility that the bedroom could get claustrophobic. Even though 75 percent of the film takes place in that bedroom it is laced with outside scenes. We have the sheriff tracking the case and trying to determine what happened to Paul Sheldon. But I've got to tell you, when we were shooting the film we were in that bedroom so long that when Paul Sheldon is able to pick the lock and get out into the hallway the whole crew was like, wow, we're in the hallway! It was like kids being let out to the playground for recess. Yeah, the hallway! The hallway was more cramped than the bedroom but it was a different location so we were all excited.

A Few Good Men (1992)

Tom Cruise; Jack Nicholson; Demi Moore; Kevin Bacon; Kiefer Sutherland;
Kevin Pollak; James Marshall; J.T. Walsh; Christopher Guest; J.A. Preston;
Matt Craven; Wolfgang Bodison; Xander Berkeley; John M. Jackson;
Noah Wyle; Cuba Gooding, Jr.

A Few Good Men was in development at TriStar. Aaron Sorkin, the author of the play the movie was based on, had written a draft for them. We were looking for a writer on a project called *Malice,* a thriller that Alec Baldwin and Nicole Kidman eventually starred in. A writing sample was sent to us and it was Aaron's play, *A Few Good Men.* A couple of people in the company read it and suggested I go see the play. I thought it was really powerful. I hooked into it because it's about a guy who's trying to extricate himself from the shadow of his father. I could relate to that and it was also a strong story. I suggested we try to get the rights from TriStar and develop it as a film.

With the strong cast we had you would have thought there were a lot of strong egos on that movie. But I'm a very strong-willed person. I'm physically big and I command some attention on the set so there's not a lot of acting out around me. Secondly, and most important, was Tom Cruise and Jack Nicholson. Tom Cruise is the consummate professional. So is Jack Nicholson. Tom Cruise comes to work to do his job. It's not about ego. He had respect for the material that we were doing. With Jack Nicholson you have a veteran actor that everybody looks up to. When he walked into the first day of rehearsal and sat down and was prepared and gave a full out performance, it sent a message very quickly to everybody there, especially the younger actors, that we were not screwing around. He set the tone. It's like a ball team that comes out to batting practice. Everybody gets in the cage and gets their seven swings and everybody's doing what they're supposed to do. Then Babe Ruth steps in the cage. And this is Jack Nicholson. And he starts hitting them into the upper deck. This is the first reading and he's hitting them into the upper deck. You're kind of in awe. So it says to everybody, no fooling around. We're going to do our work here. And that set the tone and we never had any ego problems.

North (1994)

Elijah Wood; Jason Alexander; Julia Louis-Dreyfus; Marc Shaiman;
Jussie Smollett; Taylor Fry; Alana Austin; Peg Shirley; Chuck Cooper;
Alan Zweibel; Donavon Dietz; Teddy Bergman; Michael Cipriani; Joran Corneal;
Joshua Kaplan; Alan Arkin; Dan Aykroyd; Reba McEntire; Bruce Willis.

It's funny you say *North* was a bump in the road of my career because up until then I had such critical success and then I made a film that people kind of dismissed. It got bad reviews and it didn't do business. I remember I had lunch with John Travolta when he was in the doldrums. I mean, he was, as they say, box office poison. He said to me something so great. He said, "I wasn't that good, and I'm not this bad." And it resonated for me because it was like they build you up so big and then they tear you down. And the fact is you weren't that good and you're not this bad. And if you look at *North*, it's not that bad. Some of the funniest things I've ever done in a movie are in that movie. It's a slight little fable. Because of the fact that I had done *When Harry Met Sally, Misery,* and *A Few Good Men,* everyone was expecting me to give them another big movie. Well, I didn't and everyone said, "What's the matter?" I said, "Well, nothing's the matter. I wasn't that good, and this isn't that bad."

You have to take it all with a grain of salt. I know why I wanted to make that movie and I did what I wanted to do with it. You have to think of things in terms of a body of work, you know. When you finish your work, you step back and look at it and say, "Here's my body of work." And I don't think there's a filmmaker that doesn't have what's either regarded as a clinker or stinker, or for that matter a few of them. And I'm sure I'll make other films that are not well received and that don't make money.

The American President (1995)

Michael Douglas; Annette Bening; Martin Sheen; Michael J. Fox; Anna
Deavere Smith; Samantha Mathis; Shawna Waldron; David Paymer;
Anne Haney; Richard Dreyfuss; Nina Siemaszko; Wendie Malick;
Beau Billingslea; Gail Strickland; Joshua Malina; John Mahoney.

This film was the most difficult of all to make because I was trying to blend politics, romance, and comedy. Romance and comedy make a very difficult genre. Anybody who is trying to make a romantic comedy will tell you it's a very difficult kind of film to make. Now we're adding politics into the mix and we want it to be serious and we want it to give a feeling of what really goes on in the White House and not make it too much of a fairy tale, even though there's a Cinderella quality to it. We also want to have a bed of reality underneath it. That is a very, very tough mix to put together. And it worked.

People watch the movie and they kind of just love it and are taken in by it. I liken it to watching somebody like Joe DiMaggio. They never give him credit for being a great outfielder. He always got credit for his hitting because he ran so gracefully without any histrionics. But he would also get to the ball and just catch it and make it look easy. And people would say, well that was an easy catch. So the object of a film like *The American President* was to make it look like an easy catch. It's all there. There's political themes being expressed and there's romance and comedy and conflict and it all kind of goes along and it's done and you've enjoyed yourself. But to be able to mix that was God Almighty difficult. But, remember it's not the job of the filmmaker to make it look difficult. My theory about filmmaking has always been you shouldn't notice the acting, the script, the camera, the sets, or the photography. All of those things should be seamless. They're all part of telling a story and having you be swept away.

I think the people look to a president to be both a prime minister and a king. There is an aspect of being a president that the public needs to feel is heightened and above them and superior in some way. But at the same time, they need to feel connected in a very human way. So a president has to be able to project both things. You hear all the time advisors and media people saying, "He looked very presidential doing that." Well, that's the part that the audience and the public want to see of a president. They want to feel he's larger than life. That he's a star, in a certain way. But at the same time they want to feel connected to him and feel that he's human. And that's the trick in being a successful president and that's the trick in creating a character of a president in a film.

I must tell you that the White House was extremely cooperative. They were so generous in allowing us access. I visited the White House five or six times in the preparation of the making of the film and they gave unusual access to my production team. They were allowed to really scour the entire White House and take pictures. It's why the film is as detailed as it is. It's an exact replica. People who have spent a lot of time in the White House and then came to visit the set were just spooked by how spot-on-accurate it was.

> *With Rob Reiner the passion is there. He doesn't care what other people think about it. I honestly believe that Rob Reiner, as professional a filmmaker as he is, and as responsible a financial entity he is as a partner in Castle Rock, was going to make the story either way* [Ghosts of Mississippi].
>
> James Woods—Actor

Ghosts of Mississippi (1996)
Alec Baldwin; Whoopi Goldberg; James Woods; Craig T. Nelson; Susanna Thompson; Lucas Black; Joseph Tello; Alexa Vega; William H. Macy; Ben Bennett; Darrell Evers; Yolanda King; James Van Evers; Jerry Levine; Sky Rumph; Wayne Rogers.

I'll tell you one thing about that film. *Ghosts of Mississippi* was the toughest film for me because it was the first film that I'd made that was based on historical fact. I was very, very religious in adhering to the historical accuracy of the film. I understand that people get their history through movies and I took the responsibility to be accurate very seriously. A lot of the people who were part of that story are still alive. It was very difficult to try to make it work on a dramatic level. When you're given a blank slate and a free hand, you can make up all kinds of stuff with the characters and story and how the plot twists and turns so that you can heighten the drama.

I'll give you an example. Here you've got a story of Byron De La Beckwith, a white supremacist, who in 1963 murders civil rights leader Medgar Evers in front of Evers' wife and children. Not many people know it but Medgar Evers was a very prominent civil rights leader in Mississippi and head of the NAACP in Mississippi. Beckwith murders Evers and stands trial twice in 1964. At that time no white man had ever been convicted of killing a black man. Beckwith faced two all male, all white juries, both of them hung juries. He's let out.

Twenty-five or twenty-six years later a young district attorney, Bobby DeLaughter, gets enthused about the case after Myrlie Evers comes to him and says there's a report that there was some jury tampering back in the early trials. Is this grounds for reopening the case? Now you've got the hero, Bobby DeLaughter, who is unearthing all of this evidence and information and who becomes obsessed with bringing this Beckwith down. So now I have the protagonist, Bobby DeLaughter, trying to bring this guy to justice and I've got the antagonist, Byron De La Beckwith, who is this evil, misguided, ignorant white supremacist.

In the first two trials Beckwith took the witness stand. Well, if I'm a filmmaker and given a blank slate and allowed to do whatever I want to, I'm going to have a showdown in that third trial. But Beckwith didn't take the stand in the third trial and I felt I couldn't take that license. So now I don't have that face off. I don't have that great dramatic tension there. I've got to find other ways to do it.

That happened all the way through the film. Plus I had things that happened in reality that were so outrageous and so outlandish and so unbelievable that nobody would have bought it. For instance, Bobby DeLaughter actually found the murder weapon that had been lost for twenty-five years in his own father-in-law's house. Bobby was married to Dixie Moore, daughter of Judge Russell Moore, who had passed away. Russell Moore was a famous racist judge of the time. He didn't preside over the trials of Beckwith but he attended them and he took the gun home as a souvenir. This gun had been sitting in his house for twenty-seven years. It's preposterous and yet it's part of historical reality and historical fact. So, I'm struggling in trying to make it accurate and still entertaining and still dramatic. It was the toughest thing I've ever done. I think it worked but in the end that's for an audience to decide.

The Cost of Making Movies

The cost of making movies is so out of hand now. Not just making them, but releasing them as well. Every movie you make is anywhere from $50 million to $150 million. It's too much money to plunk down with a roll of the dice each time. And the marketplace is too crowded. That's the reason that the price for stars has gone up. The marketplace is crowded and everybody's looking for an advantage to poke through so they all want Tom Cruise and Arnold Schwarzenegger to star in their films. If we don't have guys like that who can draw attention to our pictures, we're not going to open strong enough. We're not going to get sampled. There's going to be a bunch of pictures coming in on our heels and they're going to knock us out of the theaters. The competition is so heavy we're willing to pay the stars even more money.

You've got this feeding frenzy where people are so desperate to carve out that first weekend to get a foothold that the cost of making films has been completely inflated. The obvious answer is to make fewer movies. Once you make fewer movies the marketplace thins out and a picture that is good has a chance to stay in the theaters for a little while longer and make its money back.

Let me give you a good example. *Stand by Me,* which was released in 1986, never did more than $3.5 million on any given weekend and wound up doing $55 million in America for a picture that cost $7.5 million to produce. That was an enormous success. Yet if that picture were released today and only did $3.5 million the first weekend, it's thrown out of the theater because there's so many more pictures that are coming that are going to gross more than $3.5 million the first weekend. The theater owners don't care if they've just kicked you out because if the picture they've just put in to replace you does not do well they've got another one to replace that.

Flash Dance is another example. The picture made $100 million and never did more than $4 million on a given weekend. Now, $4 million by today's standards is a disaster. *When Harry Met Sally* opened to $8 million and we were thrilled! We were ecstatic with $8 million. The film went on to make $93 million because it stayed in the theaters. You have to have good movies. You can't just put crap out there. If you make a good movie people will come to it, but you have to give it time to build.

What's New in His Life beside Movies?

I'm actively involved in trying to launch a national awareness campaign on the importance of early childhood development. The first three years of a child's life are critical to whether or not he or she becomes a toxic or non-toxic member of society.

I believe what happens to a child in his first three years of life is going to determine who they are for the rest of their life and whether or not they're going to be a positive or negative influence on society. I believe that child abuse, drug abuse, teen pregnancy, welfare rolls, and people going through the criminal justice system—just about every social ill that you can think of—comes from the foundation that's laid inside a child in its first three years of life. I believe that in the deepest part of my being. If I could make a good living doing that I would devote the rest of my life to that.

How Does He Want to Be Remembered?

I hope they remember me as a man of my word. I believe I am a man of my word. I always do what I say I'm going to do. And I hope I'm remembered as a guy who accurately portrayed on film some part of the human struggle.

The only other parting words I have is that when I die I want my tombstone to read NOW I'M IN THIS PLACE!

Filmography

This is Spinal Tap (1984)
The Sure Thing (1985)
Stand by Me (1986)
The Princess Bride (1987)
When Harry Met Sally . . . (1989)
Misery (1990)
A Few Good Men (1992)
North (1994)
The American President (1995)
Ghosts of Mississippi (1996)
I Am Your Child (TV, 1997)
The Story of Us (1999)

EDITOR'S NOTE: Since this interview, Reiner has completed *The Story of Us*, starring Bruce Willis and Michelle Pfeiffer.

Awards

Academy Awards, USA

A Few Good Men, Best Picture (nominated, shared with David Brown and Andrew Sheinman), 1993

British Academy Awards

When Harry Met Sally..., Best Film (nominated), 1990

Emmy Awards

All in the Family, Outstanding Continuing Performance by a Supporting Actor in a Comedy Series, 1978

All in the Family, Outstanding Continuing Performance by a Supporting Actor in a Comedy Series (nominated), 1975

All in the Family, Best Supporting Actor in Comedy, 1974

All in the Family, Outstanding Performance by an Actor in a Supporting Role in Comedy (nominated), 1973

All in the Family, Outstanding Performance by an Actor in a Supporting Role in Comedy (nominated), 1972

Golden Globes, USA

The American President, Best Director—Motion Picture (nominated), 1996

A Few Good Men, Best Director—Motion Picture (nominated), 1993

When Harry Met Sally..., Best Director—Motion Picture (nominated), 1990

Stand by Me, Best Director—Motion Picture (nominated), 1987

All in the Family, Best Supporting Actor—Television (nominated), 1977

All in the Family, Best Supporting Actor—Television (nominated), 1976

All in the Family, Best Supporting Actor—Television (nominated), 1974

All in the Family, Best Supporting Actor—Television (nominated), 1973

All in the Family, Best Supporting Actor—Television (nominated), 1972

Independent Spirit Awards
> *Stand by Me,* Best Director (nominated), 1987

People's Choice Awards, USA
> People's Choice Awards Honoree, 1997

Razzie Awards
> *North,* Worst Director (nominated), 1995
> *North,* Worst Picture (nominated, shared with Alan Zweibel), 1995

Walk of Fame
> Star on the Walk of Fame, 1999

The Films of Joel Schumacher

Joel Schumacher was born and raised in New York City, where he studied design and display at Parsons School of Design. He began his career in the entertainment industry as an art director for television commercials before becoming a costume designer for such notable films as Woody Allen's *Sleeper* and *Interiors,* Herbert Ross's *The Last of Sheila,* and Paul Mazursky's *Blume in Love.* He then wrote the screenplays for *Sparkle* and the hit comedy *Car Wash.*

Schumacher made his directing debut with the television movie *The Virginia Hill Story,* starring Dyan Cannon in the title role and Harvey Keitel as the mobster Bugsy Siegel.

This was followed by his award-winning telefilm *Amateur Night at the Dixie Bar and Grill. The Incredible Shrinking Woman,* starring Lily Tomlin, marked his feature-film directing debut, followed by *D.C. Cab,* for which he also wrote the screenplay. Schumacher directed the successful Chicago theatrical run of David Mamet's scorching Hollywood satire, *Speed-the-Plow.*

The amazing and successful career of Joel Schumacher is still going strong with two new feature films released since this interview took place: *8MM,* starring Nicolas Cage, and *Flawless,* which he wrote as well as directed, with Robert De Niro in the lead role.

Joel likes to laugh. He maintains an easygoing set, preferring to work closely and openly with everyone involved in the making of his films. He subscribes to the theory that if he surrounds himself with the best talent in front of and behind the camera, they will always make him look good. His successful career is proof of that.

He creates a set where everyone is very happy, and the crew is very, very happy, and that makes a huge difference when everybody seems to be having a good time, enjoying what they are doing.

Alicia Silverstone—Actress

The Conversation

I was born in New York City. I grew up in Long Island City, which is right over the 59th Street Bridge where there are a lot of factories, behind a movie theater called the Sunnyside Movies, and I went to the movies every day. I used to cut school to go to the movies and my mother would come and drag me out. This is going to be hard for a lot of people to believe, but I actually grew up in a time before television. And even when television came out, we were too poor to have one. So, I was a movie addict and wanted to direct movies since I was seven years old, and I am a person who got my dream.

I grew up at a time when there really wasn't a movie colony at all in New York. Los Angeles was a far piece away, especially for a poor kid from the streets of New York. So I didn't think it was possible to get into the movie business with my background.

I went to art school and I worked in the fashion business for a while in the sixties, but I wasn't happy doing that. Like a lot of people in my generation, I had a very reckless, dangerous life in the sixties and was lucky to survive it. When I got out of that world I decided I would start my life all over again and I would pursue my childhood dream and direct movies. I'd had enough success in the fashion world and the art direction world to talk Dominick Dunne, the author, who was an independent producer then, and director Frank Perry into giving me a two-week trial as a costume designer. So I started as a two-hundred-dollar-a-week costume designer in L.A. in 1972.

A lot of what a costume designer does depends on the movie you're working on, but for the most part in a contemporary film you can shop with the actors. In 1973 I did *Sleeper* with Woody Allen, and that was a sci-fi comedy where we had to make up a whole world and there's a lot more invention and ingenuity. But dressing people in contemporary clothes and serving the story properly is also a challenge.

His First Script Did Not Sell, But His Second Did

There's an old joke which is everybody wants to direct. And it is a great job. So I did costumes, I did sets, I did art direction, production design, and I didn't feel any of that would lead to directing. It didn't seem to be possible to make that leap. But I did see some writers getting the opportunity to direct because they had written something that someone wanted to make. Ignorance is bliss. I sat down and wrote a script for television. Barry Diller and Dion Barkley were running the *ABC Movie of the Week* then, and they bought it for nine thousand dollars, and it was called *Actress Model Found Dead*. It didn't get made, but I sold it. So, fueled with that success, I wrote a feature on spec called *Sparkle* and it was made at Warner Brothers for about $750 thousand. It was Irene Cara's first movie as well as Dorian Harewood's and Phillip Michael Thomas's. It was Sam O'Steen's first feature as a director. Sam was a very well-known film editor before he began directing. So it was a lot of firsts for all of us. I can't say it was a wild success, but it's become a big cult movie.

Writing Can Get You in the Door

Then I wrote *Car Wash* in 1976, directed by Michael Schultz, and it was a huge hit. Thank you God! He did a wonderful job with it. It was shot in twenty-eight days. I think it cost under a million dollars and they're still showing it on television, so success helps. It certainly got me a lot of attention. Although after *Sparkle* and *Car Wash* a lot of producers were shocked that I wasn't black when I walked in the room. But I was able to use my writing to eventually start directing. I started with television movies.

The Virginia Hill Story (1974, TV)

Herbert Anderson; Robby Benson; Dyan Cannon; Liam Dunn; Allen Garfield; Conrad Janis; Harvey Keitel; John Quade; Tom Reese; John Vernon.

I didn't like the way I directed *The Virginia Hill Story*. I was under the illusion that since I had wanted to be a director ever since I was a child I had a great calling to do this. So when I started directing I thought I'd be a genius and I really, really wasn't. I thought I needed to learn more before I directed again and of course writing movies and working on other directors' movies helped me enormously in the learning process. It was time for me to take some time to learn and not direct again. Also, I don't think *Virginia Hill* set the world on fire so I don't think the opportunities were flying in either. So a lot of it was my own shock at not being as talented as I thought I should be and also probably a lot of other people thinking the same thing.

Dyan Cannon starred in *Virginia Hill* and she did a wonderful job. Dyan was going out with director Hal Ashby at the time. He came to visit me on the first day and told me that on his first day directing *Harold and Maude* he shouted "Action" and threw up. He said if I hadn't thrown up yet, I was doing better than he had done.

I had a wonderful cast, all of whom took a chance on a first-time director. They helped me enormously. All of them were veterans and far greater directors than I was. I've always been blessed with great casts.

Amateur Night at the Dixie Bar and Grill (1979, TV)

Jeff Altman; Pat Ast; Ed Begley Jr.; Dennis Burkley; Candy Clark; Jamie Farr; Victor French; Henry Gibson; Joan Goodfellow; Don Johnson; Roz Kelly; Louise Latham; Melinda Naud; Sheree North; Dennis Quaid; Kyle Richards; Timothy Scott; Tanya Tucker.

The Incredible Shrinking Woman (1981)

Lily Tomlin; Charles Grodin; Ned Beatty; Henry Gibson; Elizabeth Wilson; Mark Blankfield; Maria Smith; Pamela Bellwood; John Glover; Nicholas Hormann; Jim McMullan; Shelby Balik; Justin Dana; Rick Baker; Mike Douglas; Sally Kirkland.

I had directed *Amateur Night at the Dixie Bar and Grill* and it was a much, much, better creation than *Virginia Hill* and got a lot of attention and a lot of great reviews. Robert Redford gave it an award at Sundance as one of the best television movies made. It wasn't, of course, but we were very honored.

I started getting features then. The first was *The Incredible Shrinking Woman*, which starred Lily Tomlin. I thought it would be fun because Lily's such a brilliant comic talent and the idea of big sets and the comic book, cartoon style of it would be fun to do. But it was way too ambitious a project for a first movie. I was coming off a nineteen-day television movie and I suddenly went into special effects hell. I really needed an education that I hadn't had in special effects to do that picture.

For a first-time feature movie I really don't think I did a great job. I think I was so green and it was so overwhelming a challenge that I don't think I could have done the best job possible. Lily Tomlin and her partner, Jane Wagner, and I really didn't see eye to eye on a lot of things. Although they were very kind to give me my first opportunity, I think in the long run they either should have gone off to make their movie or I should have gone off to make my movie. I think a lot of the way we made the film was to compromise with each other and I'm not so sure that's always the best way to make a film. I'll always be grateful to Lilly and Jane because they okayed me and although I don't think I was the best director for the job, you have to start somewhere.

D.C. Cab (1983)

Max Gail; Adam Baldwin; Mr. T; Charlie Barnett; Gary Busey;
Gloria Gifford; Marsha Warfield; Bill Maher; DeWayne Jessie; Paul Rodriguez;
Whitman Mayo; Peter Paul; David Paul; Irene Cara; Diana Bellamy; John Diehl.

I was so disappointed with the experience of making *The Incredible Shrinking Woman* that I was going to give up directing because it wasn't very good. I'm sure a lot of people still think I'm not very good. But a very interesting thing happened. At Universal there was a mandate from the Black Producers' Guild that they wanted to see more movies being made at Universal by black producers. And so two wonderful African-American producers, Topper Carew and Cassius Weathersby, had an idea to do a movie about a basically African-American cab company in Washington, D.C. I think Universal thought they would ask for an African-American writer and director, but instead they wanted me, I think probably because of my work on *Car Wash*.

A lot of people who go to Washington, D.C., don't really see it. They just fly right into the airport, stay in a nice hotel, and go see the monuments. It's really bordered by a struggling population and we were able to tell a lot of that story in a funny way. We had a very short shooting schedule and almost no money and a wonderful cast made up of mostly stand-up comedians. You can't not have a good time when you're making a movie with comedians because they're always in competition to top each other all the time, so we had a lot of fun. Fortunately the film did well and was received well. It was a much more positive experience for me than *The Incredible Shrinking Woman.*

Then I started to get offered every wacky comedy in town and that was nice because before that I wasn't being offered anything. But I wanted to write a movie. I thought perhaps I could write something better than what was being offered to me. So with my assistant at the time, Carl Kurlander, I wrote *St. Elmo's Fire.* Then things started to happen.

St. Elmo's Fire (1985)

Emilio Estevez; Rob Lowe; Andrew McCarthy; Demi Moore; Judd Nelson;
Ally Sheedy; Mare Winningham; Martin Balsam; Andie MacDowell;
Joyce Van Patten; Jenny Wright; Blake Clark; Jon Cutler;
Matthew Laurance; Gina Hecht.

St. Elmo's Fire came about because while I was doing *D.C. Cab* I lived in Georgetown. Georgetown in the early eighties was a kind of city of yuppies. It was the Disneyland of yuppie-dom. There were bars and restaurants and clothing stores that were all geared to people who were either in college or coming out of college. I started to think how tough it must be coming into this yuppie world. These young people were expected to be mature adults, do huge jobs, make big salaries, get the right car, have the right Ralph Lauren clothes, but how immature and young these people still were when they came out of college. I wanted to tell a story about a group of friends who had gone through the college experience together, then they realize that when they got into real life there were a lot of cold, hard facts they weren't willing or hadn't been used to dealing with. That is how *St. Elmo's Fire* was born. Thank you, God!

I've been asked a lot of questions about the cast from *St. Elmo's Fire,* including how they got the name The Brat Pack. David Bloom of *New Yorker* magazine did a cover story calling them that. Although that title has stayed to this day I think it was unfair because I believe every one is an individual. I don't think people are packs. And certainly the cast of *St. Elmo's Fire* were very, very, very unusual individuals. I can't say that I knew all of them were going to become stars, but I certainly knew that they were unique and that I wanted them in the movie very badly.

I had to fight really hard for some of them. The studio okayed Ally Sheedy and Rob Lowe right away because they had already made names for themselves. I had to screentest Demi Moore, Judd Nelson, Andrew McCarthy, and Emilio Estevez. Then I had to fight for them. And no one wanted to hire Andie MacDowell. She had been re-voiced by Glenn Close in *Greystoke*. The rumor was that she couldn't act. But if you look at *Greystoke*, Glenn Close is doing the voice, but Andy is doing the emoting. I forced everybody to let me use her and she showed them.

Rob Lowe was nineteen and Mare Winningham was the oldest. She had already been married for a while and had a couple of kids, so the age ranges probably went from nineteen to close to thirty and everything in between. We had a great deal of fun. You know, it's very hard to make a movie with a lot of young people and not have fun. There's something very exciting working with people where their life hasn't all happened yet, where their career hasn't all happened yet. When they don't know if success is going to happen to them or not. There's freshness, irreverence, and a spontaneity that's very exciting that I think keeps me young.

[*This interview took place on the set of* Batman & Robin. *At this point in the interview actor Chris O'Donnell came up to us wearing his Robin suit and flung the cape over Joel's head in a playful gesture. Joel started laughing.*] This is one of the unfortunate things about working with young talent. You take these needy young actors who need a job, you give them a job in a movie, and then you buy them shoes and they walk all over you [*Chris hugged Joel at this point.*] Look at that. Oh, God. The lovely Chris O'Donnell, ladies and gentlemen! He was nothing until I found him. See what they do to me? If you feed them, they will love you.

As I was about to say before we were so rudely interrupted, it's interesting how Demi Moore got the part in *St. Elmo's*. I shared a common hallway with writer/director John Hughes at the studio we were working at. Demi was actually there for an interview with John. I think she got tired of waiting and decided to leave. I just happened to step out of my office and saw this gorgeous creature with jet-black hair down to her waist that flew like the tail of an Arabian horse. This sounds like some movie line, but I said to my assistant, follow that girl and find out if she's an actress.

He came back and told me her name was Demi Moore and she was on *General Hospital*. I brought her in and she read for the role. Demi rode a motorcycle in those days with no helmet and all I could think of was she was going to get her hair caught in her motorcycle. So I stopped her from riding her motorcycle at night when we were making *St. Elmo's Fire*. She was fabulous in the movie. Sometimes when I come home late at night and *St. Elmo's Fire* is on cable and I see her I think of the extraordinary performance she gave for someone so young. It was a very complex performance.

She's very beautiful and very glamorous in it as well as being very funny. She carries most of the humor. She has a full-tilt nervous breakdown and suicide attempt in the movie and yet is funny about it. She did a marvelous job. She certainly helped my career, too.

> *It's really a pop film. It's not really a heavy thing, but Joel has a wonderful talent in helping actors trying to find something a little deeper in anything they're doing. He's very articulate in that way.*
>
> Kiefer Sutherland—Actor

The Lost Boys (1987)

Jason Patric; Corey Haim; Dianne Wiest; Barnard Hughes; Edward Herrmann; Kiefer Sutherland; Jami Gertz; Corey Feldman; Jamison Newlander; Brooke McCarter; Billy Wirth; Alex Winter; Chance Michael Corbitt; Alexander Bacon Chapman; Nori Morgan.

The success of *St. Elmo's Fire* got me more offers than I'd had before. In the mind of Hollywood I had become the yuppie-angst director. So I got offered all the yuppie-angst movies. *Bright Lights, Big City; Less Than Zero;* any social disease and any spec project. I definitely felt I had made those movies already, although Tom Cruise and I flirted with *Bright Lights, Big City* for a while. Then along came director Richard Donner, a great friend of mine. His wife, Lauren, had produced *St. Elmo's Fire*. Lauren also produced *Amateur Night at the Dixie Bar and Grill*. She's a wonderful producer and I really admire her very much.

Dick was going to do the *Lost Boys* after *Goonies*. I think he got cold feet, but he also fell in love with *Lethal Weapon*. Lucky him! He was going off to do *Lethal Weapon* with Mel Gibson and Danny Glover and asked me if I would take on the *Lost Boys*. I read it and was going to say no because basically it was about nine-year-olds. There were no girls in it and it was very G rated. It was very much *Goonies* go vampire. That was the tone of it. As charming as it was I'm too corrupt to do G rated movies. I actually called Dick and told him I didn't want to do it.

I went running in my neighborhood one day and thought about the cave scene in the script. I thought gee, wouldn't it be interesting if the cave was in the San Andreas Fault and an old Venice baroque hotel had fallen into the crack so that the cave, instead of just being just a cave, had these very baroque touches to it along with gargoyles, etc. Once I saw that then I started getting other ideas. Then I went back and told them I wanted to do it, but not as it was written. I asked them why the lost boys couldn't be teenagers, and why couldn't they ride motorcycles, and why couldn't the star be a girl, and why couldn't they dress like an English rock band, and why, why, why, why? And they said, "Great, just do it. Just go make it." So that was a wonderful experience.

We really didn't know what we were doing and we made up an awful lot of it on the spot. Jeff Boam did a wonderful job with the script and the rewrites, but a lot of the jokes in the movie and a lot of the inside humor was made up on the spot by the cast and me or the crew. We were kind of finding it as we were making it, once again not knowing that the movie would be as successful as it was.

Mark Canton, who was running Warner Brothers then, used to come and see me from time to time and say, "You know, the heads of the studio are a little worried, Joel. Are you making a comedy or a horror movie?" And I'd say, "Yes!" There was a worry that the two genres wouldn't go together. Fortunately they did.

I think when you're dealing with pop culture you're always going to get a certain group of critics and audience that it doesn't appeal to. It is the same with the *Batman* movies. There are people who are attracted by very fine art, not pop art. I think the *Lost Boys* is a case of you either get the joke or you don't. I think that whenever you deal with mass media entertainment you have to figure some people aren't going to like it. Any director who expects every single human being who sees their movie to love it is in for a lot of disappointment and rejection in life because the audience is never wrong. Everyone who sees the movie is entitled to his or her opinion, especially the paying audience. More so than the critics, even.

I think sometimes critics, as much as I admire some of them, are very much out of step with what pop culture really is and what entertainment really means to people in the movie theater. I think, and rightly so, their job is usually to be the last bastion of some classical ideal and I don't think that's always what people go to the movies for. I think people go sometimes to just have a really good time.

Not Everyone Loves His Work,
But It's Part of the Game

I don't think I'm ever totally happy with my work because I would always like to be more talented than I am. I always feel like I've done the best I can with my current movie, but I must do better on the next. I think I probably answered more questions in interviews about the *Lost Boys* than almost any other movie because it seemed to have enormous staying power and a huge cult following. I'm very proud of that. I'm proud that people enjoyed *St. Elmo's Fire*. A lot of young people were very, very much influenced by *St. Elmo's Fire* at a certain time in their life and, you know, moving people, making them laugh, giving them an experience in the theater is what my job is.

Sometimes my work pleases all the critics. That's icing on the cake. No one likes to be criticized in print. But if you're not willing to accept those criticisms, you can't be a director. You have to be willing to be called an asshole every time you go out there, the same as if you're in sports you have to accept being booed as well as accepting the cheers. I feel that it's part of the challenge. If you knew everyone was going to love everything you did every time, it wouldn't be quite as exciting.

I think the most hurtful criticisms are the ones that seem almost too personal, when the critics second-guess what you've done and then criticize something in your character for it when they don't even know you. Or when they miss the whole point of the movie. I think those are always the most annoying criticisms because they don't seem fair.

You know, the guards at the studio gate are not there to keep us in. We can walk out of the movie business any day we want. No one asked me to get into the movie business. There were no ads saying, "Director wanted." I decided I wanted to be a director. I'm the one who knocked on doors and asked people to give me a chance. And I'm living my dream and part of the dream is the audience is never wrong. And anyone who sees a movie has a right to his or her opinion. Also, we're very overpaid. We're very overprivileged. We're very overstimulated. And the same press that feeds us with all that self-aggrandizement has the right to slap us down once in a while. I think it's fair.

Cousins (1989)

Ted Danson; Isabella Rossellini; Sean Young; William L. Petersen;
Lloyd Bridges; Norma Aleandro; Keith Coogan; Gina DeAngeles;
George Coe; Katie Murray; Alex Bruhanski; Stephen E. Miller;
Gerry Bean; Gordon Currie; Saffron Henderson.

Jean-Charles Tacchella, the director of the original French film, gave me an award at the Douville Film Festival for the remake of *Cousins.* So his honoring my version of his movie was very thrilling for me. I also had a great cast and a wonderful French classic movie to play around with, and because it is so specifically French we were able to make an American version that was slightly different yet still honoring the great work that he had done.

There's a very, very delicate balance in *Cousins* because you have a leading man who isn't ambitious, who doesn't want success, who doesn't care how much money he makes. He just wants to be happy and to have a loving relationship. That's not too American. It's risky because a lot of the people think the character is a loser because he's not ambitious for money. When we made it in the late eighties that was almost un-American.

I just felt that Ted Danson understood the role so totally and was winsome and charming. You know, before Ted Danson became a big television star, he had a very small role in the *Onion Field,* one of the great American films, and was brilliant in it. Then he was a ruthless lawyer in *Body Heat* and he did a tap dance on a dock. He had this wonderful lanky body and I just thought he would be a wonderful combination with Isabella Rossellini. She has this beautiful Scandinavian mystery, beauty, and elegance, and I thought Ted was such an American American that they would be very sexy, very charming, and very lovable together.

The character that Isabella played in *Cousins* was the most dangerous, because you're dealing with a wife and a mother who commits adultery. We live in a very hypercritical, puritanical society. We like to think there's an awful lot of adultery in Europe but none in the United States. I met many wonderful actresses who wanted the role. Then Isabella came to see me in New York. We had a long conversation and she left the hotel room, and then I called Paramount and said, "If she doesn't do the movie I'm not going to make it. I know I can make this movie work if she plays Maria." So fortunately she said yes.

Isabella has enormous focus. She's very intelligent and extremely sensitive, but she has a ferocious dignity, an ethical integrity that probably comes from her mother and father (Roberto Rossellini), who were both great artists. I met her mother, Ingrid Bergman, only once late in life, but from all the stories Isabella told me Ingrid was a very staunch individualist and a very focused and disciplined woman. Isabella has that same wonderful combination. She's capable of staying up all night washing the floors and making sure that everything's clean, and at the same time she has the Italian part of her father where she is very fluid and spontaneous and romantic. It's a wonderful combination and I think she brings that to every role that she plays. I think she's shown people ever since *Blue Velvet* that there's much more to her than just a beautiful face.

> *It is always entertaining being on a set with Joel. I mean, it's always a great ride.*
>
> Kevin Bacon—Actor

Flatliners (1990)

Kiefer Sutherland; Julia Roberts; Kevin Bacon; William Baldwin;
Oliver Platt; Kimberly Scott; Joshua Rudoy; Benjamin Mouton;
Aeryk Egan; Kesha Reed; Hope Davis; Jim Ortlieb; John Duda;
Megan Stewart; Tressa Thomas; Julie Warner.

I was in New York shooting a documentary for the Center for Living, which is a wonderful organization that assists people with terminal illnesses. At one point I rushed back to the hotel to shower and there was this urgent message from my agent saying that Columbia wanted me to do this movie call *Flatliners*. During the filming of this HIV-positive weekend, many people were talking about death, their fear of death, and also of amends and the completion of relationships with the people around them. I read the script for *Flatliners* and saw that that was what it was about. It was about people taking responsibility for their actions and what it was like to die. So it seemed like I was supposed to do that movie. It also was the most original script I've ever read. And all the credit for that belongs to writer Peter Filardi. I think *Flatliners* was his first screenplay.

When Peter was a young man in Boston, one of his friends had had a near-death experience. Nothing like we showed in the film, but that's where Peter got the idea. What he added to the near-death idea, and this was brilliant, was that not only did the characters perform these near-death experiments, but they also brought their sins back with them. So they needed to make amends and take responsibility for their actions. Keifer says to Julia Roberts at the end of the movie, "Everything we do counts. We're responsible for everything we do." And I believe that.

The movie was a big success, thank you, God! I remember a young man in Miami came running up to me and said, "Mr. Schumacher, Mr. Schumacher, I loved that movie. Where'd you shoot it? Rome?" We actually shot it in Chicago and Burbank. But I know what he meant because it had very baroque touches.

I felt that *Flatliners* was a tremendous leap for the audience. They had to go with us on an incredible journey, and I wanted to do everything I could to assist that journey. I felt we should give it a very surreal, very gothic look. I thought if we did it in a little white hospital room, it wouldn't work. What you've got is one actor lying on a table and four other actors standing around. That's not the most cinematic idea. One of the secrets of directing is hiring people more talented than you are. I hired a genius production designer, Eugenio Zanetti, who designed those fantastic backdrops, and a genius cinematographer, Jan de Bont, who has since become the director of such films as *Speed* and *Twister.*

I was working with a great young cast, all of whom have an outrageous sense of humor. It's very hard to do serious scenes when everybody's laughing. Kevin Bacon, who has a brilliant wit, would make Julia Roberts laugh before takes and sometimes in the middle of a very serious take. It's very hard to do serious life and death scenes when everybody's laughing. And you know it becomes contagious when Julia goes on with that famous laugh of hers. So I remember a lot of the laughter and I remember how shocked the Jesuit fathers were when they saw what we were doing on their campus.

Dying Young (1991)

Julia Roberts; Campbell Scott; Vincent D'Onofrio;
Colleen Dewhurst; David Selby; Ellen Burstyn; Dion Anderson;
George Martin; Adrienne-Joi Johnson; Daniel Beer; Behrooz Afrakhan;
Michael Halton; Larry Nash; Alex Trebek; Richard Friedenberg.

In retrospect, I think I was attracted to *Dying Young* for all the wrong reasons. I don't think that I was the best director for it, and I don't know if I did the best job I could have done. I was on my way to Europe to do *The Phantom of the Opera* for Andrew Lloyd Webber. The film had to be postponed because he was divorcing Sara Brightman and the rights to the show were tied up in the divorce settlement.

It was at that time that Julia Roberts had planned to do *Dying Young* at Fox and asked me to direct it. I don't think if anyone else had given me that script I would have said yes. But I was so in love with Julia. To know her is to love her, but I learned a painful lesson and maybe she did too. You don't do a movie because you're in love with the star. You do a movie because you're in love with the movie. So I don't think it's my best film, but I'm still proud of it and proud of the wonderful work that Julia and Campbell did.

Falling Down (1993)

Michael Douglas; Robert Duvall; Barbara Hershey; Tuesday Weld;
Rachel Ticotin; Frederic Forrest; Lois Smith; Joey Hope Singer;
Ebbe Roe Smith; Michael Paul Chan; Raymond J. Barry;
D.W. Moffett; Steve Park; Kimberly Scott; James Keane.

Falling Down is one of my favorite movies. I did one of my best jobs with it. But I think the credit really goes to Ebbe Roe Smith who wrote it. He touched a nerve. This was written about a year before the riots. And I think the tale of a disgruntled defense worker who's been laid off, who wreaks havoc throughout L.A., and who eventually holds a gun on his ex-wife and child was so obvious when the movie was made that I think the credit really belongs to the writer.

Many times, too many times, you'll see a story in the news where a seemingly average person goes berserk and shoots everyone on the street. Then you see the interviews with their family or friends or co-workers insisting he was the nicest guy in the world. But something was going on just beneath the surface all that time. Something was brewing, which Barbara Hershey as the wife senses so she gets a restraining order. She knows this man is to be feared because she's frightened of him. We tried to tell that story.

When we first showed it to an audience, the marketing people at Warner Bros. predicted we'd get sixty to a hundred walkouts because people would not tolerate that kind of politically incorrect tone in a film. No one left. They cheered. That was one of the most surprising, most frightening things for me. When Michael Douglas walked into that Korean grocery store and started beating this guy the audience cheered. When he took a baseball bat to the street gang they cheered. When he took out the gun in the Wham Burger, which is my favorite scene in the movie, there was pandemonium in the theater. It's exciting as a filmmaker to create that kind of response.

At the same time, that wasn't the point of the movie. *Falling Down* became a news story in itself. It was on the cover of *Newsweek*. Ebbe's script had touched a nerve in the culture. There was a lot of ink in those days about the fading white middle-class American male, which is what the *Newsweek* cover story was about. They used Michael's character in the film as an example of that. That's some of what the movie was about also. There was endless debate, some of it pro and some of it con, about whether Michael Douglas's character was the good guy or the bad guy. Not for one minute did Michael or I ever think he was the good guy. We always knew he was the bad guy. He's a man who winds up on the end of a pier waving a loaded gun at his ex-wife and child.

I know Michael Douglas thinks it's his greatest performance and I do too. I think he was very brave. There aren't too many leading men who would have taken that role. And he never asked me to soften it, either. A lot of male superstars never want to be seen in any flawed situation. They want to be perfect. Michael let me cut off his magnificent hair and he was not shy about doing the role.

Michael's performance is so brilliant, so flashy, so theatrical, and so stimulating that Robert Duvall gets overlooked a lot of the time. But it's really the story of two men and Robert Duvall is equally brilliant in a very restrained, very subtle performance. Equally brilliant are the performances of

Rachel Ticotin, Barbara Hershey, Tuesday Weld, Frederic Forrest, and the rest of the cast. It's the one thing that's consistent in my movies. I've been blessed with the greatest casts for each one of my films and a lot of the credit goes to them.

The Client (1994)

Susan Sarandon; Tommy Lee Jones; Mary-Louise Parker;
Anthony LaPaglia; J.T. Walsh; Anthony Edwards; Brad Renfro;
Will Patton; Bradley Whitford; Anthony Heald; Kim Coates;
Kimberly Scott; David Speck; William H. Macy; Ossie Davis.

Brad Pitt and I were going to do *The Devil's Advocate* together. By then I had worked with many young actors and actresses who were in the same position that Brad was at that moment, which was right on the cusp and one movie away from big stardom. And, although in the past I had maybe thin scripts, or strange projects like *Flatliners,* I'd always been able to say to the young actors and actresses, "Trust me, we're going to be okay." I sat Brad down and said, "Brad, I can't say that to you." I told him that he was at too crucial a stage in his career for me to ask him to take a chance on material that I didn't think was there yet. So we aborted the project. The film was later made with Keanu Reeves and Al Pacino.

The minute I aborted that project, producer Arnon Milchan called me and said that he had just bought the rights to John Grisham's new novel, *The Client.* He asked me to read the eight hundred pages of galleys that night and let him know first thing in the morning whether I would do it or not. I was hooked from the very opening scene and I accepted.

I got the incredible Susan Sarandon to play Reggie Love and Tommy Lee Jones to play the Reverend Roy Foltrigg. Then Mali Finn, a casting genius, saw over six thousand boys in nine states and through the help of a police officer in Knoxville, Tennessee, found Brad Renfro, who played Mark Sway. I'd like to say I molded that performance and I slapped it out of him. But the truth is Brad is a wonderful, natural actor, with God-given talent. You can't make talent where there is none.

I had wonderful allies on that film. John Grisham who befriended me right away, his wonderful wife Renee, their two children, and their best friends, Billy and Julie. They really embraced me. They always made me feel that *The Client* was in the right hands. Also Akiva Goldsman who wrote a wonderful script (along with Robert Getchell and John Grisham). She also did a fabulous job of condensing the book with me and working with the actors, which is one of the things Akiva does brilliantly. As we get each cast member in I like to change the material and tailor it to their talents. I'm very cast dependent. I really encourage them to take risks and be spontaneous and bring in their own ideas. Akiva is very good at interpreting that.

How He Chooses His Projects

A long time ago someone very wise said to an actor, take a part that only you can play. I think that's true of filmmaking. When I'm reading a book or a script I have to feel I'm the right director for it. Sometimes someone gives me a brilliant script or a brilliant book and I know I'm not the right director. Like *Forrest Gump*. Wendy Finerman had this little book and she waved it in my face a hundred times and said, "Please do this movie, it will be a great movie." I read it and I didn't know what she was talking about. The great film that she made with Bob Zemeckis and Eric Roth, who wrote the screenplay, is not that book. It's what they did with it. So if anyone were to say, "Don't you regret now you didn't do *Forrest Gump*?" I'd say no, because I wouldn't have made that movie. I couldn't have made that movie. Not only would I have regretted making it, but also so would the audience. You have to have the passion and a vision for what you're making.

I usually know by the first or second page of something whether it's my material. Sometimes it's a road I've been down before and it feels right to me, but I don't want to make the same movie again, so sometimes I turn those down too. I feel they'll be too easy to do.

The audience doesn't have to know my name because it's not important to know who directed. Audiences are interested in the stars or the story or something else they find interesting about that particular film. What I want to be sure of is that they get their money's worth. No one goes to the movies because they think they're going to have a terrible experience. Except, of course, critics and people who go to Hollywood premieres. But the audience says let's go to that movie because it looks like fun, or it's scary, or it's sad, or I'm going cry my eyes out.

Batman Forever (1995)

Val Kilmer; Tommy Lee Jones; Jim Carrey; Nicole Kidman;
Chris O'Donnell; Michael Gough; Pat Hingle; Drew Barrymore;
Debi Mazar; Elizabeth Sanders; Rene Auberjonois; Joe Grifasi;
Philip Moon; Jessica Tuck; Dennis Paladino.

I was just about to shoot *The Client* in Memphis when I got a call from Bob Daley and Terry Semel who run Warner Bros. I call them "the brothers." It's Warner Bros. Studio, so we must have brothers, so we have Bob and Terry. They said they were sending one of the Warner private planes to pick me up because they wanted to have breakfast with me. I thought something very important was up or I was going to be fired. But maybe if you're getting fired they don't send the plane, they send the Greyhound bus. So I figured they were going to offer me something.

Then someone at the studio leaked that it probably was going to be *Batman*. And I wondered to myself on the plane back if I was going to say yes or no. So the next morning we had breakfast and they said, "We'd like to offer you the corporation's largest franchise." I said, "Oh, that must be Mel Gibson. I'll take him! I'll turn him into a gynecologist in Beverly Hills and I'll make so much money that I could buy Time Warner."

What they were offering me, of course, was the Batman franchise. I actually didn't know it was the corporation's largest asset. My first instinct was, oh, what fun, to do a *Batman* comic book. Tim Burton and I are friends so I said, "Look, I will not do it if Tim doesn't want me to do it because we're friends and he created it." So I went to see Tim and he seemed glad that one of his friends was going to do it and was very supportive of that notion. So I said yes.

Then I woke up in the middle of the night and thought, "Oh my god, what have I done? This could fail so miserably and this could be such a public failure, what have I done?" Then I changed Batman from Michael Keaton to Val Kilmer, which increased the risk. But we got lucky. And you know, my initial instinct was right. It was the most fun I ever had in my life. I've been working since I was nine years old and making *Batman* is the most fun I've ever had. It's a flight of fancy and fantasy and you can let your imagination soar with it. It attracted fantastically talented people in front of the camera and behind the camera.

As I said, I changed Batman from Michael Keaton to Val Kilmer. I'd always been a fan of Val's. I saw him in *Tombstone* and I thought, "Gee, he would make a great Batman." So when we decided to replace Michael Keaton, Val was my only choice and fortunately he said yes. It took several days to find Val. He was in a bat cave in Africa when they reached him by cellular phone. He said yes over the phone. He didn't read a script. He didn't meet with me. We knew each other. He said yes long distance. And I'll always be grateful to him for saying yes because I didn't have a second choice. He was my only choice.

Jim Carrey is totally unique, totally original. I don't think I've ever worked with anyone who comes in more prepared. He will work all night at home in front of a mirror and come in with such a polished performance that still allows all the spontaneity in the world in it. And you can go up to Jim and say, "I think you should do it this way instead of this way," he's not rigid at all. But you know, besides being so brilliantly funny and mischievous and evil in *Batman Forever* he did all his own cane tricks, hat tricks, and he wears sixty pounds of makeup. He couldn't eat a morsel of food so he could fit into that suit. His body language is extraordinary, and he acts with every fiber of his being. He's an extraordinary talent and also a total joy to work with. Having him around was wonderful.

I think part of what's great about being Batman is that he's a very sexy character, but I did not feel that the Batman suits were sexy enough. So we set out to make them into extremely aggressive, sexual male costumes. I only put the nipples on because they're part of the anatomy. I had no idea that I would be doing worldwide press over why there are nipples on the batsuit. I didn't think people would notice that much. Do you know why that was a source of controversy? I don't. I thought it was silly. But I also thought it would look sillier if there was nothing there.

The women in *Batman Forever* and *Batman and Robin* are very overtly sexual too, but it's all done in good wholesome fun. There's a tongue in cheek to all of it. It's not just to be sexual; it's to enjoy the comedy of the whole piece.

The pressure of doing a film like this is more in how the movie will be perceived and received and the way the audience will ultimately accept it. But the pressure of making it is the fun, because you don't climb Mount Everest unless you have a passion to climb Mount Everest. If you climb Mount Everest I would assume you get the best people and you tie your rope onto theirs and you would all go together. So I got geniuses to come and help me make the Batman movies. People like John Dykstra, who's a special effects genius, Barbara Ling, my favorite production designer, Bob Ringwood and Ingrid Ferrin to do the costumes, Elliot Goldenthal to do the music.

Sometimes the greatest work is invisible because it's seems like real life, so you don't notice what someone has done because it is invisible. In a Batman movie everyone gets to show off, so it attracts enormously gifted and brilliant artists and special effects geniuses. They all make me look good.

I had no idea that *Batman Forever* would be as successful as it was. Thank you, God! When we started to do *A Time to Kill* in Mississippi, I got a call once again from the brothers Warner, my esteemed bosses, and they asked if I would do another one and I said, sure. So here we are on the set of *Batman and Robin* and we have two more weeks of shooting to go. It's been a wonderful experience being involved in Batman again.

A Time to Kill (1996)

Matthew McConaughey; Sandra Bullock; Samuel L. Jackson; Kevin Spacey;
Oliver Platt; Charles Dutton; Brenda Fricker; Donald Sutherland;
Kiefer Sutherland; Patrick McGoohan; Ashley Judd; Tonea Stewart;
Rae'ven Kelly; Darrin Mitchell; LaConte McGrew.

A Time to Kill is John Grisham's best novel. He always said he didn't want it made into a movie, and I asked him if he'd allow me to make it. He and his wife Renee went through twenty-five reasons why they didn't want it made. And I tried to address each one, but in the long run when people have twenty-five reasons why they don't want to make something, well, hey, it's his book. He wanted to keep it private and personal. It was dedicated to Renee.

Then I took *The Client* down to Oxford, Mississippi, to show him after it was finished. The next morning we went to breakfast in the town square and we started talking about making *A Time to Kill* as a movie. I think he was probably waiting to see *The Client* before he made up his mind. I'm thrilled he gave me the opportunity because I loved making *A Time to Kill.*

I had an extraordinary cast. But I think a lot of that credit goes to the characters created by John in his book. None of the actors in *A Time to Kill* needed a job. They chose those roles over many others they could have taken. Some of them took small roles. They obviously wanted to play those characters or they wouldn't have been down in a hundred-degree weather in Canton, Mississippi, if they didn't want to be there. We certainly weren't throwing money at them to do it. And then I think everything was made better because of my choice of Matthew McConaughey for the lead. Not only was Matthew the perfect choice for the movie, but I think his integrity, his character, his charm, his work ethic, his humanity, stimulated all of the other actors in the piece because I think they wanted Matthew to do well too. I think they also enjoyed acting with him enormously. That was something magical about it.

I had no idea that Matthew was going to shoot to overnight stardom. I've been accused many times that this was some carefully worked out publicity plan. It wasn't. He was the best actor for the job. I am very grateful that John Grisham and Bob and Terry at Warner's saw that also. John Grisham and I had co-approval over that role and if John didn't approve, it wouldn't have been Matthew, so I'm glad John was able to see it also.

During filming we lived in the small town of Canton, Mississippi, which is the town you see in the movie. It is a town of about eight thousand people, most of whom were either in the movie, worked on the movie, or supported us and visited us during the making of the film. You can't make a movie in a small town without getting everybody involved. Aside from the great story and the incredible cast I will never forget as long as I live the experience of living in that town and being with those people. I was talking to Sandra Bullock and Matthew McConaughey recently and we all agreed that God willing we'll all make a lot of movies, but it's never going to be like that again, ever. And it won't be because, well, it's always hard to repeat any experience, but that was very, very, very unique and very moving on all kinds of levels.

> *He's got very specific tastes and very definite opinions about things, and when you've got a film that's this big, you need someone who has an opinion, that'll make a decision, who isn't going to hem and haw over what you should do.*
>
> *Chris O'Donnell—Actor*

Batman and Robin (1997)

Arnold Schwarzenegger; George Clooney; Chris O'Donnell;
Uma Thurman; Alicia Silverstone; Michael Gough; Pat Hingle;
John Glover; Elle Macpherson; Vivica A. Fox; Vendela Kirsebom;
Elizabeth Sanders; Jeep Swenson; John Fink; Michael Reid MacKay.

I was asked to do *Batman and Robin* because of the success of *Batman Forever*. There's always pressure to do better with such a high-profile project. Now, I think people expect us to be successful. That's an added pressure, but a sweet pressure in a way. I think we have the best cast of any *Batman* movie. As I said before, I'm very cast dependent. I also think we have the best story and I think we have a lot of fun and games and surprises in store for people.

Whether we'll be a hit or not I don't know. How much money will it make? I don't know. I had no idea that *St. Elmo's Fire* or *Flatliners* or *Lost Boys* or *Falling Down* would earn me the career I have today. That's part of the thrill of filmmaking. You don't know what's going to happen. There are so many sure hits every year that fail. And many sleepers that come out of nowhere and become huge successes. I'm here because of one— *Car Wash.* I remember a friend of mine who's very famous and very rich saying to me, "Joel, surely you're not writing a movie about some guys washing cars. No one wants to see a movie about people washing cars!" And I thought, you know, he's right. Who would want to see a movie about people washing cars? Fortunately they did. I hope people will want another Batman movie. I hope they will enjoy what we plan for them. But we don't know. We could have an earthquake right now and who knows what would happen.

I had never seen an episode of *ER* nor was I aware of who George Clooney was. I was on a plane looking through the newspaper, and I saw this ad for a film called *From Dusk Till Dawn*. There was a big picture of George Clooney and for some reason I took out a black magic marker and drew the bat cowl on him and I thought, God, would this guy be a great Batman. Then I went to see *Dusk Till Dawn* and I thought George had an

---

EDITOR'S NOTE: This interview was conducted during the shooting of *Batman and Robin*.

incredible screen presence. Very dynamic! Obviously very handsome! And that was when the idea was hatched. Right there and then.

Val Kilmer and I were having problems, and I was anxious to say goodbye to Val and I think he was very anxious to say goodbye to me. That gave me the opportunity to get the Batman I really wanted for *Batman and Robin*. So, Val did me two great, great favors. He said yes when I needed him and he said no when I needed him to say no. I'll always be indebted to him for that.

Besides George's great looks and his obvious screen allure, there's a humanity to him that I think has given Batman and certainly Bruce Wayne more humanity than I think we've seen before, plus a sense of humor and an accessibility. We have a much less dark, self-absorbed Batman. I think that he and Chris O'Donnell are not only believable as partners, but in life, as well as in the movie, they have a great sense of humor and camaraderie that I believe plays beautifully on the screen.

I have had so much success in finding new actors in the past. This time I found this big Austrian bodybuilder by the name of Arnold Schwarzenegger and I'm going to give him a break in the Batman movie. I hope people will accept him [*laughs*].

Arnold plays a great bad guy. He was a bad guy in *The Terminator*. He is both funny and scary in *Batman and Robin*. One of the great things about the character he plays (Mr. Freeze) is that there is a real Achilles' heel as well as tenderness and a love story deep within him. It's a very interesting character. Arnold had a chance to do a lot of dimensions with this one character. He and Uma Thurman team up and they're very funny together. Very wicked and very funny.

A Little Humility Is a Good Thing

Arnold Schwarzenegger is someone that I wish would give movie stars lessons in how to be a human being. He is a fantastic person. He handles his fame and fortune so easily, so beautifully. He's very generous to other people. He understands the responsibility of privilege. I think he sets a great example.

I'm going to quote someone much wiser than me here. I believe if you don't set a good example, you have no defense for privilege. And if you are a person of great privilege and cannot set a great example, then perhaps the privilege should be given to someone else. It is very disturbing when I run across an actor, actress, producer, director, studio executive, agent, or sometimes a manager, all people of privilege, who has not learned the most important lesson in life which is the entire universe does not revolve around any one of us. None of us is more important than anyone else on the planet.

I think it's particularly hard for movie stars because the audience and the press are always telling them that it is all about them. But those that can deal with it—keep their feet on the ground—I admire very much. Arnold is like that, Tom Cruise is like that, Tom Hanks is like that, and Sandra Bullock is like that. There are a lot of wonderful people in our business like that. Too many times the jerks and the abusers get the press because of their abhorrent behavior. But I admire people who are privileged who do set a good example, who get the joke about themselves, and Arnold is that man.

How Has the Industry Changed?

The way the film industry has changed the most is we make so much more money than we used to. Salaries on all levels seem to have no ceiling. That's kind of the good news and the bad news. Movies are becoming so expensive to make. The good news is we all take home more money but I think it may be limiting certain opportunities. There also seems to be an enormous glut of product. Everybody complains they're too expensive, and yet there seem to be more and more movies coming out.

On the very positive side, there is a new breed of young actors and actresses who are coming along who are really focused on the work and the movie star part of it is secondary. Which is thrilling for someone like me because we went through a long period of the grunge, attitude, grumbling, chain smoking, mumbling-through-scenes movie actors. That wasn't getting any of us anywhere. There was a certain amount of tolerance in the industry for lateness, and perhaps for a lack of sobriety and bad habits and people who didn't know their lines. It seemed like the whole job was about sunglasses, autographs, and limousines. The work ethic didn't seem to be there and that was particularly distressing. It was hard to get inspired by certain young actors and actresses.

It's very different now. I'm sure there are still some exceptions. But the new breed is very professional. They want to be great in their work. They want their accomplishments to be more important than their recognition. They work hard. They know their lines. They come in early. They deliver.

They care about the actual process of acting and it's very exciting for some-one like me to go to work with people like that.

How Does He Want to Be Remembered?

I'm not interested in people remembering me as a director. I hope that some of my films will continue to give people good experiences when they go to the theater. As a man? I hope people think I can take a joke. I hope I was fair. That I had a defense for my privilege. I'm a poor kid who dreamed of being a movie director when I was seven years old. I got the dream bigger than I ever could have dreamed it. And with the reckless, careless, damaged life I lived in the sixties, seventies, and eighties, I shouldn't even be alive. I'm privileged to be alive. I'm privileged to have this wonderful career and to have people actually go to see my movies.

There are a lot of wonderful movies made each year that people don't see. I've been very fortunate to have audiences find my movies and accept them. So I want to be somebody who didn't abuse the privilege, who was grateful, who was unpretentious, and who wasn't an asshole. But of course I am, every day. I fail. So, I hope I'll be judged on the percentages, on the average, anyway. I hope people remember me with a laugh and had some good times.

What Does the Future Hold?

The future's never in our hands but I would like to continue making movies until they throw me out of Hollywood. I'd either like to be making movies forever or until I shouldn't be making them anymore, and I hope I know when that day is.

I always think it's important that if someone is reading one of my inter-views, and they may be dreaming of becoming a director, that I tell them what Woody Allen said to me in 1973. We were making *Sleeper* in the Rocky Mountains of Colorado and I was a two-hundred-dollar-a-week cos-tume designer and I was sitting in a field with Woody Allen. I was telling him about my dream of becoming a director and he said, "You'll do it." And I said, "You're just saying that because you like me." And he said, "No, I would never tell you that. It would be too cruel if I didn't think you really could do it. But you'll do it. You have it." "But," I said, "here I am, this two-hundred-dollar-a-week costume designer. Directing seems so far away." And he said, "Take a good look at the industry. There are only a handful of geniuses touched by the gods. As for the rest of them, if they can do it, you can do it, and you can do it better."

So what I like to say to people is, if I can do this, you can do this, and you can do it better.

Filmography

The Virginia Hill Story (TV, 1974)
Amateur Night at the Dixie Bar and Grill (TV, 1979)
The Incredible Shrinking Woman (1981)
D.C. Cab (1983)
St. Elmo's Fire (1985)
The Lost Boys (1987)
Cousins (1989)
Flatliners (1990)
Dying Young (1991)
2000 Malibu Road (TV series, 1992)
Falling Down (1993)
The Client (1994)
Batman Forever (1995)
A Time to Kill (1996)
Batman & Robin (1997)

EDITOR'S NOTE: Since this interview, Schumacher has completed *8MM* (with Nicolas Cage, Joaquin Phoenix, James Gandolfini, Peter Stormare, Anthony Heald, Christopher Bauer, Catherine Keener, Myra Carter, Amy Morton, Jenny Powell, Anna Gee Byrd, Jack Betts, Luis Oropeza, Rachel Singer, and Don Creech) and *Flawless* (with Robert De Niro, Philip Seymour Hoffman, Barry Miller, Daphne Rubin-Vega, Wanda De Jesus, Wilson Jermaine Heredia, Nashom Benjamin, Scott Allen Cooper, Rory Cochrane, Skipp Sudduth, Christopher Bauer, Kent Fuher, Richie LaMontagne, and Michelle Robinson). He was scheduled to direct *Tigerland* (with Clifton Collins Jr., Matthew Davis, Colin Farrell, Tom Guiry, and Shea Wigham) and *The Church of the Dead Girls* in 2000.

8MM (1999)
Flawless (1999)
Tigerland (scheduled, 2000)
The Church of the Dead Girls (scheduled, 2000)

Awards

Berlin International Film Festival
8MM, Golden Berlin Bear (nominated), 1999

Razzie Awards
Batman & Robin, Worst Director (nominated), 1998

ShoWest Convention, USA
Director of the Year, 1997

The Films of Robert Zemeckis

Born May 14, 1952, and raised on the South Side of Chicago, director Robert Zemeckis began making films with an 8 mm camera while
in high school. He attended Northern Illinois University before transfer-
ring to the School of Cinema at the University of Southern California. A
student Academy Award for his film *Field of Honor* brought Zemeckis to
the attention of directors Steven Spielberg and John Milius who made it
possible for Zemeckis and his USC writing partner, Bob Gale, to get a development deal for their original screenplay, *1941,* which Spielberg chose
to direct.

Zemeckis made his directorial debut in 1978 with a screenplay he co-
wrote with Bob Gale—*I Wanna Hold Your Hand,* the story of a group of
teenagers who are out to meet the Beatles on the eve of their first appearance on *The Ed Sullivan Show.* He then went on to direct another
Zemeckis–Gale screenplay, the critically acclaimed *Used Cars,* starring
Kurt Russell. But it was Zemeckis's third film that proved to be the turning point in his career. Starring the team of Michael Douglas, Kathleen
Turner, and Danny DeVito, *Romancing the Stone* became the number one
box office hit of 1984.

He followed this success by re-teaming with Bob Gale in directing the
duo's screenplay *Back to the Future.* The film earned over $350 million
worldwide and emerged as the top grossing film of 1985, as well as gar-
nering an Academy Award nomination for best screenplay for Zemeckis
and Gale. Zemeckis topped himself again with his next feature, another
box office smash, *Who Framed Roger Rabbit?* The film became the top
grosser of 1988, also passing the $350 million mark. For this achieve-
ment Zemeckis was honored with an award from the Directors Guild of
America.

Back to the Future Parts II and III followed next, back to back. In its opening weekend, *Back to the Future Part II* took in a staggering $47 million, and went on to earn a worldwide gross of well over $300 million. The later release of Part III completed one of the most popular film trilogies of all time.

Zemeckis has gone on to direct *Death Becomes Her, Forrest Gump,* and *Contact,* all highly successful and innovative films. He has proven he can work a serious story around great effects, a feat many directors cannot achieve. At this writing he has several new projects in the works.

Zemeckis's interview took place at his spacious offices at Universal Studios in California. He proved to be congenial, ready and willing to answer all questions put to him, and struck this interviewer as somewhat shy.

> *Well, I think everybody knows, and I certainly found this out, that Bob Zemeckis is probably the greatest technician director that I've ever worked with, ever. He walks onto the set every single day and invents something new and people scurry around trying to figure out how to make it. He just has one of those amazing brains that he really can translate the storytelling of the movie into a very epic, very technical, very visual sense, very visual style.*
>
> Jodie Foster—Actress

The Conversation

I grew up on the South Side of Chicago in a very working, lower middle class neighborhood. My father was in construction and my mother was a housewife. I grew up watching a lot of television and going to movies.

I would say I was fascinated by the illusion of the movies before anything else. I was always trying to figure out how they did something, like a visual effect, or how they did an action sequence, and I became obsessed with how they synched sound up with the picture. I tried to do that with home movies. So I guess my passion for film came from the technical end first.

While I was studying at U.S.C. I won a Student Academy Award for a film I made called *Field of Honor*. That was called a 480 Project. That's where you direct for a semester and you have to put a crew together of five people and you make a film. Color; synch sound; sixteen millimeter; and it's supposed to be somewhere between three and twenty minutes. At the time it created quite a stir at the university because it had action in it. That was pretty interesting.

Bob Gale and I got to work for Steven Spielberg as screenwriters. I had met Steven briefly at USC, and then we met him formally when Bob and I pitched John Milius this idea for a screenplay called *1941*. When John read that screenplay, he gave it to Steven. Steven loved it and said he wanted to make it as his next movie, but he was about to start this movie in Alabama called *Close Encounters of the Third Kind*. So, he invited us down to Alabama. He had this huge house that we stayed in. He directed *Close Encounters* during the day and together we rewrote *1941* in the evenings.

I showed Steven my student film. I think the combination of that and then reading the screenplays I had written with Bob Gale gave him the courage to suggest that I should be a director. Doing a short student film isn't enough and writing a screenplay isn't enough, but the combination of the two I think gave Steven the confidence that I knew my way around a camera, could direct actors to some extent, and could edit.

I Wanna Hold Your Hand (1978)

Nancy Allen; Bobby Di Cicco; Marc McClure; Susan Kendall Newman; Theresa Saldana; Wendie Jo Sperber; Eddie Deezen; Christian Juttner; Will Jordan; Reed Morgan; Claude Earl Jones; James Houghton; James Hewitson; Dick Miller; Vito Carenzo.

While we were down in Alabama rewriting *1941*, we came up with an idea that became *I Wanna Hold Your Hand*. We pitched Steven the idea but he didn't get it at the time. So Bob and I kept working on it. We came back to Hollywood and set the project up at Warner Bros. as screenwriters only because Warner Bros. had a policy of not making movies with first-time directors at that time. Anyway, I gave Steven the screenplay to critique. When he read it he suggested I direct it. He got Sid Sheinberg at Universal on the phone and told him I had potential. And I believe that what he said to Sid was, and this is my assumption, that if Zemeckis cracks up or if he doesn't finish the movie, I'll be there to finish it. So at worst you'll end up with a movie that I (Steven) half direct. Luckily that wasn't the case. But I think that made Sid feel secure, so between the two of them, that's how I got my directing break.

I thought *I Wanna Hold Your Hand* was pretty good. One of the great memories in my life is going to the preview. I didn't know what to expect. I had never been in a situation like this. My very first preview was at the Directors Guild. The audience just went wild. They were laughing and cheering. It was just great. Then we learned a really sad lesson. We thought we had a hit. But just because a movie worked with a preview audience didn't mean anyone wanted to go see it. But the preview audiences loved it. Then, twenty-four hours later you go into a complete crash when the movie opens and no one goes to see it.

Used Cars (1980)
Kurt Russell; Jack Warden; Gerrit Graham;
Frank McRae; Deborah Harmon; Joe Flaherty; David L. Lander;
Michael McKean; Michael Talbott; Harry Northup;
Alfonso Arau; Al Lewis; Woodrow Parfrey;
Andrew Duncan; Dub Taylor.

This was actually an idea that John Milius came up with which was basically just a title. He thought we should make a movie called *Used Cars* with nothing but despicable characters in it. Bob Gale and I thought that was a really great idea. So we wrote the screenplay and made it for Columbia. Steven Spielberg and John Milius both executive produced that. Bob Gale produced it and I directed. Again, that was another movie that had tremendously successful previews. People just loved it. And for some reason it didn't connect with the public. So that was my second box office disappointment.

What happens in the industry is you start getting the reputation of being unlucky because you make these films that are entertaining. They work when people see them, but they don't make any money. Suddenly people take notice that you make films that don't make any money. You start to become stigmatized—labeled.

Romancing the Stone (1984)

Michael Douglas; Kathleen Turner; Danny DeVito; Zack Norman;
Alfonso Arau; Manuel Ojeda; Holland Taylor; Mary Ellen Trainor;
Eve Smith; Joe Nesnow; José Chávez; Evita Muñoz "Chachita";
Camillo García; Rodrigo Puebla; Paco Morayta.

I was very fortunate in that Michael Douglas, who is a good friend of mine, is also a very, very savvy producer. He was one of the few people who saw beyond the box office of my films. He really pressured 20th Century Fox to allow me to direct *Romancing the Stone* in spite of the fact that my other films hadn't made money. He told 20th that this was the type of directing, the type of energy, he wanted in his movie. Look at the film, don't look at the box office, he told them. So, he convinced the people at 20th to let me direct that film.

It was a very crippled screenplay by Diane Thomas at the time. But when I read it I really felt that I could make that movie. But it needed a lot of work so we rolled up our sleeves and got into it.

We searched for the Joan Wilder character for a long time. Kathleen Turner agreed to screen-test with Michael. Prior to *Romancing the Stone,* Kathleen's only on-screen performances were femme fatale, vampy characters. We had a sense that she was a movie star. I mean, we knew that. But we didn't see anything that she had done which was the really soft, charming side of the character she played in *Romancing the Stone.*

Kathleen was very smart. She said, "Look, Bob, don't cast me because of what I haven't done. Cast me because I'm right. Just tell me where you want me to show up and I'll show you I can do this part." We shot a screen test; she did the character and got the part.

At that point in my career I must say that I was finding my way. I think that in my earlier films I felt compelled to tell the actors more than they needed to know. I talked a little more than was necessary. And then I realized later that actors, really good actors, basically just needed to know what the character is feeling at a particular moment in the screenplay and where they go and get that is their work. That's what they do. I would do things that could have been very nerve-wracking. Just before rolling the camera I would say, "Now remember to hit that mark and lean into the light," and I would drive them crazy. Because I didn't want the take messed up because of some mechanical thing that I wanted them to remember to do. I stopped doing that.

In my previous experiences I was used to going to the preview having audiences love the film. But then what? How do you get anyone to go see the movie? But with *Romancing the Stone* we were in the right place at the right time. In those days no one at 20th Century Fox knew what we were doing. They weren't sure what the movie was going to be. It burst onto the scene, and it was like, whoa, where did this come from? They'd had a string of unsuccessful films at that time. So all the energy of the studio got behind it. And Michael Douglas pushed it quite a bit. He went out and did a lot of publicity for it. They really worked hard to market that film really well. So we finally had a situation where we had a movie that really worked and a campaign that made people want to go see it.

Romancing the Stone was the most difficult film I've made, physically. It was a very complicated and miserable physical environment. We were down in the jungle in Mexico. It rained every day. We were always standing in mud up to our knees, just moving the company and shooting in these really difficult locations where it was difficult to get equipment and props in. I told Diane Thomas, the writer of the screenplay, that if I ever again saw a screenplay that starts off with "exterior, jungle, rain, night," I'm not going to read anything further than that. And so she had this slug line blown up and framed, and gave it to me as a gift. It was very hard. That was a hard shoot.

Back to the Future (1985)

Michael J. Fox; Christopher Lloyd; Lea Thompson; Crispin Glover;
Thomas F. Wilson; Claudia Wells; Marc McClure; Wendie Jo Sperber;
George DiCenzo; Lee McCain; James Tolkan; J.J. Cohen;
Casey Siemaszko; Billy Zane; Harry Waters Jr.

After *Used Cars* we wrote *Back to the Future*. And there was that three-year span where I couldn't get a job directing. I wasn't offered anything I wanted to direct until *Romancing the Stone* came along. I was offered teen comedies and things like that but my heart just wasn't in it. We wrote *Back to the Future* in that period of time. I have a stack of rejection letters from every studio in town. At the time the critique was that nobody is interested in time travel. The movie is too soft, it's not for the teen audience, it's not "R" rated enough, and it's the kind of story that's too tough for young kids. No one understood what the movie was trying to do. Except one guy, and that was Steven Spielberg, who read it and said, "Yeah, I'll make this."

At the time he had produced my first two movies, and they were failures at the box office. So I told Steven that if he produced this movie and it didn't make money I would probably never work again. I'd be perceived as a guy who could only make a movie if Spielberg produced it. He agreed. But after I made *Romancing the Stone,* I was really hot as a director and I was offered a lot of stuff. Then everybody who had rejected *Back to the Future* wanted to make *Back to the Future.* So I felt it was only appropriate to take it to the one guy who had faith in it from the beginning. I had selfish motivations too, because by this time Steven's name had become synonymous with a certain type of film. I mean, he had become a brand name, and to have him associated with *Back to the Future* was like a perfect fit. I turned out to be right because the movie was wildly successful.

There's an interesting story about how Michael J. Fox got the role of Marty McFly. I had already cast another actor in the part by the name of Eric Stoltz. You see I was given an ultimatum by the studio that if the movie couldn't be delivered by a certain release date, they didn't want to make it. What that did was back us into a start date. Now, my first choice for the part of Marty Mcfly was Michael J. Fox, but I couldn't get him out of his TV show in enough time to make the film and make the release date. So I cast Eric Stoltz. I thought Eric was going to be right in the part but it wasn't working. I was seeing the movie in a different way than Eric was performing it. I assembled all the footage after shooting for three or four weeks and realized I had made a tremendous mistake. Eric's a wonderful actor, but wasn't comfortable doing this type of part. So I went to Steven and told him how I felt. We then went to Michael J. Fox and asked if he would work twenty-four hours a day by doing *Family Ties* during the day and then *Back to the Future* at night. He agreed and we went back and reshot the scenes we had done with Eric. That's how Michael ended up starring in the movie.

Letting Eric go was terrible. It was awful. It was the hardest meeting I've had in my career and it was all my fault. I broke his heart. I learned, sadly, that you couldn't make decisions for the wrong reasons. You can never make creative decisions because of corporate reasons, because someone's going to get hurt.

Casting is an interesting thing. You just know it when it's really right. For me, casting falls into two categories. There's the time when someone comes in and before they even say one word, you know this is the guy. It's just a feeling that washes over you. The other is when you're struggling and you cautiously cast someone and then you hold on. You know someone is really close, but you've got to make a decision because they're going to go do another project if you don't make a decision. In the case of Christopher Lloyd he walked in and that was it. He's very shy. In an interview he doesn't say much. But he just had that look. I can't describe it. He came in and he was the guy.

In the early drafts of the screenplay, the time machine was built out of an old refrigerator, like a chamber you went in. We were concerned that kids would start locking themselves in refrigerators if the movie became popular. Bob Gale and I thought that if you're going to make a time machine, you could make it out of anything. So it would be wise to make it a vehicle because if you went back into the past, to a period of time where there weren't motorized vehicles, you'd at least be able to get around. You'd probably want to make it into some giant, sci-fi, four-wheel-drive huge truck, a giant off-road vehicle or tank. But we had a lot of jokes we could do with the DeLorean car, so that's what we went with.

Interestingly enough, there are not that many special effects in the first *Back to the Future*. There are only thirty shots and most of them are lightning. But because of the subject and because of the energy and the story, it's considered to be this giant special-effects movie. But in fact, the time machine only travels through time twice in the whole movie. And all of the optical effect shots are mainly lightning bolts and things like that. It isn't my most special-effects movie. I think there is more special effects in *Romancing the Stone*, actually—stunt type things and action sequences. Now, *Back to the Future II* and *III* are a different story. Those are giant special-effects movies.

We had no idea that *Back to the Future* would be so popular around the world. But I think it touches something. The idea of going back and seeing your roots and seeing where you came from and seeing what your parents were like when they were your age is something that everyone understands. Everyone has a family of origin so that's a universal theme.

Who Framed Roger Rabbit? (1988)

Bob Hoskins; Christopher Lloyd; Joanna Cassidy; Charles Fleischer;
Stubby Kaye; Alan Tilvern; Richard Le Parmentier; Lou Hirsch;
Betsy Brantley; Joel Silver; Paul Springer; Richard Ridings;
Edwin Craig; Lindsay Holiday; Mike Edmonds.

I wanted to do *Roger Rabbit* when I read the first three pages of the screenplay. The idea of mixing animation and live action was something that I always hated. I couldn't stand early attempts at this—*Pete's Dragon* and things like that. They just didn't work. And they didn't work, I felt, because they were a technique. They were a film technique. It worked fine with Gene Kelly dancing with the little mouse back in the forties. But to do a film story, I always felt, was a problem with the suspension of disbelief.

Then I read the *Roger Rabbit* screenplay. The inspired idea in the screenplay is in the first three pages where the cartoon character steps out of a cartoon and we realize that slowly, visually, it takes us into this unbelievable world where cartoon characters interact with human characters, and I said, "That, I understand. That works." At least technique grew from the original concept of the story.

And then I thought it would really be great to celebrate that Tex Avery, Warner Bros. type of cartoon humor that got destroyed a little bit by Saturday morning television. It became limited animation, everyone clamoring that the *Road Runner* cartoon was too violent for children. That sort of thing.

I found the idea of combining Looney Tunes with film noir was just so wild. I had to figure out how to do it. And then Steven Spielberg was incredibly instrumental because he's the only guy on the planet that was able to get all the competing cartoon characters from all the competing studios in one movie. You'll probably never see that again. Ever!

Making *Roger Rabbit* was a labor of love for a lot of people. Sometimes when you make a movie, everyone's in the right place at the right time. I was at the right place to do this. Disney was at the right place to do this because this screenplay was, or the book was, bought by the old regime, before Michael Eisner and Jeffrey Katzenberg. I was interested in it way back then, but I had meetings with those guys and they didn't get it at all. You just saw it being destroyed by whatever the Disney philosophy was in those days. So Jeffrey had now taken over the studio and all this new energy was there, but of course he was terrified of the idea. It was an outrageously expensive movie, and, of course, there was the question of is this going to work and was anybody going to buy the idea. Everybody was just walking around knowing that you didn't know until the movie was completely finished. There was no way to pre-test anything because when we actually did attempt to preview the movie very early on, it was a disaster. Only half the cartoon characters were in it. I mean, it just didn't work.

When I finished the live-action part of the movie, it was only half a movie. Again, I had a wonderful cast. I mean, Bob Hoskins was so great as Eddie Valiant. Not only did he give a great performance, but he believed that those cartoon characters where there when he was acting with nothing. That is the real illusion. The trick to the illusion in *Roger Rabbit* is not the mechanics or the technique. It was the live-action actors believing that the cartoon character is really there. Basically, Bob Hoskins was always acting for two. And that was what made the real illusion work.

Would I do another live-action/animated film? Not as a director, I wouldn't. They're way too painful. Animators are like actors, so for three years you have to direct animators. They just don't perform like real actors. They do it one frame at a time and they do it through their pencil. But they need direction, so it was really exhausting. It was like directing in ultra slow motion. You would give direction and then four weeks later you see a pencil test. Then you go back to the animator and refine the performance, and then four weeks later the change would come back. It is like watching paint dry. It's really a slow, slow, incredibly tedious process. It's a wonderful art form when it's finished, but it's hard to do. It took three years to do *Roger Rabbit*.

> *I think he has a clarity of vision. I think he knows how to pop up above the whole thing and look down, not just get lost in the center of it. I think what you call that, in the end, is he's really a good storyteller.*
>
> Mary Steenburgen—Actress

Back to the Future Parts II and III (1989, 1990)

Michael J. Fox; Christopher Lloyd; Mary Steenburgen; Thomas F. Wilson; Lea Thompson; Elisabeth Shue; Matt Clark; Richard A. Dysart; Pat Buttram; Harry Carey Jr.; Dub Taylor; Hugh Gillin; James Tolkan; Christopher Wynne; Sean Gregory Sullivan; Jeffrey Weissman; Casey Siemaszko; Billy Zane; J.J. Cohen; Charles Fleischer; E. Casanova Evans; Jay Koch; Charles Gherardi; Ricky Dean Logan; Marc McLure; Wendie Jo Sperber.

I actually think *Back to the Future Part II* is incredibly unique, in my opinion, in the history of cinema. Here we have this situation where we had a sequel, which is a strange form in itself. It's not really a motion-picture form. It's corporate real estate. It's a franchise. It's a TV series–type situation. In a TV series the characters stay the same and the adventure changes. Or in great movie sequels, like *James Bond*, James Bond is the same but the villain changes.

With the original *Back to the Future* film everyone thought we had designed the end of the movie for a sequel. But we only did that as a joke. Everyone made the assumption that this was all by grand design. It wasn't. The fact that Marty and the Doc fly off at the end, we thought, was just a good button for the end of the movie.

Then Bob Gale and I looked at it and thought we could do something that you couldn't do under any other circumstance. We could go into the first movie from another point of view and make it integral to the story of the second sequel. Now, to me that was an incredibly exciting idea, because it gave us exactly what a sequel was supposed to deliver. The same movie, but different. That's what audiences want in a sequel. The same movie, but different. I thought that was like the perfect fit. Otherwise I don't think we ever would have considered sequels.

Sequels are really hard to do. Everybody has an opinion. Everybody has his or her own perception of a sequel. Audiences have a real love-hate relationship with sequels. They love those characters so much and they love the experiences they had so that they want it again and more. And that's understandable. But they don't want it too much the same.

What we really wanted to get to was Part III, because Part III was like the perfect sequel. It was almost like redoing the first movie, but in the

West. So we wrote the elaborate screenplay and the budget was astronomical. We were in a meeting with Sid Sheinberg at Universal, who said he was not going to be responsible for making the most expensive film in the history of mankind. Of course, that budget's been eclipsed many times over since then by other films. Bob Gale suggested we just cut the screenplay in half and make it into two movies. Sid thought about it and said that it was either the most brilliant or the craziest idea. But he gave us the go-ahead. So we didn't really make them at the same time. We just made them back to back without stopping. They did overlap when I was in production on the third film and editing and doing the sound finishing on the second film. That was the hardest part. I wouldn't recommend that.

We were shooting *Back to the Future Part III* in Sonora, California. And we were doing the sound dubbing here at Universal. So I had a jet at the little airport in Columbia, California, and I would wrap when the sun went down. Then I would go to the airport, get on the jet, fly to Burbank, drive to the dubbing stage, dub *Back to the Future Part II* until midnight. Then I check into the Universal Hilton, get a few hours sleep, then get up at six, fly back to Columbia and be on the set for the call at 7:30. I had to do that for like three, four weeks. It was very hard. I do not recommend it. That is not good for you.

I don't know how I am able to juggle so much work. I think about it every once in a while and I describe it like having a high-speed VCR in my head. I'm always scanning back and forth the movie I'm making while someone's doing their performance and I'm able to see and review what I've already shot and imagine what I hope to shoot and then try to fit that piece in. I'm always checking myself back and forth. That's the best that I can come up with. I don't really know how else to explain it.

I had a bad time with the horses in *Back to the Future Part III*. I'm one of those people that do not like horses. I like to look at them. I think they are great animals, but I don't find riding them to be very comfortable. I don't remember being as terrified as I was having my actors on horses, doing scenes where you get next to a horse and you realize that if the actor falls off that horse and sprains his thumb, you have to shut the movie down. So, that's scary enough. But when I'm in a situation where I've got a steam train and two horses galloping at high speed with actors on them, and actors say they can ride, you think twice about that.

Then there are things like having another horse right outside the camera frame because horses are more comfortable following another horse.

And then you've got a camera car boxing them in. So you've got a steam train, horses galloping at high speed with real actors on them, and a camera car. I mean, I just wanted to get that stuff done. That was very, very terrifying for me.

Death Becomes Her (1992)

Meryl Streep; Bruce Willis; Goldie Hawn; Isabella Rossellini; Ian Ogilvy;
Adam Storke; Nancy Fish; Alaina Reed Hall; Michelle Johnson;
Mary Ellen Trainor; William Frankfather; John Ingle;
Clement von Franckenstein; Petrea Burchard; Jim Jansen.

I've always loved black comedy. If you look at *Used Cars,* if you look at my student films, there's something about my bent in comedy that is black. My favorite comedies are *Doctor Strangelove* and movies like that. I read the screenplay that Martin Donovan and David Koepp wrote for *Death Becomes Her* and I just got it. I thought it was really funny and something that I believed I could really do. I just loved the outrageousness of the whole thing. I had a blast making that film. It was great.

Here is the problem with black comedies in America, as opposed to Europe, for example. People love black comedies, but they will never admit it. It is a guilty pleasure. People feel embarrassed to say they laughed at that kind of a movie. You can't generate word of mouth when you do a black comedy because everyone is ashamed to admit they really thought it was funny. So you have to make black comedies for very little money. People really enjoy them, but they're afraid to say that they did.

So you sit with an audience testing these movies, which is kind of a ridiculous thing to do in the first place. You're sitting in a theater testing your film, and people are howling, screaming, and laughing. Then the scores come back and they are all like average and below average because people will say they are not going to admit it was excellent. They'll say it was just okay. They cannot admit they were laughing at such despicable characters and subject matter.

With *Death Becomes Her* it has been suggested that I was taking a shot at Hollywood's vanity, because Hollywood is always the extreme. You know, Hollywood, Beverly Hills. It's the perfect setting. But I think it's everywhere. I think it's this generation's obsession with aging. It's sort of what I was hoping for.

There are a lot of visual effects in that film. To me, visual effects are just another tool in the director's bag of tricks. That's what we do. The camera is a technical device. A lens is a special-effect technique. Those are all cinema effects that we use, when used correctly, for emotional impact. So doing something a little more elaborate is just an extension of this art form. For example, the Academy is called the Academy of Arts and Sciences. It isn't just emotion, acting, and music. It's also incredible technique and a lot of research and development. A lot of machinery. I guess that's why I love it so much, because it is a blend of the two. It's a wonderful way to deliver these incredibly powerful images and performances.

Bruce Willis was wonderful in the film. You saw a different Bruce. I didn't have to convince Bruce to do the film. Bruce wanted to do it. He wanted to do it so badly. At first I was concerned that Bruce was too buff and too good-looking. That was my initial concern. But the thing that's great about Bruce as an actor is he's got one of the most interesting bodies of work. Bruce is an actor, and he will do the character. And if he loves the character, vanity, stardom, and whatever never get in the way.

I knew Bruce was going to be great when we did his wardrobe fittings. Bruce modeled everything lying on the floor like he was passed out because he said the character was supposed to be a drunk. So he put on his sport coat and lay on the floor in a heap and asked me how he looked. And I thought to myself, working with Bruce is going to be great. He's not afraid to play a villain or a weak character. He's not afraid to play a schlumpy guy.

What actually has happened in my career is that every movie I've done so far is more complicated than the one previous. I don't know if that's a good trend or not. *Death Becomes Her* was for me my first step into computer imagery. We had built this motion-control camera system for *Back to the Future Part II* where Michael Fox was playing all these different characters in the same shots. He was playing his son, he was playing himself old, and he was playing his daughter. Those shots were done with this motion-control camera. We had to glue everything down on the set and we had to build a camera on a cement foundation. Nothing could move. All the lights had to be nailed because it was all optically blended together. So we used that same motion-control system in *Death Becomes Her*, but now we started to introduce the computer imagery. I believe it was the first time that the computer ever generated human skin. Meryl Streep had to act backwards with a blue bag over her head on the motion-control set. Then she had to do all the acting from the neck up on a blue screen stage four months later.

And then they built a sculpture of her twisted neck and scanned it into the computer to blend the two pieces together.

When Meryl had to do this scene where she stretches her head up, we had two hand doubles that put their hands in the sleeves of her dress and Meryl was crunched down on an apple box. And then she mimed this action and these two hands went up and had to come out where the shoulders really were. You see, the problem in dealing with anything about the human head is always the shoulders. So as we were doing this, I told Meryl that with all those Academy Awards she had won, and all the tremendous performances she had given, this was the clip that would kick off her American Film Institute Life Achievement Award ceremony.

Goldie Hawn in the fat suit was a riot because this thing was made out of silicon and it was great, because it had big, heavy arms. This fat suit weighed a hundred fifty pounds or something. Goldie had to bear the weight on her shoulders. It was like a backpack. She had to step into it. She was sweltering, so we had to cut a hole in the back and stick on an air conditioner to keep her cool. She was carrying around an air conditioner like an astronaut does with a tube going in her back, kind of like a tail. She couldn't take it off to go to the bathroom or anything because it took an hour and half to put on. It's a big deal. So she was stuck in it. But she was great. It was a great illusion. There was a lot of cool stuff in that movie.

> *His detecting system of what is right and what is not right is so fine that by the time you get up and start making the movie, it's like a Geiger counter, like a finely tuned instrument that he knows what is right and what is wrong.*
>
> Tom Hanks—Actor

Forrest Gump (1994)
Tom Hanks; Robin Wright; Gary Sinise; Mykelti Williamson; Sally Field;
Rebecca Williams; Michael Conner Humphreys; Harold G. Herthum;
George Kelly; Bob Penny; John Randall; Sam Anderson;
Margo Moorer; Ione M. Telech; Christine Seabrook.

I got a call from my agent, who said that there was this really quality piece of material that Wendy Finerman has been developing for nine years. I distinctly remember reading the screenplay and not being able to stop reading it, even though it had some problems. I've never done a movie from a screenplay where you could just shoot it without working on it. But it was so compelling. I was just reading and reading it and I couldn't figure out why, because it didn't have any typical movie conventions in it. It didn't have ticking bombs, it didn't have a villain, and it didn't have anyone chasing after the diamond. There didn't seem to be any compelling, dramatic conflict to keep me so interested in it. And then I realized that the true suspense was what was going to happen to this character. Whenever that happens, I know that's a major signal. I read it again and I said I wanted to do it. It was that fast.

I can't think of anyone living or dead who could do it as well as Tom Hanks did in that part. Possibly a young Henry Fonda would have done something interesting with it. But who knows. I don't think it would have been as good as what Tom did. I don't think it would have been as perfect. That's my opinion. Tom is brilliant.

I knew we didn't want him walking around with an affected southern accent. We just didn't want that. Tom came up with the ultimate idea of what Forrest should sound like. I think the young actor who played the young Forrest inspired him. He just had a very unique way of putting the consonants in the wrong place or something. So Tom took that and really ran with that.

We didn't want Forrest to physically move in an awkward way. I think what I did for the character had less to do with directing Tom than what I did in the scheduling of the movie. Because right smack in the middle of the film, right after we had done all the young Forrest stuff, the Vietnam scenes, as well as some key scenes with Forrest and Jenny, we shot Tom narrating the whole movie from the park bench.

Before we went to South Carolina to do the bulk of the movie, Tom went into the recording studio and performed all the park bench narration from beginning to end. That way I could get a feel for how long the scenes were going to play, since I had never done a narration film before. Then, as I said, we filmed in Savannah. And I remember Tom telling me that was the perfect thing that he needed to do at the perfect time. He said that at that point he just stepped into that character like he was stepping into a warm bathtub.

Tom got the flu during filming. It was on the day that he had to run a hundred yards, from one end of the football field to the other. This was one of those situations where I had two thousand extras that I had to make look like a hundred thousand in the computer, and it was in December near the winter solstice, which meant we had only six hours or so of light. We had seven cameras and I had to move these two thousand people to all these different sections of the stadium to make it look like it was a full stadium.

Tom comes to me that morning and tells me that he feels terrible. He said he had the flu and couldn't breathe and really felt lousy. I told him that was too bad because he had a lot of running to do that day. That was how we greeted each other that morning. But he was great. We had real football players, we had real running backs, and we had sprinters. And nobody was as fast as Tom. All that running in the movie was Tom, sick. And he was better than all the other guys. He's really in great shape.

When the movie came out everyone was blown away by the scenes that showed Gary Sinise without legs. Gary's a tremendously talented actor. He really gets into research. He would go and look at and hang out with people who had lost their legs. And then we had illusionists come in, like Ken Ralston, who was also going to redo the illusion on the computer for us. We had a magician make a chair that could hide Gary's real legs. The hardest thing for Gary was to not use the lower part of his leg. He had to manipulate his legs so that it didn't look like there was anything under his knee. It was ultimately all performance and we were watching it very, very closely. And then we would do little tricks to make the illusion even more spectacular. There is a scene where Gary's in his shabby New York apartment and he spins his stumps around on the floor. And of course he has real legs when we shot him doing that. Then we took the coffee table and optically put it where his legs would have had to go through. Those little subtle things just make the illusion more real.

Tom with the presidents was a challenge. We had to pixilate the mouths of the presidents so they would say the dialogue from our movie. That was hard. This was cutting-edge computer graphic stuff. For me, this was the film where opticals were no longer used. I think we used one optical. When I say optical I mean the old-fashioned way of making a composite in an optical printer. We did that with some rain. But everything else was done on the computer.

I'm very proud of *Forrest Gump*. I've thought about it a lot. Of all the movies I've made, you have to take pause and think, my God, what is it that I've done that's connected with so many people? I guess for me it was the first time that I could say everyone who was making this film made the right choices. Everyone was inspired. Everyone rose to the level of what the film was. The art department, wardrobe people, they all made the right choices. Everybody was really making exactly the same movie. From Tom's performance, or Robin's performance, Gary's performance, everybody was 100 percent on the money. I don't know if that will ever happen again. It was really, really great. Looking back on it, it was ultimately about grieving and I think that's what the ultimate connection is for everyone. It touched the part which is so important to the human experience. It's about loss of all types. Grieving the loss of a mother, grieving the loss of a friend, grieving the loss of a lover, grieving the loss of your legs, and ultimately grieving the loss of innocence of an entire nation is kind of what the whole thing embodied. And I wish I had known that when I was making it. I look back on it and say that is kind of what really connects us all.

Tom Hanks is like a dream for a filmmaker. He was always prepared. I remember one morning he was up to his neck in swamp water in the Vietnam scenes. Then I noticed the sky and the light was right. Everything was right for the scene by Jenny's grave. So we told Tom to take a shower after lunch, change his wardrobe, and get ready for the scene at the grave. I was able to get the wind blowing perfectly through the trees with perfect light and a perfect sky, and here's Tom ready and willing to switch gears and he does the scene without a hitch. That's a dream. But you can only really do that when you have a crew and a cast who can do it with you. I was able to do good things in *Forrest Gump* because everybody was always ready and prepared and willing to work.

Contact (1997)

Jena Malone; David Morse; Jodie Foster; Geoffrey Blake; William Fichtner; Sami Chester; Timothy McNeil; Laura Elena Surillo; Matthew McConaughey; Tom Skerritt; Henry Strozier; Michael Chaban; Max Martini; Larry King; Thomas Garner; James Woods; John Hurt; Angela Bassett; Rob Lowe.

Contact was a project that I kind of knew about. I was a big fan of Carl Sagan's and I got to meet him right around the time that he published the book. When I read Michael Goldenberg's screenplay, it was so different from your typical movie that deals with extraterrestrial life. It wasn't about the aliens. It was about what happens here on Earth and how everybody wanted to own it. Of course I saw this whole thing as this metaphor for religion, spirituality, and questions, unanswerable questions, which we feel compelled to answer both spiritually and scientifically. That was the beauty of what Carl was trying to say. But the truth is, in my opinion spirituality and science are totally compatible and they do not have to be in conflict. That was what I thought was wonderful about the piece.

It's tremendously sad that Carl passed away before the film was finished. I was really looking forward to those last weeks of Carl looking at the movie and duking it out with him as far as what was going to stay in and what wasn't going to stay in. He did see most of it. Three-fourths of the film was shot before he passed away. He came to the set a couple of times, even though he was very ill at the time, and made notes on all the script revisions to the very end. Every time we rewrote something, it always went to Carl for him to check the science and make sure we were doing it right. He knew what the film was looking like. He knew what Jodie was doing with her character. He was thrilled with that. Her portrayal of Ellie was just great, beyond my wildest imagination.

Do I believe in extraterrestrials? First of all, I don't believe they've landed on earth anywhere. But is there life somewhere else in the universe? Intelligent life somewhere in the universe? I believe in the mathematical probability that there has to be. If you believe in the truth of mathematics, the universe is so huge and so beyond our comprehension that I believe that there is a very good chance there's got to be some kind of energy out there somewhere. Maybe not.

The thing that Jodie brought to the character which was just so right on the money was that she never fell into an acting cliché. What she was able to do was maintain humanity, a wounded humanity, vulnerability, and still be intelligent. One never outweighed the other. It was a perfect balance. And that's what Carl and Annie Sagan were always saying. Jodie obviously got it. She played it with dignity and she played it with grace, and she never lost her femininity, and she played it with incredible intelligence. I mean, there's not a lot of actresses who can do that. She did a very good job.

The thing that was fun on *Contact* was that a lot of things were new to Jodie. She never had a harness on before. She'd never had to act in reverse before. She never had to be hung upside down for hours at a time before. But she loved it. But when I realize what I put my actors through in these movies—turning sets upside down, flipping them over, even vibrating her in that chair. That was the part that got to her after three days. That was like torture. That vibrating gets to you after a while.

I loved working with Matthew McConaughey. He is a really smart young man. He's very serious about his acting and his career. He was a joy to work with and he works incredibly hard and really gets into the character. Really figures out what he has to have. He's going to be a gigantic movie star. Screen presence is something that you can't create on your own. You either have it or you don't. But we know it when we see it. Matthew's got it.

It was the worst weather luck I've ever had on a movie. Thank goodness most of it was inside. Every time we went outside it was terrible. We only had good weather when we did the big scene outside the gates of the Very Large Array with all the people camping out. Every other time I put the cameras outside, the weather was awful. It was either foggy, snowing, raining, windy, or freezing.

I got a letter from the White House about the scene in which I used President Clinton. They asked me not to do that again. But I also heard that personally the president didn't have a problem with it. What I think happened was the news media got upset because, you see, we were exposing their game. You see, I was making a movie about fiction. The news guys present television images as true journalism, so if I can do this in a movie, then it makes everyone think, "Wait a minute, how do we know they're not doing that on television?" So for some reason the news media got really upset. They got more upset than anybody. I think that because they got so bent out of shape, the White House felt compelled to disapprove of it. But we presented President Clinton in a very favorable light.

On the State of the Industry

As far as the current state of the industry, I'm excited that people are going to movies more than they ever did before. And I'm excited that they seem to have gotten over the necessity for all movies to have happy endings. I think we can make movies with ironic endings. There was a point in the eighties where I was really fearful of that. If a movie didn't have a giant, totally heroic, send-them-out-of-the-theater-screaming ending, no one would go see it. But I think that's changed.

I think the biggest problem in the industry is the cost of marketing a movie. Because a movie has to be marketed on such a large scale, quickly, and has to be released now on thousands and thousands of screens in order for that marketing dollar to do its job, it's going to start affecting the type of movie being made. Big movies have to open on four thousand screens in one weekend. You can't do that with a little movie that needs to find its audience. Plus, I think we're making too many movies, which means the audience is just bombarded with movies weekend after weekend. The summer is just one giant movie after another.

So there's a section of the audience that would really love to see the number four movie in the country. But they never get to it because they've got to go see the next blockbuster that weekend, and the next blockbuster. They're missing out on a movie that they would really enjoy seeing because the marketplace is so full of movies and not enough screens to show them all. And I worry that the movies themselves will have to become homogenous. It's almost like movies will become what network television used to be. They have to appeal to everybody. And of course, if you have to appeal to everybody, then everything gets boring. That's my concern.

Where Things Are Going

I think that in our lifetime, maybe sooner, you won't need anything except a computer keyboard to create any type of spectacle. And then it's ultimately going to come down to the vision of the filmmaker because he'll be able to do anything. He'll have actors working in these virtual sets. There may be a form of storytelling that we don't even know about yet.

I believe that where we are today with digital imagery is where the car was back in the days of the Model T Ford. We can't even imagine the tremendous impact this is going to have on the world.

Bob's Parting Words

I just feel privileged that I'm able to make movies that I enjoy making. I just hope my body of work is always one of stretching. I don't ever want to go back over any familiar territory, just always trying to do different things. And I don't mean that in terms of spectacle and effects. I'm just talking about trying to do interesting stories and present interesting characters and if there's a way to create a really spectacular illusion along the way, I'll do that too.

How He Wants to Be Remembered

How do I want to be remembered? As a good father. That's how I'd really like to be remembered.

EDITOR'S NOTE: After this interview, Zemeckis was scheduled to begin work on *What Lies Beneath,* starring Harrison Ford and Michelle Pfeiffer, and *Cast Away,* starring Tom Hanks.

Filmography

The Lift (1972)
Field of Honor (1973)
I Wanna Hold Your Hand (1978)
Used Cars (1980)
Romancing the Stone (1984)
Back to the Future (1985)
Amazing Stories (TV series, 1985)
Who Framed Roger Rabbit? (1988)
Tales From the Crypt (TV series, 1989)
Back to the Future Part II (1989)
Back to the Future Part III (1990)
Death Becomes Her (1992)
Johnny Bago (TV series, 1993)
Forrest Gump (1994)
Contact (1997)
The 20th Century: The Pursuit of Happiness (TV, 1999)
What Lies Beneath (proposed, 2000)
Cast Away (proposed, 2000)

Awards

Academy Awards, USA
    Forrest Gump, Best Director, 1995
    Back to the Future, Best Writing, Screenplay Written Directly for the
       Screen (nominated, shared with Bob Gale), 1986

British Academy Awards

Forrest Gump, Best Film (nominated, shared with Wendy Finerman, Steve Tisch, Steve Starkey), 1995

Forrest Gump, David Lean Award for Direction (nominated), 1995

Back to the Future, Best Film (nominated, shared with Bob Gale and Neil Canton), 1986

Back to the Future, Best Original Screenplay (nominated, shared with Bob Gale), 1986

Directors Guild of America

Forrest Gump, Outstanding Directorial Achievement in Motion Pictures, 1995

Golden Globes of America, USA

Forrest Gump, Best Director—Motion Picture, 1995

Back to the Future, Best Screenplay—Motion Picture (nominated, shared with Bob Gale), 1986

Los Angeles Film Critics Association Awards

Who Framed Roger Rabbit?, Special Award, 1988

ShoWest Convention, USA

Director of the Year, 1995

The Films of Alan Pakula

On November 19, 1998, Alan J. Pakula was killed in a tragic auto accident in Melville, Long Island. It was his twenty-ninth year of producing and directing exceptional feature films.

Alan Pakula was born on April 7, 1928, in the Bronx, New York. He received his B.A. degree from Yale University, majoring in drama. After graduating, he went to Hollywood and became assistant to the head of Warner Bros. cartoons. He also joined the Hollywood Circle Theatre, where his directing work brought him to the attention of MGM executive Don Hartman. Hartman made him a production apprentice at the studio. When Hartman became head of production at Paramount, he asked Pakula to join him there as his assistant.

Pakula's first production at Paramount was 1957's *Fear Strikes Out*, directed by Robert Mulligan. This resulted in the formation of Pakula-Mulligan Productions, which created such notable films as *To Kill a Mockingbird, Love with the Proper Stranger, Baby the Rain Must Fall, Inside Daisy Clover, Up the Down Staircase*, and *The Stalking Moon*.

Pakula had always wanted to be a director, and although for a dozen years he had noteworthy success as the producing half of Pakula-Mulligan Productions, it wasn't until 1969 that he realized his great ambition when he directed the memorable *The Sterile Cuckoo*. He went on to win critical acclaim for the direction of *Klute, The Parallax View*, and *All the President's Men*, and his romantic comedies and dramas *Starting Over* and *Sophie's Choice*.

Under Pakula's direction, Jane Fonda, Meryl Streep, and Jason Robards have won Academy Awards. Liza Minnelli, Jane Alexander, Jill Clayburgh, Candice Bergen, and Richard Farnsworth all received Oscar nominations for their acting.

This interview was conducted approximately one year prior to Pakula's untimely death.

Some people work to a different clock. They have different priorities. But one thing, I think, that characterizes Alan as an actor's director is that he is in love with the process of directing. He loves the encounter with actors.

Meryl Streep—Actress

The Conversation

I had a crush on the theater since way back, back to when I was around the age of fourteen, when we moved to New York, and I used to sneak into matinees of Broadway theaters on Saturday. I would sneak into the second act, the intermission, so I missed a lot of first acts. I've always said that maybe that's why I have trouble with first acts, most people have trouble with third acts but I saw a lot of third acts.

I had a very, very strong fantasy life. As a child I used to have this running mini- or maxi-series that I used to create. I would come home from the movies on Saturday night and I would draw on some of the characters I had seen in the movies. They were usually war movies I created, in which I was a bugle boy in the first World War or the Civil War or something and I would go off into battle and then I would proceed to save all the young leading men in the troops. I would die on the battlefield or come close to dying and they'd all be running around saying we had no idea how brave he was. It was very satisfying. I used to lie awake at night continuing this series of adventures which was a little like my own little personal *Indiana Jones*, you know. I found it very rewarding. It all kind of collapsed when erotic fantasies began to take over and I would fantasize that when I hit the bed at night some fantasy woman was there but who was always beyond my reach.

I think that as a filmmaker people say, well, why do you make this film or that film or that film? You make films for yourself. I make films because I want to see them. And that goes way back with me. So in a sense, in my own fantasy world, I've been making films since I was seven or eight years old.

My father's oldest friend was president of Warner Bros. Cartoons, but I really didn't have that much interest in animation. This man knew I was interested in getting into film—live action film and the theater. He said,

"Would you be interested in working and seeing how the cartoon company works?" I said yes. Meanwhile I worked at night at the Circle Theater. I was stage managing there. It was a little theater in Hollywood, which was run by a man named Jerry Epstein and by Sidney Chaplin, who was the son of Charlie Chaplin. It was Charlie's last year or two in America before he moved to Switzerland and there I was, twenty years old, watching Charlie Chaplin direct. He would also come in sometimes to re-direct. I saw him direct some scenes from *Caligula* and improvise three or four minutes of the most remarkable performances I could imagine.

I was staying up late at night at the Circle Theater and then I would go to work at Warner Bros. Cartoons during the day. I didn't last very long at Warner Bros. Cartoons. It was not really where my interests lie, although I must say, talking to men like Chuck Jones was a remarkable privilege. When he runs into me it's always, "Well, how are you, lad?" To Chuck I will always be this young lad of barely twenty years old.

I learned simple storytelling, or I think I had an instinct for it, because I knew what satisfied me and I created stories for my own personal satisfaction and fulfillment, Walter Mitty-esque as they were. I remember being in a story session and they would have all these cartoonists come in and critique the storyboard before they animated it. And one of the rules they had was that Bugs, this very brash character, had to have some justification before he did all these brash, outrageous things. Usually a hunter or somebody else had to do something that was not strictly kosher, something that was endangering Bugs, and then, from that point on, having gained the audience's sympathy, Bugs could now be the underdog who becomes as outrageous and as brash as you want to make him. The whole essence of it was to first get the audience on your character's side and then you can do what you want to do. I found all of that fascinating.

I met a wonderful man named Don Hartman who was a writer/producer and director. He had written the Road pictures for Bob Hope and Bing Crosby and had done a lot of the Danny Kaye pictures for Sam Goldwyn. I met him through a mutual friend and he introduced me to Dore Schary, who at that time was the head of production at MGM. I got a job as an apprentice with Don Hartman at MGM when he was going to produce and direct. Within a year, Mr. Hartman was made head of production at Paramount, so at the age of twenty-two I found myself as assistant head of production at Paramount Pictures. It sounded rather more important and grandiose than it actually was. It didn't pay a lot by any means, but I was near the power and I would read everything that came in and I would attend story meetings and I would very often see dailies.

It was an extraordinary time at Paramount in that Billy Wilder, George Stevens, Alfred Hitchcock, and William Wyler were making films there. I would say that's where I learned. I also learned the difference between what you read in a script and what you see on film. And if I had any doubt of the importance of a director and the difference a director can make, I found it out then. Because you would see good scripts done by competent directors made into good films; made by less competent directors, good scripts were made into bad films; and you would see scripts that seemed acceptable but not extraordinary made into extraordinary films by remarkable directors. Like George Stevens. I remember when a very intelligent man read the script to *Shane* and he said to George Stevens, "Why would you want to make that into a film? It's an okay Western, but it's just another Western and you're a great American director." It clearly was not just an okay Western, and Stevens saw that. So as a learning experience, it was extraordinary.

I wanted to be a director but I was working with producers and writers. I was an executive and that is how I was perceived. Don Hartman used to say to me, "Well, you're an executive. Why don't you try my job, and why don't you try to be another Irving Thalberg?" I told him I didn't want to be an executive, I wanted to be a director. And he said, "Well, if enough people tell you you're drunk, maybe you should lie down." Well, I lay down for about six years as a junior executive and then I got a chance to produce my first film, *Fear Strikes Out*. It was a chance I fought hard for. Ironically it was a baseball film. I had been a tenth-rate athlete as a child. And yet, not at all surprising, it was the story of a real baseball player, Jimmy Pearsall, who has a manic-depressive breakdown. It dealt with a combination of elements that I think, without my being aware of, upset me from that time forth, and it was a great deal of the kind of work I did in later years.

Here was the story of an American baseball player who was a wildly gifted player, who suffered from a manic-depressive illness. Those kind of contrasts between light and dark, between strength and weakness, between the constructive and destructive and self-destructive, those elements existing in one character appear in a lot of my work, for whatever the reason. Look at *Klute* and there's a girl who is a prostitute who is very self-destructive. At the same time she had this great capacity for life.

The girl in the first picture I directed, Pookie Adams in *The Sterile Cuckoo*, was a girl with great humor, great wit, great originality, great life, and yet also great self-destructive elements. Look at Sophie in *Sophie's Choice* and Nathan in *Sophie's Choice*. You look back on your films and you begin to realize that there are things that seem to haunt you as a director, as a filmmaker, whether it's material that you have written or material you have chosen. Somewhere there are these underground rivers that keep pulling you to things. Even when you think you know why you've chosen to do a film, you look back years later and you think, "That wasn't the real reason, there was something else that is much more irrational that seems to fascinate me." I guess that's the change from the little fantasy films I made up as a child, where there are heroes and villains and very often they exist within the same person. I seem to have a fascination with Dr. Jekyll and Mr. Hyde in many varieties.

His Affiliation with Robert Mulligan Begins

I met Bob through the first film that I produced, *Fear Strikes Out.* I read the book and I encouraged the studio to buy it, and I told them that I would love to produce it, so they gave me the chance. I wanted to use a young director. I thought if I used a very established film director I would disappear into the woodwork, not in terms of credit because that was not the issue. The issue was I had very passionate feelings about this material and what kind of filmmaker should be directing it. I really wanted somebody from my generation because I felt there would be a rapport and a collaboration that I wouldn't have otherwise.

I met with several very interesting directors and Bob Mulligan was one of them. Bob was one of the best directors in live television in its heyday. I also knew I wanted to cast Tony Perkins as the baseball player. I knew that very early on in the development project. I had seen some scenes from William Wyler's film *Friendly Persuasion* with Gary Cooper, Dorothy McGuire, and Tony Perkins. I found Perkins very appealing. He had a lanky, Jimmy Stewart quality as well as a kind of mystery and darkness and sensitivity.

I talked with Tony and I said, "Listen, I'm considering Bob Mulligan to direct this picture, how would you feel about Bob?" And he got on his knees in my office and put up his hands in prayer. He didn't have to say anything else. I went back to New York and I met with Bob and that turned out to be a very fateful decision in my life. Several years later I was going to produce *To Kill a Mockingbird* and I sent the book to Bob and that became the beginning of Pakula-Mulligan Productions. It was a wonderful period for me in one way, because I loved working with Robert. In another way it postponed my directorial career because producing was satisfying.

The Sterile Cuckoo (1969)

Liza Minnelli; Wendell Burton; Tim McIntire; Chris Bugbee;
Sandy Faison; Austin Green; Elizabeth Harrower.

After Bob and I did six or seven pictures together, I thought if I didn't start directing soon, I never would. I had read a book called *The Sterile Cuckoo* by a young college graduate named John Nichols. I had taken an option on it with my own money, and I thought it should have a young director directing it. I got Alvin Sargent to write the screenplay, which was about an affair between a simple, naïve young man and a complicated, fascinating, self-destructive girl and the effect she has on him.

So now Alvin, who had become a successful screenwriter, is writing the script and I finally thought, the hell with another young director, what about me? I'm getting less young by the hour and by the day. If I don't do it now I'll never do it, so I cast myself. Liza Minnelli called me and said she read the book and loved this part and would I meet with her. I tested her with the young boy by the name of Wendell Burton who played the guy in the film.

I was hitting forty and I had been waiting for years to direct and I was very sophisticated about what directors did and what they didn't do on one level. Yet when I went to direct that test, which I have somewhere in some dark bin, I made every mistake that a young, very naïve director would make. I tried to do too much. One of the rules of directing is and should be that a story is told as much as by what you don't see, what you don't show, as what you do show. If you show everything, nothing has importance. Well, I did this very dramatic scene and I had these two wonderful actors. We worked together for a weekend and if I said stand on your head and whistle Dixie they would have stood on their heads and whistled Dixie. And if I had said cry and laugh at the same time, they would have done that. It almost went that far, but not quite. At one point, after Liza did a piece of the scene, the crew broke out into applause. I thought, this is gonna be absolutely brilliant.

Well, I've since learned to be cautious about what happens when the crew breaks out into applause. It very often means you're over the top. It's very dramatic to the naked eye but the camera looks at it and says, too much, too much, too much, when you see it on film. I ran the test for the two companies that were going to finance the project and they started to lose interest in the project and dropped it. They had a point. Not that Liza

was not gifted in it; it was just over the top. It was too much. I was pushing them all to do too much and I cut it so that every moment was shown.

Paramount was looking for a film so my agent sent over the script and they
loved it. I met with Bob Evans, who was head of the studio, and he said they
loved the script and he said, "You're a very successful producer, you've never
directed before, but okay, fine. We'll take the chance. Who do you want?" I
said, "I want Liza Minnelli." And he said, "Don't you think you should test
her?" He didn't know I had tested her. Hollywood is a small place and it also
is a big place. It's amazing how people don't always know what's going on in
another place. And I quickly thought, if I tell him I've tested her, he'll ask to
see the test and the ball game is over. On the other hand, if I lie he may find
out that I did the test and then I'd look like a damn fool. So I said, "Well Bob,
I don't feel I have to test her. I know she's right for it. I've met with her and
we've read it together." With much trepidation they agreed.

We did the film and I told Liza that it was such a delight working with
her that I always thought it was going to be like that. Very often it is, but not
always. During the shooting of the film every once in a while Liza, who always called me "boss," would ask me to come into her trailer and just tell
her the story. She knew the script backwards and forwards but it helped her
and I would do it as if I was doing it to my stepdaughter. I'd say, once upon
a time there was a young girl who lost her mother and she didn't know how
to be a woman. And she'd be very, very funny so that people didn't make fun
of her. But she didn't know what it was like to be a woman. She had no security in that. And she was very scared and her father was very remote and
lonely and she was lonely but she hid it. Then she met a very quiet boy and
she fell, etc., etc. I'd tell her the story this way and it helped her to know
where she was in the piece. I did it several times during the filming.

There was one moment during the film when Liza, who was one of the
most concentrated people I knew when she was acting, suddenly lost her concentration. We were shooting outside in upstate New York on this college
campus and she was waiting for her boyfriend in the film to come out of a
bus. She was standing up in a car with a sunroof, with her head and top half
of her body sticking out, and we went through a take and it was strangely un-
focused and I stopped and I said, "What is it? What happened?" She said, "You
know what happened? I was suddenly thinking how happy I was doing this.
How happy it made me to do this work." Well, as a director that moved me
because that's what the work does for me. When it is working for you, when
you sit on your little apple box and you see actors do a scene and it comes to

life, it has surprises, it has what you wanted it to have and things that you wouldn't have thought of as well. On the other hand the downside is that when it doesn't work you're in a depression because the difference between something working and not working can sometimes be a hair's difference.

During the filming Liza kept asking when I was going to show her the original screentest we had shot. I waited until after we completed shooting and she looked at me afterwards and she said, "Well, why did you hire me?" I said, "No, the question is, why did I hire me?"

Klute (1971)

Jane Fonda; Donald Sutherland; Charles Cioffi; Roy Scheider; Dorothy Tristan; Rita Gam; Nathan George; Vivian Nathan; Morris Strassberg; Barry Snider; Betty Murray; Jane White; Shirley Stoler; Robert Milli; Anthony Holland.

The first draft screenplay of *Klute* by Andy and Dave Lewis was sent to me, and I had just met with Jane Fonda weeks before about a film that her agent was interested in having her do. It was an interesting project but I did not want to do it. And then *Klute* came through my transom and I could only see Jane in it. I sent it to Jane, who was in New York publicizing Sydney Pollack's *They Shoot Horses, Don't They?* Then I flew to New York after she read the script and she said, "Well, why do you want to do this? This could get awful cheap, call girl and all that stuff." And I said, "Because I think you'd be wonderful in it and I think that it's a remarkably written character. I think there are things in the story that need work but the character is there now and the rest we can work on." To this day I think that she said yes because she wanted to get rid of me because she had to do all these interviews.

There was no way I would have done that picture without Jane. Every picture depends upon casting and the wrong casting can destroy any story, no matter how good it is. I thought where Jane was in her life then, in a very transition time, was actually right for this character. It turned out to be more of a transition than I realized because she broke up with Roger Vadim a few months later, and then she became radicalized a few months after that and politicized, and became a very different woman in many ways. I thought this would be a wonderful time for her to be working with material about a woman who is trying to change her life and then is forced to change her life.

Then my agent called and said Warners was not going to make the deal with Jane and did I want to go with anybody else? I said, "Absolutely not."

So we were both out. My reaction was, *que sera, sera*—what was meant to be was meant to be. Now, somebody just told me last week that Barbra Streisand was on Larry King and he asked her what pictures she turned down and then regretted and she mentioned *Klute*. I knew Warners had sent it to her but I was not involved at that point. So as great an admirer as I am of Barbra Streisand, that's not a film I would have done with anybody but Jane. Several people turned down Warners then, and they came back to us and that's how Jane Fonda and I got to do *Klute*.

I remember this disastrous moment in the making of this film, which was at the end of the last day of rehearsal. It was Friday and we had been rehearsing for three weeks. I had rehearsed four weeks on my first film and I thought that's the way to go. We were gonna start shooting on a Monday in New York. At the end of the day on Friday, Jane came up to me and she said, "Alan, I want out. I don't know what I'm doing. I just think I'm wrong for this. I don't think it's going work. Get somebody else." And I said, "I'm not letting you out. I think you're going be wonderful in this." Her panic was real and genuine. She had no faith at that point for whatever the reason.

I then met with my production manager and the whole production team and I said we have to change the entire schedule for next week. We were set to do a major scene inside a set that we had rehearsed. I thought it would give everybody confidence. But because Jane had no confidence I felt we had to get her into it very gradually. So I said, we have to start with little bitsy scenes, just until she gets over this stage fright. That means doing walks in New York and going into phone booths and other little scenes. Well, that poor crew and the location people went through hell because that meant shooting in actual locations on New York streets and that meant getting all the necessary permissions. It made for a terrible weekend and a terrible week for a lot of the crew because I was demanding it from them. But it was right. By the end of the latter part of that first week, Jane did a scene where she auditions to be an actress, and I could feel her confidence really coming back again.

As a director you always have to be ready and do a lot of planning and then you have to be prepared for everything changing at the last second. Here is another example. There is a psychiatrist in *Klute* and this call girl goes to him and they're actually crucial scenes to really understanding this woman and to believing in the changes that take place in her character. I cast a very good male actor for the role of the psychiatrist. Jane came to me and said, "You know, Alan, he's a very good actor. I don't want to sound unreasonable, but I think it would be better for me if I had a woman as a psychiatrist. I think it is something a woman would relate to on a different level." Well, when I told some people I was going to change the role to a woman because of Jane they said why give in to an actress? It wasn't a question of giving in to an actress. The fact is I should have asked her before. She was operating out of instinct and nobody knows what works for them better than the person themselves. It's their unconscious, it's not my unconscious—up to a point, that is. Vivian Nathan became the psychiatrist and made all the difference in the world.

Klute was also a picture where I got my visual style from cinematographer Gordon Willis, who was a huge influence on my life, artistically. Gordon gave me the courage to believe in my eye. I had a rather disturbing visual concept for that film. It was like the characters were subterranean; they were like in these caverns, lived at the end of a long tunnel with just a big long studio room and very often photographed like a long tunnel. It was the underbelly of the world. We tried to photograph it that way. It was a world where people were all the way in the bottom or all the way on top.

There was the killer, played by Charles Cioffi. Here was a man who was a sexual killer who killed a prostitute. A sexual killer means that some way or other he's hot-blooded or has no control of his emotions. But what did it come out of? It came out of the fact that the man is totally out of touch with his emotions, could not relate to other people, is isolated, cut off from other people. So I would show him hiding in the basement or I would show him in his office all the way in the top on Wall Street in this glass office, sealed off from the world of people who were nothing to him but little gnats down below. Gordon really encouraged me in that visual style.

Love and Pain and the Whole Damn Thing (1972)

Maggie Smith; Timothy Bottoms; Jaime de Mora y Aragón; Emiliano Redondo; Charles Baxter; Margaret Modlin; May Heatherly; Lloyd Brimhall; Elmer Modlin; Andrés Monreal.

Love and Pain and the Whole Damn Thing, the film we did after *Klute*, was really a film I started working on before *Klute*. It had a screenplay by Alvin Sargent, who did *The Sterile Cuckoo*, and it was a picture that was a failure. It was a very bizarre little picture and I have great fondness for it. I have a rule that when you have a success people don't see the bad work and when you have a failure, people don't see the good work.

This was the story of a woman and a boy. If you look at my pictures there are lots of odd couples, and in this case it was the oddest couple of all. It was the story of a young boy, played by Timothy Bottoms, who meets this English spinster who's dying in Spain and they fall in love. At the end of the picture they get married. It's all about the absurdity of love and it's very romantic. I did it in a very romantic, fairy-tale, fable style. It's full of castles. It's an absurd fairy tale that was roundly rejected.

I have people who still write me about that film. A professor of film in Philadelphia says he teaches that film. But by and large it didn't get much of a release. I don't think it ever was released in Europe. Maggie Smith gives an absolutely remarkable performance as the absurd spinster. She's the original woman who slips on a banana peel and then is busy protecting her pride and her dignity and is terrified of becoming undignified. And then she finds herself dying of a neurological disease that makes her fall down all the time. The ironies of fate. And then she finds herself in this very undignified affair with this very insecure young boy-man. It was about taking chances and it was a very romantic, picaresque piece. While there were charming, outrageous, farcical things in it, it didn't work at all and critically it was not well-received. But there is a little lonely minority out there that seems to still remember it.

> *There are directors who feel that they have to direct even when there is no direction needed. You get the feeling that they don't feel like they are doing their job unless they are busy telling you what to do or suggesting things. Alan has the experience and the wisdom, certainly, as a director to leave you alone when it's going well. I very much like working with him.*
>
> Bonnie Bedelia—Actress

The Parallax View (1974)

Warren Beatty; Hume Cronyn; William Daniels; Kenneth Mars; Walter McGinn; Kelly Thordsen; Jim Davis; Bill McKinney; William Jordan; Edward Winter; Earl Hindman; Bill Joyce; Stacy Keach Sr.; Ford Rainey; Joanne Harris.

The Parallax View was a whole other kind of filmmaking for me. In many ways it's the most visually stylized film of anything I've ever done and it has three sequences which I think are the best visual storytelling I think I've ever done. It dealt with an America that was in the post-Vietnam syndrome and the Watergate syndrome. It was made during the Watergate hearings. It's a world that has become almost surreal in itself. It is America that has become Kafka-like, in which you never meet the bad guys. You never know who the Parallax people are, some fascist organization of some kind that seems to be assassinating people.

Warren Beatty, who plays a journalist and the hero, is trying to infiltrate and find out who's assassinating moderate candidates. It's actually candidates trying to construct a new political system. So Beatty answers an ad and tries to infiltrate this organization because he thinks they are looking for trained assassins. They put him through a test to find people who are potential assassins. So I designed this kind of free-association test sequence from still photos and about the viewer's reaction to images of mother, father, and country. It is designed to rip you into a kind of a frenzy of rage if you are one of the people who have been left out of society and to see if you are one of the ones who have been unwanted, one of the tragic people who are the unknowns of society, people society doesn't care about. That was a fascinating sequence.

And then there's an assassination at the end, which takes place in a huge convention center. They are running a sound system test for a big nomination show of some kind. The whole place is decorated in red, white, and blue. There are these college drill teams marching and we had big cards with pictures of Thomas Jefferson and George Washington—the great icons of America. There's the candidate who's rehearsing and they show him where he's going to be and then he gets in the golf cart and goes down through this whole row of red, white, and blue bunting and is shot in this golf cart.

It's interesting that several years ago a now extinct film magazine had an article about pictures that misuse patriotic symbols and make fun of them. That's not what I was doing at all, but they mentioned *The Parallax View* in the article. It was meant to be a cautionary tale and I was saying, beware, anybody can hide behind these symbols. Symbols mean nothing; it's what they stand for. So in many ways it may be the most stylized film I've ever done, I think. And yet it was very political. It was very Kafka-esque in a curious way because suddenly the hero not only didn't win, he was killed. And not only are the heavies not killed, you don't know who they are at the end.

The last moment in that film is in court, something that resembles the Supreme Court making a decision about the whole thing and after they make the decision, they disappear. They pop off and we are left with just empty chairs, like there's no justice. All you hear is this John Phillip Sousa-like march and we dubbed it so it didn't sound to you like it was marching across the screen. And you hear cheering crowds along with this cheerful music. But you know it's the sound of evil. It's being used to make you think they are patriotic.

All the President's Men (1976)

Dustin Hoffman; Robert Redford; Jack Warden; Martin Balsam; Hal Holbrook; Jason Robards; Jane Alexander; Meredith Baxter; Ned Beatty; Stephen Collins; Penny Fuller; John McMartin; Robert Walden; Frank Wills; F. Murray Abraham.

One critic referred to *The Parallax View* as the death of the American hero. Well, in my next film, *All the President's Men*, the hero is reborn. Two ordinary guys, two unknown journalists, Carl Bernstein and Bob Woodward, exposed the story of the Watergate conspiracy and the conspiracy to prevent the truth from getting out. It is a story that ended with an American president being forced to resign.

Bob Redford came to me and asked if I wanted to direct *All the President's Men*. He was the producer. I read the first draft and I couldn't go with it. On the plus side, he chose where to end the story and I think he was right about that and there were certain basic structural decisions I thought were right. But I thought the tone was wrong. I was not alone in thinking that.

All the President's Men is a true story about a major piece of American history and I didn't think it should be dressed up for entertainment value. I didn't think these two men should be made into more conventional wise-cracking film heroes in a buddy picture. So there was that problem and Redford had the same problems with the script. Bill Goldman did several rewrites and in the end we really kept going back to the book. Even while we were shooting I would have Redford go out and call Woodward and ask what his memory of a certain scene was. And Dustin would go out and call Carl Bernstein and ask him questions like that.

Here is an example of that. After the film was released and Carl Bernstein had seen it several times, somebody asked what it was really like when he met the bookkeeper for the Committee to Re-Elect the President, a character in the film played by Jane Alexander. Carl said, "It's like it was in the film." The film, with its great power, actually reflected reality.

Anyway, we'll get back to making the film. We worked on the script and tried to really give it a certain kind of documentary reality although I had no intention of shooting in a documentary film style. It's not documentary style at all. It's making a story point. Like the opening and closing of the film, which I'll talk about in a second. It's the kind of thing that I got the courage to do from the stylization of *The Parallax View*. The studio became nervous when they saw what was the shooting script, although we changed it a lot as we went along. We would keep going back to the book and back to what we thought was reality. And they felt it was not looking like an entertainment piece to them. They said, "Oh God, this looks it's some television documentary, some CBS white paper."

Frank Wells, who was chairman of Disney, called me on the Friday before the week we were going to begin shooting. Frank says, "Alan, we've all just seen the final draft and it looks like it's going be as dry as dust and dull as dishwater." I told him things would come together as we shot. There was nothing they could really do about it because Redford was producing and starring in it along with Dustin Hoffman. I was directing it and we were committed up to our kazoo and there was no way they were going to cancel the picture two days before we began shooting. So Frank said, "Alan, I want to know that you plan to make a theatrical motion picture that has some entertainment value." I said, "Well, I do." He said, "Would you mind if I came to Washington to hear it from you in person?" And I said, "No, Frank." He said, "Everybody thinks I'm an idiot to be doing this." I said, "You're not being an idiot at all. You're putting up all this money and you should be able to talk to me in person." So Frank came to Washington and I told him that Redford and I planned to make a theatrical, entertaining film. It will maintain a sense of truth, but it will be a theatrical film that will be exciting to watch and a rewarding theatrical experience for the audience. He said, "You mean it?" I said, "I mean it." He said, "Okay." That was the end of that.

I opened the film with just a white screen and silence and nothing else. Then suddenly out of the silence comes whack—and this typewriter key slams on the screen and puts down an "A," and then slams "L," and it's *All the President's Men*. What was I trying to say? This was a story of the power of the word. This was the story of the power of the typewriter. It's a story of the power of writing machines. Then I used it again at the end. In the last scene on television, Nixon is being inaugurated and everybody is watching in the newsroom, and Woodward and Bernstein are writing this major story about Halderman, this story that's going to break the whole thing wide open and we know it. The camera moves in and you hear the twenty-one-gun salute take place for the president. The guns are loud. In the background you hear Woodward and Bernstein's typewriters going. Now the camera moves in closer and closer to them and past the television screen. The sound of the guns gets softer and softer. By the end of it the sound of the typewriter keys overpowers the sound of the guns coming from the television. And what is it saying? It's saying that the power of the word turned out to be stronger than the power of the presidency. It's mightier than the sword. So in that way, there was stylization in a lot of places.

I had a wonderful cast to work with in that film. The irony is I don't think Bob Woodward is a role that Redford would have wanted to play if he hadn't really wanted to see the film made. He knew that he had to be in it to get this film made commercially. Redford was used to playing more colorful parts, like in *Butch Cassidy and the Sundance Kid* or *The Sting*. He had just made several of those kinds pictures that were wildly successful films and he was wonderful in them.

The two things that were committed before I became involved in the project was that Redford was going to play Woodward and Dustin was going to play Carl Bernstein. When I met with Redford I said, "You know Bob, I'm very interested in doing this material but I'm not crazy about the casting." He said, "You mean Dustin and me?" I said, "Yes, because to me the power of this story is that these are two unknowns. You and Dustin may be better known than Nixon." That became an acting problem for them. But in the end, as we all know, it worked.

A lot of people asked us how we could make that picture when everybody knew how it was going to end. Well, Redford and I were nervous about that. But I think what happened was something I couldn't have predicted. Part of the power of the film was that people knew how important the story was and the suspense came from realizing how close it came to the story never getting out. So in a way, it worked for us.

We had a very interesting experience when we previewed that film. The first night in Denver, Colorado, we knew we were successful. We knew the audience was really with Woodward and Bernstein and really with the film. The next night, feeling pretty cocky, we went down to Louisville, Kentucky. You could feel that audience was more southern, resenting these pushy reporters. Same film and yet it played entirely differently and we came out of that thinking, well, who knows? That's what's fascinating about making a film. An audience changes the whole tone of the film.

Sophie's Choice (1982)

Meryl Streep; Kevin Kline; Peter MacNicol; Rita Karin; Stephen D. Newman; Greta Turken; Josh Mostel; Marcell Rosenblatt; Moishe Rosenfeld; Robin Bartlett; Eugene Lipinski; John Rothman; Joseph Leon; David Wohl; Nina Polan.

There are some people who say I've made two kinds of films. One type is political—*Parallax View, All the President's Men*. Then I make a certain kind of personal, romantic film. In many ways, *Sophie's Choice* was both. It's another loss of innocence story. Go back to what I did as a producer. Go back to *To Kill a Mockingbird*. It's a story of how two children lose their innocence when their father handles this case and they are exposed to this terrible crime and the cruelty of human beings and the unfairness of human beings. Then they come through it with their beliefs and humanity intact because it's an absolutely wonderful father they have. *Sophie's Choice* and *Sterile Cuckoo* had some of that.

I was very moved by the book when I read it. I was concerned about doing a story about the Holocaust, because while I'm a Jew, I was born in America and raised in America. I had a very protected American middle-class upbringing. I was worried about making the school band while the Holocaust was going on. Sad to say, but true. And so I said, "Do I have a right to make this film?" On the other hand, I related very strongly to Stingo and the portrait of the artist as a young man and the education of the artist into his first experience with evil and with passion. And there is something else I strongly relate to. Maybe many men do, I don't know. The whole idea of being in love and thinking you can save somebody. For me the tragedy is when you can't and you have to realize the limits of your power. Several of my stories have that as a sub-theme worthy of the stories I've dealt with.

Sophie dealt with all those things and it dealt with, in a sense, a political issue, as Bosnia is political. The human problem in Bosnia is political and it is more than just problems of a territory and ethnic groups. The human pain and the human price paid, and the final evil is that the victim is made to feel responsible for being the victim. And the victim is left with the guilt. To be destroyed, to have your loved one destroyed, and you are left feeling that you are the guilty one. And of course, that's the story of Sophie. I felt so strongly about the story I decided to do the screenplay myself.

The big question was who the hell was going play Sophie. I went and met with Meryl Streep. I had just started the screenplay and I had no idea what she would do with the part. I couldn't imagine her in it, yet I knew she was a great actress because I had seen most of her work. I said, "You know Meryl, if you want to run the risk of committing yourself to do this film before I finish the screenplay, I'll run the risk of committing to you without knowing what you'd be like with a Polish accent." She said she would like to wait until she saw a screenplay. I said, "Fine, but you have to know that since I can't be sure you're going do it, I have to go look elsewhere."

Meanwhile I had Doug Witt going around looking for the ideal girl to play Sophie. Of all of them I found one that interested me a great deal, a young Slovakian actress who eventually became the Czech ambassador to Austria. Then I finished the screenplay and the difficulties of getting financing with an unknown were enormous. Meryl's agent finally called me and said, "You know, Meryl's embarrassed because she's read the screenplay but you didn't send it to her. But she's read it and she desperately wants to do it and would you meet with her?" And I said, "Well, who am I not to meet with Meryl?"

Meryl remembers our first meeting and recalls going home and telling her husband that she didn't think I liked her. I reminded her that I had offered the role when I first met her. She doesn't remember that. I've said this before and I'll say it again, I've worked with some of the most gifted people—actors who were geniuses—but Meryl's the one. She has it, period. The biggest thing I did for her in that performance was getting her a coach to teach her Polish. She said to me one day, "You know Alan, I made a Polish sound today and I suddenly felt the character." Well, I understood that because that's how some actors work.

We sat down for a reading of the script when we started rehearsal and Kevin Kline, who I had cast months before as Nathan, had just come out of doing *Pirates of Penzance*. We sat around for about an hour, just talking and drinking coffee. Then we began to read the script. Suddenly Meryl begins to read and now somebody else appears. It's not the woman I was talking to ten minutes before. My first reaction was, "Oh no, nobody will believe this." It was so different from Meryl and it was such a shock to me that it took me a while to get used to it. I realized how extraordinary she was. Kevin was awed by this, as were we all. Now he had to play catch-up. What is interesting to me is when I saw the film recently I was reminded once again how good Kevin was in that film.

There was an almost disastrous moment when we were shooting one of the most important scenes in the picture. We were in Yugoslavia and shooting the scene in which Sophie has to make a choice between her two children. I came on the set that night and somebody said that the man who is playing the Nazi commandant who makes Sophie choose between her children is quartered right next to the little girl and they have been talking with each other. And I said, "Get that man away from her. She's got to be afraid of him. Don't let him near her. She's a child, she's got to be terrified of him." Well, she was, as it turned out. But if they had spent much more time together off-camera that child would have felt comfortable with him when he came and asked Sophie to make a choice. She might have said, "Oh, there he is, and he's that nice guy I talked to over there—hi!" That would have been disastrous. Meryl was quite remarkable in that scene because in many ways she controlled the child's performance because she was holding the child. Children really don't understand directions at that age. They understand about the person who is supposed to be their mother. Meryl would spend a lot of time with her so that she would love her and feel safe with her, and foster that maternal feeling.

> *He really is an artist in a community where that word is abused constantly. He's an artist in the sense that he has a vision of popular film as a way of expressing general ideas, ideas and emotions that we can all respond to.*
>
> Brian Dennehy—Actor

Presumed Innocent (1990)

Harrison Ford; Brian Dennehy; Raul Julia; Bonnie Bedelia; Paul Winfield; Greta Scacchi; John Spencer; Joe Grifasi; Tom Mardirosian; Anna Maria Horsford; Sab Shimono; Bradley Whitford; Christine Estabrook; Michael Tolan; Madison Arnold.

Presumed Innocent was a film from a successful novel. Again, it had a similar problem as in *All the President's Men* in that you have a suspense picture where millions of people know who did it. In the book Scott Turow dealt with a very passionate, hot, violent sexual crime and dealt with it in the cool voice of a lawyer. It was told in the first person by the man who is accused of the murder and who is also a lawyer. It's told with a remarkable amount of legal detail. It is the story about the most unreasonable, irrational, emotional act told by a character in the voice of reason. I wanted to keep that kind of dryness about that kind of hot material intact. The difficulty of doing that in film was that very often the character is defined by how the author wrote the story. And when you take that out, you lose a sense of the dimension of the character, the specificity of the character. And film is film, not prose.

One of the core problems for an audience in *Presumed Innocent* is that you are expected to spend most of your screen time with a man whose guilt or innocence you do not know for a great chunk of the film. And at the same time, you must care about this man because he's the one who's going to take you through the story. If they don't care about him, it's a very cold experience. And again, going back to childhood, I like to put myself in the experience. I wanted the audience to relate to this man and say, what is it like to be accused of this kind of a murder and to have done something that's so outside your character. Turns out not to be true, but you have to go through this horrifying experience with this man. It became very important that there be a man that you know is basically decent, even if he did something horrendously indecent out of some uncontrolled passion or madness. But you must in some way care about him to have that film work. So the respect for this lawyer and the casting of that role became very important.

Harrison Ford is an idealization of the average American male, as he'd like to think of himself. There is an extraordinary sense of decency that comes through about Harrison on the screen. That's one of the reasons I think he's such a great star. I think it's in the man. It's rare that an actor becomes known for qualities that are totally opposite of himself. And so he became crucial to the film too. Harrison thought of the idea of getting a very short haircut so he would look less glamorous. I thought it was not necessary. All I know is he gave a damn good performance and if it helped him give that performance, then it was necessary.

Because I wanted to get the kind of tone the book had, I decided to do it in a very dry visual style. I wanted a very objective, controlled character. I did not want to soup this up. We live in a time when some people believe the more you soup something up, the more that's going on, the more the audience is going be involved. That's not necessarily so. So in a way I tied one of my own and one of Gordy Willis's hands behind our backs by saying I don't want a lot of camera movement in this. I just want to present it. Here it is. I want the camera to be very controlled. And then maybe in some way we get a sense of the dryness of that narration in the book. Dryness may not be quite the word, but the controlled, rational quality. I chose to do it in an understated way because I felt the events themselves were so flamboyant that I wanted the camera to be a counterpoint to that and just be there as an objective reporter. If I were doing it again today would I do it that way? I might find another way of doing it. It worked, but other ways could have worked too, I think. I found it a fascinating discipline at the time.

There is a problem at the end where Bonnie Bedelia has this huge soliloquy in which she explains what happened. This happens in a lot of detective stories and very often can be anti-climactic. It demands a certain suspension of disbelief to believe that this bourgeois woman had been so desperate that she could have committed this crime in this incredibly inventive, extraordinary way, although Scott Turow is very clever in the way he sets it up. But it is a shock. This takes place in a very long speech. Now you're really in the hands of your actor there because she had to make all of this exposition work and bring it some personal emotional quality that makes you believe her and even feel compassion for this woman. I thought she accomplished this remarkably. But you come to realize that the whole picture's in the hands of this actress and if she can't make this work, the picture will come apart at the seams. It's one of those terrifying moments when you realize how fortunate you are to have a consummate actress like Bonnie.

I remember hearing during a preview of the film, someone said, "Well, why doesn't he cut to somebody else and show us what's going on here instead of talking about it?" Well, I'm a great believer in point of view, to the point possibly of getting too literal about it at times. The point of view was Harrison. I was doing this in this understated way with Harrison's character, and to suddenly cut into a flashback of what she did, I thought, would violate the reality and in some ways would make it less believable. Because what she did was so bizarre and operatic for anybody who read the book or saw the film. Clues she left after murdering this woman were gynecological evidence to prove that it was a man, done by a man, essentially her husband. Her evidence was her husband's ejaculate. I felt that if you showed some of that it would be absolutely ridiculous. But beyond that I wanted to stress a personal humanity, that this woman did it out of her own pain and, yes, madness.

It's a film full of some wonderful actors. There was Brian Dennehy and there was Raul Julia who was an interesting, wonderful actor. God, do we miss him. Raul was a wonderful actor and had this wonderful Latin flamboyant quality to him. But here he was playing this very controlled defense lawyer. Very different than what Raul usually played. And again, I was asking him to be terribly controlled and I thought he turned in a remarkable performance.

The Pelican Brief (1993)

Julia Roberts; Denzel Washington; Sam Shepard; John Heard; Tony Goldwyn;
James Sikking; William Atherton; Robert Culp; Stanley Tucci; Hume Cronyn;
John Lithgow; Anthony Heald; Nicholas Woodeson; Stanley Anderson; John Finn.

I read John Grisham's book *The Pelican Brief*. I read *The Firm*, too, and thought, "God, he just tells a wonderful yarn." He's a wonderful old-fashioned storyteller, and I say old-fashioned in the happiest sense of the word. You can just sit in it and bathe in it and have a wonderful time. It's like being a kid again. When I read *Pelican Brief* I saw Julia Roberts all over the place. I saw *Pretty Woman* and I asked to meet with her. My wife would say to me that every time I had meetings with Julia she could always tell because I'd have this smile, this sort of beaming face. Going back to Liza, there are people who do that to me. And Julia certainly does. She was really, really strong in the role. Julia went from being this delicious girl to being this mysterious, remarkable woman with a certain other kind of maturity that happened right there in that film. And then I was blessed with Denzel Washington, a spectacular actor who is at the top of his form.

There is a scene in this hotel room between Julia and Denzel. She sits there and tells Denzel her story. She was so controlled, like an animal that doesn't move. So contained and so the opposite of the Julia we all know who seems to be so alive and free. In the stillness, which was her choice, was a feeling that if she ever let it all out she would just fly apart, she would be destroyed. So that containment and that control was, I thought, extraordinarily powerful and I looked at that scene and I thought, there's Julia Roberts, the woman, instead of Julia Roberts, the girl. It's quite extraordinary.

One of my personal favorite scenes in that picture is a very simple scene in which she suddenly feels terrified after she has been to the offices of the people who are the conspirators—the people who are after her. She returns to the hotel and is lying on this bed. Denzel is there and he sees the pain she's going through. He, of course, is the one who had insisted that she remain involved in the case and not run away. He sees her pain and he finally just says, "I think it's time for you to leave." And all she says is, "I'm going with you." He now cares enough about her that he wants to protect her, that she's more important than the story. And she's changed in that he and the story have become more important in her own mind. It's a love scene in which neither one touches. No one ever says "I love you," but for me, if you look at those two people, it's a total love scene. And that, to me, is a much more interesting love scene than the usual clinch and the usual, "I love you, I love you, I love you, and I love you." When people say "I love you" too much on screen, I begin to question it. It's always more interesting if the emotion is so deep that it can't be said that easily or if the audience feels that they're saying it for them. It was, for me, an entertaining project made again with a superb cast and great fun to do.

Looking Back at Some of His Other Films

I've done fewer comedies than I've done dramas. I did *See You in the Morning* which was an original screenplay that was really a valentine to the happiness I've found in a second marriage, which I have great fondness for, for a lot of reasons. I did a picture called *Starting Over* that was based on a screenplay by James Brooks, in itself reason enough to celebrate. It starred Burt Reynolds, Jill Clayburgh, and Candy Bergen in what might have been her big comic role.

Jim Brooks came to me and he knew I had been divorced and had just gotten remarried and was happy, and I think he had just gotten divorced also. I was cutting *Parallax View* at that point. We talked about working together. He was in television at that point and he called me and he said, "You know, I have a book called *Starting Over* which I have an option on." And I said, "I know the book, it's an interesting book, but I always thought if I did a picture about divorce I'd do another story, not my own story." And he said, "I have an idea of what I want to do with this, will you listen?" And I said, "Sure." So I he came over and I said, "Why don't you work on the screenplay and I'll act as if I'm producing and directing it and then you just give me first call on the right to direct it."

We worked that way and he came up with a wonderful script. We went to cast it and there was Burt Reynolds who really hadn't done that kind of a part, which was a rather ordinary man being rejected by a first wife and going on to have to lick his wounds and get on and make a new life for himself. It's hardly the great leading man part. Burt is an extraordinarily endearing man and there is a genuine sweetness in him. He has all the complications we all have. I don't relate to people that don't have complications. But the essence of the man that I worked with was genuine. I mean very caring, vulnerable, and technically, as a comic actor, highly skilled.

I would say one of the most difficult directions I've ever had to give was to Candy Bergen in that film. She played a songwriter who fancied she could sing. Marvin Hamlisch and Carol Bayer Sager wrote these kind of outrageous songs for us. Candy worked very hard at studying singing with a coach and then she had to make these recordings for the film. So it was a Sunday and we're shooting and she said, "Don't come down in the morning, just come down later; let me rehearse and let me present you something that at least you can make some judgment on." So I came down in the afternoon and she sang and she was not displeased with it. Nor was anybody.

My reaction was, "Oh, God, it's not bad enough." I said, "It's not wonderful singing, but it's not bad. It's just neither here nor there. What is supposed to be funny about this character is her outrageous belief that she's a wonderful singer when reality does not back that up." And she said, "You want me to make a complete fool of myself?" And there I am, looking at one of the most beautiful creatures that God has ever created and having to say, "Yes, that's exactly what I want you to do." I could see her face fall, but by God, sport that she was, she went out there and she sang her lungs out with this naïve belief that she could sing and let it all hang out. And out of it came one of my favorite comic moments. She sings to Burt thinking that she is doing this absolutely stunning thing. It's remarkable.

Charlie Durning was in the film. If Charlie were English he would have been knighted by now. He is one of the great hidden resources of America and incredibly endearing. There's a relationship between Burt Reynolds and him that's just a wonderful friendship. I would love to see them make a film together that's really about a relationship of two men who really care about each other.

I haven't talked about several other films of mine. There was a film I made that didn't get released called *Dream Lover* with Kristy McNichol. There were a lot of things wrong with the film and the story it dealt with. But she is absolutely remarkable in it. There are a few visual sequences in that film that I find some of my more interesting work. Other things about the film just don't work. But I learned a lot of things from that film. Then there's *Orphans*, which I call crudely my attempt to make a play that still kept its definition and form as a play. I worked with Albert Finney, Matthew Modine, and Kevin Anderson on that one. Albert Finney is—well I've said it about Meryl and I would say it about Albert too—if there is a heaven for directors and if I get there and they say you can direct Meryl Streep all for eternity, well you could direct Albert Finney for eternity too.

I have been fortunate. I've worked with a bunch of great actors and I hope to keep doing just that.

Filmography

The Sterile Cuckoo (1969)
Klute (1971)
Love and Pain and the Whole Damn Thing (1972)
The Parallax View (1974)
All the President's Men (1976)
Comes a Horseman (1978)
Starting Over (1979)
Rollover (1981)
Sophie's Choice (1982)
Dream Lover (1986)
Orphans (1987)
See You in the Morning (1989)
Presumed Innocent (1990)
Consenting Adults (1992)
The Pelican Brief (1993)
The Devil's Own (1997)

Awards

Academy Awards, USA

Sophie's Choice, Best Writing, Screenplay Based on Material from Another Medium (nominated), 1983

All the President's Men, Best Director (nominated), 1977

To Kill a Mockingbird, Best Picture (nominated), 1963

British Academy Awards
All the President's Men, Best Direction (nominated), 1977

Edgar Allan Poe Awards
Presumed Innocent, Best Motion Picture (nominated, shared with Frank Pierson), 1991

Golden Globes, USA
All the President's Men, Best Director—Motion Picture (nominated), 1977

Golden Satellite Awards
Outstanding Contribution to the Entertainment Industry, 1999

Hamptons International Film Festival
Distinguished Achievement Award, 1996

National Board of Review, USA
All the President's Men, Best Director, 1976

New York Film Critics Circle Awards
All the President's Men, Best Director, 1976

Robert Festival
Sophie's Choice, Best Foreign Film, 1984

The Films of John G. Avildsen

During the course of his career, John G. Avildsen has directed everything from offbeat cult classics like *Cry Uncle!* to *Rocky, The Karate Kid,* and *The Karate Kid Part II,* three of the most popular movies ever made.

Born in Oak Park, Illinois, on December 21, 1935, Avildsen and his family moved to New York City when he was ten. He attended New York University at night while working in an advertising agency. In 1961, after two years of military service as a chaplain's assistant, Avildsen met up with his former ad agency boss, who was starting production on a film, *Greenwich Village Story.* Avildsen was hired as his assistant director.

Over the next few years, Avildsen took on various film production assignments on such films as *Black Like Me,* Arthur Penn's *Mickey One,** and Otto Preminger's *Hurry Sundown.* While supplementing his income making industrial films for such clients as IBM and Clairol, Avildsen produced, photographed, and edited several theatrical shorts, including *Smiles* and *Light-Sound-Diffuse.*

After answering a newspaper ad ("Wanted, Film Director"), Avildsen directed and photographed his first feature, *Turn on to Love.* This was followed the next year by the comedy *Guess What We Learned in School Today?* which he also co-scripted, photographed, and edited. Then came the controversial *Joe,* which became the sleeper film of 1970 and launched the careers of Susan Sarandon and Peter Boyle. Just a few years later, in 1976, he would win the Oscar as Best Director for *Rocky.*

It is noteworthy that Avildsen's filmmaking background has led him to continue to function on many projects as cameraman and film editor as

---

* As an unbilled assistant.

well as director. He remains a multi-talented filmmaker whose films display the mark of a professional.

> *Maybe the most fortunate thing in my career is the fact that I've had such great parts with great writers and great directors. I've worked with the best and I consider John one of the better directors I've ever worked with. I think he's terrific.*
>
> Jack Lemmon—Actor

The Conversation

In the early days I think I was much more of a master of my fate than in recent years. In the beginning it was much more the hustler aspect of things—going out and beating the bushes and getting jobs and reading the want ads and reading the stories about movies that were going be made and trying to figure out how I could get a job on one of them. This was before directing. This was when I was working as an assistant cameraman or a boom man or a production manager or an assistant director or a gofer. There was a lot of scrambling in those days.

Well, when I was a kid I wanted to do the Gene Kelly story and play him in the movie. I was going be a dancer and he was my hero. So movies were something I went to but I had no desire to make them. My father was always making home movies. He made home movies long before I was born. He had a Bell & Howell camera and one of my earliest memories was holding up the sign with the date and the place that would start off each of the home movies. So I grew up looking at this guy with this camera in front of his face. I used to play with the camera and we used to take a lot of still pictures.

But movies and making them was not my dream until I was in my mid-twenties and I got out of the army. The fellow I had worked for in the advertising business, Jack O'Connell, had worked in Italy for Fellini and Antonioni while I was in the army. When I got out of the army he made his first movie, a picture called *Greenwich Village Story*, which came out in 1963. I worked for him as his assistant director and had a great time. Jack put together a general partnership and raised, oh, I'm not quite sure how much, maybe fifty, sixty thousand dollars, and we made this movie. I said that this sure is a lot more fun than advertising and never went back. The movie bug had bitten me.

After that I started doing all sorts of jobs on various non-union, low budget movies, working as anything and everything. But eventually I couldn't get arrested. So I went back into advertising but this time making industrial movies for clients like IBM and Clairol and Shell Oil. That took me all around the country making these movies that were designed to keep all their salesmen awake early in the morning at these sales meetings. These films presented the new product, the new game to play, whatever it happened to be, and the purpose of it was to keep these guys excited about their jobs and what they were doing. So I had a great time doing that. That's when I started photographing and editing myself. So for the same eight bucks you got three guys.

I got to work for Preminger and Penn. There's a big difference between Otto Preminger and Arthur Penn, from my observations. One was constantly looking through the camera and the other one hardly ever looked through the camera. Otto was a great one for setting the shot and riding on the dolly and getting everything just the way he wanted and yelling unmercifully at the actors and the crew. He was always very nice to me except one time. But he was quite a dictator in general. Penn, on the other hand, was very, very soft-spoken and never looked through the camera. I worked for him on a picture called *Mickey One* that Warren Beatty and Leslie Caron made and it was a very unusual, offbeat picture.

For Otto Preminger I worked on *Hurry Sundown,* not one of his better pictures. But he was very generous in allowing me to observe what was going on and then one day he took a liking to me and he said, "John, you go and you shoot a sundown shot. Find a nice place and go and shoot it." So I went around for weeks looking for that perfect place with a sunset and finally found it and told him and showed him some pictures and he said, "Good, you do that." And next thing I knew, I turned around and I had about fourteen trucks behind me along with this huge army who followed me out to get this very simple shot. Then they realized that I had directed a scene and wasn't in the Director's Guild. I had to join the Guild and it was expensive. They kept sending me bills and at a certain point I had to go down there to plead with them to let me out of the Guild. I was in as a production assistant and at that time, I was working on lots of non-union, low-budget movies in New York and the last thing I needed was bills from the Director's Guild. So I was finally released.

Like I say, my dad was always shooting home movies and I looked at them if I wanted to eat. And so it became something I figured everybody did. He would buy me still cameras and pay for the film and developing and I would take a lot of pictures and that's something I've always enjoyed doing. And then when I started making these industrials, rather than hire somebody, I started photographing them myself and hired a good assistant who took care of the technical aspects of the camera and I would point it and shoot it and cut it together. I found that very satisfying.

I think the director belongs behind the lens. The reason that there are directors of photography is in the beginning it was all you could do to just take care of that besides having to have people go where they had to go and say what they had to say, or whatever. As the camera became simpler, the mystery of it went away. By the time I started making movies it was a much simpler affair. It's also something that I loved and had a knack for so it was a natural move for me. And like I said, for the same amount of money you got somebody who directed, photographed, and cut it.

I always figure that there's nobody that's gonna stay up as late as I am to cover all my blunders, and you do that in the editing room. I could never figure out how anybody would have the same motivation that I would have because when I become the editor I look at all this footage that I've given myself and I say, "My God, look at all these blunders. This guy is terrible. Now it's my job to take all this footage and try to make it into something." So I stop being the director and become the editor. I feel I am more motivated and that I would be more ruthless than somebody else would. On a lot of occasions I realized, wait a second, I don't need that. The story works fine. This has happened so many times and each time I say, in this movie I'm only going to photograph what I really need and it never works. There's always something extra you end up with.

I started going to the movies at a pretty early age. The movies of John Ford and Frank Capra were very indelible in my early movie-going experience. I think they had a big influence on me. So did Fellini and Kubrick. I think the first movie that I remember seeing as a small boy was a John Ford picture called *They Were Expendable*. It was a John Wayne movie and was very exciting and it made a big impression on me.

Turn on to Love (1969)

Sharon Kent; Luigi Mastroianni; Richard Michaels; Jackie Riley.

My first directing job in feature films came from answering a want ad. I was looking through this newspaper called *Backstage in New York* and there was an ad that said, "Wanted, Movie Director," so I answered the ad. The guy who put the ad in the paper, a man named Leonard Kurtmann, had never produced a movie before. He worked in an advertising agency in the mailroom and he wanted to be a producer. So he advertised for a director and I answered the ad and we made a horrible movie called *Turn on to Love* for about seven thousand dollars and it made money and led to the next one.

I didn't cut it because I went off and worked as a cameraman on another picture and wasn't able to cut it but I don't think that anybody could have made it much better than it was. It wasn't a very good script and I don't think it showed a lot of promise. It was very cheap and was done in seven days and shot on four-years-out-of-date TriX black and white 35 mm film. All the guys that made these industrials with me worked on it. The acting was terrible. The story was equally as bad. But it worked and had a beginning, middle, and end and it made some money and got me the next picture.

After I finished *Turn on to Love,* I vowed that I would never make another movie like that one. Back in those days they were called exploitation films. A lady and her bare breasts were flashed occasionally in this really dumb story and I thought I would never do that kind of movie again and fortunately I've never had to.

Guess What We Learned in School Today? (1970)

Iris Brooks; Richard Carballo; Stanton Edgehill; Robert Emery;
Larry Evers; Devin Goldenburg; Zachary Hains;
Yvonne McCall; Jane McLeod; Diane Moore;
Rosella Olsen.

Guess What We Learned in School Today? was the result of being broke the summer that everybody was going to Woodstock. I had a little baby boy and a lot of films I wanted to make, so I said, "I've got to be able to come up with a story that people will see the obviousness of and want to make." Around that time I had gotten involved with a group called SICUS, Sex Information Counsel U.S., that advocated sex education. Quite a lot of its literature made sense to me, so that became the basis of the story. It's what happens when sex education comes to this conservative suburban town. It was a very broad comedy and it worked. It was successful and made some dough and I was very pleased with it.

Okay Bill (1971)

Bob Brady; Gordon Felio; Roz Kelly; Nancy Salmon.

Okay Bill was originally called *Sweet Dreams*. It was the second picture I made but it wasn't released. It won the Atlanta Film Festival prize but it couldn't find a distributor.

It was the result of this friend of mine coming to me and saying, "Gee, you're in the movie business, I want to be in the movie business too. How do I do it?" And I said, "Raise some money and I'll make you a movie." So he raised about seventy-five thousand dollars and we made this movie that had no dialogue. He said, "Well, shouldn't there be dialogue?" I said, "Dialogue is tricky and expensive and if we just shoot it silent, we can put in the dialogue later, we'll get the actors to improvise and we'll edit that and that will be on the soundtrack and it will be much easier." So he did that. He didn't know any better. We made this movie with no synch dialogue* and the dialogue went in later. We brought the actors in and showed them the picture and then they would start to improvise the scenes and it was an abstract Fellini-esque movie that did pretty well and I was very pleased with it.

Later I realized that dialogue was better to have in synch than not so that was one of my first lessons. I think that every time you make a movie you learn a lot. I know I do. I think the more you do it the better you get at it. The more things you absorb the more you see what works and what doesn't work and you say I'm never gonna do that again, but sometimes you do. But the doing is the learning.

---

* Filmed without sound.

Joe (1970)

*Susan Sarandon; Patrick McDermott; Tim Lewis; Estelle Omens; Bob O'Connell;
Marlene Warfield; Dennis Patrick; Audrey Caire; Mary Case; Jenny Paine;
Peter Boyle; Reid Cruickshanks; Rudy Churney; K Callan; Robert Emerick.*

My good friend Norman Wexler, who was a fellow copywriter in the advertising business, started doing industrials around the same time that I did. He
and I ran into each other at the office of this fellow that we were doing industrials for. He told me about this article he read in *New York Magazine*
called "Speed Is of the Essence" and then how he had heard Spiro Agnew talk
about the silent majority. I said, "Gee, that would be a terrific movie." So I
pitched it to the Cannon Group, for whom I was making *Guess What We
Learned in School Today?*, but they turned it down. So I kept working on *Guess
What We Learned in School Today?* Then Cannon came back and said, "Listen,
we've raised money to do this other script and we realized that this other
script is horrible. So we don't want to do it. But we have to do something;
otherwise we'll have to give the money back. So what can you do?" I said,
"Remember that story that Norman Wexler had? That could make a good
movie." They said, rather reluctantly, "Do it." I started casting and working
with Norman in the evenings and in a week we had a script and two weeks
later we were shooting a movie. And that was Susan Sarandon's first movie
and the movie that brought Peter Boyle to everybody's attention.

The picture caught the moment. The picture was made in January 1970.
In May 1970 the construction workers down on Wall Street did battle with
the peace protesters and the term "hard hat" was coined, and in July *Joe*
opened with the quintessential hard hat. The timing couldn't have been
better. So we were very fortunate.

It was Norman Wexler's story. This was the first movie script he had written so I worked with him and we got it down on paper. It was very much
about that time in our history and whether people of Joe's persuasion were
right or whether the young people who were against the war were right.
People's feelings were running very high at that time and it caught all of that
in a very dramatic story. It was the first time I had a script of any real caliber. You can't do anything if you don't have a good script and good actors
like Susan and Peter. I remember they didn't want to use Peter Boyle because they thought he looked too young. He didn't look like he had been

in World War II. I had done a lot of casting and I thought Peter was by far the best candidate for the role.

I would have the actors come in and audition. There was a scene in the movie where we first meet Joe and he was working in this bar. He's had a few boilermakers and he's spouting off about the hippies and how they had ruined the music. He had a line that went, "You show me a welfare worker who's not a nigger lover and I'll massage your asshole." That was the line. So when they came into read, I said to them, "Now, if you want to change the words or improvise or whatever don't feel restricted by the dialogue." So when Peter Boyle came in to audition and we came to that part in the script he said, "You show me a welfare worker who's not a nigger lover and I'll massage your asshole," and then he added, "and I ain't queer." And I knew right away that this was the guy because a guy like that would say something like that if he started talking about the rectum.

I told Peter he had the part but Cannon wouldn't let me use him. So we went with another older actor who was also very good. When my friends heard that I had cast this other fellow they said, "My God, you don't want to use him, he's a drunk, he'll get into fights, he'll be terrible." I said, "Well, gee, he auditioned so well, maybe he'll be all right." Two days before we're supposed to start shooting this fellow urinated on the escalator at Bloomingdale's and punched out this little sales lady and I said, "Folks, let's go with Peter Boyle." And out of desperation they did and it worked out great.

When Susan Sarandon first walked in—I think she was about nineteen—and auditioned she was just terrific. She was a real strong actress. She looked just right.

It was all shot on location during a very cold winter for about $250 thousand and we did it in about twenty days. It was the first time that I had dealt with violence in the movies and I felt that a little bit of that goes a long way. I found that you didn't have to dwell on lots of close-ups of blood coming out of the body to make the impression that this guy's not around any longer.

I photographed the picture myself too, so I was behind the camera a lot. This one day we were shooting out in the country and there was a school bus that we used to ferry the crew around and the motor was running and it was interfering with the sound so I said to one of the assistants, "Kill the bus." And he said, "Okay it's done." I had these microphones on so I couldn't really tell if the bus was still running. So I said, "Well, how do you know it's dead?" And he said, "Well, it's lying on its back and its wheels are up in the air." Now I don't know why I remember that but that's the only funny thing I remember about making that movie.

Cry Uncle! (1971)

Aaron Banks; Ray Barron; Jackson Beck; Maureen Byrnes; Allen Garfield; Devin Goldenberg; Pamela Gruen; Lloyd Kaufman; David Kirk; Marcia Jean Kurtz; Madeleine Le Roux; Debbi Morgan; Bruce Pecheur; Chuck Pfeiffer; Jan Saint; Nancy Salmon; Reuben Schafer; Paul Sorvino; Melvin Stuart; Dean Tait; Frank Vitale; Sean Walsh; Patricia Wheel; Joe Young.

After *Joe* was finished I was anxious to make another picture. So before *Joe* was released I made *Cry Uncle!* Steve Tisch, who produced *Forrest Gump*, was a gofer on *Cry Uncle!* We shot the film on Long Island at this motel. We had this night shot to do so we were waiting for it to get dark. Everybody was in their various rooms at the motel whiling away the afternoon. Steve drove this police car up from the city because it was gonna appear in the shot at night. As he drove up to the motel he hit the siren. Now this was in the sixties, you understand. When the cast and crew heard the police siren there were toilet flushes in every motel room and when it turned out that it was a false alarm, they ran Steve out of town.

The Stoolie (1974)

Jackie Mason; Dan Frazer; Lee Meredith.

I did the movie with Jackie Mason. It was after *Cry Uncle!* and it was during the time that *Joe* was coming out. It was a real sweet story about this second-rate stool pigeon from Hackensack who double-crosses the police, takes the money, and goes to Miami. The original title was *Roger of Miami Beach*, not to be confused with *Lawrence of Arabia*. Jackie played the stool pigeon. He meets a girl whose morality changes him and he turns out to be a good guy. We had a lot of fun making it in New Jersey and down in Florida.

Towards the end of production we had a scene where Jackie and the girl are falling in love and they were having dinner as the sun was setting on this beautiful hotel. I was also supposed to shoot a scene with Jackie sitting ringside during a big floor show at this fancy hotel, so we had a band, dancing girls, and lots of extras standing. Well, I kept shooting and shooting the sunset and meanwhile the band and the dancing girls and all the extras were growing very impatient and started wanting more money. Now, Jackie was subject to people whispering in his ear and he was convinced that I was trying to sabotage the movie. It was really my error. I should have shot the big scene first and then after all those people went away shot the simple scene of two people at the table. I didn't do that. So Jackie fired me.

I remember the next morning, lying on the floor of the hotel hall talking to him under his door because he wouldn't talk to me face-to-face. I pleaded with him not to pull the plug at this point and offered to pay for the last few days of shooting myself rather than to have it stop and have him try to resurrect the whole show a few months down the line on his own. But he wouldn't hear of it. So the movie stopped and I went away and we did *Save the Tiger* with Jack Lemmon and a year or two later Jackie had somebody else finish the picture. He wasn't such a hot producer but he was a terrific actor.

Jackie had a very Chaplin-esque quality to him and he did a terrific job with this character. He was very touching and funny and when we needed straight dramatic scenes, he could do that too. Comics are often very good actors, as Chaplin was. So I was very disappointed that the picture never got finished and put together properly because I think it could have launched Jackie Mason's movie career a lot sooner and I think he would have surprised a lot more people. He had an opportunity that slipped by and it's unfortunate.

Save the Tiger (1973)

Jack Lemmon; Jack Gilford; Laurie Heineman; Norman Burton; Patricia Smith; Thayer David; William Hansen; Harvey Jason; Liv Lindeland; Lara Parker; Eloise Hardt; Janina; Ned Glass; Pearl Shear; Biff Elliot.

Joe had just opened and I was doing *Cry Uncle!* and I get a phone call late at night from Jack Lemmon who I had never met or spoken to. He had just seen *Joe* and said he was blown away by it. He said, "Kid, I've got to make a movie with you." I thought somebody was putting me on. But it really was Jack. So I read Steve Shagan's script for *Save the Tiger* and it was beautiful and easily the best script I had read.

I went out to meet Jack and audition for him and I said to him, "I've always been a fan of your work but if you choose me to direct this movie I don't want to see you in it. I want to see this character; I don't want to see Jack Lemmon." He knew just what I was talking about and told me to keep

my eyes open. While we were shooting, if he had a mannerism or something that I didn't like, I would cut. He'd look at me and say, "You want me
to do it without the eyebrows." I'd say, "Yeah, try it without the eyebrows,"
and he would do the line without the eyebrow and it would be terrific.

I've always said that Lemmon was a peach. If he had an idea and saw that
I didn't react to it immediately he'd say, "Now listen, if you want to do that,
you go ahead. Me? I think it's a terrible idea." He made it very easy for me
because I was fresh off the farm and had never been to Hollywood before.
This was a great opportunity for me and he allowed me to do what I do and
gave me his support, which I couldn't have done without. When Jack won
the Academy Award for Best Actor I couldn't have been more pleased because working with him was such a pleasure. And it was a tough part to
play, too. It was hard to maintain that level of depression day after day and
it was quite a strain on him but he did it like the pro he is.

I remember Jack and I were standing in downtown L.A. one night while
the crew was setting up the lights. It was very late at night and there was
nobody around. This little Mexican lady came out of the shadows and ran
up to Jack and asked him for his autograph. He looked around, then looked
at her and he said, "Gee, I thought you'd never show up." And I said, "Gee,
what a funny line." But then a few days later the same thing happened and
he said the same line and I realized he had used that line a few times before. He was delightful. He's a terrific actor and in this town I was fortunate
to get his support as well as his talent.

W.W. and the Dixie Dancekings (1975)

Burt Reynolds; Conny Van Dyke; Jerry Reed; Ned Beatty; James Hampton;
Don Williams; Richard Hurst; Mel Tillis; Furry Lewis; Sherman G. Lloyd;
Mort Marshall; Bill McCutcheon; Peg Murray; Sherry Mathis;
Roni Stoneman Hemrick.

I had actually read Tom Rickman's script, *W.W. and the Dixie Dancekings,*
when I was doing *Save the Tiger,* and I thought the script was terrific and I
thought that James Caan should play the part of W.W. I thought he was a
real good actor and I thought it would be something quite different for him.
But Burt Reynolds was part of the package. So I said no, thank you. Well,
time went on and *Save the Tiger* came out and didn't make a lot of money
and my bills were piling up and I needed a job and the only one that was

still around was *W.W.* So I thought, well, maybe Burt Reynolds won't be so bad. But much to my chagrin I said yes and Burt Reynolds proved to be a handful. He was the total opposite of Jack Lemmon and it proved to be one of the unhappy experiences of my movie-making career. Burt refused to let go of his own persona and get into the part that he was playing. You know, nobody ever knew who Laurence Olivier really was because he was never visible in the characters he played. Whereas Burt didn't want to let go of who he really was and play the character that had been written. I didn't have the knack of being able to get what I wanted and make him happy at the same time and we just did not get along. Now Burt might have a whole other take on it. He may be dying to work with me again.

Fore Play (1975)

Zero Mostel; Estelle Parsons; Pat Paulsen; Jerry Orbach; George S. Irving;
Andrew Duncan; Laurie Heineman; Deborah Loomis.

Well, after *W.W.*, I had two movie ideas that I wanted to do. One was called *Naked* and it was a documentary. We found people coming out of a porno theater and asked them if they had directed the film, what would they have done differently. It gets more involved than that, but essentially we made a documentary on that subject. The same guy who financed that strange idea also financed another strange idea I had about the Vietnam War.

Nixon had become president and the question was what would happen if somebody kidnapped Tricia and the ransom was that Nixon and his wife would have to appear on television and make love if they wanted their daughter back. I figured this would sort of render Nixon impotent, as it were. So the investor responded to that idea. David Odell, who had written *Cry Uncle!*, responded to the idea too. He wrote this story about the President and the head of the Mafia. Zero Mostel played both parts. I wanted Rodney Dangerfield but Rodney wouldn't appear in his underwear. Zero didn't have such reservations.

So the President gets in office with the help of the Mafia who financed his campaign. The Mafia did this because the President promised to make pornography illegal so that the Mafia could make a lot of money selling it. But the Mafia is getting impatient because the President isn't moving quickly enough so they kidnap his daughter and announce to the media what the ransom would be. Estelle Parsons played Zero's wife and they eventually agreed to appear on television to get their daughter Tricia back. It was a great experience working with Zero and making that picture.

> *I never knew what we had. No one ever knew what we had. The studio did not know. They had to see screening after screening to believe that they had a million-dollar movie looking like a thirty-million-dollar movie. That was all John Avildsen.*
>
> Burt Young—Actor

Rocky (1976)

Sylvester Stallone; Talia Shire; Burt Young; Carl Weathers; Burgess Meredith; Thayer David; Joe Spinell; Jimmy Gambina; Bill Baldwin Sr.; Al Salvani; George Memmoli; Jodi Letizia; Diana Lewis; George O'Hanlon; Larry Carroll.

We had been doing some location scouting on a picture that I was going to do with either Michael Caine or Richard Burton. But before any film was shot the production company ran out of money and the movie never got made, which was probably a good thing because the script was marginal. It was at that time that an old friend of mine, Gene Kirkwood, sent me Sylvester Stallone's script about a fighter called Rocky. I said, "A prizefighter? I'm not interested in prize fighting. That's really dumb, two people getting in a ring and slugging at each other." Gene said, "Do me a favor and read it." So I did and on the third or fourth page Rocky is talking to his two turtles, Cuff and Link, and I became totally captivated. I had auditioned Sylvester a few times prior to this for other pictures. *W.W.* as a matter of fact. He came in to audition as a hillbilly but somehow he didn't convince me. But he was a good actor and *Rocky* was a terrific script. It was ninety-eight pages and it never stopped. So I said, "Yeah, let's do it," and fortunately it worked out well.

Robert Chartoff and Irwin Winkler were the producers of *Rocky* and I had done some work for them some years before fixing one of their turkeys. I shot a couple of weeks of new footage for this particular picture and got to know them as a result so they made a deal with me and we made the movie in twenty-eight days for about $950 thousand.

Sylvester was very smart but he took a big gamble. He said, "If you want the script I go with it." He had been offered a lot of money to sell it but only as a writer, not to play the part himself. But he hung in there and to the credit of Chartoff and Winkler and United Artists, they decided they would shoot crap and give him that opportunity and it worked for everybody.

I think Sylvester told me that he rewrote the equivalent of about three hundred pages. We were constantly rewriting. He was very receptive to my suggestions and we were constantly changing it and making it better. I remember the day we were gonna shoot the scene where Rocky is called into the promoter's office and given the opportunity to fight Apollo Creed. The fight promoter says, "Well, Rocky, you have an opportunity to fight Apollo Creed, what do you think about that?" And Rocky said, "Oh boy, I'll give you a good fight." And I was thinking, wait a minute, Rocky's a smart guy. He may not be educated but he's smart and he knows that he has no business fighting a guy like Apollo Creed. He's totally out of his league. So he would say, "No, I'll do a good job for you as a sparring partner, but I'm not in this guy's league."

Now the promoter has got to talk Rocky into it and Rocky becomes the victim of this guy's sales pitch. We as the audience now feel more sympathy for Rocky because he's being taken advantage of. He says the right thing, he says, "No, I don't belong in the ring with this guy." And the promoter talks him into it. So we feel for Rocky. Sylvester responded to the idea and changed a couple of the lines and we shot it that way.

Since it was low-budget and we only had a short shooting schedule we didn't have a lot of time to make a lot of mistakes. We didn't have enough money to go to Philadelphia and shoot it with a full union crew so I talked the producers into going there with a smaller, non-union crew, which was very much what I was used to working with. We started shooting all of the exteriors and it went very well for a few days.

Rocky and Adrian's first date was originally written in a restaurant where they sat looking at each other for about five or six pages while Rocky was seducing her. I suggested that we not shoot that in a restaurant because it was a static situation. I suggested that maybe they could go bowling or ice-skating. They liked the ice-skating idea and we went to this rink in downtown Philadelphia. But before we had a chance to shoot it, the producer said we had to get out of town because the unions were going to find out we were there and we'd get in a lot of trouble. So we left without shooting that scene.

When we get back to Hollywood the producer said, "Well, we have to put it back in the restaurant." "Why?" I asked. And he said, "Because we can't afford all the extras we would need for the ice-skating scene, so let's put them in the restaurant and they can be sitting in a corner and you won't see anybody there." I said, "No, no, hold on. Maybe they go to the ice-skating rink and it's closed and that's why there's nobody there and they have to sneak in." Sylvester liked that idea and rewrote the scene because we couldn't afford the extras. But I think that made the scene so much better. So there were a lot of examples where our low budget and lack of money forced us to do things in a different way and I think it came out better.

Before I did that film I had never seen a boxing match. I'd seen a little bit of it on television, but I had never been to a boxing match until I started working on the movie. I started looking at a lot of boxing movies and I found that the boxing didn't look at all real. I realized that if we were going to make it look real we were going to have to practice a great deal. I've found that a lot of rehearsal really pays off. So I convinced the producers to give us a lot of time to rehearse the fight. We started that rehearsal process even before we started shooting the movie. We were going to shoot the fighting sequences at the end of the movie to allow the actors to learn it.

The first day that Sylvester and Carl Weathers get in the ring, they started bouncing around and one guy says, "I'll do this," and the other guy says, "No, I'll do that," and I said, "Wait a second! This is never going to work." I suggested to Sylvester that he go home and write it out—"Write it all out and we'll learn it like a ballet. Whatever it is that you want, put it on paper and we'll learn that. We'll break each round into sections. There will be four or five sections in each round and we'll know that in the first section, there are three rights and a duck and a punch and a this and a that and you guys will learn it and anticipate each other and it will look great."

Sylvester came back the next day with about thirty pages of lefts and rights and we started learning it. I was shooting 8 mm in those days, before tape, and I would photograph these rehearsals and then show them the footage. I said, "We've got to get a lot better than this because otherwise it's going to look like the film I shot and you don't want it to look like that." That motivated them and every day for an hour or two they practiced. They knew that there was a left and a right and then a this and a that and a jab and a punch and they got it down so they were coming very close to one another with their punches and it looked real.

Bill Conti's music made a tremendous contribution to *Rocky*. I used it to cut to. I would show Bill my 8 mm footage. I put some Beethoven on the record player and I said, "You see, you slow it down and you put Beethoven behind it and it's like a ballet. Give me something like that." So that was Bill's inspiration to write that beautifully classical score for *Rocky*. I think the whole budget for the music score was around twenty-five thousand dollars. That was his fee, paying all the musicians, renting the hall, paying the mixer and buying the tape. The average composer would have taken that money and given me music on a piano. But not Bill. He brought in this thirty-piece orchestra and the producer said, "Bill, how are you ever going to make any money paying all these guys in the orchestra?" Well, thank God he did it that way because the score of *Rocky* was a big factor in its success.

Before we leave Bill Conti, let me tell you another story. He brought me the music for the end of the movie and it was inspiring. I said, "Bill, I don't have any footage that would go with this music." Originally it was written that Rocky would be carried out of the ring on the crowd's shoulders and he would reach down and pull up Adrian and they would go out on the crowd's shoulders. When we came to shoot this, the crowd carried out Apollo and the assistant director said that we didn't have enough extras to carry out Rocky. Well, obviously the same people that carried out Apollo were gonna carry out Rocky. But Sylvester heard this and he said, "Wait a second, that gives me an idea. Maybe he's not carried out. Maybe nobody pays any attention to him. He lost the fight." A lot of people don't realize that Rocky lost, but he did. But he won because he wanted to go the distance and he did do that. But he lost the decision.

So Sylvester said, "Why don't we just have him walk down the aisle by himself after everybody else has left? He'll see Spider Rico, the guy he had the first fight with. Spider will say, 'Good fight, Rock' and Rocky will thank him. He and Adrian will join hands and they'll walk away from camera and that will be the end of the movie." That sounded very poetic and I said, "Great. Let's do that." And if you remember the poster of *Rocky*, that was the image, the boy and the girl holding hands walking away from the camera.

But after listening to Bill Conti's music, I said, "Wait a second. We need to keep Rocky in the ring and bring Adrian to him. Have her fight through the crowd and she finally gets into the ring and they embrace. Then I can use Bill's music, because this music with the footage I've got makes no sense at all." So I was able to convince the producers to do this. But we had no money. Now, Marty Scorsese was about to do a picture for the same producers. By the way, when Marty was a student at NYU, he worked for me on a short film I made. So anyway, unbeknownst to Marty, I think, the producers took his camera gear that he was supposed to begin using the next day. They gave us about four hours to take this gear and about twenty extras to create a crowd and we went back to the sports arena and shot this footage of Adrian calling out to Rocky and Rocky bellowing, "Adrian!" It was Bill Conti's music that inspired that.

When I first learned that *Rocky* had been nominated, I think in eleven or twelve categories, it was the same day I was getting fired from *Saturday Night Fever* because the producer of that film and I did not see eye to eye. I was sorry I was losing that job because we were just about to shoot it, but I was very pleased that the picture got nominated. I had no dreams of winning because nobody was in *Rocky* that anybody had ever heard of and it was very low budget. Needless to say when it won it was a great surprise. I remember jumping up and hugging Sylvester and running up to accept the Oscar and it felt great. I also remember reaching into my pocket to get the envelope with all the names of the people I wanted to thank but my perspiration had run the ink so the envelope looked like a Monet—totally indecipherable. But fortunately I was able to remember all the folks that I wanted to thank. I had a great time at the party that night. I highly recommend it.

And Then There Were the Sequels

While we were doing the first *Rocky,* Sylvester and I had an idea for a sequel. Actually, it was going to be a three-part story. But Sylvester didn't want to go in the same direction as I did so I took a pass on *Rocky II* and that was the end of the *Rocky*s for me. Many years later, *Rocky V* came down the pike. Sylvester wanted me to do that one because he was going to die at the end of it. He was going to have lost all his money and go back to the old days in Philadelphia and he thought what I did in the first one was what he wanted to do in the last one.

I read his script and it was beautiful and had a very touching death scene where he'd be riding to the hospital in the ambulance and die in Adrian's lap. She would come out at the end and speak to the press and announce Rocky's death and say, "But as long as people continue to believe in themselves, Rocky's spirit will live forever." As she's talking we would see Rocky running up the steps from the first movie and that would be the end. I thought that was a classy way to end the series. So I agreed to do it. We started shooting the movie and the studio got cold feet and changed their mind. They figured it was not a good business decision to have one of their big assets die. James Bond doesn't die so Rocky doesn't die. So Rocky didn't die, but the movie died, because the movie was written for him to die at the end and when he didn't, it didn't work. So it ended up being an unhappy experience for me. The moral of the story is, there's nothing like a starving actor.

In the first *Rocky* there was nothing on Sylvester's mind except that movie. On the fifth *Rocky,* he had lots of other things on his mind. Fame and fortune often takes its toll. It was a totally different experience working with the very rich and successful Sylvester in the fifth film, having worked with the unknown and impoverished Sylvester in the first. It was very hard to get his attention in *Rocky V* because he had so many distractions in his life. He's a very good actor, but he's also human. The kind of success that he enjoyed in such a short amount of time was a lot to deal with.

The Formula (1980)

George C. Scott; Marlon Brando; Marthe Keller; John Gielgud; G.D. Spradlin; Beatrice Straight; Richard Lynch; John Van Dreelen; Robin Clarke; Ike Eisenmann; Marshall Thompson; Dieter Schidor; Werner Kreindl; Jan Niklas; Wolfgang Preiss.

The Formula was a big mistake. I had read the book and couldn't quite understand it. I had just left a movie that I was going do with Peter Sellers called *Fu Manchu.* At the last minute Peter decided that he was going to direct it. So they paid me a lot of money to go away. I said, "Hey, this is terrific. You get all this money and you don't have to make the movie. This could be a good living." So I figured maybe the same thing would happen with *The Formula.* Somebody, somewhere along the line, would realize this thing doesn't work and they'll have to pay me to go away and I won't have to make the movie. Well, I was wrong. They didn't realize that it didn't make any sense. Then I made a big mistake in hiring George Scott who made Burt Reynolds look like Shirley Temple. So that was a disaster. Marlon Brando, on the other hand, was great fun. He was a pleasure to work with.

But the movie didn't do anything because it ultimately didn't make any sense. My cut was about an hour and a half. But the version that got released was a much longer version and had a lot of stuff in it that made it even more confusing and it didn't do very well. So it's not one of my happier experiences.

I got to Berlin in February with George Scott, who had a drinking problem in those days, and it was a workout. I remember when we were in Switzerland in St. Moritz, a beautiful place, and snow everywhere you look. I'd show up in the morning and George would come in and he'd say, "I want to drink today, I'm not working. I'm going to be in the bar." I said, "Oh, great." So it was a tough experience. Had a great time in St. Moritz going down the toboggan slides, but the movie was a nightmare. And it's too bad because it was about the oil barons and about the exploitation of the American consumer and it was well-intentioned, but it was a very convoluted story that was not easy to follow.

I remember when I first went to Marlon Brando's house to try to get him to be in the movie. The studio was getting cold feet over George Scott. So I thought if I could get somebody like Marlin Brando to go up against Scott to play the part of the oil guy, maybe the studio would respond, and sure enough they did. They liked the idea. They said, "You get Brando and we'll do it with Scott." So we go up to meet with Brando and he's very cordial and he said, "Listen, this is the way I'd like to play this guy." I said, "Oh, what's that?" Now remember, in the script the guy was written as somebody you would expect to find on the cover of *Time* magazine, a three-piece suit type of oil mogul. Brando said, "I see this guy as a sort of Howard Hughes character living out in the desert and he's got a beard and a straw hat and he's very eccentric," and I said, "Gee, maybe, but I don't think so. I think this guy should look like he's the head of General Electric—he's the establishment." And Brando said, "Okay, I was just testing you." He and I got along very well after that and he was a great source of humor.

I told Brando that I had heard all the stories about how he likes to change the dialogue, so I suggested we change it then so that when it comes time to shoot it we wouldn't have to spend any time changing it. He said, "Good idea." So we spent a lot of time together going over the script and he had a lot of good ideas and a lot of good lines. So we finally said, "Okay, this is the dialogue." I show up the first day to start shooting his scenes and the assistant says, "Brando wants to see you in his trailer." I walk in, say good morning and ask how he is. He said, "I can't say this shit." I say, "Okay, let's find some shit you can say." Well, we spent the morning going over it again, with him telling me marvelous stories, and we finally came up with dialogue that he did like. But he didn't want to memorize it. He thought that somehow memorizing it would spoil it and not be spontaneous. He liked to have it written on cards.

There was one scene that was about four or five pages long between him and George Scott. The way it was staged it had him and Scott walking down this road near the oil field and behind them would be coming Brando's entourage—limousines and bodyguards and so forth. It would be a two-shot and there would be no cuts. Marlon had this hearing aid as part of his character because he was playing an older guy. So what he would do is record his dialogue on this tape and he would be listening to it through the earphone and he had a pressure device inside the waist of his trousers and by flexing his stomach muscles he could turn the tape on and off. So he'd be walking along, flexing his stomach, listening to his dialogue and repeating it. We're walking along this endless shot and at a certain point he said, "Sorry fellows, I just ran out of tape." So it was back to the drawing board.

Neighbors (1981)

John Belushi; Kathryn Walker; Cathy Moriarty; Dan Aykroyd; Igors Gavon; Dru-Ann Chuckran; Tim Kazurinsky; Tino Insana; P.L. Brown; Henry Judd Baker; Lauren-Marie Taylor; Sherman Lloyd; Bert Kittel; J.B. Friend; Bernie Friedman.

Neighbors was a terrific novel that Tom Berger wrote that I was very taken by. I wanted to option it and I learned that Dick Zanuck and David Brown had optioned it ahead of me, but we decided that we would make it together. My first choice for the role of Earl was Rodney Dangerfield because the character got no respect. Nobody was interested in working with Rodney. He hadn't made any movies. I had worked with him for a week and he did a great screen test. By the way, he was terrific in Oliver Stone's *Natural Born Killers*. It was a shame that he wasn't nominated. So they didn't want to do it with Rodney and we ended up doing it with John Belushi and Dan Aykroyd. We ended up doing it with them playing the opposite characters than they would normally play.

John and Dan worked together great. They were very, very tight friends, but John was really going through a lot of ups and downs with his substance abuse problems at the time so you never knew what you were going to get when John showed up. Sometimes he was okay and sometimes he was not . . .

There was a scene where John is supposed to sink in this quicksand. We had built a big tank and put tapioca pudding in it and he was supposed to sink in it. We had this little elevator platform that he would stand on and it would sink into the quicksand. Well, we put him on it and it went down and of course he floated. So I said, "Okay, we'll put on a couple of straps that you can slide your feet in and that will take you down and then once you're under, count to three and slip your feet out from the straps and you'll come up." He didn't want to do that. He wanted big heavy weights put around his ankles. I said, "John, if something goes wrong you're going to sink in there." "No," he said. "I know what I'm doing, blah, blah, blah."

On movie sets you have these big heavy sandbags that hold lights in place. So he had two sandbags taped around each ankle and put over the side. Sure enough, he slipped and went in the pit and his stand-in had to pull him out. If that guy hadn't caught him he would have gone down to the bottom of that pit. I don't know how deep it was but it would have been very, very difficult to get John out of it with all these sandbags strapped on him. It was a definite workout.

A Night in Heaven (1983)

John Archie; Judy Arman; Christopher Atkins;
Anthony G. Avildsen; Sandra Beall; Danny Belden; Tina Belden;
Harold Bergman; Fred Buch; Linda Lee Cadwell; Karen Margaret Cole;
Don Cox; Spatz Donovan; Alix Elias; Dan Fitzgerald; Veronica Gamba;
Andy Garcia; Joseph Gian; Robert Goodman; Eric D. Henderson; Bill Hindman;
Will Knickerbocker; Amy Levine; Robert Logan; Rosemary McVeigh; Gail Merrill;
Sherry Moreland; Brian Mozzillo; Tiffany Myles; Craig Nedrow; Charles F. Pastore;
Cindy Perlman; Hope Pomerance; Sally Ricca; Deborah Rush; Brian Smith;
Carrie Snodgress; Scott Stone; Mary Teahan; Pam Tendal; Deney Terrio;
Butch Warren; Lesley Ann Warren; Bobbie Wolf.

Gene Kirkwood, the man who brought me *Rocky,* brought *A Night in Heaven* to me. He took me down to Orlando where these Chippendale-type clubs were just starting out, and women were going to see guys dance and strip down to their jockey shorts. That was the premise of the movie and the studio wanted us to use Chris Atkins, who had just made *Blue Lagoon.* I saw that it could be a story about forgiveness where both the husband and wife discovered the other's infidelity. The wife was a schoolteacher and Chris was a student of hers who she runs into at this male strip joint and has a brief affair with. Meanwhile her husband has an affair with an old friend and they each discover the other's infidelity and they talk it out and they forgive one another. I thought that would make a pretty interesting story.

The script wasn't finished but the writer assured me that she would write this scene where each would discuss the other's infidelity and there would be forgiveness. As luck would have it she never did write that scene. The movie turned out to be about this guy who didn't know his wife was screwing around on him and she never told him and the picture ended and you sat there saying, well what was that about? Well, it was about a movie that never had an ending written for it. So it was not one of those happy experiences, you know.

> *John said to me, "Why don't you get yourself into some classes, get yourself in shape?" I said, "Do I have this part?" He said, "Well, not yet, but unless we find Spencer Tracy out in Los Angeles, it's yours."*
> *Ralph Macchio—Actor*

The Karate Kid (1984)

Ralph Macchio; Pat Morita; Elisabeth Shue; Martin Kove; Randee Heller; William Zabka; Ron Thomas; Rob Garrison; Chad McQueen; Tony O'Dell; Israel Juarbe; William H. Bassett; Larry B. Scott; Juli Fields; Dana Andersen.

When I was sent the script for *The Karate Kid* I said, "Wait a second, how can I do *The Karate Kid,* I did *Rocky!* I can see it now; they're going to call it *The Karocky Kid.*" But I read it anyway and was very taken by Robert Kamen's script because, just as Sylvester's script wasn't really about boxing, I didn't think that *The Karate Kid* was about karate. I thought it was about this young boy who was growing up and the bullies were after him and he meets this father figure, Mr. Miyagi, who is everybody's dream of what a father should be, and it was just a terrific story.

I had the good fortune of working with casting director Caro Jones who has done practically all my pictures. She brought me some great talent. The first one was Pat Morita, who played Mr. Miyagi. I wasn't aware of Pat. I had never seen him in *Happy Days* and I had never seen his nightclub act. He had a nightclub act where he billed himself as "the Hip Nip," and people who had heard about Pat Morita said forget it, he's not an actor. Well, he walked in and I videotaped the audition and he nailed the part of Mr. Miyagi. I told the producer we were not going to find anybody that would do it better than him. But they didn't want to know that. They brought people in from Japan. But we did a screen test with Pat Morita and that convinced them that he was the guy.

I had seen Ralph Macchio in a couple of pictures. He came in to audition with Elisabeth Shue who had done hamburger commercials up until then. The two of them really hit it off. I called them the cannoli and strawberry shortcake. They were opposites to the nth degree and they were perfect together.

I had one problem with the first *Karate Kid*. It was written that at the end of the tournament the last scene would take place out in the parking lot. Mr. Miyagi and Daniel would be walking and Kreese, the bad karate teacher, would accost them and challenge Mr. Miyagi and Mr. Miyagi would level him. Then he and Mr. Miyagi and Daniel would go off arm in arm. But the shooting of the tournament went so well that I suggested that it would be the right place to end it. We didn't need the scene in the parking lot. Everyone agreed and that is what we did.

More Sequels

Robert Kamen had a real good idea for a sequel and I was in love with the characters and so off we went to do it. The sequel was much more Mr. Miyagi's story as we go back to Okinawa and meet his father just before he dies. Miyagi is finally reunited with the woman he loves and Daniel learns from this and he has his first love affair. It was a beautiful story.

I went to Okinawa with the idea of shooting there. But because of all the typhoons they've had it is not a very pretty place. All the buildings are like cement bunkers and there are not a lot of trees because the typhoons keep blowing them down. So we went to Hawaii which stood in for Okinawa. What a pleasure it was to shoot in Hawaii. People who liked the first film liked the second one even more, so that was very satisfying.

Then came the question of the third one. Robert Kamen came up with this idea that Miyagi and Daniel would time travel back to ancient China and we would discover where the ancestor of Mr. Miyagi learned the secret of karate. I wanted to shoot it in China. Coca-Cola, who owned Columbia at the time, was excited about the idea. China was excited about the idea. Everybody was excited about the idea. But the producer didn't want to go to China. He wanted to stay in the U.S. and we ended up basically making the first movie all over again and it was dreadful. Nobody showed up and I don't blame them because it wasn't very good. If the sequel is a good story, it's a good idea. If it's not, it's a bad idea.

> *I worked in the school where Joe Clark actually was. That's how I shaped my character—I shaped it around Joe himself. What I will give John in terms of credit is the ability to do that. We had discussed it early on. But he did give me that latitude.*
>
> Morgan Freeman—Actor

Lean on Me (1989)

*Morgan Freeman; Beverly Todd; Robert Guillaume; Alan North;
Lynne Thigpen; Robin Bartlett; Michael Beach; Ethan Phillips;
Sandra Reaves-Phillips; Sloane Shelton; Jermaine "Huggy" Hopkins;
Karen Malina White; Karina Arroyave; Ivonne Coll; Regina Taylor.*

When Norman Twain, the producer of *Lean on Me,* showed me a news story on Joe Clark, who was the principal of East Side High in Patterson, New Jersey, I was very taken by it. I found the character very charismatic and what he was doing with the kids was terrific. I met him and toured the school and was very impressed. Michael Schiffer wrote a terrific script. Then I met Morgan Freeman, who I had recently seen in a film called *Street Smart,* for which he was nominated for his performance. I thought he would be the perfect actor to play Joe Clark.

I remember the first time we showed it to the public and handed out the cards on which they rate the picture. Ninety-six percent of the people who saw the picture rated it either excellent or very good. So I couldn't have been more pleased and the picture did very well. That was an experience that I'll always have very fond memories of.

It was a very tough film to make. They didn't want me to shoot in East Side; they wanted me to shoot at a school in Manhattan. I went around and looked at all these various schools and none of them were as good as East Side and none of them would have given us the cooperation that East Side did, so we ended up shooting there, but it was very, very difficult. There was no air conditioning. The kids were dropping like flies. It was very tough but we received great cooperation and terrific performances from the actors.

I've had the pleasure of working with Morgan Freeman twice now and he is the consummate artist. He's a professional, always knew his lines and always had great ideas. He was always making contributions and never got tired. He is a really good actor and I was very blessed to have worked with him.

School was going on while we were making the movie and Joe was speaking over the loudspeaker and carrying around his bullhorn and we'd run into him in the halls every so often, so the real guy was constantly inspiring Morgan. It was very strange where reality stopped and fantasy began. I think the picture was very true to life and there wasn't very much fiction in it. All the students there played themselves and we got some real good performances out of kids who weren't professionals. There was a singing group at the school that we incorporated into the movie. They went on to make a number of CDs. They've got a group called Rift but they were known as the Playboys at East Side. They're the kids who sing in the movie.

The Power of One (1992)

Nomadlozi Kubheka; Agatha Hurle; Nigel Ivy; Tracy Brooks Swope; Brendan Deary; Winston Mangwarara; Guy Witcher; Tonderai Masenda; Cecil Zilla Mamanzi; John Turner; Robbie Bulloch; Gordon Arnell; Jeremiah Mnisi; Armin Mueller-Stahl; Paul Tingay; Morgan Freeman; Simon Fenton; Stephen Dorff.

The Power of One came down the pike after Robert Kamen read the book and recommended it to me. I read the book and I found it very compelling. Arnon Milchan, who financed it, took a big gamble in doing a very non-commercial subject because any movie that had anything to do with apartheid up until then didn't do well. *World Apart, Dry White Season*—none of them made any money. But Arnon believed in the story and wanted to do something about South Africa, so we went to South Africa and did a lot of research. I went around the townships there and it was really quite an eye-opener. It was staggering how these folks were living, how they were treated. This was while Nelson Mandela was still in jail. So it was quite a challenge.

I had the good fortune of having Dean Semler as my director of photography. He had just received the Academy Award for shooting *Dances with Wolves*. He brought his talent and energy to the picture. Morgan Freeman played the part of the convict who had been in jail most of his life. Morgan learned a South African accent for the part. I worked with John Gielgud again, whom I had worked with previously in *The Formula*, and my wife, Tracy Swope, played the part of the young boy's mother.

8 Seconds (1994)

Luke Perry; Stephen Baldwin; James Rebhorn; Red Mitchell; Ronnie Claire Edwards; Linden Ashby; Cynthia Geary; Cameron Finley; Carrie Snodgress; Dustin Mayfield; Clyde Frost; Elsie Frost; Gabriel Folse; Joe Stevens; Clint Burkey.

Just as I had never been to a boxing match before I got involved with *Rocky*, I had never seen a rodeo until I got involved with *8 Seconds*. Lane Frost, a young man from Oklahoma, won the World Championship bull riding contest when he was twenty-five or twenty-six years old. A few years after that he was killed while riding a bull in Cheyenne, Wyoming.

Luke Perry, who played Lane, learned to ride bulls on his own. He convinced me that it was safe because I thought it was nuts to have our star really doing this, because after all we were doing a story about a guy who got killed doing it. But he convinced me that he knew how to do it and he did. He rode those bulls himself.

I had seen the rodeo movies that had been made and they looked about as bad as the boxing movies that had been made and they didn't look real. I knew that we had an actor, Luke Perry, who was really going to ride the bulls and I knew that that was going to make things look a lot better. I also asked the bullfighters, the clowns who were in the ring to try to keep the bull away from the rider once the rider got off, to film for us. We gave them cameras so that we could get a wide-angle lens very close to the action. You couldn't put a cameraman in there because cameramen are smart and they wouldn't get into a bullring, whereas these bullfighters would. We put a wide-angle lens on a very small camera and they didn't look through the camera, they just pointed the camera and they practiced a lot. They got it down so that by moving the camera a little bit they were able to frame it well and we got some very exciting shots.

After we finished filming, my editor, Doug Seelig, suggested that we get some more footage of Luke on the bulls. He also suggested we get some footage of Stephen Baldwin, who played Luke's pal. There was a rodeo in San Diego so we went down there to get the shots. Steve, who had never taken lessons, was a real good sport and got on the bulls twice. Then we shot some footage of Luke riding. When he finished riding the last bull, Luke jumped off and the bull kicked and missed his face by inches and dislocated his shoulder. It was a real close call.

The death scene was difficult because in reality Lane's wife wasn't there to witness his death, whereas in the rest of the movie, she was always there when he rode well. When their relationship was good, she was there and he rode well. When their relationship wasn't good, she wasn't there and he didn't ride well. So at a certain point I said, "Well, even though she wasn't there, why don't we have her there? That way she can witness the death and we don't have to have an anticlimax of her getting a phone call and being told about the death." There was a lot of consternation about that and we eventually shot it both ways. In the end it made a lot of sense to have her there.

How Does He Select His Projects?

The first thing I look for is a script that I can get through. You start reading a script and it becomes pretty obvious if it's any good early on. If it doesn't keep you turning the page, it's not a good script. And it's got to be a story that you'd want to see, that you can relate to, and that you can endorse. If I read a script that has a lot of violence in it I don't get enthusiastic about it. If the script is not about something that I can relate to or care about, I don't respond. But sometimes you're lucky and you read a script that you put down and you say, "Wow! Don't change anything; let's shoot it!" That doesn't happen very often. So you're very much at the mercy of the script and without a good script you're in trouble.

The Studios

Big corporations now own the studios. They're not owned or run by individuals whose only business is that of making pictures. I think that's taken a toll on the caliber of pictures being made. Independent movies are often the best movies around. This year is a real good example. The independents got many more nominations than the majors did. But still a lot of great movies come out of the major studios over the years. So it's changed in one way and in another way it hasn't. It's not the days of the dream factory, where there were contracts and you had all those terrific actors under contract and they made a lot of pictures. That isn't the way it is any longer. So a director will make fewer films now than he made in the old days. In the old days you walked out of one sound stage and went across the street and started directing another picture that was all prepared for you. Now you have to be very involved in the preparation and often you are responsible for getting it financed.

What Does the Future Hold for John G. Avildsen?

Beats me. It's celluloid roulette. You're at the mercy of all sorts of things. It's a business where luck plays a huge factor on what you say yes to and what you say no to. I said no to *Kramer vs. Kramer,* I said no to *China Syndrome.* I made a lot of big mistakes and had a lot of regrets about things that I could have done that I didn't—that I had the opportunity to do and for one reason or another I blew that opportunity. So I hope that next time when I get an opportunity I'll be smarter and I won't blow it. But luck is a big factor.

Filmography

Turn on to Love (1969)
Guess What We Learned in School Today? (1970)
Joe (1970)
Okay Bill (1971)
Cry Uncle! (1971)
Save the Tiger (1973)
The Stoolie (1974)
W.W. and the Dixie Dancekings (1975)
Fore Play (1975)
Rocky (1976)
Slow Dancing in the Big City (1978)
The Formula (1980)
Murder Ink (TV series, 1980)
Neighbors (1981)
Traveling Hopefully (1982)
A Night in Heaven (1983)
The Karate Kid (1984)
The Karate Kid, Part II (1986)
Happy New Year (1987)
For Keeps (1988)
Lean on Me (1989)
The Karate Kid III (1989)
Rocky V (1990)

EDITOR'S NOTE: After this interview was completed Avildsen directed *Coyote Moon* starring Jean-Claude Van Damme and *A Fine and Private Place* starring Richard Dreyfuss.

The Power of One (1992)
8 Seconds (1994)
A Fine and Private Place (1998)
Coyote Moon (as Danny Mulroon, 1999)

Awards

Academy Awards, USA
Traveling Hopefully, Best Documentary, Short Subjects (nominated), 1983
Rocky, Best Director, 1977

British Academy Awards
Rocky, Best Direction (nominated), 1978

Directors Guild of America, USA
Rocky, Outstanding Directorial Achievement in Motion Pictures (shared with Ted Swanson, Fred Gallo, and Steve Perry), 1977

Golden Globes, USA
Rocky, Best Director—Motion Picture (nominated), 1977

Razzie Awards
Rocky V, Worst Director (nominated), 1991
The Karate Kid III, Worst Director (nominated), 1990
The Formula, Worst Director (nominated), 1981

The Films of Garry Marshall

Garry Marshall (Masciarelli) was born on November 13, 1934, in the Bronx in New York City. In the four decades since his career first began, he has established himself as one of Hollywood's most respected writers, producers, and directors of television, film, and theater.

Marshall made his directorial feature debut with *The Young Doctors.* He went on to such hits as *Pretty Woman, Frankie and Johnny, Beaches, Nothing in Common,* and *The Flamingo Kid.* He hasn't stopped since.

Marshall has also created and executive-produced some of the longest running and most celebrated sitcoms in American television history. Among those are *Happy Days, Laverne & Shirley, The Odd Couple,* and *Mork & Mindy.* Marshall has developed and created fourteen television series and executive-produced more than a thousand half-hour episodes. In addition to enjoying critical and commercial success across the board with his film and television projects, Marshall has also helped launch the careers of such well-known Hollywood personalities as Julia Roberts, Robin Williams, Pam Dawber, Matt Dillon, his sister Penny Marshall, Jason Alexander, Henry Winkler, Mayim Bialik, and Crystal Bernard among others.

A graduate of Northwestern University, Marshall began his career in 1961 as a writer for *The Tonight Show,* starring Jack Paar. He went on to write for such hit television programs as *The Lucy Show, Dick Van Dyke, I Spy, Love American Style, Gomer Pyle U.S.M.C.,* and *The Danny Thomas Show.*

Marshall's sense of humor is boundless. Hang on to your seat because this interview will leave the reader in stitches.

> *Garry's a very somber guy on the set. Very serious, very cold. Really not much fun. I'm lying of course. He is funny and goofy and silly. You kind of forget that you're making a movie. Certainly he does.*

He's got all his little quirks that we've all come to know and love. The tuna fish that appears four, five times a day, and the tooth picks. He's great. I don't think anybody comes off of a Garry Marshall picture, whether the picture is good, bad, or indifferent, without having had a wonderful time.

Jason Alexander—Actor

The Conversation

The key to directing is don't take it too seriously. I started in this whole field of directing never having any interest in it. I grew up in the Bronx, New York. I was a very sickly child. I was just trying to get out of bed. That was my ambition, not success—just to get out of bed and to stop coughing and sneezing. I lay in bed as a sickly child, and also a clumsy child, mind you, because I played a lot of sports and would always get hurt. I had stitches all over the place. So I used to lie in bed a lot while the other children played and I would think of stories just to amuse myself and sometimes if I thought of a scary story, I would get scared. And if I thought of a depressing story I would feel worse. So I started mostly thinking of amusing stories and looking at life comically. I guess I have done it ever since.

He has fourteen type-written pages of allergies. How he got in the army, none of us knows. When we go out now, or go to a party, he has a taster with him. Can I eat this? You got to say, "No, it's got mustard, no, it's got mayonnaise, and it's got ketchup." He's allergic to everything.

Penny Marshall—Actress/Director/Sister

My sister's name is Penny Marshall. Her real name was Carol. It's a whole insight into her directing, if you know her real name is Carol. She was named after Carol Lombard. But this is my interview, why talk about my sister's directing career. I have another sister named Ronnie who is a producer now, and the three of us all were hopefully going to be dancers because my mother was a dance teacher. Turned out none of us were any good at dancing and so we went into other endeavors. We grew up in the Bronx, New York, in a small apartment with a lot of people. We had a large family with the grandpas and the grandmothers. In those days they didn't take old people and put them away, they just kept them in the house and in your way. So we were all bunched together. If it was a dysfunctional family it was so crowded you wouldn't know it was dysfunctional. We were all very happy. That's pretty much how I grew up, with no big interest in show business other than dancing.

My dad was in advertising and my mother was teaching. Now when I say she taught dancing, she was not with the ballet, she taught dancing in the cellar of our building. She taught little kids. So we were all in the shows. I was such a bad dancer she made me the drummer. To this day I play drums and I worked my way into college playing drums. But we saw shows and we saw how entertainment affected an audience. We saw how people cheered for their own children and they cheered for people they liked and knew, which helped us later in our careers to be around people that were likeable.

In those days it was five cents to come to my mother's recitals in the basement. We sort of liked the entertainment business but since we were bad dancers, we didn't know what to do. So I went for journalism because I figured I could always think and use my brain.

At Northwestern University Journalism School I was a sports editor on the school paper. I thought I could be a journalist. I got in the real world, working for the *New York Daily News,* and found that I was no good at being a journalist because I fooled around too much. People ask me how to get started. I feel you get started by kind of bumping into it. People try to get started by staying in their house and thinking, "How shall I get started?" The best way to get started is to go out in some arena and just get close to what you think you want to do.

I tried writing all sorts of stuff. A columnist at the *New York Daily News,* Robert Sylvester, said, "You could write humor, kid." So I thought maybe humor was the answer to my career and I started writing stuff. I was playing drums in various nightclubs and would try to give the comedians jokes. Most of the time they said, "Get back to the drums and shut up, kid." Once a comedian took my page of jokes and took out a cigarette lighter and lit the page of jokes on fire, so I realized that if I was to pursue this particular field of entertainment, it could be depressing and there would be a lot of rejection. I think accepting rejection is the key to directing, writing, or whatever you do in entertainment. To be able to accept rejection you have to feel it's noble to fail. You talk yourself into that. Then you have to be comfortable living with chronic emotional pain for a period while your work gets rejected. I must say I learned this very early.

After being rejected a lot and playing drums in nightclubs and giving comedians jokes, I finally got a job on a TV show called *The Tonight Show with Jack Paar,* writing jokes. I met a lot of comedians including Danny Thomas and Joey Bishop. They brought me to Hollywood to write for a new thing called situation comedies. It was just luck that I was a joke writer at the point where television executives said, "Let's get the joke writers!" That's how I came to Hollywood as a top joke writer. They were gonna teach me how to write a story and they did.

I wrote for a lot of TV stars and their shows. Like Danny Thomas, Joey Bishop, the *Dick Van Dyke Show,* and Lucille Ball. I became trained in writing physical and verbal comedy. After I had written for everybody else I created my own TV series. Now, when you create a TV series you also are the show runner. Because "show runner" is not a very cute title to have on the ending credits they began calling us producers. At first they called us executive producers. Executive producers were really writers who ran the show. My first show was called *Hey Landlord.* It was ninety-ninth in the ratings so I was neither a good show runner, nor writer, nor executive producer. I was no good at any of the three. But through failure and just doing the job I learned, and my next shows became successful. *The Odd Couple* came first, then *Happy Days, Laverne & Shirley, Mork & Mindy, Angie, Joanie Loves Chachi,* and on and on. There were also a few failures like *Me and the Chimp* and *Blansky's Beauties.* So when people ask me how I became a director I basically became a producer and hired myself as a director because nobody would hire me because I had never directed before. So that's how I broke into directing.

I learned in my mother's dancing school that if the audience knew the person they were more prone to welcome them into their hearts and to clap for them and enjoy their entertainment. Fred Silverman, who was head of a network, was never at my mother's dancing school, but he seemed to understand the same concept. So we did a lot of what we called spin-offs. From *Happy Days* we spun-off *Laverne & Shirley* and *Mork & Mindy.* Penny Marshall and Cindy Williams, who played *Laverne & Shirley,* made their first appearance as those characters on *Happy Days.* Robin Williams' debut was on *Happy Days* as Mork. The trick is always to associate one thing with something else. For example, "*Frankie and Johnny*, made by the director who directed *Pretty Woman*." This goes back to the TV spinoff days. Penny and Cindy were the original *Laverne & Shirley* on *Happy Days* and went on to do the series. *Laverne & Shirley* ran for eight years, *Happy Days* ran for ten seasons, *Mork & Mindy* five years. So I realized that good characters lasted a long time.

After twenty years in TV my shows were winding down. I wanted to do something else and my first choice was theater. Jerry Belson and I did a play called *The Roast* on Broadway but we closed in three nights. So I said, "Let's rethink this a minute. Maybe theater is not right for us yet. What else can we do?" There was the writing of clever cocktail napkins that Woody Allen once did. It wouldn't pay very much and sometimes they would blur when you put a drink on the napkin. A blurry joke on a cocktail napkin is not so funny. So that was not good. Where could I go for my new career?

I always liked movies but I did not grow up, like many of the great filmmakers of our time, walking around as a four-year-old with a camera, shooting my mother taking out the garbage. I did none of that but I always enjoyed the fact that you could actually get some reactions from a film. In TV I had number one shows because they told me I had number one shows. But I could not see the reaction of the audience. To this day when I make a film I go and watch it and face the audience so I can see their reaction.

How Sweet It Is and *The Grasshopper* were my first movies. I wrote and produced them with Jerry Belson, and Jerry Paris directed them. But then you could watch a movie and know it was dull as soon as the cigarettes started lighting up, because that was back when you could smoke in the theater. Now there's no smoking so you have to do expensive research with people pushing dials and writing on cards. Smoking is bad for you, but it was great to tell how your movie was doing.

> Young Doctors in Love *was invented between set shots, I think. At least my role in it was. We were shooting a round of basketball and he says, "We're doing a movie, and what do you think is funny? Is a monkey suit funny, like a gorilla costume?" He gives me a couple of choices. "A mobster who dresses in drag, but who really is a very tender and sensitive fellow. That's funny."*
>
> Hector Elizondo—Actor

Young Doctors in Love (1982)

*Sean Young; Michael McKean; Gary Friedkin; Kyle T. Heffner;
Rick Overton; Crystal Bernard; Ted McGinley; Saul Rubinek; Harry Dean Stanton;
Pamela Reed; Taylor Negron; Patrick Collins; Dabney Coleman;
Titos Vandis; Michael Richards; Demi Moore; Hector Elizondo.*

What was the question? Oh—movies. After failing in the theater, I said, "Let's see about movies." I wanted to direct movies. But at the time it was very difficult. I had never directed a movie so nobody wanted me. ABC liked me a little bit because I made them a big hit with all my shows. So they gave me my first shot at directing. *Young Doctors in Love* was kind of a crazy comedy that I had a terrific time doing, but it was only successful in Sweden for some unknown reason. In Sweden it killed them. And we were big in Madrid where they had a terrible rainy season, but other than that *Young Doctors in Love* did not do too well.

That film got a lot of actors started. See, you got to start some place. Michael Richards' first real movie was *Young Doctors in Love*. Demi Moore's first movie was *Young Doctors in Love*. Hector Elizondo, the first time I got to work with him was on that film. So even a failure helps you find an actor that you use later. That was how I got into movies. *Young Doctors in Love* was my first picture as a director. After that, they said, "Look, he finished the picture; it looks like a movie. It killed them in Sweden. Maybe we should give him another picture."

I like to work with young people and we had a lot of them in that picture. I once said that I like to get people just as they're beginning and before rehab—that's when you get the stars. And I've gotten a lot of them in that slot. So these kids were so eager and they would try anything. It was really delightful working with them. They weren't veterans of the screen and all that, but they just did a wonderful job. So it was the blind leading the blind in a way, but we had a good time and we knew how to make it funny.

A Little Advice on Directing

As a film director, it's much different than TV directing. After a show has been running for a while, if the TV director doesn't fall down and faint, usually the cast and crew can kind of maneuver around on their own. I remember the late director George Marshall. I studied his stuff. He was almost God to us. As an old, old man he directed *Odd Couple* episodes of Tony and Jack and myself. We loved George Marshall. Sometimes he fell asleep in the middle of directing. But because we were so trained we could go on. You can't do that in movies. In movies the director is the king, the whole ball of wax, so everybody is looking to him and asking him what to do. I was petrified directing my first film. I went to work every day scared to death. I was petrified and couldn't make decisions. And yet that's all you have to do, is make decisions.

There was a day on *Young Doctors in Love* where it rained, so we quickly moved indoors to a locker room that was our cover set. I had never seen the set before because it wasn't finished. It still wasn't finished. We had a couple of walls to work with. So we rehearsed the scene and it was very, very dull and bad. Not only was the scene no good but the crew was not liking me very much. Not only didn't they like me but they were mumbling to themselves. Now I've got to figure out a way to impress them so I said, "Wait, I'm going to do this scene. I'm gonna come up with a shot. Maybe I'll get a crane or I'll come through the ceiling, or maybe come through the floor. I'll shoot through glass, I'll shoot through bubbles, I'll do something sensational."

I couldn't think of what to do so I walked around the block and said, "How can I show them I'm a great filmmaker?" And as I walked around the block I realized—you've got to talk to yourself when you're a film director—I realized that I wasn't a great filmmaker so how am I going to convince them that I am? I walked back to the set and asked them to give me the widest lens they had. I told the crew to put the camera low on the floor and I said to the actors, "Say what's written, just say the lines." And then I put a telephone on the wall and I got one actor who was very small and I said, "While the scene is going on, you do this." And I said, "Ready, action." We rolled and after the first take everyone was startled because it was so funny. Then take two was even funnier and then I yelled, "Cut—perfect!" And then they all said, "Oh, that's what he does. He's not a great filmmaker but look, with a phone and a guy he made a dull scene hilarious. Look at how he did that, this person." Suddenly I got a little respect and they started to help me and it worked out much better. I still was frightened but at least I had them on my side.

I guess the lesson I learned is you can't be something if you didn't learn it yet. Do what it is you do. Do what you did that got you to the dance. My key was I could make things funny and they were gonna have to help me capture it on film. After we laid those ground rules it was a terrific experience. I truly believe that film directing is the most difficult job of any job I've ever done in my whole life, because film directing is an art form that is based on how artistic you can be when you're exhausted. That's the whole key to it. So anybody can direct if they're fresh as a daisy every day and hopping around and they get a week off between shots. Sure you can direct. But how to direct exhausted at four in the morning, that's the key to directing. People ask, "What do you need to know as a director?" There's many things you need to know but one is stamina and two is have the right shoes. Without the right shoes your feet hurt, everything hurts. Before I directed my first picture I talked to Francis Coppola and he put his arm around me and took me for a walk and I waited for all these genius things about filmmaking and he said, "Change shoes at lunchtime." Remember, you got to have two different pairs of shoes or else you'll die altogether.

The funniest thing in *Young Doctors in Love* seemed to be where I put the phone on the wall and said, "This is what I do, folks. I don't give you fancy shots."

> *I mean it really was like a pie in the face kind of thing on the set. He comes off real casual, like hey, we'll make a movie, it'll be fun. But in fact everybody's energy is put into making that film and it's very much a Garry Marshall film.*
>
> Matt Dillon—Actor

The Flamingo Kid (1984)

Matt Dillon; Hector Elizondo; Molly McCarthy; Martha Gehman; Richard Crenna; Jessica Walter; Carole Davis; Janet Jones; Brian McNamara; Fisher Stevens; León; Bronson Pinchot; Frank Campanella; Richard Stahl; Joe Grifasi.

One of the keys to directing is communicating. To communicate, people have to understand what you're saying. So once in a while you've got to take water. Drink a lot of water while you're directing—very important—and then you can communicate. After *Young Doctors in Love*, in which I made a lot of mistakes, the next film I did was called *Flamingo Kid*. I had a very good producer by the name of Michael Phillips who had been walking around with this script for eight years. Because *Flamingo Kid* was about playing gin rummy, nobody wanted to make it because they thought that it would be visually dull. I saw *The Flamingo Kid* script and I thought it was very visual, very exciting. It didn't have four hundred camels going across the desert, there was no guys rioting, there was no yelling and jumping around, they were just men playing cards. So nobody wanted to do it.

I thought it was terrific because I saw the story not about gin rummy but about a boy who chooses between his father and somebody else. It happens. Mark Twain wrote once that when you're twelve years old your father suddenly becomes very stupid and he doesn't get bright again until you're twenty-two. This was the part of life that we captured in *Flamingo Kid*. The son turned against his father toward a flashier image.

The *Flamingo Kid* script was written perfect and we were all set to go. Matthew Broderick agreed to star in it. Matthew says words so beautifully. Suddenly Matthew Broderick went out the door. Where did he go? The deal fell through. Didn't work. Now we got Matt Dillon, a man not known for his verbal skills. The man spoke through his shoes quite a bit and went to mumbling school. So now we had a talking script for a mumbling actor. This could give you quite a headache no matter how many times you changed your shoes.

We started and we had to fix the script every other day for Matt. Luckily I brought along Richard Crenna and Hector Elizondo, two veteran actors, who were very helpful. We also had a lot of newcomers. I love to work with the newcomers, that's one of my favorite things, and in *The Flamingo Kid* you had first-timers Marisa Tomei, Bronson Pinchot, and Fisher Stevens. Then there was León whose name was Leon Robinson, but he became so big his name is just León now.

This was a very good shoot even though we had to rewrite every day so Matt Dillon could say the lines that were written for somebody else. So the key to that experience, I must say, was to learn that a director must adjust. It's never the way it's supposed to be. Actors fall out, somebody else comes in. You just have to adjust to it. But I truly think *The Flamingo Kid* is the funniest thing Matt Dillon ever did because he is a funny guy.

Sometimes Matt would be late or do something odd and I always would say, "Why is he doing that?" Then I realized, "Oh, yeah, he's nineteen." Nineteen-year-olds do things like that. When I did the makeup and hair and wardrobe tests his face came alive on the camera. His eyes, those cheekbones, it was just awesome. I feel every director should fall in love with the male lead and the female lead. That is a very good thing to do because then you want to make them as beautiful as possible. In *Pretty Woman* I tried to make Richard Gere as beautiful as Julia Roberts. I think you have to do that.

With Matt Dillon it was easy. He just lit up the screen; he had that "camera loves him" kind of thing. We surrounded him with a supporting cast that made him feel very comfortable. You have to put in the cast a couple of adults who set the tone. That's why I always use Hector Elizondo, because he comes on the set and he says, "This is the way you behave on a movie, folks." He behaves a certain way and he has a certain professionalism that the kids pick up on. I did that way back on my TV shows. Each show has an adult. I think if you're an actor, you're allowed to be temperamental, you're allowed to be a little childish, because some of it's a little silly, you know. Making mad, passionate love with a whole bunch of guys looking on is a little silly. So you have to let the temperament rise and a little crankiness occurs, but if you have an adult, at least it's under control.

Some Advice on Eating Habits

Oh, and it's very important that you hire an editor with the same eating habits as you. This is what Penny and I discovered very early. When I interview I always ask besides their credits what they had for lunch. What? Mexican food! Well, I don't do much Mexican. Thai food? Gee, I don't know if we're gonna get along. Because you have to eat every day, sometimes three meals a day with the editors, so you might as well have food that agrees with both of you. Then you get this bonding going. On *The Flamingo Kid* my editor was Priscilla Ann Nedd. At first she was eating such things as goulash. She finally learned to eat pasta and a nice piece of chicken. We got along real good after that.

On *The Flamingo Kid* I got writing credit but the man who did a terrific job rewriting got no writing credit. His name was Bo Goldman. But it said Neal Marshall and Garry Marshall wrote the script and Neal Marshall's real name is Markowitz and my real name is Masciarelli, so there were no Marshalls involved at all. It just happened to say Neal Marshall and Garry Marshall and we're not related in any way. Neal Marshall wrote the script years ago based on his own experiences working at these little resorts on Long Island and he carried the script around for eight years before I got it.

Another exciting thing about *Flamingo Kid* was a girl named Janet Jones. Many of my newcomers went on to great stardom. Janet Jones went on to a great marriage. She married Wayne Gretsky and she has wonderful children. Wayne Gretsky, for those filmmakers who are too busy in the editing room, is probably the greatest ice hockey player who ever lived in the world. Janet Jones was a quite a find. My wife and I were playing in a celebrity tennis tournament and I looked across at the other court and I saw a girl that had a body that was startling. I said to my wife, "You see that girl over there? If she can say hello I think we'll put her in the picture." So I went up to Janet and she said hello and I put her in the film and she did a great job.

> *Garry is forever fascinated by family. I think it is the root of almost all of the stories that he tells. And I think there is the sound of a Garry Marshall movie that is the sound of familiar people talking to each other. It ends up being, I think, the fingerprint of his films.*
>
> Tom Hanks—Actor

Nothing in Common (1986)

Tom Hanks; Jackie Gleason; Eva Marie Saint; Hector Elizondo; Barry Corbin; Bess Armstrong; Sela Ward; Cindy Harrell; John Kapelos; Carol Messing; Bill Applebaum; Mona Lyden; Anthony Starke; Julio Alonso; Jane Morris.

After I finished *The Flamingo Kid* they said, "Well, maybe he can make a film, who knows." The film did pretty well. I felt I had done two kinds of comedies and I wanted to do something a little more serious. And along came a piece called *Nothing in Common*. It was attached to Tom Hanks. I knew Tom from the softball days and he had also appeared on *Happy Days* so we knew each other. Producer Ray Stark brought me in and said, "I saw your work, it's not bad, let's see what you can do here." So I got my chance to do a more serious picture.

We shot a lot in Chicago and we worked extremely hard on it but I loved the results. The movie was about a father and a son and I wanted the father to be Jackie Gleason. Everybody said, "Don't be crazy, you can't get Jackie Gleason, he doesn't work anymore. He's retired." But Ray Stark said, "You want Gleason? We'll go get Gleason." Ray went to Florida and he simply said to Jackie Gleason, "Jackie, if you never do another film your last film will be *Smokey and the Bandit, Part Two.*" Gleason leaped out of bed, grabbed a pen, signed the contract, and said, "I'm coming. I'm gonna do the picture." We got him in and he was a little ill but I thought he was terrific.

It was just a delight for me to shoot that film. If you saw the picture you know it was quite serious sometimes. Now, being from comedyland you can't just say, "That's it, Tom, be serious now." I remember we were doing a very emotional moment where Tom gets teased by his father who is supposedly dying in the hospital. We started into the scene but it wasn't working. Gleason said, "You know what's wrong? We're all from comedy. These are serious scenes but we're in comedy set. We've all done hospital jokes and here we are in a hospital." So I said, "Yeah, you're right," I said, "so we're going to have an exorcism. We're going to get rid of all the jokes in this room." The three of us ran around this hospital room doing every joke we ever heard about hospitals. We did them all. The crew was having a wonderful time. We ran around for like fifteen minutes and finally Jackie said, "This room is now void of any humor. Let's shoot the scene." And then we shot the scene and it worked.

Nothing in Common was the first time I worked with big stars. I mean, Tom wasn't really a big star yet. In *Bachelor Party* he ran around in his underwear, so it wasn't like he was a great dramatic star. But he's a fine actor. People don't know that Tom Hanks studied Shakespeare. He went to acting school. He did the Shakespeare Festival in Cleveland. They have a very good Shakespeare Festival in Cleveland. He is also part Portuguese and you always say to yourself, "Ah, Portuguese, no wonder he's funny. He comes from a long line of funny Portuguese people." When's the last person from Portugal that made you fall down laughing? Not often. But the fact that he wanted to do dramatic parts and be serious helped me. Working with Tom Hanks was always a delight for me as it is for most directors. My sister Penny directed him in *Big* and *A League of Their Own*. He doesn't come in lazy. He gives you a shot and tries different things and then if he's dead in the water and you got no other way to go, he just commits to it and that's what's always needed from an actor.

Jackie Gleason was mostly known as a comedian from TV but he was also a heck of an actor and he did some wonderful work in films and probably did not receive enough accolades as an actor. Tom and I asked him if we should call him Mr. Gleason. He said, "Call me 'The Great One,' that's what you should call me." So we called him The Great One. "Great One, you want to come over here for a minute?" As I said, he was a little ill during *Nothing in Common* so you had to work with him so he wouldn't have too much physical stuff to do. But he always knew where everything was. Because he didn't feel good he asked me to get him out of there every day by five in the afternoon. So every day I would get out by five except once in a while, and this is where it takes a little finesse. I would say, "Jackie, you got out at five every day for six days. Today I'm a little behind. Can you give me an extra half-hour?" He always gave in. I see directors that say, "We'll be out by six," then the first day they go until nine, then the actor gets very aggravated. That's no good. You got to show that you're at least trying to deal with who you're dealing with.

I would always make it fun for Jackie because every day at five over the sound system we would play his exit music from his TV show and so he would get up and he would exit to the music. He loved that. And everybody would clap as he went off. So we had some fun doing it.

Over the years I have also found a way to work with stars. In the film Gleason is a salesman and he loses his job. He had just got these pens made that had his name on them and he's going to give them out to customers. But that's the day they fired him. So he goes on this ferryboat for a ride and he's supposed to be sad. I said, "Jackie, there's not a lot of dialogue in the scene. You're just thinking about losing your job, right?" And he said, "Yeah." "So remember, you got those pens. Maybe you got a few in your pocket. What would you do with the pens?" He said, "Throw them in the water or something." I said, "What a wonderful idea, let's do that! Jackie has a great idea! Let's shoot it!" And we shot the scene. "Cut!" I said to Jackie, "What great idea am I gonna get tomorrow?" You see, sometimes rather than just say, "Here's what you do," you kind of work with them. That always served me well. I always felt that if you can make people feel good they'll do better work.

Tom Hanks was very helpful to a wonderful new actress named Sela Ward who went on to big television fame in *Sisters*. But this was her first film and Tom helped her a lot in it. In one scene Tom had to get emotional. He said to me, "Just give me a minute and I'll nod when I'm ready." So he went away for a few minutes and he came back and he nodded and I said, "Action," and we shot it. Sela was watching this. Now she has an emotional scene, so she said, "I need a moment." She went away and then she came back and I asked her if she was ready. She whispered to me, "What did Tom do when he went away?" "Well, let's ask him," I said. "He went away and I don't know what the hell he did." So we had to discuss it with Tom. Tom explained that he was trying to reach down into his memory or whatever they learn in the various acting schools. But it worked and he was helpful and she was wonderful. So the actors helping each other was a big facet of *Nothing in Common*.

A Fine Line between Comedy and Drama

As a director one of my aims with almost every picture is to walk the line between comedy and tragedy. Because that's what I think life is. On the same day you're doing something funny, something sad happens. My mother was very ill and Penny and I were with her at the hospital. Penny was at the height of her fame in *Laverne & Shirley*. My mother was lying there, Penny was crying, and a couple of nurses came in and they said, "Ah, Laverne is crying. Could we have your autograph?" Now in the middle of this she doesn't want to sign an autograph. So there's always this comedy and tragedy working. I've tried to walk that line. Sometimes I walked it very well, sometimes the audience and I walked it well together. The critics don't always get it but I have always tried to combine it and not go too far. Sometimes I go too far and I immediately know it from the audience's reaction. Even when something is hysterical I cut it out because maybe it went too far the other way and you don't believe the story anymore.

One more thing. Often I lecture at film schools and I always say probably technically all of you people know more about making films than I do. But I know more about how to get the star out of the trailer than you do. That's a big part of filmmaking. You've got to get the actor on the stage. You got to get them to want to do the scene.

Overboard (1987)

Goldie Hawn; Kurt Russell; Edward Herrmann; Katherine Helmond; Michael G. Hagerty; Roddy McDowall; Jared Rushton; Jeffrey Wiseman; Brian Price; Jamie Wild; Frank Campanella; Henry Alan Miller; Frank Buxton; Carol Williard; Doris Hess.

I had a crisis in my life in the mid-eighties involving money. You can make money in show business but then there are people who come and they get you mixed up and you lose your money. Through some bad investments I lost a lot of money so I had to do a picture. Because I was known for handling actors very well I was offered a film called *Overboard* which starred Goldie Hawn and Kurt Russell. Besides being known as a filmmaker that was amusing and could finish a film I was also known as someone who could handle any kind of star. I think one of the biggest things in handling big stars is you can't be frightened. I have no fear of anybody. Bette Midler told me after the movie *Beaches* that I was the first director who wasn't afraid of her. I come from the streets of the Bronx. I'm afraid of nobody. What are they going to do, yell? I've heard yelling you wouldn't believe. You should meet my father. So I was looking for a job and Goldie Hawn, happily, had a picture and also knew me so I was hired.

What made that picture not so special was it came out at Christmas and that was not a good time for the film to come out, but it did all right. It's funny because most people have seen it on video or TV and they know every joke in the picture. A lot of stuff that I had practiced on *Laverne & Shirley* and learned from Lucy I put in that movie. Goldie is a consummate actress and brilliant as a comedian. She didn't have to always figure out what her motivation was. In one scene she's on the back of a truck and Kurt's taking her to his home and she's all mixed up and I thought it was dull, just a truck driving along. So I took the bullhorn and I said, "Goldie, flies are here in the woods. Swallow a fly!" She did a whole bit swallowing a fly. She did so good she almost choked. Another actress would stop the truck, get out and say, "What does that mean? What is my motivation? Why would I swallow a fly at this point? Is it in defiance of society or am I say-ing something at the establishment?" And my answer would be, "No, no; you're just swallowing a fly. It's a little something on the way home."

I remember the big scene at the end of the picture took place in the water and she had to swim in this beautiful gown. We couldn't let her wear a wet suit because of the gown and the water was very chilly. She did the scene but because the boat changed positions, which they do in the water, we didn't get the shot. She did it twice and we still didn't get it. So I said, "Goldie, you got to go in the water again," and she said, "I'm not going! That's it! It's freezing!" We're all out there in the middle of this ocean and I was trying to think of what great speech I could give her. Like how impor-tant the scene is to the film and it has to do with the ending, and all that stuff. Before I could say anything Kurt said, "Goldie, for the money you're getting you got to get in the water again." I wanted to say that, but as soon as she heard Kurt say it she jumped right in the water and we did four more takes and she was great.

Kurt Russell is one of the best actors I ever worked with. Kurt is the kind of star who when you say, "We're losing the light" and you run with the equipment, he picks up the equipment with you. He carries the stand, he carries the lights, because he's one of those kind of guys. So I love working with him. Kurt comes prepared. He does his homework.

I almost owned the man, you see. Ron Howard and I owned a baseball team for a while. We owned a team called the Portland Bees in Portland, Oregon. On that team Kurt Russell played second base. The year before we bought the team he left so we were one year away. We could have owned him. Then I could have made him do anything because I could have said, "I own you, you're the second baseman on my team." He's a great athlete and tended to do all his own stunts. He's also very strong so he could lift girls and other things and move things. He's not afraid of anything. I have always said that if you need a team player Kurt Russell is probably the best around.

Beaches (1988)

Bette Midler; Barbara Hershey; John Heard; Spalding Gray; Lainie Kazan;
James Read; Grace Johnston; Mayim Bialik; Marcie Leeds; Carol Williard;
Allan Kent; Phil Leeds; Lynda Goodfriend; Nikki Plant; Michael French.

I had worked with Michael Eisner from the old days on *Happy Days*. He suddenly became head of Disney. He said to me, "If there's two people that can make a hit picture for Disney it's Spielberg and you." I said I would bet on Spielberg.

They had a picture called *Beaches* that had a very sad ending. It was about two girlfriends. One is very sick and starts to throw up all over the place and has diarrhea all over the place and her friend has to clean it up. Disney got a little scared of that. "Where's the Mickey Mouse here?" they asked. They called me and said, "We love the script but we don't do this here at the moment. Maybe you could just give it a little lighter touch." I said, "You mean the character has to get well at the end?" "No," they said, "she doesn't have to get well but it just shouldn't be so horrifying."

Bette Midler and I met and we got along and we decided to do the picture. The casting of Barbara Hershey was very hard because we screen-tested about twelve people and we couldn't make a decision. I said, "You know, it's driving me crazy, we can't pick. Run the screen test without sound." I watched them all without sound and it became very obvious to me that the two that seemed the most friendly were Barbara Hershey and Bette Midler. I was trying to show the friendship between two women. I think it's fascinating because girls' friendships are much different than boys' friendships. Girls can say the worst things to each other and an hour later they make up. Guys hold a grudge for twenty years. Girls seem to get on with it all.

I used color to shoot the film in four sections. The first part of *Beaches* is done in pastels. It's youthful and it's like kiddy. Then they go into a very sad part of their life, they're struggling, so it was very dark and everything was black. Even the wardrobe was dark. Then suddenly Bette Midler's character becomes a big hit and becomes an overbearing star who is a pain in the neck, so we made it nouveau riche. We made it glitzy and everything was shiny. The fourth segment of the picture is when the illness occurs. That was the last hour of the film so we made that gold. We shot it as much as we could at magic hour and tried to make it kind of ethereal during the character's demise there at the end.

We saw a lot of kids to play the part of Bette as a child and of course Bette brought in two girls that were the most gorgeous girls you ever saw. They looked just like Michelle Pfeiffer. "Well, Bette," I said, "they're very nice but they don't seem to have your fire." We had this one kid that I felt looked just like Bette. She looked like a young Bette but she didn't have the fire and she was very nervous at the audition. I auditioned her four or five times until she finally just let it loose. It took a lot of coaching but we finally chose Mayim Bialik, whose name I couldn't say right to this day. I thought it was something you buy in the bakery in the Bronx. Give me a Mayim Bialik, please, and a little cream cheese, yeah.

> *The key to imitating Garry Marshall is, whatever you're going to say, you have to end the sentence with the noun of the sentence. So you say, it was good, the thing. Or, you could be good in the thing, the part. It's always the noun is at the end. I can't believe he's not Jewish.*
>
> Jason Alexander—Actor

Pretty Woman (1990)

Richard Gere; Julia Roberts; Ralph Bellamy; Jason Alexander; Laura San Giacomo; Hector Elizondo; Alex Hyde-White; Amy Yasbeck; Elinor Donahue; Judith Baldwin; Jason Randal; Bill Applebaum; Tracy Bjork; Gary Greene; William Gallo.

Pretty Woman was another Disney picture. They had an ending where a prostitute and a rich man get together and fall in love. The prostitute's in her late thirties and this is her last shot at life. In the original script she tells the guy not to leave because she loves him. He says he's got to go and he hands her three thousand dollars for her services. She takes the money and throws it in his face. He slaps her and knocks her down in the street and he drives away. She goes upstairs and her roommate ODs on drugs. That was all in the original script.

Disney calls. "Oh, Garry—we got another script here. It's a little dark at the end so maybe you could lighten it up here." I read it and I loved it. The writer, Jonathan Lawton, had done a wonderful job. Maybe it should have been a harsher script but they hired me to not do that. I said, "I'll find an ending," and eventually I did with the help of a rewrite lady by the name of Barbara Benedict, who suggested that maybe Gere's character is afraid of heights. And that was the ending rather than the girlfriend overdosing.

My wife's the head nurse at the L.A. Free Clinic and she gets all the street kids in there. Julia actually stayed with my wife for a couple of days to learn about real teenage prostitutes and young girls walking the streets of Hollywood Boulevard. But it was important for me to say that the kid should get out. If you remember the story, she quits prostitution and is going back to school before he comes and rescues her. Some of the feminists said she's waiting for the guy to rescue her. Well, she rescues him right back because she does change his life as much as he changes hers. So that worked out very well. It was a $14 million picture that made $286 million, so that's good business. If you ever get it right it works out nice in the end.

When I came to the project no actors were attached. We did screen tests and I thought Julia was the newest, freshest face. I didn't think she was particularly funny. Then I put her in a screen test with Charles Grodin and simply said, "Julia, this man is twelve times funnier than you and he's gonna blow you out of the scene, so you got to hold your own." I saw her as she was trying to hold her own with him. She was amusing and charming and that's where, unfortunately, Charles Grodin didn't get the job.

We took Julia around to meet various stars to see who would be interested in being in the film with her because she wasn't anybody yet. I remember when she met with Richard Gere. It was in an apartment in New York and I always let the actors talk a minute and I go to get a drink of water or something. I remember looking down the hall of this very railroad-type apartment and there was Richard and her talking to each other. I couldn't hear a word that they were saying but just watching them I said, "Ooh, they're getting along and that's a heck of a two-shot there." It just happened to work out.

At one point in *Pretty Woman* Richard said, "You know, you don't really need me. Julia's so wonderful you just need a suit, so why don't you just shoot my suit and let me go home." I said, "No, no; you're a key to this." There was a wonderful moment where, at the end of the opera, Julia gets up and says, "That was so wonderful I peed in my pants." It was very funny and she did it so honest, so sincere, and so charming. Richard said, "Now, that's a great ending." I said, "You want a line, I'll give you a line." He says, "You can't top that line." I said, "I can top anything." So Julia says her line and then the woman in the next seat says, "What did she just say?" And Richard says, "She liked it better than *Pirates of Penzance*." When Richard saw the picture and that scene he came over and hugged me and said, "You know what you're doing sometimes." Working with him was the key to *Pretty Woman* because he gave her the room to fly. You could have had another actor who says she's got too much to do, I want to be the star. He was lovely and they were nice together.

Frankie and Johnny (1991)

Al Pacino; Michelle Pfeiffer; Hector Elizondo; Nathan Lane; Kate Nelligan;
Jane Morris; Greg Lewis; Al Fann; Ele Keats; Fernando López; Glenn Plummer;
Tim Hopper; Harvey Miller; Sean O'Bryan; Goldie McLaughlin.

I think the best script I ever directed was *Frankie and Johnny* written by Terrence McNally, who Paramount did not want to have write the script. It's always like that. Terrence wrote the play *Frankie and Johnny in the Clair de Lune* and I said, "Let him write the screenplay." They said, "He never wrote a screenplay, we don't want him." I said, "He knows the characters, for heaven's sakes, let him try and I'll work with him." Well, Terrence wrote a brilliant screenplay and we got Al Pacino and Michelle Pfeiffer.

Al was almost going to do *Pretty Woman* so we knew each other. He wanted to do this. Michelle Pfeiffer arrived in this office where I'm sitting and said, "I'm gonna do this picture." She went on and on for an hour and a half telling me why she would be great for this role. I thought she would be great because I wanted it to be about a pretty girl who had some adversity in her life, a pretty girl who gave up dating. Everybody said, "Oh, it's got to be a homely girl." In the play it was not so much a homely girl, it was Kathy Bates who is not homely. It was kind of a different spin on the subject. Some of the critics felt those two good looking people wouldn't have these problems, but critics who said that were critics who really were not that handsome or not that good looking. But the audience in general liked the film.

Frankie and Johnny opened during the Anita Hill, Clarence Thomas hearing so it was very hard to get people out to the theater. The critics really were very kind to *Frankie and Johnny* and it was very well received critically. But not a lot people went to the theaters. They were waiting for the video to come out. Then the day the video came out was the day of the L.A. riots. The poster and cassettes were in the video stores and as I watched on television, in the store I was watching the poster was on fire. I like to say that *Frankie and Johnny* was not the highest selling cassette, but *Frankie and Johnny* truly was the most looted cassette. Nobody looted a cassette more than *Frankie and Johnny* because that was the night the looting went on.

Stars very rarely have the same process. Michelle Pfeiffer learns the stuff and does it in three or four takes and that's the best she's going to get. She knows that and that's how she works. Al Pacino on the other hand is Mr. fifteen, sixteen, seventeen takes. That's where he's at! So you got to have two people trying to address each other's process and be kind through the process. And you must kid a lot. Kidding with stars is always very important. We played a lot of pranks on Al because he's a very serious actor. In one scene he bursts through a door and he thinks he's going to see certain people there. I brought in the entire cast of *Star Trek* that was shooting next door in full uniform and put them in the room. Al bursts into the room and there was the *Star Trek* cast, but his presentation is so strong he got out his first line. He did the line very straight, then he realized—what? Mr. Spock is here!

It was a very internal film. Every scene had dialogue and intensity so it was one of my hardest jobs. But you know, the film that I thought I came closest to being the filmmaker I wanted to be was *Frankie and Johnny*, and I'm still trying. Sometimes you need that chemistry. The three of us got along very well.

Exit to Eden (1994)

Dana Delany; Paul Mercurio; Rosie O'Donnell; Dan Aykroyd; Hector Elizondo;
Stuart Wilson; Iman; Sean O'Bryan; Stephanie Niznik; Phil Redrow;
Sandra Taylor; Julie Hughes; Laurelle Mehus; Tom Hines; Alison Moir.

As a filmmaker you want to do a good body of work. Noel Coward once wrote that the best way to survive in show business is to pop out of a different hole every time because you don't want to get typed. So after *Frankie and Johnny* I wanted to do different things. The times were changing in movies. People wouldn't go to see just anything. Now, all my themes celebrate something in boy-girl relationships, the celebration of some sexuality or some loving. In *Pretty Woman* it was the kiss. That was the key to the whole lovemaking. In *Frankie and Johnny* it was the noise of lovemaking. Each one had a different kind of feel to it.

Somebody brought me the book *Exit to Eden* and I thought to myself, how can I make a different form of lovemaking accessible because it's the time of AIDS, it's a time of people not really getting married and everything, so sex took a whole different turn. It was a time of feminism. The girl is aggressive, the boy is aggressive, and they don't know what to do anymore—who's in charge? There's so much confusion in the sexuality of the country that I thought that maybe I could bring a different kind of sexuality that might be interesting.

S&M is such a dirty word. So my job was to try to make it accessible to the regular public. Well, it didn't work out so well. Some people thought it was distasteful. I know for a fact that in all the research women seem to accept *Exit to Eden* better than men do. Who knows why? Maybe women can deal with it better. Also, the woman was dominant in the film and so maybe men didn't like that too much.

It became more of a comedy because Rosie O'Donnell and Dan Aykroyd were in it and that made it a little more acceptable to the studio that was paying for it. It might have been miscast in some places because I did not get the chemistry I got in *Pretty Woman* or with *Frankie and Johnny*. I think when you're doing a love story you have got to get that chemistry. The actors were great, but it just didn't work. I always say, if it didn't work it's my fault. I picked the wrong project, I shot it wrong, I did whatever. But to this day when I go on book tours—I have a book, *Wake Me When It's Funny*—women will say, "I saw *Pretty Woman* seven times, *Frankie and Johnny* was my favorite, *Overboard* makes me laugh," and then they lean real close and say, "I also liked *Exit to Eden*." They look around so nobody can hear what they say because people will think they're a strange, bizarre person.

I always say about *Exit to Eden,* "I made a picture about S&M and the critics spanked me." Still, I liked making that film and the author, Anne Rice was happy, but maybe I should have done the vampires instead. I think to be a true filmmaker you have to try different things. Hit or miss, try and see if you can do it. I thought walking the line between drama and comedy in *Exit to Eden* caused me to slip over the edge. I think that if I had to do it over again I wouldn't have made it so funny.

Dear God (1996)

Greg Kinnear; Laurie Metcalf; Maria Pitillo; Tim Conway; Hector Elizondo; Jon Seda; Roscoe Lee Browne; Anna Maria Horsford; Kathleen Marshall; Isadora O'Boto; Felix A. Pire; Donal Logue; Sam McMurray; Nancy Marchand; Larry Miller.

I wanted to write my own screenplays again and I was doing that but I was too slow. I was getting kind of interested in doing another film and *Dear God* came along. They had an actor who was new and I was known as somebody who could handle the newcomers. They had a great ensemble cast and I figured I could put a lot of new kids in this film. We did it and I thought it was very funny. But *Dear God* was not particularly successful and the audience turned their back to the film. I think the title might have been off. They might have thought it was *Oh, God* and they were looking for George Burns. George is alive, by God! And I think they pushed Greg Kinnear too hard. I think Greg is good and I think he truly will be the next Tom Hanks as the years go by. He's very charming. Then maybe there were too many TV stars in it. Whatever the reason people did not flock to the theaters. I wanted to do it because I thought maybe there was time for a nice sweet picture but the audiences didn't go to it. But I was hoping to make a low-budget picture that was successful and it's very hard. You always have to make an art picture or say, "Hello, I'm really from Canada and I shot this in Toronto and it cost almost nothing. I used my credit card and now I'm going to jail but here's the film." So it's different ways to do it.

His Thoughts on the Movie Industry

The movie industry has become an industry of marketing. It's not really whose picture is best; it's whose picture is marketed the best, whose trailer is the best, whose ad campaign is the best, and who the critics seem to like. I have always been very successful in most of my work, but certainly not all of it. People say, "Well, you had a lot of things that worked out, what do you attribute that to?" I say I attribute a lot to the fact that I never thought the audience was stupid. Many times the critics think the audience is stupid because the audience doesn't agree with them. So a movie like *Porky's* becomes a hit after every critic puts it down.

People like to watch films on the videocassette, the foreign market is booming, so there is no middle ground any more. If you make a picture for under $25 million you got to make your money back on video and foreign and if ten people see it domestically you got a shot. If you make an $80 million picture usually you can get an audience because they advertise it. You make a picture for $35 to $40 million and unless you're really lucky you don't have a prayer because you have to make so much back and you can't make it back through video and the foreign. Most of the filmmakers today are still artists trying to do what they believe in. I'm a little sad that the state of the movie industry at this moment does not have a lot of room for nice, pleasant pictures. It's mostly for quirky films with big explosions.

I always felt art was something that lasts a long time. I'm sure that just as the man was painting the *Mona Lisa* another guy says, "What is that? First of all we're not sure that's a girl; it could be a boy in a wig. And not a nice smile with teeth—she's got rotten teeth—this could be a bomb!" So we don't know what art really is. But we know that American pictures are the best-made films in the entire world. The world marketplace is always looking for American product and it's up to our filmmakers to make stuff that has impact and artistic content.

Pretty Woman ran in a theater in Pakistan every day for a year. Now right away you say, Pakistan, the home of films. But that's how powerful our movies are. So that's the good news. The bad news is domestic release is very tough to get and it's tougher to get a hit. Everybody gets great reviews, everybody is the greatest picture—there's too many. So to get a picture out there domestically is very hard today. I think it's a great time to be in the film business because of all the new cable channels. There are so many outlets where a film can be shown, that it's a great time to make films. And we'll see which ones last and are around after the year 2000.

Listen, I have been doing this interview so long my sweater went out of style and it has faded. I now have to get another sweater to end this interview because this is gone already. I've been here forever.

His Parting Words

There were two Siamese twins—two fellows—and they wanted to be racecar drivers. They lived in Indiana and the dream of these Siamese twins was that someday they would drive in London so the other brother could drive the car.

I think dreams are very important even if people don't understand them. Somebody once asked me, what is power in Hollywood? Is it being on the list of the most powerful people, many who are in rehab? Or is it that you have the most money and you're paying a lot of alimony? What is power in Hollywood? I think the power in Hollywood is to have passion for the project you're doing so much that you cannot conceive of anybody doing it the way you would. The power in Hollywood is to get what you see up there on the screen the way you see it. That's the real power of Hollywood. Whether it's a hit or miss is irrelevant. But to get it up on the screen, that's the power of a filmmaker, to get it up on the screen the way he wanted it. And I wish that everybody who makes a film gets that power.

I think that I've enjoyed this interview. If you at home enjoy this, remember my name is Garry Marshall. If you didn't enjoy it, my name is Larry Kasdan.

Filmography

The Odd Couple (TV series, 1970)
Me and the Chimp (TV series, 1972)
Laverne & Shirley (TV series, 1976)
Mork & Mindy (TV series, 1978)
Young Doctors in Love (1982)
Herndon (TV series, 1983)
The Flamingo Kid (1984)
Nothing in Common (1986)
Overboard (1987)
Beaches (1988)
The Lottery (1989)
Pretty Woman (1990)
Frankie and Johnny (1991)
Exit to Eden (1994)

EDITOR'S NOTE: After this interview was completed Marshall directed *The Other Sister,* starring Juliette Lewis, Diane Keaton, Tom Skerritt, and Giovanni Ribisi. He also directed a re-teaming of Julia Roberts, Richard Gere, and Hector Elizondo in *Runaway Bride.*

Dear God (1996)
The Other Sister (1999)
Runaway Bride (1999)

Awards

British Academy Awards
Pretty Woman, Best Film (nominated, shared with Arnon Milchan and
   Steven Reuther), 1991

PGA Golden Laurel Awards
Honorary Lifetime Membership Award, 1998
Lifetime Achievement Award in Television, 1998

Women in Film Lucy Awards
Lucy Award, 1996

His television programs have been nominated for numerous Emmy and
Golden Globes Awards. In addition, Mr. Marshall and Jerry Belson won an
Emmy for their writing on the *Dick Van Dyke Show.*
   In 1990, Mr. Marshall received the Lifetime Creative Achievement Award
from the American Comedy Awards. In 1992 he received the Publicists
Guild Motion Picture Showmanship Award. He received the Television
Showmanship Award in 1979. In 1995 he received the Valentine Davies
Award from the Writers Guild of America, West, Inc.

The Films of John McTiernan

John McTiernan was born on January 8, 1951, in Albany, New York. At the time of this interview McTiernan had only directed seven feature films. Yet those films have established him as one of the industry's foremost directors of action-adventure movies. His work has gained him a world-wide following, significant critical acclaim, and has set the standard for an entire genre of films. His expertise at presenting stunning visual cinema images, combined with outstanding performances from his actors, has set him apart from the crowd.

McTiernan has a reputation of being his own man—knowing what he wants and pursuing it with a vengeance until he masters the exact effect he set out to achieve. He is a demanding director who demands the very best of himself.

Early on McTiernan received a fellowship from the American Film Institute. With a grant from AFI, he made a short film, *Watcher.* From there he honed his skills and made his living directing commercials and eventually some television films while writing his first screenplay. That script, *Nomads,* became his feature directorial debut in 1986 and starred Pierce Brosnan and Lesley-Anne Down.

McTiernan's first big-budgeted studio film was the 1987 production of *Predator,* starring Arnold Schwarzenegger and Carl Weathers and produced by Joel Silver. *Predator* clearly established McTiernan's reputation as a major director of action-adventure films.

John McTiernan is an interesting and complex man and speaks freely about what is on his mind, as this interview will prove. For this interview we met with John on a warm, sunny day in Wyoming on his four-thousand-acre ranch, where he kicks back when not on location directing a film.

He is probably one of the most inventive individuals I have met. He is brilliant, but in addition to being brilliant he is a great actor's director and I was so taken by that because John is so action-oriented that you think of him as a great action director.

Colleen Camp—Actress

The Conversation

I was going to Juilliard in New York and wanted to be a theater director. It seemed like most theater directors were wealthy to begin with and had a trust fund and a large proportion of them were also gay. I felt somehow that I didn't fit. Also the world of Juilliard was just hermetically sealed. It was a school that had the same carpets running up the wall that it had on the floor. You'd spend twelve or fourteen hours a day in this environment and in the same corridors where the same carpet is on the walls. It was almost as if it was contrived to be disorienting.

I met some people who were working on films. I think they called themselves independent filmmakers or some pretentious nonsense. I started thinking about it and I saw that there was a lot of technology involved in making films. It was essentially theater but with a lot of technology. One day I played hooky from Juilliard. I went to the Symphony Theater on 95th Street and Broadway. Now absences at Juilliard were counted, you only got so many in a semester. You could be absent for three days and then after that you were in deep doo-doo. Anyway, I went to see *Day for Night* and I sat and I watched it all day long and through most of that night. I think I saw it eight times that day. I was trying to see how a movie worked. What's in each picture and how does one picture connect to the next? Where is the story in this? What's the technology of it? I wanted to watch a movie long enough so that I got past story, got past the acting, and got past the "Oh, I love that bit" and just try to get as distant and cold toward it as possible. I learned to sit in the back row of the theater. You never ever watch it close if you want to see what's there or if you want to learn to try to reproduce what's there. I think at one point I learned *Day for Night* shot for shot from memory so that I could simply write it down. I sat down at a table and said,

"Okay, this is the first shot, the next cuts to this, cuts to that, it goes to this"—just every shot, so that you learned to think in the vocabulary.

Anyway, I watched that film all that day and then I went back the next day and watched it again. Somewhere after that I found an experimental college in the State of New York that had a good film program. I went there and just made up my own program. I made a long movie that was called *Poor Richard's Almanac* that was supposedly everything that went through the mind of this guy named Richard who was sitting in an apartment in New York City stoned on his ass and all sorts of stuff went through his brain. Anything I wanted to try to learn about could be part of what was going through his brain. I just tied it together later. I did it over the course of a year or so.

I worked as an assistant to Jan Kadar for a year at the United Film Institute. That was a particularly good experience because I'd have to prepare his class work for him. Or he'd try out things on me before he'd get in the class.

There were three or four films of Robert Altman's that I was very fond of, certainly *McCabe and Mrs. Miller*. That film was about the building of a village in the wilderness. The movie company built the village and shot in the village as they were building it. So it had this bizarre sense of reality. I also think Altman was consciously working on the sound rather than the picture. It might have been cinematographer Vilmos Zsigmond who was contributing the picture aspect of it. That was the time when Altman was working with multiple soundtracks and that sort of thing. At times it got him in trouble because he let significant things drift through the soundtrack instead of being pointed up. But the basic idea was this was recorded, it wasn't presented, so it would sound as if it wasn't the microphone in somebody's face but something you just overheard. Like this was wasn't pointed at the camera. The camera happened to see and hear it. I think I pursued that idea a lot since. I toyed with it an awful lot in *Die Hard: With a Vengeance*.

I think I chased AFI for a while before I got in. It seemed to have the reputation of being the best film school in the country. The part that I liked about it was that they had contrived a program that was pretty much self-taught and they drove you toward things that they thought were specifically necessary to teach. They didn't teach any technology at all. They figured that if you were good enough to survive in the movie business you would get that on your own. They pursued telling a story in a picture or in pictures. And they pursued dealing with actors. And that's all. They would take technology away from you. You couldn't get into the technology and hide in it. You simply told your story in just the crudest black and white video.

And if there were a story there, it would show up and if there weren't, it would also show up. I don't know that the other schools are as good about pursuing that. They let people get so involved in the prose of filmmaking that most filmmaking is all prose anyway. There are an awful lot of places where people can hide and deceive themselves, pretend they're doing something when they're actually wasting their time.

Ironically one of the most important lessons I learned at AFI might have been to control my temper, or a particular way of controlling my temper so that it didn't destroy me, which is what I usually manage to do with it.

Nomads (1986)

Lesley-Anne Down; Pierce Brosnan; Anna Maria Monticelli; Adam Ant; Josie Cotton; Frank Doubleday; Héctor Mercado; Mary Woronov.

I had done a fair amount of film work by the time I got to that moment so it wasn't like the first time I walked onto a movie set or, it didn't feel foreign or like this was a completely different experience. It essentially was a student movie that was a little bit longer and hopefully it was going to be distributed. It was particularly nice working with Pierce Brosnan. I liked him and continue to see him periodically. He's a very good actor—a much better actor than he's given a chance to show.

I think the main thing he and I worked on was the killing off of Remington Steele. He had this particular manner that he used in *Remington Steele*. It was all bright and chipper. He described it as imagining that you have string coming from the top of your head, so everything happens like this [*McTiernan bobs his head up and down*]. Basically our work was to get rid of the string and to add gravity to him and put him on a diet where he would drink four or five beers a day to thicken him up. He loved all of that stuff. He loved changing himself. It was a shame that when they first cast him in the Bond thing the network stepped in and wouldn't let him do it. It was a shame because he was perfect for it. And now he is doing it.

I was happy with the film to a point. I mean, I'm never particularly pleased with my own work. I think Stanley Kubrick once said that if he was getting 50 percent of what he set out to get, he was doing very well. He was happy with himself. But when you first start out in films if you get 10 percent of what you had in mind, you're doing well. I mean, once a film is finished it's done and I don't want to see it for a while.

Predator (1987)

Arnold Schwarzenegger; Carl Weathers; Elpidia Carrillo; Bill Duke; Jesse Ventura; Sonny Landham; Richard Chaves; R.G. Armstrong; Shane Black; Kevin Peter Hall.

I was in the middle of editing *Nomads* and I showed Larry Gordon, the producer, some of the movie. I think they offered me a film called *Commando* or something like that that was the first Schwarzenegger movie at Fox. I had another movie that I wanted to do so I turned down the Fox film and went off. They came back to me for the next Schwarzenegger movie, which was *Predator.* They packed me off to South Carolina where Arnold was shooting *Raw Deal* or something and I met him and they sort of sniffed around me to see if I would do and that sort of thing.

The most difficult thing about *Predator* was that I was coming into an organization that had its own notions and to some extent, its own corruption. The production designer worked for Joel Silver, one of the producers, and he insisted that we go to Puerto Vallarta in Mexico. I found out later that it was because he owned a house there or something. But the guy did no research and since that was my first studio feature I wasn't adept enough to do his research for him. What the guy didn't bother to find out was that the West Coast of Mexico is deciduous. The leaves fall off the trees at a certain time of the year and it happened to be when we were shooting. So it all turned orange on us. The cameraman and I wanted to go on the East Coast of Mexico that wasn't deciduous. It was green and it actually had jungle but there were no resort hotels and it wasn't trendy. We weren't able to convince Mr. Silver that we should shoot down there. So the hardest thing was trying to pretend that there was jungle around Puerto Vallarta.

Then, fortunately, the monster came in and it was bad. We shut down to get a better monster and by then I had a chance to cut the first portion of the film together. The studio saw it and so that gave me a little bit of credibility. When we went back to shoot we went to the East Coast like I wanted to in the first place. That's where anything that looks like actual jungle came from. It's a very odd thing. I mean, you so often wind up wearing other people's mistakes. But they were mistakes that you saw going in but couldn't stop it and so you try and maneuver out of other people's mistakes, which is one of the hardest things to do.

A Red Suit in the Jungle

Getting the monster effect was not easy. This was when motion control systems were not as simple as they have since become. We had this guy in a red suit running around in the jungle. The idea is that you shoot a picture of the guy in the red suit and then you would reproduce the exact same camera movement on just the jungle without the guy in the red suit in the shot.

The computer-driven camera finally showed up on location. We had about sixty-five of these shots scheduled to do. They set camera up the first time and it took them three days to put it together. We multiplied that out and figured it would take us 180 days just to get the special-effects shot. I said the hell with the exact reproduction. Why don't we just go for it? We threw out the computer and I would shoot the shot with the guy running in the red suit and then I'd shoot three versions of the same thing. I'd just have a cameraman reproduce it. We'd time it as close as we could and we would also have landmarks in the frame as a reference. We just shot two or three or four speeds of it to try to get one that was as close as possible to the original. We eliminated all the computer nonsense and that's the way we ultimately wound up doing a lot of the shots.

Jean-Claude Van Damme had just come to Hollywood and was represented by the William Morris Agency. They came to me and asked if he could play the monster. So Jean-Claude came down to Mexico and they sent him off with the special-effects guys who fitted him out with a red suit. Jean-Claude came out and he was so angry that this string of obscenities came out of him. You couldn't get a word out of him that wasn't with "fuck" or "shit"! I think that lasted maybe about a day before we all realized that this wasn't really Jean-Claude's big break in the movies and that this probably shouldn't be his first film. You see, he had been told that it was a significant part and then he discovered that he was basically a technical. We also at one point tried to dress up a monkey in a red suit so I could get pictures of a creature jumping through the trees. The monkey wouldn't keep the suit on.

Arnold Schwarzenegger obviously competes at everything he does. Carl Weathers was an experienced actor and a well-trained one and Arnold was really just sort of learning. So Arnold used to come down and watch Carl work just to learn how from him. That was probably the most significant competition going on. They used to compete a lot about how many miles each of them could run and this sort of nonsense. There was a lot of that. But ultimately the thing that was most significant in the long run was Arnold watching Carl and trying to learn about acting, because he did learn. He went at it with the same attitude that he might have gone at a body building competition or some sports thing. He's got a great attitude that way.

Working with Actors

There are some directors who create a performance or at least attempt to. I basically try to create an environment where you choose professionals, people who have skills. By and large I've been, with one or two notable exceptions, successful at knowing when I've got a professional or not. If you have a professional then you just let them do their job. Try to be a mirror for them, try to be an advisor, try to understand what they're doing and help them get to it. You maybe discuss concepts in the beginning. There are other directors, I suppose, who actively try to make a performance, like Elia Kazan who might start with a neophyte actor and help them make a performance out of it. I don't pretend to do that. I'm not sure that's particularly successful on film, because the audience can always see who the person is.

Let me back up on that. The main thing that an untrained actor can't do is put a persona on film. It will come out as a sort of no-person there because they haven't learned to put it out there, to let it show up. Then there's a second step when you have a trained actor. They can't really deceive the audience about who they are, about what their basic nature is. You can't really pretend on film to be someone else, someone other than you are. You can find aspects of yourself and point them up or bring them out but you can't really do what they do in theater, which is create and become a completely different person, or in effect put on a mask and become someone else. There's enough distance in theater and enough illusion there that an actor like Olivier can get away with that. But you can't do it on film because the audience somehow always knows the basic character, the basic nature of the person they're looking at.

There are some directors who use that brilliantly. Robert Redford uses it all the time and he's incredible at it. He did that in *Ordinary People* where the story is about what's wrong with this family. He cast Mary Tyler Moore who is perky and smiley. But somehow the audience would always know that behind the eyes of Mary Tyler Moore was the soul of Rommel. That dovetailed perfectly with the story he was telling which is the ultimate reveal. What was wrong with that family was that woman. You think it's everybody else who's screwed up and it turns out that she's the one that's driving the whole thing and you don't see it until the very end. That was a very astute use of that phenomenon if you will.

If someone is involved in cold action, in a dangerous or life-threatening or physically very difficult activity, their emotions don't shut off. I mean, it will have an emotional context. It takes you right back to that question about are we really here. What happens if we are really standing here on the edge of this building? Or if we really must get across this gorge or get across this elevator shaft or something like that. If you, the actor, are not simply a superhero who just does things like that but is actually standing there saying, "Jesus, I'm scared out of my wits but I have to do this," what is the emotional thread through the middle of all this activity? You try to make sure that those beats are in there. Hopefully the audience experiences the emotional thread through the middle of all the physical activity. If you ask the actor to walk across the room and pick up a cigarette, you try to fill in what the emotional context is. Just because you ask the actor to swing on a fire hose across the top of a building it doesn't mean that suddenly you don't have an emotional context. It's the same thing. It's another moment in your play so the actor better know what he's doing or why, even if the actor really isn't really doing it and a stuntman is. Somewhere you'd better fill in the emotional context, you'd better get to a shot where the real actor appears to be doing it.

His Thoughts on Critics

Critics are not genuinely trying to inform their readers about movies. It's more about how important they are and that sort of thing. It also makes them vulnerable to manipulation. There are a number of people who invest a great deal of time in their press things. For a while I was this person that critics liked. I was a young filmmaker, did inventive things, and came from nowhere. The fact that I was succeeding meant somehow that it was more likely that they would succeed. That there would be air and life and new things in the industry, which usually translates to they'll get a chance too. But now I've become one of those horrible monsters. I work with the studios and I'm paid too much and I work on stupid movies. By and large all those things are true. But I'm still basically the same person. I was the hero then and a monster now.

It was interesting going to Cannes and seeing a festival of critics. In essence it's a giant television studio. And seeing the way one is treated there makes me believe I do better with European critics than American ones. You're farther away from it somehow so the interactions are less emotional. Jerry Lewis and I do well in Europe. I don't know what else I can say about critics without getting myself in tremendous trouble. The guy who writes for the *Wall Street Journal* seems to have a genuine care for movies. He seems to actually enjoy movies, which is, to some extent rare. He seems to genuinely be trying to inform his audiences about them. I respect the guy for that.

How Does He Prepare to Direct a Film?

The particular way I work—or the particular way my brain is set up—is that I have pre-visualized the whole movie to a great extent. I actually have seen the whole movie in the back of my eyelids. I think it's maybe connected to the fact that I'm left-handed. I find a lot of cameramen have the same thing. A very disproportionate number of cameramen are left-handed and they wound up being cameramen because they were bright but they didn't gravitate to word-based things.

I discovered that when I was first messing around with a camera I could, for instance, hold in my eyes the image upside down or backwards and it made no difference to me. I could just say, okay, there it is, and I can still operate the camera upside down and then I could just switch it around and it would still click. I didn't know where all of that was leading except that I do pre-visualize just about everything to the extent that it gets me in trouble so I try not to do it. I don't storyboard most things because to try and get what I want in a single picture frame is difficult because you have to understand lenses and most storyboard artists don't. It takes a long time to teach them how the distortion will work. You invest more time trying to get the damn picture drawn than you can do in two minutes with a camera.

I do storyboard things that must be discussed specifically with other people, like special-effects shots. If you're going to contract a shot with the special-effects house, you have to make it explicit. You have to be able to discuss it with other people so what you do is you storyboard what you want. I have had at one point or another storyboarded many other things and basically found that it was a waste of time. It also tends to keep you from paying attention to what's right in front of you.

The hardest thing is to stand there in the here and now and in the moment and find the image that advances your story—units that you need now, at this instant in the movie. It has to cut to that picture you're coming out of and go to this picture you're planning to go to. See it here, now. This is what we've got; I don't care what we planned. The hardest thing is to stop planning—stop thinking about the movie that I've already run on the back of my eyelids and instead deal with the movie that's in front of me.

Die Hard (1988)

Bruce Willis; Bonnie Bedelia; Reginald VelJohnson; Paul Gleason;
De'voreaux White; William Atherton; Hart Bochner; James Shigeta;
Alan Rickman; Alexander Godunov; Bruno Doyon; Andreas Wisniewski;
Clarence Gilyard Jr.; Joey Plewa; Lorenzo Caccialanza.

I had just finished *Predator* and the studio had seen it and liked it, so they started giving me scripts and *Die Hard* was one of them. I think I turned it down a number of times because the original script was really a terrorist incident. It had very little humor and seemed to take itself very seriously. It seemed to me that terrorism wasn't entertaining. Eventually we found a way to think of it as something other than a terrorist incident. I had this notion, although I didn't really tell the studio this, that you could turn it into a sort of Shakespearean comedy, that it would become a panorama of the people involved in the incident. I basically structured it as a comedy and it was actually *A Midsummer Night's Dream*. That is, something happens on a festival night that turns the world upside down and all the princes become asses and all the asses become princes. In the morning the true lovers are reunited and everyone goes on but the world is better than it was the night before.

So I started making changes in the script along those lines. The original time period of the film was three days long. I moved it into one night and just tried to find ways to expand the comedy and involve other characters. I guess the major change we made was turning it into a robbery and that was when I said, "Yes, I'll do it." As I said, I never found terrorism entertaining but a good robbery is fun, whether it be bad guys or the good guys, people love to watch a good caper. I thought if I could put that in the center of it then it would take away the meanness. So many action movies are mean at their heart. I personally find them uninteresting and unentertaining. They're just no fun.

If I remember correctly we were initially talking about Richard Gere in the title role. I don't know how the change came about. Gere turned it down, or something. We changed it a great deal once we started working with Bruce. Then I had a working class hero and I just tried to use what Bruce was about.

We had very little preparation time. I think we had five weeks from a go. We were lucky in that we were working right next to the studio and we didn't really have to go anywhere. A lot of it evolved as it went along. I think when we started shooting we only had thirty-five pages of the finished script. I think we got the script finished when we were about halfway through shooting. We kept making up things and managing to incorporate things we'd discover into the movie. In a way it was a very creative environment because everyone knew we were making up a movie as we went along. All I had to do was keep in mind where we were ultimately trying to go and what was the ultimate style that we hoped it would fall into. I would encourage people to make up their own dialogue and change what they wanted to with character things. A lot of the better lines just happened on the set. When you get into the physical situation it's a lot easier to think of something that actually fits it. Bruce very often would come up with a great thing once he got physically there and he could see how it would work. It's like in the other one I did with him. He comes up with the line about the burn inbetween his toes and the athlete's foot when he was talking to the FBI guy. He came up with that on the spot.

So, How Dangerous Was It?

I get asked all the time about how dangerous it was to shoot that film. Part of the nonsense of shooting a movie is you have to pretend that it was incredibly dangerous. It's basically a sales illusion. These are movies made by major corporations that have to function in the real world of lawyers and insurance policies and lawsuits and that sort of stuff, so you don't do things that are dangerous. If they are dangerous by definition, you can't do it, and certainly not with a star. Often stars will talk about all the incredibly dangerous things they did, and I suppose many times the things they do are at least frightening. For an inexperienced person getting into it for the first time it's scary. But if you have a stunt you have to work on it and work it out to the point where you are pretty damned certain of how it's going to work and that it is safe. You can't proceed with something if it's not safe.

When you are doing a stunt it slows the process because you have to break it all down. When you fire a weapon you have to use ear protection for the actor and ear and eye protection for everybody out front. All of that is a very, very time-consuming procedure. There's nothing like, well, you run in here and go bang, bang. You have to split those sequences up into little pieces. You can't shoot action sequences as I love to shoot some other scenes when I have dialogue and I just shoot it with a hand-held camera and tie shots together with the camera movement. You can't do that when you have stunts or firearms or explosions. You have to change the dialogue so that the cuts won't stand out. What often happens in special-effects films is that the language changes at the moment of the special-effects shot. The shot itself did not fit into the cinema language of the sequence and consequently it looks false. It stands out even though viewed on its own, and when you cut it into the sequence, it's as if you're playing a Mozart melody and all of a sudden there's one note from John Philip Sousa. But if you can match the effect shot to whatever language style that you want to be in at that moment, you can get away with much more than you think you can.

How Does He Choose His Projects?

I don't necessarily always do movies when I have started the project, or rather, not every project that I start necessarily culminates in a movie. I can't simply snap my fingers and say, "I want to do this," and it's done. But I don't take things for a job. I never did. I mean, I could have made a living doing commercials or I could have made a decent living writing but it wasn't what I wanted to do. You sort of always have to be willing to keep yourself poor. I never made any money at all until I was thirty-five or so and every cent, just about, that I made up to that time I put back into movies. Initially, it would be put into projects, trying to learn how to make films. Later on it was put into buying books that I wanted or paying a writer to work on something. I continually reinvested. As soon as you do it for the money, then it's death.

What I was going to say was that I continually checked myself to make sure that I was shooting a movie and not shooting a deal. That's very dangerous. Things get a bureaucratic life of their own in a studio structure. Very often people are shooting a deal. They go out and they buy expensive talent. They'll buy me or they'll buy Schwarzenegger and think well, they'll straighten it out. We have purchased the best to turn our deal into a movie. So far I've been willing to stay hungry. And I hope that about the time that I'm tempted to do something for the money, the way I'm trying to set it up is that's the day I retire; that's the day I go do something else, find another career.

I tend to gravitate toward movies I'd like to see, and the movies I'd like to see are often, by and large, sort of boys' adventure movies. Big boys, little boys, they're still boys' adventure movies. So if that makes me an action director, they can label me that way, I don't care.

I didn't like the first *Die Hard* sequel's script. They wanted to go out and make the same movie over again, which I thought was silly. It's a hack intention. That's a sort of producer's intention—we've made a certain amount of money, now we can make some more money. We'll just do exactly the same thing. I passed on that one.

The Hunt for Red October (1990)

Sean Connery; Alec Baldwin; Scott Glenn; Sam Neill; James Earl Jones; Joss Ackland;
Richard Jordan; Peter Firth; Tim Curry; Courtney B. Vance; Stellan Skarsgård;
Jeffrey Jones; Timothy Carhart; Larry Ferguson; Fred Dalton Thompson.

I chased that project for a long time. I tried to buy the book and I missed by about a week. They sold it to somebody else. So then I had to chase that somebody else for a while. They developed six or seven screenplays that were hopeless. I just waited and eventually convinced the studio to let me take a whack at it. The people who had worked on it before thought it was some sort of international thriller or thought it was about bombs or thought it was about tough action stuff. What it really was about was *Treasure Island* and that's what Tom Clancy started with, basically—an intuitive recounting of *Treasure Island* in another format 150 years later. It's about a boy. He's thirty-five years old and he's a boy in the environment he functions in—in the bureaucratic, political world that he's in. He's the kid at the end of the table. He comes to possess a piece of information or an insight and he's swept off with a bunch of bizarre characters and something in his innate nature helps him to solve whatever the crisis is. He comes back from sea forever changed.

Sean Connery's character is basically Long John Silver in a lot of ways. It's a person who is potentially very dangerous and that you don't trust but whom you come to love in the end. So writer Larry Ferguson and I just used that as the paradigm to go through a six- or seven-hundred-page book and say, this bit goes in, that's irrelevant, that goes out, this is in, that's out, da da da da da da. You can just ask, does this incident have anything to do with our basic story line? Does this have anything to do with *Treasure Island*? And if it does, it's in; if it doesn't, it's out. If you reorder the script that way or just go through and select out of the novel that way, then it all ties in very easily. It didn't take us very long. I think we got through it in six weeks or less. The studio read it and said go immediately.

The thing that is ironic is that I tried to get Harrison Ford to play the part that Alec Baldwin ended up doing. We pursued him something awful, chased his agent and chased him. I buttonholed him at the premier of *Working Girl*. I tried desperately to talk him into it. He said he might be interested in playing the Russian captain. Then, after Alec played the role of Jack Ryan, Harrison was apparently interested. There was a great deal of scheming that went on to push Alec out of that part. It's not a pleasant subject and I probably would offend a lot of people if you get me into it too far.

Working with Sean Connery is a joy. You don't have to help him develop his role. Sean's too good a professional. You just better run fast enough to keep up with him. That's the hard part because he doesn't suffer fools well. If you're not paying attention and keeping up with him he'll eat you alive. Sean and I just talked about the role. I talked about the notions I had and then I tried to listen carefully to what he was thinking about. He did some very astute things, ways in which he could sort of control the way other actors related to him.

On the first day of shooting we had scheduled a relatively large scene. There were a lot of actors on the set and they were all kids, Russian kids that we got and trained. We sort of ran a navy school and gave them specific tasks so they could run long routines. We actually trained the crew to behave like submariners. Actually, there were a number of real submariners in the crew. Anyway, on that day Sean was working and he called the assistant director to the side of the stage and he dressed him down something royal. He just gave him one hell of a talking to. It was in a place where everyone could hear. He wasn't yelling but it was a very stern, hard voice from a major star who was cutting the AD a new orifice. I thought, "Sean's really in a bad mood and boy, are we going to have trouble." As soon as Sean walked onto the set this little Russian kid involuntarily stiffened. I watched it go down the line and every actor and non-actor on the set stiffened involuntarily when Sean got anywhere near them. And that was when I caught on that he did it deliberately and it was all staged. What he was doing was setting up all of the other actors in the scene to behave toward him as if he really were the captain. And it was so simply done. So that's what I meant about you don't help Sean with his role. You just make sure you keep up.

I spent quite a while on real submarines and the problem is that the engineering on a real submarine is designed to be extraordinarily durable and, in effect, battle-worthy. It's all made of steel and it's often very simple and it looks old-fashioned. Everything is in a particular place because they've learned this is the best way to do it. Almost every piece of equipment on a submarine is there in that particular way because somebody probably gave his life to learn that it was a mistake to put it some other way.

I told the designers to have every piece of equipment in the submarine function the way it really does so that we could use real submariners, which is what we did in terms of the American crew. We could use real submariners and they would know exactly how every piece of equipment worked. All the dials were in the right place and everything was accurate except the style in which it was built. Then I just said, upgrade it. It's as if the navy went in and said, "Instead of steel, we're going to build this with aircraft technology. We're going to use plastic and pre-formed things so it will look like the flight deck of a 747," for instance. The irony of that was when some of the navy brass came and were visiting the set they looked around and they asked two or three times how we arrived at these changes in the set. I explained that we just applied aircraft technology instead of shipbuilding technology. They sort of relaxed at that point and then explained that that was exactly what they had done in the design of the Sea Wolf submarine that they were just turning out the first copy of. It was supposed to be supersecret at that point and we had stumbled into it. They thought they had a leak or something.

Medicine Man (1992)

Sean Connery; Lorraine Bracco; José Wilker; Rodolfo De Alexandre;
Francisco Tsiren Tsere Rereme; Elias Monteiro Da Silva; Edinei Maria Serrio
Dos Santos; Bec-Kana-Re Dos Santos Kaiapo; Angelo Barra Moreira; Jose Lavat.

I had heard a lot of horror stories about actually trying to work with a movie company in the Amazon. In the areas where there is some jungle left, you also have huge health problems. So I found a place in southern Mexico that had reasonable facilities and no health problems. I mean, having typhus and resistant malaria in a crew is not a romantic experience. That was why I wanted to find a facsimile of the Amazon in a better area. Also, the trees in the Central America area are much bigger than in the Amazon. Out on the flat of the Amazon the trees go 100, maybe 125 feet. In Central America you can get them up to 200.

To get up in the trees we developed a system of cables that allowed us to move in trees, and then we had to teach the actors how to do it. They had a couple of weeks invested in learning how to move safely in the trees and we had to teach most of the crew. We wound up spending, I don't know, six or eight days where we really just lived in the trees. That was a tough film to shoot. I wish there were more tree scenes in the film because I like that stuff.

I think actually as an environmental movie we did extraordinarily well. I think we did about $60 million domestic box office and $170 million or so total internationally. We had gotten a lot of flak from someone calling environmental groups around the world saying we were doing all this damage to trees. There were continual stories in the press about that. We eventually discovered that it was a particular person in Hollywood that was voicing it. It's astonishing how carcinogenic some people are.

Last Action Hero (1993)

Arnold Schwarzenegger; F. Murray Abraham; Art Carney;
Charles Dance; Frank McRae; Tom Noonan; Robert Prosky; Anthony Quinn;
Mercedes Ruehl; Austin O'Brien; Ian McKellen; Professor Toru Tanaka;
Joan Plowright; Jason Kelly; Noah Emmerich.

The studio environment on *Last Action Hero* was not a particularly good one and it was ultimately destructive. We were making a movie that was about a fairy godfather. It was suppose to be a very childish, PG-13, kids movie. Somewhere in the middle of it the studio said, "Now, wait a minute, we're making an action movie." I held a meeting and said, "Gentlemen, can you please sort this out? I'll make one movie or the other, but how can we do both at the same time?" They began rewriting the script in the middle, after it was already shooting. We'd come in each day and wonder what the studio had in mind for us to shoot the next week. How were they planning to change the end of the movie when we'd already started the front end of it?

It was probably my only negative studio experience, primarily because the people involved weren't very supportive. They're simply dumb and don't understand the process of making a movie. This was a case where some of the studio people were making a deal and not a movie. They had sold it to themselves and to each other by making it as vague as possible about what they were really doing. It was all things to every person. Then when it began to become specific you'd have people charging in different directions saying, "No, we're doing this, no, we're doing that." You can't do that while you're shooting.

What we learned about press poisoning is that it is an active competitive activity in Hollywood, and very often when you see negative stories about a movie, they're planted. Most of the negative stories about *Waterworld,* or a fair number of them anyway, were helped along by people at other studios. And there are, you know, young journalists who will cooperate in anything like that because they think it's gonna help their own careers as screenwriters or whatever. We should probably go on to another subject.

If this interview goes on much longer you're going to have to be present at my divorce because my wife isn't going to speak to me.

Die Hard: With a Vengeance (1995)

Bruce Willis; Jeremy Irons; Samuel L. Jackson; Graham Greene;
Colleen Camp; Larry Bryggman; Anthony Peck; Nicholas Wyman; Sam Phillips;
Kevin Chamberlin; Sharon Washington; Stephen Pearlman; Michael
Alexander Jackson; Aldis Hodge; Mischa Hausserman.

As I mentioned, they had been sending me scripts. I think Jonathan Hensleigh was up here at the ranch. We were working on another project and I asked him what other material he might have in his drawer. He came up with this thing and we read it and he said, "You know, you could turn that into *Die Hard.*" It sort of put back in, for me, what was missing in the second succeeding attempts at sequels. It was a movie all by itself. It wasn't simply reproducing something you had already made. I wasn't going to make the original *Die Hard.* I wouldn't try to top myself. I wouldn't try to do the same thing again because I think it's a fool's errand. I deliberately threw a curve ball and made it different than the original *Die Hard.* Whether it topped it or whether it didn't I don't know.

You can't tell the story of John McClane over again. You have already told it and the audience already knows it. So you have to spin another story out of it. Again, you always have the politics or the swirls around stories, and as stars get more power there's more negotiation and maneuvering. Often one of the most difficult things about dealing with a star is the entourage, because you will have a group of people who make their living out of sucking on this one person, and they're often dangerous because they make themselves important by frightening the principal, frightening the star. They trade on the star's insecurities. So if you have somebody like Sean Connery who isn't insecure, you got no entourage. Nobody around. He doesn't put up with people like that. Some other stars have phalanxes of them around. They're always getting advice from their hairdresser or from the guy who pumps out the toilet in their motor home or something like that, and often you have to deal with those folks.

What are my goals? In a way that's like not talking about a project until I've done it. I'm not going to talk about what my goals are in filmmaking until I've achieved them—almost for superstitious reasons. Things are a lot better if you just do it and then have other people talk about it. There's enough people in Hollywood doing that—enough people posing. I think

that things that are in the nature of the whole breadth of a career are subject matter for film festivals when you're sixty. I've got a while and I think
I'll take my time getting there.

How Would He Encourage Newcomers?

There's a joke about how you get to Carnegie Hall—practice. There was
something in *The New York Times* about realizing a cumulative number of
hours of practice in any particular field is often determinate: If you want to
be a nationally ranked swimmer, for instance, you have to start by the time
you are ten. If you want to be internationally ranked, you have to start by
the time you're seven. So it's sort of like, if you're nine, don't bother. I'm
making a joke out of it but the essence of what they were saying was that
in both sports and musical activities and in anything where it's a specific set
of skills, you have to spend time working on it. So, if you want to be a filmmaker, then make films. And keep making films. It has to become your life.
It has to be the only thing you think about or work on for at least twenty
years. It takes twenty years to get a film style from the time you start.

Have There Been Influences?

People who were most influential for me? Larry Gordon and Ned Tannen and
Andy Vagna. And I don't think I've had a mentor in a specific way, and it's
probably a problem or failing of mine. I should have arranged a mentor relationship. Some of those mentor relationships are very, very good. Steven Spielberg's relationship with Sid Sheinberg at Universal, for example. I think he
gained a lot of information and a lot of training about how to behave in the industry and how things work. I think it sustained him and gained him tempo,
and he learned much faster than he might have had he not had that relationship. Most of the men I've worked for I still have a good relationship with.

His Parting Words

Well, we're planning on getting an irrigation system in out here. We're raising the dam in the reservoir later this fall. Stuff like that. With that I better
depart because my wife is getting anxious.

EDITOR'S NOTE: Since this interview was completed, McTiernan has directed two
more films: *The Thomas Crown Affair,* starring Pierce Brosnan, Esther Cañadas,
Denis Leary, and Rene Russo; and *The 13th Warrior,* starring Antonio Banderas,
Vladimir Kulich, Maria Bonnevie, Omar Sharif, and Diane Venora.

Filmography

Nomads (1986)
Predator (1987)
Die Hard (1988)
The Hunt for Red October (1990)
Medicine Man (1992)
Last Action Hero (1993)
Die Hard: With a Vengeance (1995)
The 13th Warrior (1999)
The Thomas Crown Affair (1999)

Awards

American Film Institute, USA
Franklin J. Schaffner Award, 1997

Razzie Awards
Last Action Hero, Worst Director (nominated), 1994
Last Action Hero, Worst Picture (nominated, shared with Stephen J.
Roth), 1994

The Films of Martha Coolidge

Martha Coolidge was born on August 17, 1946, in New Haven, Connecticut.

Coolidge did not emerge, full-grown, out of nowhere in 1983 to direct the amiable sleeper *Valley Girl;* by the time of this "debut," she had nearly two decades of experience to her credit. She began making short films at the Rhode Island School of Design, then moved to New York to work in commercials and continue her film studies at the NYU film school, and for a while produced a Canadian children's program (*Magic Tom*).

Her award-winning documentaries include *More Than a School,* and *Old-Fashioned Woman,* a study of her grandmother, which debuted at the New York Film Festival in 1974. Her first feature-length film was *Not a Pretty Picture,* the autobiographical story of a high school date rape, which debuted at the Kennedy Center in Washington, D.C., winning a Blue Ribbon Award at the American Film Festival and a Gold Ducat at Mannheim.

It was during this period, as a much-honored documentarian, that Coolidge helped to found the Association of Independent Video and Filmmakers.

During Coolidge's first venture into Hollywood, she began a long association with Francis Ford Coppola, developing a project with his American Zoetrope company, before returning to Canada to direct a mini-series and the dramatic feature *City Girl.* It was the great response to this film (which Peter Bogdanovich executive-produced) at various film festivals that ultimately led to Coolidge's opportunity to direct *Valley Girl* in Hollywood in 1982.

As the co-chair of the Directors Guild President's Committee, Coolidge helped lead the fight against colorization and for moral rights for filmmakers. She is a member of the Board of Directors of the Directors Guild, Women in Film, the American Film Institute, and was named to the Dean's Advisory Board of UCLA's School of Theatre, Film, and Television.

The reason that I wanted to work with her was when I saw Rambling
Rose *I saw the mark of an artist there, and the mark of an artist is a
recognizable style. That's that assertive thing you need, because the
recognizable style comes so much out of what you need to express,
what you need to assert, what you need to put out there. The imple-
mentation is that receptive thing. I think Martha has both of those
things in a nice balance.*

Mercedes Ruehl—Actress

The Conversation

I was born in New Haven, Connecticut. My father was an architect who
taught at Yale. My mother was an architect who had a string of other children
and me. I would say that probably the most significant thing that happened
to me as a child in relationship to my career was that my father was an amateur filmmaker. He had a little 8 mm camera. I was the oldest, but we all used
to act in the movies and get in costume. He'd do special effects. We'd have
racecars that we'd stop motion and move around. It was just sort of playing.
It was always games, but it was a lot of fun. When I think back on it, it had
a deep attraction to me because my father died when I was nine years old, so
that this was a sort of fun area he was interested in and then it was gone.

I came to directing fairly early but in a very roundabout way. When I was
about thirteen, I started performing as a singer. It was just the birth of the
era of folk singers. So I got a guitar and I learned how to play the guitar and
the banjo. I started performing. I liked performing. I was popular and I had
a good voice. By the time I was fourteen or fifteen, I was virtually a professional singer in the New Haven area, which was a very musical area.

As I progressed in high school, I started acting and singing on stage in musical theater. I always found the singing wonderful. But I found acting, which
I liked, more difficult for me. I found it hard to do emotionally and very
stressful. One day in my senior year of high school I volunteered to direct a
play and I got off the stage. It was a Chekhov play. I sat out in the audience
and started directing the actors and I was home. It was just a revelation for
me. I suddenly felt free and I could think about the material and I could re-

ally help the other actors. I understood a lot about the acting because I happened to work with some very good directors even in my small experience.

By the time I got to college I was extremely involved with the theater program even though I went to the Rhode Island School of Design, which was an art school. We had a very serious theater program that was just extracurricular. But I both acted and sang professionally in clubs in the area and then also directed. I made my first movie in my freshman year, and again had another revelation that making movies is what I really liked to do. It was making the movie that was appealing to me.

Had my parents not raised me, and in particular my mother, to be an artist, maybe I would have felt some kind of gender block, but I really didn't feel it at all. I was raised to be an artist. I was raised to think that I could do what I wanted to do and not worry whether men or women could do it. It wasn't that I was raised with any particular feminist attitude, it's just that I didn't feel that there was any problem. I didn't think of Hollywood directors. I thought of filmmakers. I was on the East Coast and in art school and there were all these avant garde filmmakers. I thought, I could make movies. What's the difference between that and painting? Soon I found out the difference is money. But I just suddenly latched onto filmmaking. The acting and the singing phased out.

In my second year I made four movies at school and there wasn't even a film department. By my third year I majored in film as a special student and I was the top-ranked student in the school. So I took a program where I just took the academic classes and then pieced together, with certain advisors, my own program where I actually made a longer movie. I had certain people telling me what to do and helping me but I didn't really attend classes, so to speak. I made a fifteen-minute long, 16 mm movie that I worked on for most of the year and took academic and cinema classes that were available.

I was in my junior year at Rhode Island School of Design and I went to an avant garde cinema showing. Willard VanDyke, who at that time was the head of the Museum of Modern Art, presented it. I remember *Scorpio Rising* was shown and a movie called *Bottoms* by Yoko Ono. I thought I could do that. I was sitting in the audience and I was compelled, just compelled to go up to VanDyke and tell him that I had to be a filmmaker. I was very shy but I forced myself to go up to him and introduce myself and say, "You know, I really want to be a filmmaker." He said, "Why are you here? You don't need a degree. Come to New York. There's a great independent film community in New York. You can look me up and I'll tell you what to do."

Because I was on this sort of independent study program I actually completed the courses I needed and then moved to New York during the year and completed my movie there. I went to producers and asked if I could learn and said that I wanted to be a director. This one producer took me aside and said, "Whatever you do, don't tell anyone you want to be a director. They don't want you to be a director. You've got to get your nails done, you've got to wear lashes, you've got to wear makeup, look nice, and whatever you do, tell them all you want to be is an assistant."

I finally showed my movie to Willard VanDyke. We've since become very good friends, but he hated the movie. It's one of the most serious blows that I've ever recovered from. Having gone to this man with all of my hopes and shown him my movie, to the man who said he'd show me how to make connections in the independent film world, and then he said, "Whoever said you could be a filmmaker?" He hated the movie and suggested I do something else. That was really a blow.

I went up to Columbia Graduate School and showed my film to the head of the School of Film. He loved the film and wanted to show it to all the students. So I ended up in the spring of 1968 going to the graduate school of film at Columbia University. If you don't remember the spring of 1968, it was a very tumultuous spring with Columbia being the center of the upset. The students raged and struck and wanted to change education and shut the school down. In the end, I had a very interrupted semester, but I did begin making a very long film with actors and essentially really made a commitment to making films.

I decided to pursue film in a serious way so I applied to NYU graduate school and got in. But the schools had been so interrupted that I actually decided to emigrate to Montreal and try to get a job at the Canadian National Film Board where they made really nice movies. I didn't get a job at the Board, but did get a job at CTV, Channel 12, where I worked on all kinds of television, which was a great experience for me.

I finished my twenty-five minute movie up there and then the next year decided to come back to NYU graduate school. I made several movies in my two years there, but I produced one movie that got distribution and won a lot of prizes. I directed and produced a second movie that won a lot of prizes and finally got distribution and I sort of made my connections in the independent world and made my mark. I was immediately paid to make this second documentary, and then I made a third movie with a grant that Willard VanDyke helped me get. So I'd now made two movies about members of my family. I became very well-established in the documentary world, won a lot of prizes, and was one of the three founders of The Association of Independent Video and Filmmakers.

Then I saw a little movie about rape and I was so disturbed by it that I thought I should make a movie about my own rape. I felt ready to finally deal with it. I created this movie in my mind that was part drama and part documentary because I wanted to work with actors. I created this movie called *Not a Pretty Picture* and made it with an American Film Institute grant plus more investments and raised all the money.

It was a very complex shoot because it was a combination of documentary and fiction. I hired an actress who had also been raped because that was a very important part of the story. In the movie there's the storyline, which is my story. Then there are interviews with the actors and me about our own experiences and how they interrelate. It is a very unusual movie and ended up being feature length. I personally negotiated and got theatrical release in certain major cities for the film.

While I was making *Not a Pretty Picture* I got a call from producer Fred Roos in Francis Coppola's office. They had seen the documentaries and wanted to meet me. So I met with Fred Roos, who's been a lifelong friend, and Francis, and they said, "We're very interested in working with you. We think you're very talented. What do you want to do?"

At that point I was really thinking about going to Hollywood. What I discovered about my filmmaking was that I was not an avant garde filmmaker. I never really was. It isn't in my soul to be obscure. I really wanted to work with actors and tell stories and get back to dramatic storylines, back to my roots in the theater. Hollywood had sort of tried out a few women directors. The Ida Lupinos were prior to my being aware of any women directing at all. Elaine May at this point had directed a movie and there was some hope. So I felt that if I went to Hollywood, perhaps I could actually work.

So I took my movies under my arm and went out to Los Angeles in 1976. I became an American Film Institute intern. It was a program where you were paid a very small stipend to go into a major studio motion picture and watch the director work throughout an entire motion picture. I interned with Robert Wise, who has also ended up being a lifelong friend. It was a very significant experience but in a certain way it was also difficult because I had already been directing for almost ten years. But I was starting all over again in Los Angeles.

I learned an enormous amount interning with Robert Wise. I also took that time to make connections with agents, which was probably the most difficult part of it all. Women were not being hired. But there was sort of a buzz about me. I had made a lot of films. It wasn't like I was a student coming out with his or her first movie. I had four or five movies under my arm that I could show. And the rape movie was so unusual that people remembered it. So finally, after months and months and months of screenings and meetings, I got an agent. That agent spent months introducing me around town and I met a lot of people but didn't end up with any movies. People weren't really hiring women.

I finally got a couple of development deals. The whole Coppola group was making *Apocalypse Now* so even though they had made an early connection with me they weren't working. I came to town and made a couple of short films on my own. I wrote a story that was made into a film by Disney. But I didn't actually make a movie myself. It was such a frustrating experience.

When the Coppola people came back to the United States we reestablished our contact and I started developing movies there. I did one that fell through and then I did another that was two and a half years in development. It was called *Photoplay*, a rock 'n' roll musical love story that I was going to direct. It kept postponing and postponing, and then there were some financial problems and whatever, and finally the movie got cancelled, which was very, very frustrating to say the least. I became very disillusioned with Hollywood and decided to leave town and move to Toronto, Canada.

The only person I knew in Toronto was the distributor of my educational films. I went up and visited her and bought a house and left Los Angeles behind. It was a very emotional and impulsive move. I was just fed up. I had been in Los Angeles for about three years or so and felt there were no women directors being hired so there really wasn't very much of a chance.

The one thing I would like to mention is that while I was with Coppola I took the opportunity to study acting with Stella Adler and Lee Strasberg and every acting teacher that was respected that I could get access to. I really perfected my knowledge of acting and working with actors.

I wasn't in Canada very long before my agent got me a job. I believe I was the first woman to direct a narrative series for the CBC. I was an experienced director and they needed someone to do this mini-series segment on famous Canadians. Then I was offered an independent feature film, which ended up being called *City Girl*. I ran into huge problems. I never finished shooting it that year. I went back to New York, slept on couches for three or four months while I tried to raise the money to finish that film, which I didn't own.

I actually raised the money several times over with some financiers, but the question of ownership of that picture was very complex. I wound up coming back to Los Angeles where a friend of mine put me in touch with Peter Bogdanovich. Peter fell in love with that movie and he ended up buying it. It took him five months to do it, but he bought the movie. He produced it and paid me to finish shooting. That was the movie that was finally called *City Girl*. It was a rough-cut of that picture that the producers of *Valley Girl* saw.

Valley Girl (1983)

Nicolas Cage; Deborah Foreman; Elizabeth Daily; Michael Bowen; Cameron Dye; Heidi Holicker; Michelle Meyrink; Tina Theberge; Lee Purcell; Richard Sanders; Colleen Camp; Frederic Forrest; David Ensor; Joanne Baron; Tony Plana.

One of the turning points in my life was a dinner I had with Andy Lane, one of the writers and producers of *Valley Girl*. He told me how they had this independent film financed and how exciting it was. I thought, "How good for you." But I was really feeling blocked in my own career because even then *City Girl* was having money problems. Andy said, "I want you to read this because it's about girls. It's called *Valley Girl* and I'd like for you to direct it." I was very surprised and went home praying that I'd like the script. When I read the script, I realized that I could really make a real movie out of this. I went through a murderous several weeks trying to get on that picture because the company that was financing it decided I was too much of an artist and they didn't really want me to direct it. But Andy Lane and Wayne Crawford, who also wrote it, did not want to direct it so they worked hard to get me on it. All three of us worked and put the picture together.

The total cost of the movie was $325 thousand. That was the production cost. The music cost a little more. I called in every favor I had and every friend I knew in the business and made the best picture that I could possibly make. It completely changed my life. *Valley Girl* was definitely a hit movie and was a big financial success. After that I got offered a lot of teen comedies.

Nicolas Cage is another funny story, because, as you know, Nicolas Cage's real name is Nicholas Coppola. I'd spent three years with Francis

Coppola and knew his whole family, but the one person I had never met was Nicolas. He had spent a lot of time around Francis, so he knew who I was, but I didn't know him. He came in for an audition and apparently it was his first audition under the name Cage. When he came in he was very secretive about who he was. So I asked him where his family was from. He said, "Well, I'm half-Italian." Silence. So I said, "How did you get interested in this business?" He was very monosyllabic in the interview. But his reading was fantastic. He was perfect for the part.

I knew he was still shooting a small part for Francis Coppola in *Rumble Fish* and I said, "You know, Nicolas, I really want you in this movie. Let me call Francis Coppola. Francis is like family to me. I'm sure they'll want to help me and I'm sure he's like family to you, too. Let me call him up and see if I can arrange this because I really want you to star in this movie." He gave me the strangest look. So I called up the production manager of *Rumble Fish* and I said, "I have this guy Nicolas Cage and I really want him in my movie." Finally he said, "We don't have a Nicolas Cage, we have another Nicholas." My little red light started going up. I said, "Nicholas who?" He said, "Nicholas Coppola." I decided to keep Nicolas's identity a secret from everybody else because I felt that he changed his name for a reason.

He did eventually star in *Valley Girl,* thank God. He was great in the movie. I had a really great time working with him. He's a very inventive, intelligent actor who brings a lot to what he's doing. There's a funny moment when he looks out over the valley and he says, "She's out there, somewhere." In that scene, he pulled out this little waxed flute filled with fluid and blew a note and cried. Then he ate the flute. I had to shoot before it got dark, for safety, and when he started to eat the flute I said, "Cut, cut. Nicolas, do you have another one of those flutes?" He said, "Oh, no. I ate the note, not the flute." It was a great experience working with him.

On Working with Actors

I put my whole heart and soul into the movie. I enjoyed doing a comedy. It was a wonderful experience. But what I really found worked for me was the fact I had done a lot of improvisational work in my early movies. I wrote them and they were based on improvisation, so I found myself feeling very free to work with the actors' ideas. That's been the basic idea in all of my pictures. Work with the actors. Let them feel comfortable. Take the actors' input. I like intelligent actors who have lots of ideas and bring a lot to the table.

It's easy to say no when something doesn't work. What's really hard is when nobody has any ideas. *Valley Girl* was shot very, very quickly, in twenty days. We had to squeeze the rehearsals in on our own time, but we did rehearse it, and I never went past three takes. It was mostly done on the first take. Print, and that's it. I learned that from Robert Wise. I had no film. They gave me sixty thousand feet of film to shoot the movie on. It was a film that had to be done with an enormous amount of efficiency, but I wanted the playful aspect of the actors' input so I used rehearsals to do that. So that's how we made that film.

Joy of Sex (1984)

Cameron Dye; Michelle Meyrink; Colleen Camp; Ernie Hudson;
Lisa Langlois; Charles Van Eman; Joanne Baron; Darren Dalton; Heidi Holicker;
Cristen Kauffman; David H. MacDonald; Paul Tulley; Joe Unger;
Christopher Lloyd; Conni Marie Brazelton.

Several studios tried to buy *Valley Girl*, but in the end Atlantic Pictures kept the picture and distributed it themselves. I got a lot of offers from various studios and ended up taking an offer from Paramount. But all I was being offered was teenage comedies, which, frankly, was not what I wanted to do next. *Joy of Sex* was not a finished script. It was originally called *The National Lampoon's Joy of Sex* at the time. It was a really silly picture.

It was really only half a script but I was sick of turning movies down and thought I could be a hero, foolish person that I was, and I was anxious to get my first studio picture underway so I made this movie. The entire budget of that picture was two million. Not enough for a studio union picture, but I didn't realize that. So I went into this movie, which today I never would have done, without a full script, eight days of prep, and no money, but fortunately I had a wonderful cast.

The movie was a jumble of subplots. Me and my friend, who wrote the script, struggled through because she was writing it as we were going along. The studio insisted getting involved in what would and would not end up in the film and that left giant holes in the plot. Finally they asked me to leave the picture and they ended up cutting it all up. It doesn't mean it would have been a good picture if I had finished cutting it, but it would have been a better picture. I learned a big lesson from that experience.

Real Genius (1985)

Stacy Peralta; Daniel Ades; Andres Aybar; Louis Giambalvo; Ed Lauter; Charles Shull; Beau Billingslea; Charles Parks; William Atherton; Sean Frye; JoAnn Willette; Ina Gould; Nadine Vix; Gabriel Jarret; Paul Tulley; Val Kilmer; Michelle Meyrink.

Luckily producer Brian Grazer, who had loved *Valley Girl,* offered me *Real Genius.* The script was very silly when I first read it. Then gradually, after it was rewritten several times, I thought it was a very intelligent, smart movie and I could make something really terrific out of it.

Brian said to me, "I really believe in having fun making movies." And it was fun for me. I actually gave one of my profit points to cinematographer Vilmos Zsigmond, so I was shooting with a wonderful cameraman and had a terrific cast. It was also one of Val Kilmer's very first films. It was a lot of fun with a lot of special effects. I'm very proud of it.

What I loved about *Real Genius* is that the basic story is a real story that you can identify with. It was about these kids being exploited with money in the sciences supplied by the military of our nation. In other words, it's black money from the CIA that funds a lot of scientific research and therefore skews what the scientific research is meant to do. These kids go into the sciences because they love nature, but what they discover is that they are building a weapon. Their corrupt professor is using them to develop this weapon and get grants. The movie is based on the pranks that we've all heard about at Cal Tech and MIT, the idea that these brilliant, genius kids develop all these crazy pranks. All of the pranks in the movie are based on real pranks. At one point they turn the entire dorm into a multiple-story ice skating, bobsled rink. People are on ice skates, and sleds are coming down one story and the next. We had a fabulous time researching it.

I wanted something at the end of the movie that was not straight revenge. I didn't want the students to come out and beat the professor up or anything like that. I wanted a more inventive way. I was asking everybody for ideas. Ron Cobb, a friend and a designer on the picture, suggested we use the laser to ignite the popcorn and blow up this house with popcorn. In the movie I establish that the professor hates the smell of popcorn. The students build this giant Easy Pop in the middle of the foyer of his precious house and they use the space-based laser weapon to ignite the Easy Pop.

What we had to do was build a full-scale house in the middle of a neighborhood. It was like a Disney World prop. The house would fall apart and then we would put it back together again for take two. I forget what the tonnage was of popcorn that was in one firing, but it would explode and just pop out everywhere for about fifteen seconds. I know that we had forty-foot tractor-trailers lined up, all filled with popcorn. We used about a hundred tons outside and forty tons inside. In fact, we had to pop the forty tons ourselves, so we built six huge popping machines that popped day and night outside our stage for six weeks prior to getting outside and shooting the house blowing up. It was certainly the biggest special effect I've ever done and it was an extraordinary event to observe.

Plain Clothes (1988)

Arliss Howard; Suzy Amis; George Wendt; Diane Ladd; Seymour Cassel;
Larry Pine; Jackie Gayle; Abe Vigoda; Robert Stack; Alexandra Powers;
Peter Dobson; Harry Shearer; Loren Dean; Reginald VelJohnson; Max Perlich.

After *Real Genius* I was still offered teen comedies. It was very hard to pick and choose and find scripts that I liked. I was working on some action pictures and other genres but they didn't get made. Then *Plain Clothes* came along. It was sort of a black comedy and rather adult in tone and I liked that aspect of it. I kind of have a dark sense of humor myself. I thought the movie was quite satirical, in a certain sense. It was also a bit of a metaphor for me because the main character is a cop who hates high school and can't get out of high school because he's posing as a high school student. I remember one critic saying, "Why won't they let Martha Coolidge out of high school?" But anyway, I had a lot of fun making that movie because I had a great cast. It was my first picture with Diane Ladd, who I later did *Rambling Rose* with.

In *Plain Clothes* there were cameo roles for older actors and it just seemed like a really great opportunity to get some terrific, experienced, wonderful people. Robert Stack's one of the funniest people I've ever met. He's known for all his straight roles, but he's a very funny man. Abe Vigoda was a riot. I actually sent George Wendt and Abe and Diane Ladd to Seattle high schools where they posed as substitute teachers for the day. The only one that was almost recognized was Abe.

She has great wit about her and she has a real understanding of
humor in film and in scripts that she sees, but it's so intelligent. She's

*so savvy in her humor that somehow that's why she is able to in-
stinctively get how subtle humor can be in the saddest of moments
and still transfer it to an audience.*

Laura Dern—Actress

Rambling Rose (1991)

*Laura Dern; Robert Duvall; Diane Ladd; Lukas Haas; John Heard;
Kevin Conway; Robert John Burke; Lisa Jakub; Evan Lockwood; Matt Sutherland;
D. Anthony Pender; David E. Scarborough; Robin Dale Robertson;
General Fermon Judd Jr.; Richard K. Olsen.*

I was struggling to change genres. Right around the time I did *Real Genius*,
my assistant had found *Rambling Rose* and had gotten me to read it. I fell in
love with the script and really wanted to do it. The first thing I did was send
it to Laura Dern. I could not imagine anyone else in the part except Laura.
At that time she was eighteen years old. I tried like crazy to get that movie
made. It turned out that a lot of people had tried to get that movie made
for a long time. Then I had my son, did a couple of TV movies, and Laura
gave the script to her then boyfriend, Renny Harlin, who was an action director who had a deal with Carolco Pictures. Renny loved the script so
much that he said, "I'd like to produce it." So he took it to the head of Carolco and they had the courage to put the money up and make the picture.

The script was seventeen years old when we made the movie. I had been
involved with it for five years and yet we only had nine weeks of prep, total.
We had to find locations and cast it. I think the other great stroke of luck was
all of my first choice actors were available—Robert Duvall, Diane Ladd, and
Lukas Haas. I never bothered to think about who the boy would be because
the boy had to be exactly the right age when we started the film. So as soon
as we had the go on the picture I started looking around for the right boy.

Some people who knew the Haas family suggested I call them. This role
was a little questionable in terms of the family's taste. They really had to
trust their son a lot to let him play this part. In *Rambling Rose*, Lukas plays
a boy who's having his first sexual experiences. In the end the Haas's really
trusted Lukas. He made the choice to do the role but his family was really
behind him. Lukas is like working with any mature, incredibly knowl-
edgeable actor. He'd done something like twenty-two movies by the time
he did *Rambling Rose*.

Before I met Bobby Duvall I was a little intimidated. He'd been a little standoffish about the offer, questioning who the people involved in the project were, and things like that. Calder Willingham, the writer of the screenplay and the book, wrote a beautiful letter to Bobby Duvall in which he talked about the role. When Duvall finally accepted he had not met any of us, so I flew into Wilmington, North Carolina, to begin my prep and Bobby came up to meet me. We hit it off from the first moment we met. I really love him. He's a great guy. He's an incredible, consummate actor. I think the biggest issue for an actor like that is, do you, the director, love actors? I do love actors and I love acting and I think that was clear from the moment we met.

The idea of working with all these great actors *is* the idea. If it isn't broke, don't fix it. You've got incredible talented people who hopefully are inspired by your vision. You've got to transmit that to everybody you can in as clear a way as you can, and then be supportive of them and their creative work so everybody is at their maximum creative point. I think that was one of the great things about *Rambling Rose.* Even though the hours were extraordinarily long, it was a shoot filled with love and inspiration and everyone cried on the last day. We were all just in tears when the movie ended and I don't know if I'll ever have an experience as powerful in that way because it was so special. But I do remember Bobby Duvall asking, "Can you shoot a movie in seven weeks?"

Laura Dern and I had had many years to talk about the part. We really had been talking about this script for five years so she had many strong ideas. So by the time we got into rehearsal Laura showed with her character 100 percent, full-blown, totally, totally complete. Accent. Everything. Her mother Diane is from the South so Laura had spent time in the South. She's a consummate actress. Her process isn't as verbal as a lot of other people so that a great deal of it was she and I just sharing ideas.

I think what was most important in the rehearsal process was I went over all the relationships between the characters because we shot the movie very much out of order. On the other hand, it was very important to me that the bedroom scene between Rose and the boy be put off to very late in the schedule. I wanted Lukas and Laura to have a long relationship with each other first. They became really good friends. Lukas would bring CDs to Laura that she would play. They had this teenage friendship that developed along with a great trust, and that's what they needed to play that scene as actors.

Feature Films vs. Television Films

Essentially, I went right into a TV movie called *Crazy in Love* with Holly Hunter, Gena Rowlands, Bill Pullman, and Frances McDormand. But I far prefer doing theatrical films. What I found good about doing television, however, is that it's fast. You have to make very quick decisions. What's good about that is there's less interference because it's got to get done. Television can be difficult because you don't have the time to work on style. It's really about the material; it's not about how you do it. It's very difficult to shoot in a very creative way for television. Everything has its pluses and minuses. I think that temperamentally I prefer having more time than television allows. I like to spend more time on my rehearsals presenting the material and more time in preparing how I'm going to shoot it and from what point of view. I personally enjoy the challenge of going back and forth. But often, it's more of an economic reason.

If I'm stuck in a genre, which happens to everybody, I just won't continue in it, because every time you take a movie, it's another year of your life at least. Then what's great is to step out of that and do something a little bit different. I did some *Twilight Zone*s. Science fiction was a lot of fun and it took me way out of my normal genre and into a genre that I love to read. It has to do more with the subject matter than it has to do with what one really enjoys doing. It was a lot more fun to spend weeks and weeks and weeks and weeks shooting a feature than four weeks for a TV movie.

Lost in Yonkers (1993)

Richard Dreyfuss; Mercedes Ruehl; Irene Worth; Brad Stoll; Mike Damus;
David Strathairn; Robert Guy Miranda; Jack Laufer; Susan Merson; Illya Hause;
Calvin Stillwell; Dick Hagerman; Jesse Vincent; Howard Newstate; Peter Gannon.

I suspect that the way Neil Simon's play came to me was through *Rambling Rose*. In fact, I was getting an enormous amount of material being sent to me because of *Rambling Rose*. It made such a splash in the community. I was blessed with *Rambling Rose*.

I read the first page of the *Lost in Yonkers* script and knew I had to do it if I could. Neil had created beautiful characters and taken it out of the stage setting. Just the first page let me know the freedom Neil had worked with in his adaptation. After readying the script I felt the next step was to meet Neil Simon and see if we hit it off. We got together, and, as I recall, the meeting went on for several hours. I really think it's important to try to get inside the head of the writer. I call myself a writer-dependent director. So I try very hard to get to the source of the inspiration, to know what's behind the writer's thoughts. When a writer has the kind of gift Neil has with language, you don't want to mess with that, you just use it. Neil was on the set every day, not necessarily all day long, but always on call, and always consulted. We worked very closely together. It was an extraordinary experience to work with a writer of that stature. We had a great time.

I loved working with Richard Dreyfuss. Again, just a consummate star and a wonderful actor. He did such a transformation on himself that was really breathtaking in terms of getting into a character, because the thing that Neil does better than anyone is write good characters. We knew we had Mercedes Ruehl because she was already signed on before I came on. The big question was who was going to play Uncle Louie. I think Richard did such an incredible, whimsical, wonderful, creative job in his portrayal. One of the most difficult things in the whole movie was Richard playing Mercedes Ruehl's brother. They're not the same height. They don't look alike at all. But they were great together.

The interesting thing about *Lost in Yonkers* is that you're taking a play, a prize-winning play, that the actresses won prizes for playing those roles, and you must, in a sense, change it. Neil had really done a great job in opening it up. We had to further develop the characters and take a look at how the movie was going to be different from the play. Richard had not done the play, so that immediately threw new color into the mix in terms of the relationships with the family. There were also two very young boys. Now in the theater, they didn't go with boys that young. That also threw another piece into the mix. And I cannot say enough about the performances of Mercedes Ruehl and Irene Worth.

Angie (1994)

Geena Davis; Stephen Rea; James Gandolfini; Aida Turturro; Philip Bosco; Jenny O'Hara; Michael Rispoli; Betty Miller; Susan Jaffe; Jeremy Collins; Robert Conn; Ray Xifo; Rosemary De Angelis; Rae Allen; Ida Bernardini.

I think that the most compelling element to *Angie* was Geena Davis, to be honest. I thought that the part of this girl, who has enormous problems and runs away from her family and does some terrible things, was a very brave part for her to play. It's a funny movie but in its deepest heart it's really a very serious drama. I really wanted to work with her and liked her enormously as an actress. It was a big challenge because she's playing an Italian from Brooklyn. There was a lot of character development and work on accents and gestures.

I was very adamant about making that picture in Brooklyn. I wanted to surround Geena with the real thing. I got a lot of actors from that area who really had the background and could give support to the movie both in the look and the acting and to the relationships that would really give authenticity to it. I think the other thing that really compelled me about this film was the birth scene. I had a baby and I knew how unauthentic birth scenes are in movies. I really wanted to make one which was not only a comedy set piece, which it is, but also have a little more truth to it and how it really happens and how wacky it can get. I think giving birth is an extraordinary turning point in women's lives. And the great appeal to *Angie* is that the movie turns from a comedy into a drama in that one moment. I really do believe that the birth of a child is a complete turning point in anyone's life.

Geena is an extraordinary professional. She was a perfectionist in her accent, in her look, in her walk, in everything. She was always prepared. She's a very tall woman, so the biggest challenge in the whole movie, I think, was finding the actors who could play opposite her. Steven Rea spent a few hours on boxes, but aside from that we had a wonderful time. She's got a great sense of humor.

I think what's always disappointing is when a movie doesn't seem to hit its audience. This movie, which many people have told me they love, is really geared toward the people who have families. It is also my second movie that I consider to be particularly aimed at a female audience. It's funny. I'm a woman director and people think that what I've done are women's movies. It's not really true at all. If you think about it, *Rambling Rose* is really a man's story. *Lost in Yonkers* is certainly a man's script that has two female characters in it. It's told from the boy's point of view. These are projects that are character-driven movies so they fall into a certain genre. But *Crazy in Love* and *Angie* are movies geared toward a female audience that will be understood by women and news to men.

> *The true job of a director is to be a storyteller, and to have the ability*
> *to create magic or discover magic or even know magic when you see it.*

Martha truly has that ability. She's got technical background, but she loves the process of acting. And that's incredibly refreshing for an actor.
Patrick Swayze—Actor

Three Wishes (1995)

Patrick Swayze; Mary Elizabeth Mastrantonio; Joseph Mazzello; Seth Mumy; David Marshall Grant; Jay O. Sanders; Michael O'Keefe; John Diehl; Diane Venora; David Zahorsky; Brian Flannery; Brock Pierce; Davin Jacob Carey; David Hart; Scott Patterson.

I think *Three Wishes* is a wonderful movie. It was a really great experience making that picture. I had come across the script when I was making *Rambling Rose.* I had been talking to people at Paramount about doing it back then. There was a huge executive changeover at Paramount and it took a long time for the producers to get it going, so in the end I came back to it. What is great is it's a fairy tale. It's a modern, contemporary fairy tale. It is not a comedy. It is more of a drama and a romantic fantasy.

It takes place in 1955. 1955 is the year my father died. I guess the point I keep bringing up here is that movies have to be as personal to the director as they are to the actors or to the writer. I feel that if the director doesn't have a personal identification to the material, you really shouldn't go near it. You take too long making movies. You have to really be involved with the material. In 1955 my father died of cancer. The movie is about a wife and her two children who have lost her husband in the Korean War and the children are struggling with being fatherless children in 1955, something I remember very well. My mother became a widow in 1955 and I know the fantasy of, I wish my father could walk in the door, I wish he wasn't really dead, I wish I could be the same as everybody else, I wish that something magic and wonderful could happen to me. That's basically what *Three Wishes* is about.

It was wonderful working with an incredible young actor named Joseph Mazzello who goes right into the same category as Lukas Haas. Patrick Swayze is just a wonderful man and a wonderful actor. He's terrific in the picture. Mary Elizabeth Mastrantonio was terrific. Then we had Seth Mumy, a five-year-old terrific actor, along with dogs and visual effects. Doing a movie combining dogs, children, and visual effects was extraordinary, to say the least. The dogs were always working in scenes with Seth, so that was an incredible challenge in itself. And then Seth had to work with things that weren't there, like monsters and creatures and all the magic that was going to be put in later with visual effects.

Career Moves, Career Decisions

I have to say that perhaps my attitude towards my career is a little bit different than a man's would be. At this age, and at this point in my career, I'm very aware of how much timing and luck were involved in me ever getting to this point. Not saying I didn't have determination. I had determination beyond most people's conception of what that could be. From the time I made my first movie to *Valley Girl* was eighteen years. I had many periods where I felt I was trapped and couldn't get out of a genre and wasn't being given material that I liked and I somehow stuck it out through those slumps. I think I've been more inventive about stepping back and forth between television and features and I have a huge foot in independent filmmaking. I work between studio pictures and independent pictures. But I think the most important thing is that I know now that discrimination exists everywhere, all the time. This was something I wasn't willing to recognize when I was younger, when I blindly went forward believing that I could be a woman director.

When I applied to film school, they said, "You can't be a director. You can't name five women directors in the world. There are no women directors." In fact, at the time I could only name one. And even though there are many more women directors than ever before, there are not that many more women making movies per year. It is because we have fixed ideas in our society about what women do and who will let them, and how much money they should have control over. It's gender roles. Basically we're talking about deep changes in our social attitudes and our personal attitudes that are going to take generations to overcome. And I have to say that my career is blessed. I'm very thankful for the movies I've been able to make. I've had incredible experiences. I love every movie. There are many movies I want to do. There are many movies I wish I could make but haven't had the opportunity to do, but it is a miracle that any movie gets made at all. I feel very, very blessed that I've been able to do it. It's exacted tremendous costs and sacrifices from me. I started my family very, very late in my life. I think that my career really took off very late in my life compared to the men that I know who are lucky enough to get to do this. But I love my work.

Out to Sea (1997)

Jack Lemmon; Walter Matthau; Dyan Cannon; Gloria DeHaven; Brent Spiner;
Elaine Stritch; Hal Linden; Donald O'Connor; Edward Mulhare; Rue McClanahan;
Alexandra Powers; Sean O'Bryan; Esther Scott; Allan Rich; Estelle Harris.

Out to Sea has been a terrific experience. I've always loved Walter Matthau and Jack Lemmon. They were both attached to this picture when I came on board. I've known the producer, John Davis, for years. I really was in the mood to do a comedy. I wanted to do a straight-out comedy and this is a really funny movie, but it has two other wonderful aspects to it that I just feel lucky to be dealing with. One is romance and the other is music and dancing. The idea that this is a music and dance picture is fantastic. We spent three weeks shooting in a ballroom. We did fifteen playback numbers with choreography. It's just been an extraordinary experience.

I have a background in musical theater. I watched a lot of musical theater being put together on Broadway and you have to do it in a very similar way in the movies. It's just extraordinary working with all of these legends. Then you add the other people into the movie like Dyan Cannon, Gloria DeHaven, Brent Spiner, Edward Mulhare. I mean I had just a fantastic group of people, to say nothing of Donald O'Conner and Hal Linden. I probably never worked so hard to get two actors involved in a movie. I had to call them personally and beg.

This has been an incredible collaboration. Again, I was working on a picture where the script was going on as we were shooting, so you need a lot of feedback. A lot of the comedy is coming not just from the lines but from the inspiration of the actors.

I have to say that when Jack Lemmon and Walter Matthau are working together in a really funny scene, they can't keep a straight face. It's one of the biggest problems. They really crack each other up. They love each other and they're very respectful of each other's talent. They don't think the same way so they often surprise each other and come up with stuff that they didn't expect.

I remember one scene where Walter does one of the funniest things I've

---

EDITOR'S NOTE: This interview took place in one day on the set of *Out to Sea*. Martha would direct a scene, then, while the crew was setting up for the next sequence, she would continue doing this interview.

ever seen him do, which is cross the dance floor with a limp and a cane. Jack is shaking. He's laughing so hard. He is out of control laughing and that happens frequently.

There Are More Opportunities

There's more opportunities for women directors all the time. Not just women directors but ethnic directors. I think this is important to realize. The doors are open and society has changed. It will never be the same. I think that the next thing is huge social upheavals in terms of population breakdown and what we're going to see. The studios know there are different audiences out there and there are different directors besides stars that appeal to these audiences. But I think what's important, and what's going to be difficult, is to watch how the women and the other directors move into really big "A" pictures. That's a tough struggle. They want a certain type of person to make these big pictures. It's still a closed door.

Her Parting Words

Well, I hope that I have brought some enjoyment into people's lives. It's certainly why I make movies. I think that I enjoy the challenge of making movies and I love the struggle. I'm basically what I call a crisis-type personality, but I really wouldn't do it if I didn't think I was bringing some fun or insight or feeling into people's lives. I think that's what it's all about, our mutual humanity.

Filmography

David: Off and On (1972)
Old-Fashioned Woman (1974)
More Than a School (1974)

EDITOR'S NOTE: After this interview was completed, Coolidge directed *Introducing Dorothy Dandridge,* a TV project starring Halle Berry and Klaus Maria Brandauer, and was slated to co-direct (with Jane Anderson) the TV movie *If These Walls Could Talk 2,* with Ellen DeGeneres, Sharon Stone, and Vanessa Redgrave.

Not a Pretty Picture (1975)
Employment Discrimination: The Troubleshooters (1976)
Bimbo (1978)
Winners (TV series, 1978)
Valley Girl (1983)
Joy of Sex (1984)
City Girl (1984)
Real Genius (1985)
The Twilight Zone (TV series, 1985)
Sledge Hammer! (TV series, 1986)
Plain Clothes (1988)
Trenchcoat in Paradise (TV, 1989)
Bare Essentials (TV, 1991)
Rambling Rose (1991)
Crazy in Love (TV, 1992)
Lost in Yonkers (1993)
Angie (1994)
Three Wishes (1995)
Out to Sea (1997)
If These Walls Could Talk 2 (TV, 1999)
Introducing Dorothy Dandridge (TV, 1999)

Awards

Directors Guild of America
Robert B. Aldrich Achievement Award, 1998

Independent Spirit Awards
Rambling Rose, Best Director, 1992

Women in Film Crystal Awards
Crystal Award, 1992

The Films of Herbert Ross

Herbert Ross, one of Hollywood's most prolific filmmakers, was born on May 13, 1927.

He began his career in the arts as a dancer in musical comedy and later became a choreographer for ballet. He subsequently formed his own ballet company with his first wife, the late Nora Kaye, who was the prima ballerina of the American Ballet Theater and the inspiration for *The Turning Point*. Their company toured extensively throughout Europe, appearing at Italy's renowned Spoleto Festival.

During that period, Ross directed and choreographed Broadway musicals, including *Wonderful Town, Anyone Can Whistle, The Apple Tree,* and *On a Clear Day You Can See Forever*. Ross also devised the show-stopping "Miss Marmelstein" number in *I Can Get It for You Wholesale* that first brought Barbra Streisand to the attention of New York theater audiences.

His credits as a choreographer for film and television include *Carmen Jones, Inside Daisy Clover,* and *Doctor Dolittle,* as well as the live telecast of *Wonderful Town* starring Rosalind Russell, and *The Fred Astaire Show,* in which the legendary entertainer gave his final television performance. Ross also directed and produced *The Bell Telephone Hour.*

After Nora Kaye died in 1987, Ross became highly involved in the work of the American Cancer Society, from which he received a Lifetime Achievement Award. He and his second wife, Lee Radziwill, are also active in supporting numerous other charitable causes and social programs.

Herbert Ross has directed a number of outstanding films, from *Goodbye Mr. Chips* in 1969 to the 1995 production of *Boys on the Side* starring Whoopi Goldberg and Drew Barrymore. Herbert Ross' name may not be a household word, but as you read you will realize that he has directed some of the finest films ever put on the silver screen.

*I really give Herb credit for teaching me the techniques of acting
that I've used in my whole theatrical, cinematic life and I thank him
for that.*

Steve Martin—Actor

The Conversation

I began as a dancer, as you know, and then began to choreograph and direct in the theater. I had choreographed a couple of pictures in the sixties but I never paid any attention to them. I got a call from a man called Arthur Jacob who had seen a show that I did and who wanted me to come out to do *Doctor Dolittle*. I had already done a picture called *Inside Daisy Clover* with Natalie Wood. On *Doctor Dolittle*, the director, a very nice man called Richard Fleischer, did not want dances so I sort of just blocked scenes for the musical numbers. I got along remarkably well with the actors and I was the only person that Rex Harrison, who was a notoriously difficult man, would listen to. So they began to rely on me to handle Rex.

And after that I went to direct a musical sequence on a picture called *Funny Girl,* thanks to director Willy Wyler. I had worked previously with Streisand in the theater. I had done her first show called *I Can Get It for You Wholesale,* and then did the number that had made her the incredible star that she ultimately became. Anyway, *Funny Girl* was her first film and Willy was uncomfortable with musical numbers so he asked if I would direct the musical sequence as well and I was thrilled. I choreographed and directed all the musical sequences in that film.

Goodbye, Mr. Chips (1969)

*George Baker; Michael Bryant; Petula Clark; Alison Leggatt;
Peter O'Toole; Siân Phillips; Michael Redgrave; Jenny Runacre.*

Arthur Jacobs, who had produced the *Dolittle* picture, was preparing a movie called *Goodbye, Mr. Chips* with Peter O'Toole. The director of the picture dropped out. Arthur asked if I would go and meet with Peter O'Toole who at that time was shooting *The Lion in Winter.* I was choreographing *The Fred Astaire Show.* I asked Fred if he would let me off for this long weekend to go to Ireland to meet with Peter. I met up with Peter who interviewed me and told me that he'd heard that I was really brilliant. He had been told that Anthony Harvey, who was directing *The Lion in Winter,* had seen the show I choreographed called *Anyone Can Whistle.* I was, to say the least, very happy to hear this. So Peter and I had a couple of drinks. I had a cold and I threw up all over Peter. I came back home and told my wife what had happened, that I'd gotten sick and thrown up and I thought I'd never hear from him again. Peter, as it turned out, thought that was hilariously funny and gave me the okay to get the job and that's how it happened.

I was nervous but I had everything to gain and literally nothing to lose if I failed. I had directed a lot of live television over the years so I was familiar with that process, and I had done enough film as a choreographer and had directed parts of two different pictures. So I had some background and I was used to live TV, editing as I shot, so I always had an editing plan in mind. I also had fantastic help. A cameraman named Ozzie Morris was the cameraman on the movie and was really a kind of mentor to me. Ken Adams designed the movie, and those people are still close friends of mine and I still see them and work with them when I can.

I liked the film a lot. I thought O'Toole was just magnificent in the movie and I thought it was a very good screenplay. Unfortunately, it was oddly out of touch with its time because it came out just as the revolution happened in music. The Beatles had just occurred and pictures like *Strawberry Statement* were being made. *Easy Rider* had just opened. Those kinds of movies opened up a new door to a new kind of movie experience and ours was in another tradition. But I thought I did a good job. Even Pauline Kael thought I did a good job.

The Owl and the Pussycat (1970)

Barbra Streisand; George Segal; Robert Klein; Allen Garfield; Roz Kelly; Jacques Sandulescu; Jack Manning; Grace Carney; Barbara Anson; Kim Chan; Stan Gottlieb; Joe Madden; Fay Sappington; Evelyn Land.

The Owl and the Pussycat came to me through producer Ray Stark. We had done *Funny Girl* together and I had been responsible for directing the musical sequences. And because, I guess, of my relationship with Barbra, they thought it was appropriate that I direct the movie. I had also done a number of comedy sequences in films before. Barbra, George Segal, and I had one of the happiest times we ever had making a movie.

It was originally done on the stage with a black actress and a white actor and we were going to do the movie with Barbra and Sidney Poitier, but he bowed out of the movie. Then I tried to get English actor Tom Courtney, who decided that he didn't wish to do it, and then we were fortunate enough to get George Segal who was great in the part.

Barbra always had a clear view of what she wanted to be. We shot a screen test and we tried every angle known to mankind in every lighting condition. She was very anxious to know what the effect of light was. We discovered, and no one knew this—I guess Harry Stradling, the cinematographer, did—we discovered this extraordinary skin that she has and its ability to reflect light, which is one of her greatest strengths. So she has a very clear idea of what she wants, but I think she's an actress before she's a director. She's anxious to be informed and anxious to be directed and anxious for approval and anxious for discussion.

When we did *Funny Girl,* just to get an insight into how meticulous she is, she had a copy of every draft of the stage play that was ever written. She must have had forty-five or fifty different versions of *Funny Girl,* and she would go rattling through these versions and extract what she thought was a wonderful line or something that she thought was positive. So she's very dedicated, very hard-working, and very concentrated, and really great to work with. And Barbra used to have lamb chops, I just remembered that, she ate lamb chops for lunch. One other thing. The scene where George and Barbra are stoned in the bathtub—they insisted on getting stoned in order to play the scene, and of course it was hopeless and we had to do it again when they were slightly straighter. But that was the time, you know.

T.R. Baskin (1971)
Candice Bergen; Peter Boyle; James Caan; Erin O'Reilly;
Howard Platt; Marcia Rodd; William Wise.

That came to me through an agent who had a lot of women on her client list. One of them was Candice Bergen, who is incredibly beautiful. The agent sent me this script, describing it to me as a *Breakfast at Tiffany's*. Of course it had nothing at all to do with *Breakfast at Tiffany's.* Anyhow, I was interested, but it was a script that never had enough dimensions or enough depth to succeed. Still, there was about it something interesting because it was about loneliness. I think most people found it difficult to accept that a beautiful woman like Candice Bergen could be so lonely and not have any friends or any companions or any lovers in her life. I used to counter that by saying that Nora, my wife, and I used to have New Year's Eve dinners and this one New Year's Eve we had three of the most beautiful women in Hollywood for dinner and none of them had a date—Natalie Wood, Candice Bergen, and Samantha Eggar. Not one of them had a date.

Play It Again, Sam (1972)

Woody Allen; Diane Keaton; Tony Roberts; Jerry Lacy; Susan Anspach;
Jennifer Salt; Joy Bang; Viva; Susanne Zenor; Diana Davila;
Mari Fletcher; Michael Greene; Ted Markland.

Arthur Jacobs, who had produced *Dr. Dolittle*, sent me the play by Woody Allen. Woody had done what he thought was a draft, but he had just literally xeroxed the pages of the French version of the play and it would have stage directions in it, like, "He exits left and she comes on from right." He hadn't turned it into a screenplay at all. I did that for him—sort of put it in locations and so forth and then sent it back to him and then asked him for a number of new scenes, and he was terrific. And then I asked him why he wanted somebody else to direct it and why he didn't want to direct it himself. He said because it was a play and it was a narrative and he had only done sketch material up until then and he didn't feel he was ready for it. It was a very important turning point in Woody's life and a big step for him in terms of dealing with narrative.

We were going to shoot the picture on Long Island but there was a strike in New York. On one day's notice we pulled anchor and we went to San Francisco. And that's how we wound up there. We shot that picture in seven weeks, by the way. And I think the budget on the picture was $1.6 million, probably.

Stories about the making of *Play It Again, Sam*? Not any that I could repeat. Actually I do have one. We were shooting on the road somewhere and it was the sequence where bike riders threaten Woody. At that time we were working out of a Cinemobile. Are you familiar with the Cinemobile equipment trucks? Anyway, all of our equipment and costumes were in it and the

Cinemobile blew up. But we still had the camera so we kept working until we ended the day. That was devastating.

The Sunshine Boys (1975)

Walter Matthau; George Burns; Richard Benjamin; Lee Meredith;
Carol DeLuise; Rosetta Le Noire; F. Murray Abraham; Howard Hesseman;
James Cranna; Ron Rifkin; Jennifer Lee; Fritz Feld; Jack Bernardi;
Garn Stephens; Santos Morales.

Neil Simon and I had not worked together in professional theater. We did work together many years before at a holiday summer camp in the Poconos that had a theater. I was the resident choreographer and Neil and his brother were the sketch writers and Jerry Bock, who went on to write the music for *Fiddler on the Roof,* was the composer. We had a little stock company of people and we did an original review every week for two nights. On Saturday night people saw it and on Sunday night all of the new guests saw it. On Monday we went back into rehearsal and did another whole new review with orchestration, dances, sketches, monologues, etc. But we were working so hard, Neil and I hardly spoke to one another.

Walter Matthau was already set to play the role of Willy Clark. I had conducted a series of screen tests for the part of Al Lewis with Red Skelton, Jack Benny, Milton Berle, and a comic by the name of Lou Ayer. Jack Benny got the part. He then became ill in New Orleans and he rang me up and said, "You know, something happened to me and I can't do this picture. Would you please use my friend George Burns?" Up until then we had not seen or read George for the part. Anyhow, as it happened Jack became too ill to do the movie. The same agent, Irving Fine, represented both Jack and George. We rang up Irving, and George, by that time, was well and out of the hospital after having his heart surgery. So George came to my house and we had a reading of the script with Walter, producer Ray Stark, Neil Simon, and myself, and George was just great and he got the part. Interestingly enough, the then head of production at MGM, Michael Rosenberg, did not want George. He wanted another actor. Neil and I and Ray said we wouldn't do the picture unless we could have George. We prevailed and we made the movie.

George essentially was playing himself. Walter was giving the characterization. He was approaching it as an actor because he didn't have the same background or the same age or any of the qualities that naturally suited the role that George had. It was a question of encouraging George and not having him drop out of character to pursue a laugh. He was very intelligent and grasped that right away. I think he was already eighty-two when we shot the movie and he had memorized the entire script. He knew every word of the script by heart.

The only time that he ever made a mistake was the first day of shooting. There was a knock on the door and Walter said, "Enter" and he goes over to open the door. He opens the door and George is supposed to say his character's name and instead George said, "It's George Burns." That was the only time that he ever went up or made a mistake, but it was his first take. Never did it again.

The greatest story about George is this one. I said to him, "Gee, George, you're in such great shape and you don't have any wrinkles." He invited me to come inside his trailer. Then he took all his clothes off and there he was standing there in only his jockey shorts and I said, "It's amazing, there's not a wrinkle on your body. What do you do?" And he said to me, "Revlon Eterna 27. I've used it for thirty years." Well, it did a great job for George.

How Does He Choose His Projects?

Sometimes very carefully and sometimes it's pin-the-tail-on-the-donkey. Sometimes you choose a project that you know in your heart is not good, but you need to go back to work for a variety of reasons, sometimes economic, sometimes psychological. Sometimes you're longing to do a picture that somebody else has got that you've not been considered for. Sometimes you work very hard or you have an idea, as in the case of *Turning Point*. Sometimes you have an idea and it takes years to get it going. So there are all different ways.

Funny Lady (1975)

Barbra Streisand; James Caan; Omar Sharif; Roddy McDowall; Ben Vereen; Carole Wells; Larry Gates; Eugene Troobnick; Heidi O'Rourke; Royce Wallace; Lilyan Chauvin; Samantha Huffaker; Matt Emery; Joshua Shelley; Cliff Norton.

I believe that Ray Stark still had Barbra under some sort of contract for x number of movies. I'm not absolutely sure of that because I didn't know all the facts. In any case, this was the last movie that they were going to do together. Ray was very anxious to make the film. She was too young to play the role and not very happy with the prospect of that. I interviewed a young actor by the name of Robert De Niro who was longing to play Billy Rose. I arranged for him to read with her, but Barbra thought he was too young to play the role. She was obsessed about seeming to be too old. I kept saying to her, "Let's do this movie ten years from now. You can do this movie when you're seventy." But I think we all were so committed by that time that we just had to make the picture. We tried very hard and it worked to a degree but it wasn't her best or my best. Jimmy Caan was terrific in the picture and was nominated for his work, you know.

That movie was conceived in a slightly different tradition than one would find today in that in *Funny Lady,* song was an extension of speech. In *Chips* I mistrusted that convention so much that nobody was ever in direct synch. In this movie, because of Barbra's genius as a vocalist, the rules were different. But most of the musical numbers are meant to be a performance. So I would divide them into what was going to be a performance sequence, and then the ones that were going to be in the theater, we'd call them "book song." How to ease from speech into song took a great deal of thinking and ingenuity. In one sequence somebody had given her a new Victrola and she put on what was a record of hers and then sang along with the record and ultimately moved from the duet with her own voice to a full-out musical number. With Barbra the rules are different because of the brilliance of her vocal techniques. It justifies singing without having to explain.

Directing Musicals Is Not for the Weak at Heart

In a musical we rehearse and carefully plan everything. Take a number like "Rain on My Parade." I worked that out in 4-bar and 8-bar cuts and drew a sheeting plot with a sketch artist. I knew exactly that we were going to cut on the second beat of the fifth bar, or whatever, to make the cut. Then I would rehearse it so that I could see Barbra go through the entire sequence with minimal props to know that it was building correctly. Then we shot a lot in continuity. You have to plan way ahead.

In *Funny Lady,* I had this idea about a number called "Great Day" which turned out to be incredibly difficult. It was hard and unrewarding and in the end everyone hated it, including myself. I saw it recently on tape and I thought, "Well, it wasn't that bad, it was okay." It was just a strange idea for Barbra to do this black and white number but it was very period and that was what drew me to it. In the emotional scenes—a lot of singers feel this way—Barbra didn't want to be tied to recorded track. In *Funny Girl,* for example, she sang "My Man" once. We shot that with multiple cameras as she did a real live performance. Then whatever other pickups we had to do we shot to the track. If we didn't do it that way she could never have gotten to that emotional state in a studio, out of context.

Maybe Barbra's Been up in the Plane Too Long

There's a sequence shot from a helicopter where Barbra's little plane goes off and she's trying to connect with Billy Rose. The helicopter and Barbra's plane go off into the clouds and that's the end of the shot and I yell cut. Now I'm waiting for her plane to come back. Half an hour later her plane has still not come back and I think to myself, "Where is she? What has happened to the plane? How do we finish this? Should I call the police? Should I call Ray Stark?" All of a sudden I hear the sound of the engine and the plane comes back and I can hear Barbra screaming "Get me out of this." So the plane comes in and taxis. I wanted another take so I immediately told the cameras to roll before she could get out of the plane. We sent her right back up again and as soon as she heard the musical playback she went right into synch because she's a trooper, she's a pro, and she took off again.

Again, the same thing happened. She's gone for what seemed like an eternity. It was foggy that day and we found out later that she had gotten into a traffic control problem. She was circling Beverly Hills for over half an hour, terrified, in this little open-cockpit plane. When the plane came back the second time she was out of that cockpit before the plane came to a full stop. And quite right she was.

The Seven-Per-Cent Solution (1976)

Alan Arkin; Vanessa Redgrave; Robert Duvall; Nicol Williamson;
Laurence Olivier; Joel Grey; Samantha Eggar; Jeremy Kemp; Régine;
Charles Gray; Georgia Brown; Anna Quayle; Jill Townsend; John Bird; Alison Leggatt.

The Seven-Per-Cent Solution was a very charming book written by Nicholas Meyer. I had an idea about doing the movie so that the movie itself was bookish. I wanted the picture to be mannered so that you were always aware that these were actors playing the roles. I even used credits that said Alan Arkin as Dr. Freud, and Vennessa Redgrave as Lola Deveraux, and so on, just to remind you of the artifice of the piece. It was for that reason that

I wanted to have an all-star cast. We were lucky enough to get all these remarkable people, including the first time that Larry Olivier had worked after his terrible illness. He hadn't worked in two years. So he played the very small part of Professor Moriarty, which gave him an opportunity to test whether or not he could sustain it. I like that picture a lot because of the artifice and because I think we achieved a reality in a very stylized way, which is not so easy to do. Alan Arkin is fabulous in that movie.

Olivier was very insecure. My wife Nora had known him and Vivian in their glory days and I had worked with Vivian on the stage, so I had this kind of offbeat feeling that I knew him. He wasn't difficult, he was just nervous. He was also very concerned about earning income for this family he had started. Later on he stayed with us in our home when he was making *Marathon Man* in Los Angeles.

The Turning Point (1977)

Shirley MacLaine; Anne Bancroft; Mikhail Baryshnikov;
Leslie Browne; Tom Skerritt; Martha Scott; Anthony Zerbe;
Marshall Thompson; Aleksandra Danilova; Antoinette Sibley;
Starr Danias; James Mitchell; Daniel Levans; Scott Douglas; Lisa Lucas.

Nora Kaye was the greatest dancer that America has produced thus far and was an extremely honored artist in her career, which she gave up for our marriage. About a year or two after Baryshnikov had defected, she said she had this feeling that the timing to do something about the ballet was really right now because there's Baryshnikov, he's such a wonderful dancer, etc., etc. We spoke to the writer Arthur Laurents and persuaded him to join us in this endeavor. The picture was set up at Columbia at the time and something occurred, I can't remember what that was, but it was through Sue Mengers that the picture moved over to Alan Ladd Jr. at 20th Century Fox.

Most people thought it was autobiographical, that it was about Nora, but that's not true. It was about a woman that we knew that was distantly related to Nora who had married a dancer in the company and had gone to school in Phoenix, Arizona, and had a number of children. One of those children ultimately played Emilia in the movie, Leslie Browne. The two real dancers that the story was based on were Kelly Browne and his wife Isabelle. So it had nothing to do with Nora because by the time we made the movie we had been very happily married for over fifteen years.

There is an amazing story about this movie. Leslie Browne was not meant to play the role of Emilia. She was meant to be the dance-in because we have to have stand-ins for dancers, as you do for actors, in order to block the variations in the dancing. The girl who was supposed to play the part was extremely difficult and stubborn about turning up and not turning up and being very unpredictable. Finally she turned up with this incredible sunburn and she was peeling and was all swollen and it was impossible to shoot her. She had never attended rehearsals because she was too complicated to attend rehearsals, and I now knew that we could never make the movie with her. So I let her go and Leslie went on that Monday. We were just flying blind. If the dailies were no good the plug would have been pulled on the picture. I had only six million bucks to do that picture with, so every day mattered to me. When I was shooting the ballets and stuff I was shooting forty minutes of cut footage a day. I was shooting with six and seven cameras and I shot every pas de deux in the gala performance in its entirety. We shot some very interesting and beautiful footage on some of the great dances of that time.

We tried to limit how much text Baryshnikov had to speak because his English—he's much better now, of course—but then it was really flawed. As a dancer it was a difficult step for him to make. But I think he did. He was also at the peak of his career as an artist and a dancer so the footage on him was astounding.

Because the production had gone a day over, the studio made us shoot the big fight scene between Shirley and Anne at Century City in California instead of the Lincoln Center in New York. It was late and we were about to start the fight sequence and Shirley suddenly said, "I don't want to hit Anne, she's too small and I'll hurt her." Anne kept saying, "Hit me, hit me, hit me." I had to stop and explain to Shirley that the clock was ticking and the rooster is about to crow and why it was absolutely necessary that she hit Anne. Finally I convinced her. By this time it was four in the morning and the sun was going to begin to shine soon. Suddenly this wind blew up and the cameraman asked me if I still wanted to shoot. And I said, "Oh, absolutely." So we started and skirts and hair was flying. I did one take with two cameras and the actresses themselves—I had nothing to do with it, I wish I had—discovered that great moment when, in the middle of slugging one another, they suddenly wind up spanking each other's behinds and break up and start laughing. They knew they had to get to that but nobody knew how it was going to occur. And that's how it occurred.

The Goodbye Girl (1977)

Richard Dreyfuss; Marsha Mason; Quinn Cummings; Paul Benedict;
Barbara Rhoades; Theresa Merritt; Michael Shawn; Patricia Pearcy;
Gene Castle; Daniel Levans; Marilyn Sokol; Anita Dangler;
Victoria Boothby; Robert Costanzo; Pancho González.

The Goodbye Girl had been started as another movie, which was cancelled for reasons that I never did know about. I was eventually sent the script and I remember telling Neil Simon that I thought perhaps it would be best if he thought about what the two main characters' lives were like in New York instead of when they go to California. He rewrote it completely and it became *The Goodbye Girl*. And that's how that evolved. And it's one of the best screenplays he has ever written. It's a terrific script, just terrific.

Richard Dreyfuss was full of energy and vitality as well as being very concerned with the part. We were shooting in L.A. and he wanted to appear in a play at the same time that we were shooting the movie. It was a production of *The Tenth Man* that was being done on the equivalent of Off-Broadway. I thought that was a great thing for him to do because it was life imitating art. I also knew he had so much energy that unless we channeled it constructively he could also become distracted. So I gave him permission to do that. Everybody came down on my head but I refused to give in. I thought then, and still do, that it was the best thing that he could do for the role, and indeed it was.

California Suite (1978)

Jane Fonda; Alan Alda; Maggie Smith; Michael Caine; Walter Matthau;
Elaine May; Herb Edelman; Denise Galik-Furey; Richard Pryor; Bill Cosby;
Gloria Gifford; Sheila Frazier; David Sheehan; Michael Boyle; Len Lawson.

California Suite was a magical experience. I couldn't wait to get to the sound stage every morning. Yet it was a hard film to make. I would rehearse a week, shoot two weeks, shut down, rehearse a week, shoot two weeks—it was a very long schedule as a result of that. But the material was interesting. I liked the play that Jane Fonda and Alan Alda did a lot. And I loved the Michael Caine, Maggie Smith play. I felt the Walter Matthau play was a really funny one. I was very happy with most of that. The last play I felt was weaker than the other material. It was weak on the stage, too.

When you're working with Neil Simon's material it is hard. It's harder because you have to be so precise and there's very little latitude and you have to get it dead right. There's very little movement in the material for you to improvise or contribute to other than to get it absolutely right. The material falls apart on you unless you're right on the mark. It's like a high-wire act all the time. I found it very exhausting and very demanding and when it worked successfully, very fulfilling. But it's very disciplined. In a funny way, it's not as easy as some other material. I find it's hard to do but very rewarding.

By the time we shot it I also knew exactly where every laugh was going be. It would drive me nuts when I knew the actor wasn't getting there and I knew why. So you have to wait. It's very important to me that the actor feels that he makes that discovery himself because then he owns it, as opposed to listening to the line reading or having something imposed on him.

Nijinsky (1980)

Valerie Aitken; Alan Badel; Alan Bates; Henrietta Baynes; Colin Blakely; June Brown; Leslie Browne; Stephen Chase; Mart Crowley; George De La Pena; Vernon Dobtcheff; Anton Dolin; Carla Fracci; Geoffrey Hughes; Jeremy Irons; Frederick Jaeger; Charles Kay; Ronald Lacey; Olga Lowe; Monica Mason; Dean McMillan; Tomas Milian; Kim Miller; Siân Phillips; Ronald Pickup; Patricia Ruanne; Janet Suzman; Ben Van Cauwenbergh.

Oh, it was a nightmare. It wasn't close to my heart. It was like an O'Henry short story. I thought it was something that Nora wanted to do. Nora thought it was something that I wanted to do. I was never very happy with the script. It was a physically difficult movie to make and extremely hard. Alan Bates was one of the highlights of the picture and a terrific actor, a terrific man, but it was murder to do. We had a lot of physical problems. The set designer that I had hired, who came from the ballet, turned up and couldn't really design sets for us to work in and wasn't familiar with locations. Finally I directed the picture myself. I made errors in how to make the movie because I didn't have sets; I was determined to shoot in all the locations that were necessary. So we shot in Sicily, Monte Carlo, Budapest, and London. It was a lot of moving around, a lot of very tough stuff. It was a very, very difficult movie to make.

Pennies from Heaven (1981)

Steve Martin; Bernadette Peters; Christopher Walken; Jessica Harper; Vernel Bagneris; John McMartin; John Karlen; Jay Garner; Robert Fitch; Tommy Rall; Frank McCarthy; Eliska Krupka; Raleigh Bond; Gloria LeRoy; Nancy Parsons.

Pennies from Heaven was certainly under-appreciated, but then it was very difficult material for a general audience. Of all of my work, I think it's the best. And it's a dazzling, dazzling screenplay by Dennis Potter. I think we did it very well and it's one of those times when everything I had in my mind in terms of art direction and choreography worked out the way I planned. So we all knew we were doing very elevated work and we were dealing with very elevated material. I think Metro thought they were getting a musical because they heard all of these songs that I was going to use and they never stopped to examine the darker aspects of the material. But as far as realizing my own personal dream goes, I think it is the most successful and the most ambitious film I've ever done.

In the case of Steve Martin I can tell you it was not collaboration. Steve entrusted himself to me for seven months to prepare for the movie. He had never danced before so he took tap dance lessons for five months. I coached him for two months prior to the regular eight weeks of rehearsal. What knowledge he had of acting, which is now experience, he had as a result of the work that went on in the preparation of that movie. We then had an eight-week rehearsal period, which is normal for the choreographer to set the numbers and for me to think about how I was going to shoot them. Steve worked hard and I worked hard with him. And I must tell you that cinematographer Gordon Willis' work is also just masterful. I'm very proud to have been part of that.

> *I think Herbert knows more about comedy that just about anybody. He has an ability to find humanity in comedy. You know, he doesn't go for the joke. He goes for the reality of the situation and the humanity. I think he's just brilliant at it.*
>
> *Dinah Manoff—Actress*

I Ought to Be in Pictures (1982)

Ann-Margret; Eugene Butler; Michael Dudikoff; David Faustino;
Martin Ferrero; Lance Guest; Samantha Harper; Dinah Manoff;
Walter Matthau; Santos Morales; Lewis Smith.

Let me say that this picture chose me. It had a history. It was a stage production with Tony Curtis that was playing in Los Angeles, and Dinah Manoff was in that production. Neil was not happy about the way the production was going and let the director go. He asked me to come to see it and to take it over, and as a favor to him I did. Along the way there was a decision made to replace Tony with Ron Leibman. I redirected it for the New York opening with Ron and Dinah, who was terrified at the time of opening on Broadway. She went on to win the Tony Award for that performance.

Then it came back again as a film vehicle for Walter Matthau. I had a strange idea about the movie based on my experience with the play, because I thought essentially it was not comic material. So I directed it in a different way than I had approached the other Neil Simon material. It's bleaker and darker and it's about empty lives. I don't think my experiment was a terribly successful one. But Walter Matthau was very good in it.

Max Dugan Returns (1983)

Kiefer Sutherland; Bill Aylesworth; Matthew Broderick; Dody Goodman;
Mari Gorman; Panchito Gómez; Charley Lau; Marsha Mason; David Morse;
Brian Part; Jason Robards; Donald Sutherland; Sal Viscuso.

I thought the script had a lot of charm. Then I saw a young actor named Matthew Broderick in a play called *Torch Song Trilogy* and I thought he was just the best thing I'd seen in years—since Al Pacino. He came in to read and I thought he was just marvelous, and it turned out that on that day Matthew also got the lead in *Brighton Beach Memoirs*, another play that Neil had written. And we did the movie first. He was very young when we did the film—sixteen or seventeen, I think—and we protected him. We just wanted him to be okay, and he was.

I do seek the truth in my projects. The truth is sometimes very difficult to get to because it's the simplest thing. I have this unfortunate ability to know when an actor is faking or to know when the actor is being dishonest. I can tell when an actor is relying on material or tics that worked for him in other roles that are not germane to the part or the style or the playwright of the project we are doing. That's not always a blessing, because you then have to undo years of comfortable feelings that the actor has been resorting to. I just know when an actor is dishonest. I find that very difficult to witness and I certainly am not going to print any scene that is guilty of that. I'm going to keep going until I can get the truth.

Marsha Mason was wonderful in the movie. I think Marsha is the most marvelous actress with the most wonderful technique. I'm a great fan of hers and I think she's absolutely great. She works really hard, like a theater actress does. I've seen her do a lot of stuff on the stage, very different things, and she has great range. Marsha is first-rate.

Protocol (1984)

Goldie Hawn; Chris Sarandon; Richard Romanus; Andre Gregory; Gail Strickland; Cliff De Young; Keith Szarabajka; Ed Begley Jr.; James Staley; Kenneth Mars; Jean Smart; Maria O'Brien; Joel Brooks; Grainger Hines; Kenneth McMillan.

I had a very strange relationship with Goldie. During the war, women who worked in offices were assigned billets where they would live. My sister was one of them and she stayed at the home of a woman called Laura Hawn. Years later I get a call from my sister saying, "Laura has this daughter whose taking dancing lessons and she's coming to New York and would you see her?" I was doing *On a Clear Day* and Nora was doing the auditions for me. Nora said to me, "There's this adorable girl that came in and she's absolutely the prettiest thing I've even seen but she's not strong on pointe." There was a number on pointe in the show so I never saw her, but that girl was Goldie. And the rest, as you know, was history. So I knew her mother and she knows my sister, who went to her first wedding, as I recall, so we had this funny connection.

It was during the editing of the movie that my wife Nora became ill. So I had to finish that movie knowing that. But I had a good time making it. It was an adventure and I'm crazy about Goldie. I think she's great.

Footloose (1984)

Kevin Bacon; Lori Singer; John Lithgow; Dianne Wiest;
Chris Penn; Sarah Jessica Parker; John Laughlin; Elizabeth Gorcey;
Lee McCain; Jim Youngs; Douglas Dirkson; Lynne Marta;
Arthur Rosenberg; Timothy Scott; Alan Haufrect.

We used to call that film "a closet musical" because musicals were in disgrace at the time and this was clearly musical. So nobody ever called it a musical, but my background in musicals helped me a lot in organizing that material. The interesting thing about that movie is that the tracks that you hear in the movie were never available to me when we were shooting the movie. I sometimes had another song that I related to and choreographed to. *Let's Hear It for the Boy* I shot without any track at all, I just shot it to a click track.* I had storyboarded so I knew the construction, and then the song was written and recorded after we wrapped and edited the movie.

Kevin Bacon moved very well naturally. Lori Singer was trained as a dancer and as a musician and she played the cello. I'm very fond of Laurie and Kevin. And Kevin has a gift of motion and liked to dance socially and was very liberated about it. We not only doubled him in the film, we tripled Kevin. There are three different versions of Kevin in that movie. There's a dancer, a gymnast, and an acrobat.

An actress who joined us later and played a small role in the movie was a very young and enchanting girl and she turned out to be Sarah Jessica Parker, who is a terrific actress and now Matthew's girlfriend, I think. She's a super actress, Sarah Jessica. She couldn't have been more than sixteen or seventeen when she did the picture.

> *I think he's really wonderful with character, and I think he has a wonderful sense of human comedy. He has a sense of irony, a sense of humor that comes out even when things could be dark.*
>
> *Sally Field—Actress*

---

* A cue track—it marks timing points.

Steel Magnolias (1989)

Sally Field; Dolly Parton; Shirley MacLaine; Daryl Hannah; Olympia Dukakis;
Julia Roberts; Tom Skerritt; Sam Shepard; Dylan McDermott; Kevin J. O'Connor;
Bill McCutcheon; Ann Wedgeworth; Jonathan Ward; Bibi Besch; Janine Turner.

My wife Nora had died and Ray Stark called me and said, "You've been out of work long enough." I hadn't worked in a year and I was just beginning to come around. Ray asked me to go see a play and tell him if I thought there was a movie in it. I went to the theater and saw the play and I thought it would make a terrific movie. The author, Bob Harling, and I set to work on adapting the play into a screenplay.

It was Ray's idea to cast it all-star. There were three girls up for the role that Julia Roberts ultimately played. One of them was Wynona Ryder, who was too young, and another was Meg Ryan, who turned us down to do *When Harry Met Sally*. The third one was Julia Roberts, which is how she got the role. Most everybody connected with the project was not in favor of Julia. She had done a picture for Ray called *Baja California* that he made me see because he thought she was so bad in the picture and didn't look all that good. So we took enormous pains with Julia so that this wouldn't happen again and also to protect her in the course of making the movie.

I should say something about Sally Field's technique. She has the most amazing technical facility of any actress that I've ever worked with, and her ability to produce a performance precisely the same way every time is extremely impressive.

The women got along marvelously well with each other. I think that Sally set the tone. I endeavor to treat everybody the same. I thought it was very important that anything I had to say, I said in front of everybody. I never had a private discussion with an actress on that movie, because I didn't wish to set up any special relationships. We even went so far as to change the positions of the trailers that the girls were in so that nobody's trailer was first or second. It changed every single day.

The hardest thing with an ensemble cast is to find a communal acting style that serves the movie because different movies demand different approaches. It was very important to establish a personal friendship between the actresses because that's what they were acting out on the screen. We had to find the common naturalistic acting style to play it in so that nobody violated the texture or the tone of the piece. It always helps when a script is good and this script was.

True Colors (1991)

*John Cusack; James Spader; Imogen Stubbs; Mandy Patinkin;
Richard Widmark; Dina Merrill; Philip Bosco; Paul Guilfoyle; Brad Sullivan;
Russell Dennis Baker; Don McManus; Karen Jablons-Alexander;
Wendee Pratt; Rende Rae Norman; Frank Hoyt Taylor.*

True Colors is a script that I liked. Kevin Wade wrote a very good script. It never went the distance but I liked what it was about and I liked the actors. I thought they were good and I worked very hard on that movie even though I considered it flawed. I don't think the studio was behind it either. The regime that had wanted to do the movie in the first place had left. I never believed that kind of thing was done until it happened to me.

Sometimes there isn't a correlation between the critical reception and the public's reception of a film, so it's very nice when the movie does well in terms of the public because it makes it easier for you to do your next work. Usually the conditions you make it under are more favorable and the chances are that the material that you're being offered or will get a chance to look at is superior to the material that you would get when you are less desirable from an employer's point of view. On the other hand, there are movies like *Pennies from Heaven*. That was a commercial failure that I regard very highly and that I would do again if I had the opportunity. So it's different for each movie.

Undercover Blues (1993)

*Kathleen Turner; Dennis Quaid; Fiona Shaw; Stanley Tucci; Larry Miller;
Obba Babatundé; Tom Arnold; Park Overall; Ralph Brown; Jan Tríska;
Marshall Bell; Richard Jenkins; Dennis Lipscomb; Saul Rubinek; Dakin Matthews.*

Kathleen Turner was attached to the project; Mike Lobell, who was producing, submitted it to me. I had this feeling that Dennis Quaid was really the appropriate casting for the part of Jeff Blue, so when he agreed to do the movie I was very happy about that. He and Kathleen got along very well. They're very separate, very private, very different people but we had a very good time making that movie and I think very highly of both of those actors. I also had a special relationship on that picture with two other actors. Stanley Tucci, who played the part of Muerte, and Fiona Shaw, who played Novacek, the heavy.

I thought I did a really good job on what I knew to be not first-rate material. The movie interested me because I got to do stuff I didn't normally get to do—action stuff, fight sequences—all of which I found interesting and challenging to do. Everybody always wants to do *The Thin Man* and can never do it. But we tried.

His Casting Process

I read as many people as I possibly can. Sometimes an actor gives you an insight into the role and helps you understand things about the character that you might not have thought of by yourself. It always needs another intelligence. Sometimes I have a very special view of who I think is appropriate for the role. Yet sometimes in reading other actors they bring an insight to the part that is so devastatingly original that you can't conceive of making the movie without them. I'm very, very painstaking and meticulous about casting and I think that it's vital to the success of the movie. If you make an error of judgment it can be very damaging to the success of the picture.

A movie takes on its own life. A lot of people work on a picture and everybody affects the course and the destiny of it. Everybody has some input and all that input, however unconscious, affects the making of the movie. An actor's personality or an actor's needs affect how the picture goes. Wasn't it François Truffaut who said that every movie starts with the highest hopes but about halfway through all that is really important is completing the picture? A strong actor, for example, can influence the way you conceived the picture. He or she can take it to some other place and you have to go with it because the actor's vision may be better than what you originally thought of. But sometimes there's a conflict because you don't think that the actor's contribution is taking it to the right place, and then your job is to try to get the actor back on course.

Boys on the Side (1995)

Whoopi Goldberg; Mary-Louise Parker; Drew Barrymore; Matthew McConaughey; James Remar; Billy Wirth; Anita Gillette; Dennis Boutsikaris; Estelle Parsons; Amy Aquino; Stan Egi; Stephen Gevedon; Amy Ray; Emily Saliers; Jude Ciccolella.

What drew me to the project was the writing. I thought it was the first time I had read a script in which people spoke the way my ear heard people speak in 1995. The way they expressed themselves and forgot what they were expressing themselves about was extremely contemporary and I was interested in that. I also thought the subject it dealt with—the lack of options that people have at that age—was interesting. Also the nature of the sexual experience has changed for everybody since the advent of AIDS and sex is not liberating or easy anymore.

It was the happiest experience I've ever had making a movie. In fact it was so happy that Whoopi, Mary-Louise, Drew, and myself were so sorry it was coming to an end that we kind of slowed down in order to eke out another two or three days of shooting. All of us respected the material. All of us respected each other. All of us were very centered and very grounded in the work we were doing. All of us felt we were doing good work on a worthy project. That doesn't always happen.

Since *Boys on the Side* I must have read at least eighty to a hundred scripts. Good ones are very tough to find. There's an awful lot of dumb material out there and there's an awful lot of material that's just chasing other material. A genre that just succeeded always spawns ten new screenplays that are similar. But then every once in a while you do read something of quality and of interest.

The Changes in the Industry

I came into the industry at a time of great change. I came in at the beginning of what was the youth revolution and the change in music, when language freed itself and the biggest laugh I've ever heard in the theater was Barbra Streisand saying, "Fuck off." And the cost of films, as I've pointed out, was relatively inexpensive when I started. We were able to shoot *Play It Again, Sam* for one million six. You can't make a studio picture now for probably less than $20 to $25 million with a cast of any quality or recognition. So all that's changed. The stakes are high but also the winnings are much higher should you win. Take a picture like *Forrest Gump,* for example.

There's very little history left in film. The executives aren't connected to the past. It is all about change. And then the outlets for a movie are so different. The life of a film goes on and on as it never did before, with cassettes and television. I was in Ireland in a hotel once and there, on closed-circuit television, were five of my movies playing. It was just an accident but it was amazing to me. And now that film will be transferred to laser disc and DVDs and there's yet another outlet. And then there is this voracious appetite that cable has. The mystery and the magic and the glamour of film still exists and still draws people to it. I think that what hasn't changed is the need in people for a communal experience in which you do go to the movie theater and share the movie with all those other people sitting there. I sound like Gloria Swanson—there in the dark, laughing together, crying together, and hissing the villain—which hasn't changed.

What Does the Future Hold for Herbert Ross?

Well, I'm not a fortune-teller so I couldn't possibly know what the future holds for me, but I hope it continues to hold making more films and better films. Making films that will enlighten and enrich the audience's life, and not exploit it and not exploiting people to make them. And I would like to help young directors and be able to move into a period where I would be producing films for people that I thought were gifted.

Other than that I have no parting words. It's just a tough life, you know, and a fascinating one, and I'm very lucky to have had it.

Filmography

Goodbye, Mr. Chips (1969)
The Owl and the Pussycat (1970)
T.R. Baskin (1971)
Play It Again, Sam (1972)
The Last of Sheila (1973)
The Sunshine Boys (1975)
Funny Lady (1975)
The Seven-Per-Cent Solution (1976)
The Turning Point (1977)
The Goodbye Girl (1977)
California Suite (1978)
Nijinsky (1980)
Pennies from Heaven (1981)
I Ought to Be in Pictures (1982)
Max Dugan Returns (1983)

Protocol (1984)
Footloose (1984)
Dancers (1987)
The Secret of My Success (1987)
Steel Magnolias (1989)
My Blue Heaven (1990)
True Colors (1991)
Undercover Blues (1993)
Boys on the Side (1995)

Awards

Academy Awards, USA
The Turning Point, Best Director (nominated), 1978
The Turning Point, Best Picture (nominated, shared with Arthur
  Laurents), 1978

Golden Globes, USA
The Turning Point, Best Director—Motion Picture, 1978

Los Angeles Film Critics Association Awards
The Turning Point, Best Director, 1977

The Films of William Friedkin

William Friedkin was born August 29, 1935, in Chicago, Illinois. At an early age he became infatuated with Orson Welles after seeing Welles' classic film *Citizen Kane,* an achievement, Friedkin insists, that has motivated his entire film directing career.

But it was documentaries, first in Chicago, then in Los Angeles, that got his career off the ground. He went to work for WGN TV in Chicago immediately after graduating from high school. It was at WGN that he began making documentaries, one of which won the Golden Gate Award at the 1962 San Francisco Film Festival.

Friedkin's career has taken twists and turns in his never-ending quest to make the one film that he feels comes close to *Citizen Kane.* Some would argue that he came very close with *The French Connection, The Exorcist,* and *Sorcerer,* even though *Sorcerer* proved to be a box office failure.

No one will argue with the fact that Friedkin is an extraordinary filmmaker who strives for the unusual and the challenging. Readers will find his interview laced with wonderful and insightful information about the process of filmmaking.

> *Billy delves into areas not too many filmmakers are pleased or even comfortable about dealing with, whether it's a film like* Cruising *or whether it is* Sorcerer. *He's an intimidating fellow. He has a mercurial charm and a mercurial dangerousness and a mercurial sense of humor about him. But under the right circumstances it can be endearing, very, very powerful in a sense of what you will learn as an actor.*
>
> *Allen Garfield—Actor*

The Conversation

When I was growing up in Chicago I had no particular interest in film. I mean, I used to go to the movies like other kids, I'd go see movies that largely consisted of *Hopalong Cassidy* westerns and *Dick Tracy* and *The Phantom* and serials. Through all my formative years, I'd say, I just was entertained by films. I never had any idea that I would ever be making them. I originally was hoping that I would one day become a professional basketball player, so I worked very hard at trying to play basketball and perfect my skills at that.

When I was about seventeen or eighteen years old, I was working in the mailroom at this television station in Chicago right out of high school. I had no college education at all. One day I went to see a film called *Citizen Kane*. I had no idea what it was but somebody at the TV station said, "There's a really great movie playing over here at the Surf Theater," on the near north side in Chicago. I went to see it on a Saturday afternoon and I stayed in the theater from noon until about ten at night when they ran the last show. I was completely mesmerized by that film. It just worked on all of my senses, because the film itself is like a quarry for filmmakers in the same way that James Joyce's *Ulysses* is a quarry for writers. When I came out of the theater, I was dazzled, I was in another world, I was transported, and I had never had an experience like that in any of the other movies that I had seen.

A day or so later the idea formed in my mind that that's what I wanted to do. Whatever it took to do something like that and to organize the incredible talents of actors, musicians, writers, photographers, lighting people, sound people, and synthesize them into such an incredible overpowering work of art is what I felt I would like to aspire to. I have by no means made a film that even came near that and that's what keeps me working at it. I've seen that film now maybe two hundred times. It's the only education I ever had in filmmaking. I never had a lesson in either acting or the camera or any of the techniques; I just sort of picked it up by osmosis.

All I was interested in doing in high school was playing basketball and goofing off. I wasn't tall enough to play college ball. So I didn't know what

I was gonna do. Quite by accident, I saw an ad in the newspaper that said, "Opportunities for young men to succeed in television," which was a brand new field. You could start small in the mailroom and then work your way up and learn as you went. So I applied for this job in the mailroom and got it. In 1955 very few people knew anything about television. It was live television and it was a brand new medium and there were virtually no taped programs. There were films being made for television but most television around the United States was done live.

I was in the mailroom for about six months and after working all day the directors and the technicians allowed me to stand in the back of the control room and just observe. I watched how they put together a television show and I started to take notes. I learned that when a director gave a certain command, certain things happened. I learned that a large part of how these directors were able to get what they wanted came from the way they interrelated with people. So I took notes and I wrote things down and I learned. I got an education on how to do live television.

After about six months in the mailroom I was promoted to floor manager, which is like an assistant director in films. The floor manager was actually on the floor while the director worked in the control room and issued his instructions through headphones to the floor manager, who then tells the talent what the director wants done. I did that for about six months and then I became a live television director before I was eighteen years old. And that was a very common story. I mean, you'll hear that from people like John Frankenheimer and Sidney Lumet—they started working as ushers or whatever and within a year, they're directing live television.

I directed about two thousand television programs over a period of eight years, everything from news programs to kids' shows to dramatic specials to baseball games, and finally the Chicago Symphony Orchestra. I did a couple of kids' shows every day, *Lunchtime Little Theater* and *Garfield Goose* and *Bozo Circus,* and then at night I would do the Chicago Symphony Orchestra broadcast. You really had to have a knack for spontaneity to work in live television. There were no second takes. You had to get what you wanted and be very clear in your instructions to people from the get go.

A Documentary Brings Him Attention

In about the seventh year I came across a story about a young black man who was on death row in the Cook County Jail in Chicago. Something about this man's story intrigued me. He was literally gonna be executed in a matter of months. I arranged to meet him through the Warden of the Cook County Jail. This black man's name was Paul Crump and he had been on death row for about eight or nine years. After meeting him I felt that Paul had been railroaded, that he was an innocent man who had been falsely convicted of murder. So I got this idea to make a film about how he was tried and convicted and how the Chicago police beat a confession out of him, which was commonplace in those days. I was given permission by the warden of the Cook County Jail and by Paul Crump and his lawyer to make a film that became a kind of court of last resort for Paul.

Bill Butler was a cameraman at WGN in Chicago back then. Bill has since become one of the best cinematographers in Hollywood. He did *Jaws, One Flew Over the Cuckoo's Nest,* and *Grease.* Bill was a live television cameraman when I was working live and the two of us wanted to make a movie. So Bill and I had been talking after work about making films and then this story comes up. I went to the television station I worked for and they said, "No, we don't want to make a documentary film." But there was another station in town that wanted to hire me. So I went to Red Quinlan, who ran this other station, and I told him that if he would finance this documentary I would go to work for his station. He put up the money for *The People vs. Paul Crump.*

Bill Butler and I went to an equipment rental house in Chicago and we talked to the owner named Jack Barron and said, "Look, if you show us how to use a camera and get synch sound in this camera, we'll rent your equipment 'cause we're gonna make a film." He gave us a lesson in how to load and focus and shoot with an Arriflex 16 mm camera and how to use a Nagra tape recorder.

So Bill and I, along with two other guys, went into the Cook County Jail for six months and we made a film about Paul Crump. It won the Golden Gate Award at the San Francisco Film Festival and also a number of other international awards. The film wound up saving Paul Crump's life. It was shown to the then Governor of Illinois, who pardoned Paul Crump based on the facts in the film, even though his parole and pardon board voted 2 to 1 not to spare Crump's life.

That film brought me to the attention of David Wolper, who was making documentaries at that time. Wolper invited me to come to work for his company in Hollywood. I left Chicago and went to work for him for about a year and a half. I made three documentaries, all of which ran on the ABC network in prime time. This was like the early sixties, and Sonny

Bono of *Sonny and Cher* saw one of the documentaries. He had an opportunity to make a feature film with Cher, but he wanted to get a young director to do it. He wanted someone that he felt compatible with who was of the same generation.

Good Times (1967)

Sonny Bono; Cher; George Sanders; Norman Alden; Larry Duran; Kelly Thordsen;
Lennie Weinrib; Peter Robbins; Edy Williams; China Lee; Diane Haggerty;
James Flavin; Phil Arnold; Hank Worden; Morris Buchanan.

Now, I must say, at the time I didn't know Sonny and Cher's music from Adam, you know, and when I later heard it I didn't think it was that great. I've since come to appreciate it. I met with Sonny and we were very compatible and so he said to his producer, Steve Broidy, "This is the guy I want to direct my feature film." It was called *Good Times*. I brought Bill Butler out from Chicago to shoot it and we literally were making it like guerilla filmmaking. We had no permission. We'd sneak on the Paramount lot where they had the *Bonanza* Western street. We drove in with Sonny and Cher on a Saturday when they weren't filming. We waved at the guard at the gate and said, "Hi, Sonny and Cher," and the guard said, "Oh, go right ahead." We'd get out and start shooting on the Western street. We went to the music center and shot a big production number with Sonny and Cher. With no permission, no clearances, no police protection. We just started making this film and we had no script. We went with whatever ideas we had. Sonny would get an idea, I'd get an idea, and we'd film it and figure out how to put it together later. And that was my first feature.

Sonny was a genius. He couldn't read a note of music, but he'd hear music in his head. He'd get an arranger and say, "I hear this trumpet and it's going like this—bump bump bump bumpa-bump bump," and then he'd say, "and I hear violins going—da da da da da da da da da da da da da da," and he said, "Maybe the drums can go chee cun chee cun chee cun cun chee cun cun chee cun," and he'd literally talk out the parts while the arranger wrote them down. He'd go into a studio without a conductor and he'd say, "Okay, one, two, three—hit it!"

He'd write down the lyrics and then he would call Cher and they'd send a car to pick her up and drive her to the studio and they'd go in and record the track, make three or four takes, then he'd send her home and he'd mix it. He wrote eight or nine songs like that and I'd listen to him recording them and I'd give him ideas for filming sequences. We would then go out and basically film my impressions of his songs. We even had George Sanders acting in the film, along with a few other good actors, but we basically improvised the whole picture.

A Meeting with Hitchcock

My first day on a real set was on the *Alfred Hitchcock Hour.* I had done one of the last of the *Hitchcock* shows before I did the Sonny and Cher feature. Norman Lloyd, who was the producer, had seen my documentary about Paul Crump. He said that there was more suspense in the first five minutes of that than in anything the *Hitchcock Hour* had done that season, so he hired me.

Norman Lloyd advised me that on the first day I should set up the easiest shot I could make, do it in one take and move on. That, he said, would let everyone know I had confidence in myself and in turn they would have confidence in me. My reaction has always been to pay no attention whatsoever to anyone's advice. That's been like a knee-jerk reaction of mine. So I set up a shot that was like a four- or five-page master that involved people walking all over one set and going into another set with the camera following the actors.

I was working with a great cinematographer named John F. Warren, who had won an Academy Award for *The Country Girl* with Grace Kelly. Jack was very nervous about doing the shot because they hadn't done shots like that on this show. But we went ahead and it took me about four or five hours to get several takes. By then all the black suits from Universal started hovering like alien spacemen around the fringe of the stage to see what the hell was going wrong. Finally we got the shot and the rumor was that I was gonna be fired, that I'd never get past a day. But then the next day I was setting up another shot and Norman Lloyd came up behind me and I heard him whisper to Jack Warren that the shot was incredible. "It took forever," he told Jack, "but it was really wonderful." And I heard Jack Warren, who was a wonderful man, whisper to Lloyd that the shot was his idea. Well, right then and there I learned my first Hollywood lesson—success has many fathers, but failure is an orphan. Because that shot turned out to be a success a lot of people were willing to take credit for it.

Hitchcock actually came to the set. At that time Norman Lloyd was really producing the series and Mr. Hitchcock just read his introduction to the various segments. Norman brought Hitchcock over to meet with me and I was really shook up because, of course, Hitchcock was the master. I stuck out my hand and Hitchcock took it very limply and I said, "Oh, Mr. Hitchcock, it's really a pleasure to meet with you." And he said, "Mr. Friedkin, usually our directors wear ties." And I looked at him, I thought he was kidding me, but he wasn't, and then he turned and walked away and that's all he said to me.

Years later at the Director's Guild awards show I won the Director's Guild Award for *The French Connection* and I was wearing a tuxedo. I saw Hitchcock at a table in the audience and I walked by him with my Director's Guild award and I sort of snapped my tie at him and I said "How do you like the tie, Hitch?" He didn't remember, of course, but it gave me a great deal of satisfaction.

After *Good Times* came out I felt that I had no future in the industry. I mean, the film was terrible. It was really inept. But surprisingly it got very good reviews. A number of people in the film industry saw it, including Norman Lear and Bud Yorkin, who hired me to do my next feature, *The Night They Raided Minsky's*. This was as a result of having seen *Good Times*, which, I'm telling you, is not viewable.

The Night They Raided Minsky's (1968)

Jason Robards; Britt Ekland; Norman Wisdom; Forrest Tucker;
Harry Andrews; Joseph Wiseman; Denholm Elliott;
Elliott Gould; Jack Burns; Bert Lahr; Gloria LeRoy.

The Night They Raided Minsky's came to me because Bud Yorkin and Norman Lear saw something in *Good Times* that they thought was filled with a youthful abandon or whatever. Yorkin was originally going to direct but went off instead to direct another picture for their company. Norman Lear stayed and produced it and I guess they thought I could bring something original to this story about burlesque in the 1920s. Well, let me tell you, I had a rough time doing that one. It was a struggle. I really didn't know enough to direct a feature film at that time. I was struggling through it and I wasn't getting a lot of help, either. I was pretty much cast adrift. Although Norman Lear is a brilliant producer and writer and he did what he could to shape me up, the film has a great many flaws. I, personally, can't watch it today. It's wonderful for some of the performances and some of Norman's writing and concept, but the direction is not very good.

I never thought that the film would be successful. I had a lot of trouble cutting it together in the editing room. Believe me, a lot of things were invented in the cutting room just to cover my shooting mistakes. Burt Lahr, who was one of the great American comics of all time, had a very big role in the film. But Burt died before he could even complete half of his part. So we then had to rewrite the story and shoot around Burt. When it came out I thought once again that I had no future as a feature director. I thought I'd never get to direct another film.

The Birthday Party (1968)
Robert Shaw; Patrick Magee; Dandy Nichols;
Sidney Tafler; Moultrie Kelsall; Helen Fraser.

The next film I did was *The Birthday Party,* from a play by Harold Pinter, and that's something I really wanted to do. I saw an Actors Workshop production of Pinter's play. I asked him if I could do it as a film and after several meetings he agreed. I got on a plane to London and I cast the late Robert Shaw and Patrick Magee and a wonderful actor named Sidney Tafler. It was a great experience working with Robert Shaw and Patrick Magee and Harold Pinter. I probably learned more from that experience than anything I've ever done. I learned about how the mind of this great writer works, and he taught me a lot just by his friendship and by osmosis. We made a film that got some very good reviews, but, again, was almost sunk without a trace. It had a very limited release and is not widely seen today.

The Boys in the Band (1970)
Frederick Combs; Leonard Frey; Cliff Gorman; Reuben Greene;
Robert La Tourneaux; Laurence Luckinbill; Kenneth Nelson;
Keith Prentice; Peter White; Murry Melvin.

Mart Crowley, who wrote the play *The Boys in the Band,* had seen both *The Night They Raided Minsky's* and *The Birthday Party,* that was a film of a play.

His play was a great success Off Broadway, and he was looking for a young director to do the film. He liked *The Night They Raided Minsky's* and *The Birthday Party*.

I never thought of it as gay-oriented subject matter. It is, of course, but I saw it first and foremost as a wonderfully crafted love story with comedy. I gladly agreed to do the film with the original stage cast. We shot it all on one set in a very short period of time. We had to rethink the entire production for the screen, which was interesting because all of the actors who had performed on stage had to approach the film as though it was a brand new work and to scale it accordingly.

There was no resistance to the making of the film. After it had come out, to my great surprise, there were a handful of protests from members of the gay community who thought it was stereotyping gay people, and I never thought that it was and I was dumbfounded at that response. I can understand now what they were referring to, although it was never Mart Crowley's intention to stereotype people. He wrote from his own experience about people that he knew. If they happened to be stereotyped, well, that was too bad, and I thought of him as a really interesting and unique individual. But the film became controversial for a number of reasons. It was the first mainstream film that purported to be about gay life in America.

I remember that we had this one scene where one male actor had to kiss another actor on the lips. I remember weeks of meetings trying to figure out a way to do this and to mollify those two actors so that they both felt that their careers weren't going to end with that kiss. They were so nervous by the time they got to do it that it wasn't very good and we had to ultimately cut it from the film. Mart Crowley was there all the time and we wound up inventing a lot of moments for the film that weren't originally in the play.

I must say, though, that I would not advise anyone to film a play. At best, it's the film of a play. It's not a film. As much as you try to disguise the origins, they seem to want to come out and announce themselves to the world. Crowley's play is great and I think with a good cast it plays better on the stage than it does on film, although I think the film has some very powerful moments.

> *Nobody ever does a car chase like Billy. Billy was the first one to use the car chase in the movie* The French Connection.
>
> *Chazz Palminteri—Actor*

The French Connection (1971)

Gene Hackman; Fernando Rey; Roy Scheider; Tony Lo Bianco; Marcel Bozzuffi;
Frédéric de Pasquale; Bill Hickman; Ann Rebbot; Harold Gary; Arlene Farber;
Eddie Egan; André Ernotte; Sonny Grosso; Benny Marino; Pat McDermott.

Phil D'Antoni, a producer friend of mine, and I wanted to do a film to-gether. Phil came up with *The French Connection,* the story of two New York cops who are involved in busting a big heroin ring in the late six-ties. He brought me a book about the case involving the two cops—Eddie Egan and Sonny Grosso—a kind of a poetic combination of names. I went to New York and I met with Egan and Grosso and I knew there was a film there.

We had several screenplays written but none of them worked. For about a year or so we couldn't get anyone to make it. Can you believe no studio wanted to make *The French Connection*? By that time I was considered an American art house film director because of *Boys in the Band* and *The Birth-day Party.* On top of that we had no stars and we weren't gonna get any stars for that picture and no studio wanted to make it. It was turned down by every studio, some of them twice.

Finally Dick Zanuck at 20th Century Fox called us in and said, "I don't know what the hell this script is but I got a feeling it could be something." He said, "I've got a million and a half dollars hidden away in a drawer over here. If you guys can make this film for a million and a half dollars, go ahead and make it." At that time the film had a budget of about three million dollars because we were hoping to get Paul Newman and some big names in it. Zanuck said we didn't need any big names. He said, "Go out and make it with good actors and make it for a million and a half dollars."

I went home that night and I talked to Phil. I said, "Phil, we can't make this film for a million and a half dollars." And Phil said, "We have to tell him that we can." I said, "You mean lie?" He said, "I wouldn't use that strong a word, but yeah, we gotta tell him we can make it for a million and a half dollars." I said, "I'm not gonna lie to these people, it's wrong." And Phil said, "Look, you won't have to tell him anything, I'll take care of that. Let's just go make the picture." So we said, yeah, we can make it for a mil-lion and a half dollars.

I knew this guy who was a very popular newspaper writer in New York by the name of Jimmy Breslin. He was like a heavyset black Irishman, and he had this wonderful two-fisted drinking way about him. I liked Jimmy and I was fascinated by him. I said to Dick Zanuck, "What about Jimmy Breslin? You said you don't want any name actors in the picture, what about Jimmy Breslin because he's like an Irish cop?" And Zanuck said, "That's a great idea, go ahead, do it." So I go back to New York and I start rehearsing Jimmy Breslin in this role to play Jimmy "Popeye" Doyle in *The French Connection*. By that time I had cast Roy Scheider in the part of Buddy Russo, so I got Scheider and Breslin improvising for three weeks. We would go through various aspects of the story and try to improvise dialogue, and on Monday Breslin would be brilliant and terrific. On Tuesday, he'd forget what he did on Monday. On Wednesday, he couldn't even remember what he was doing there. Come Thursday he might be drunk or not show up at all on Friday.

This went on for three weeks and finally Jimmy said to me, "This ain't goin' too well, is it?" And I said, "Well, not really." And he said, "I gotta tell you something, kid. You say there's a car chase in this picture?" I said, "Yeah." And he said, "I promised my mother on her deathbed that I would never drive a car so I never learned to drive a car." That was it for me. I went back to Zanuck and I said, "It isn't gonna work with Breslin." He said, "All right, go to your next choice," but we didn't have a next choice. I offered the part to Peter Boyle, who had just made a film called *Joe*. He turned it down. He said he only wanted to do romantic leads.

Finally someone suggested Gene Hackman. He had never had a starring role in a picture but he was a terrific actor with a great reputation. He was best known for playing Warren Beatty's brother in *Bonnie and Clyde*. Phil D'Antoni came to me and said, "If we don't do it with Gene, we're not gonna have a picture, it's all gonna go away." And so I spent a weekend and thought it over and decided to go with Gene, partly by default. Almost every other actor that got in that picture, including Fernando Rey, got into the film by default or by mistake.

Another Casting Snafu

I said to the casting director at one point, "There's this wonderful actor in the French film *Belle de jour,* the guy who's like the Corsican guy. Find out who that guy is and let's get him to play the Frenchman." The casting director comes back and tells me that the actor's name is Fernando Rey. I said great, hire him to play Charnier. About a week before shooting begins Fernando Rey comes to America and I go to the airport to pick him up but I can't find him. Finally I get paged and I go up to this desk and it was Fernando Rey. But it wasn't the actor that I had in mind from *Belle de jour.* Fernando Rey has got a little goatee and he's very sophisticated, and that wasn't at all what I had in mind for *The French Connection.* Now I'm driving back to the hotel with him and he says, "By the way, you know I'm Spanish, not French. I don't speak French very well." And of course the guy's supposed to be French!

I get Fernando to his hotel and I immediately go to the hotel phone and call the producer, Phil D'Antoni, and the casting director and I said, "You guys are crazy, you've got the wrong actor—you brought the wrong actor in here." They said, "What are you talking about?" I said, "Who the hell is this guy? That's not the guy from *Belle de jour.*" So they do some research on the subject and they learn that yes, the guy from *Belle de jour's* name was Francisco Rabal, not Fernando Rey. It turns out that Francisco Rabal was also not French, he was Spanish too. *Belle de jour* was shot in France so I assumed it was a French picture. Francisco Rabal is the actor I'm looking for.

I said, "Okay, we're gonna fire Fernando Rey and let's get Rabal." So they immediately make inquiries and they find out that one, Francisco Rabal was unavailable; two, he didn't speak a word of English; and three, he didn't speak French very well either. So now I've got to make the film with Gene Hackman, who I didn't want, and Fernando Rey, who I had never heard of. But the god of movies really smiled on that picture because those two actors turned out to be absolutely brilliant and memorable.

I didn't set out to make a documentary, but having made documentary films I wanted to make *The French Connection* with documentary techniques—handheld cameras. You come into a scene like you don't know where the action's gonna happen and you have to find it, as you do with a documentary. I would literally stage a scene with the actors and not tell the camera operator where the actors were going. Nothing was really staged and nothing was planned. And that became the technique for the film, what we call a kind of grab-ass technique or improvisational technique that I learned from doing documentaries. And that became the style of *The French Connection.* I also sent Gene Hackman and Roy Scheider out to hang around with their counterparts, Egan and Grosso, so they'd come back with stories and dialogue that they could improvise right into the picture.

The Now Famous Chase Sequence

Everyone asks me about the chase in *The French Connection*. The first script we did, the one we sold the idea with, didn't have a real chase in it. I think we had a line in the script that said, "The chase begins here," like, "World War III breaks out," and then it's up to the director to figure out what that means. Phil D'Antoni and I had put off dealing with this chase as long as we could because we couldn't figure out what the hell to do with it. Phil had produced the movie *Bullitt* and had been involved with one of the great chases in modern film history. I told Phil I wanted to top that but we didn't really know how.

One day Phil and I left my rented apartment on Park Avenue and 86th Street in New York and started walking south on Park Avenue and kept walking until we had an idea for this chase scene. I remember that we walked for fifty-five blocks just talking and saying, "What if this happened, what if that happened, and then what if this?" And I'm walking and I hear the subway rumbling underneath me and I said to Phil, "Let's not have two cars chasing each other, let's have a car chasing a subway train." He said, "Well, how do we get a guy on a train?" "I don't know, but what about the idea of a car chasing a train?" "Well, how fast does a train go? If these trains can go two hundred miles per hour or something, then this could never happen." We had to go find out how fast the train could really go. It turned out that an elevated subway train could go at a top speed of fifty miles per hour, so that made it possible.

The New York Transit Company denied us permission. But while all this was going on, I was working out a sequence of how I could get one guy onto a train and the other guy into a car. And to make it more difficult I would let the guy get into a car that wasn't his own. He'd have to commandeer a car, just as the other guy had commandeered a train. So now these ideas start formulating and finally we convinced the Transit Authority to let us do this but they had no idea what they were getting into. Then it came down to how to do it. I never storyboarded; I never drew one picture of anything. I simply went out to the location and I improvised from shot to shot what would happened next and always thinking in terms of how I could violently invade each frame. How I could have violent action going through each frame and have the screen interrupted in various points both with light and shadow and with movement.

It occurred to me that the best chases I'd ever seen on film didn't involve bystanders. The one thing I could do that was different was to involve innocent bystanders. If you look at the chase in *Bullitt,* you'll see that these two cars whip through the streets of San Francisco and there's nobody in their way—very few other vehicles, none in danger, and no pedestrians. So I said, "Let's set this chase right in the heart of Manhattan, right in the heart of a busy community, and the car can endanger human life and the train has innocent passengers on board and their lives are in danger." What you're trying to do is so deeply immerse an audience into a sequence like that that they suspend disbelief. The way to do that is by constantly challenging the frame line and by having cuts that come at you and various incidents happening.

The key is various incidents, not just speed. A guy's going fast, there's a woman in his way pushing a baby cart, or the train's going fast and guess what? The conductor's having a heart attack, so there's various incidents happening all the time that are occupying the audience's attention, whereas if they were just watching a car go fast or a train go fast, they're gonna get bored after a while.

You have to remember that a chase, like every other scene in a movie, is made one shot at a time. No one shot at any point is really dangerous. It looks dangerous in the juxtaposition of those shots, but each shot is made with a lot of control and then you cut and you do another shot. And it's the putting together of one to another, the editing and the montage, that makes it look dangerous and difficult. So I approached it one shot at a time and I would let each incident grow out of the one before.

For example, there's a sequence in the chase where Hackman's car is going through an intersection and he's supposed to narrowly miss another car that's going in the opposite direction. What happened was an accident occurred. The stunt driver accidentally nicked the other car and then spun off of it, causing damage to Hackman's car that wasn't planned. I saw it and I said, "Hey, that's good. Let's keep it. Let's not do it again and do a near miss as we planned. Let's keep that accident because it looks so real." Several such accidents developed in the course of shooting the chase. The cars collided so many times that it was impossible for Hackman's car to continue. So I would simply use one little section of each shot where an accident occurred, go back in and repair the cars, put back the hubcaps or the fenders that came off, bend some steel back, and go again as though nothing had happened. We took advantage of the real accidents that occurred.

The most dangerous-looking sequence of the chase is where Hackman's car narrowly misses a woman pushing a baby carriage. That was the easiest sequence to shoot but it looks like the most dangerous. It's where most people go like this [covers his eyes] and yet it was shot simply. Gene Hackman was in a stationary car at that point. I had the cameras zoom in on Gene as though Gene was moving very fast. The illusion of a camera zooming to a person looks like the person is moving toward the camera. Then I turned around and made a shot of the woman crossing the street with a baby carriage and at a certain point she was to turn and look at the camera and scream and at that point her camera would zoom in to her. So in neither case was any vehicle or person in danger. In each case it was a zoom to Hackman, his reaction, followed by the woman walking, she hit a mark on the street, turns, we zoom in to her face, she screams, and the two shots together combined with the sound make it an effective near-miss.

There are any number of sequences that are done with movie magic. When you see the two elevator trains colliding they never actually collide. I put one train right next to the caboose end of another train and drew the first train away. You reverse the film so that on the screen it looks like the trains are colliding when they're actually separating.

The fact that no one did get hurt during the filming of the *French Connection* chase is something of a miracle, but a lot of it came from good planning. It's supposed to look dangerous but not be dangerous. But when we came to the last day of filming the chase I realized that we didn't have enough speed on the screen. I went to the stuntman, Bill Hickman, and said, "You know, Bill, we've been filming on this chase for eight weeks and we don't have enough speed or enough danger and I really don't think this is gonna work." He asked if I was willing to get in the car with him and he'd show me some speed. So we mounted a camera on the front bumper of his car and I operated a camera that was over his shoulder because he was doubling Gene Hackman. Bill then drove that car at about eighty or ninety miles per hour for twenty-six city blocks with no control, right through red lights, green lights—everything you see in *The French Connection*. All those pieces of those cars coming up and narrowly missing, those are not stunt cars. All we had was a gumball* on the top of Bill's car and a siren to warn people to get out of our way. It was a miracle that nobody got hurt. It is from that one take that all the speed sequences occur. It was done with no mishaps, fortunately, but there could have been. I would never do anything like that again. I was young and im-

---

* A flashing police car light.

petuous and I didn't think of the danger. And there was danger, really, to human life in that shot. We did other things like that on *The French Connection*. We had no permission to do a lot of it.

I wanted a traffic jam on the Brooklyn Bridge, but the New York Police Department said absolutely not, you can't tie up traffic on the Brooklyn Bridge. I had all these off-duty police officers with me who were the *French Connection* cops. I told them that in about an hour I wanted to shoot a traffic-jam scene on the Brooklyn Bridge. They said, "Right, you got it." So they just went out, drove their cars on the bridge and stopped. We put Hackman's car and Fernando Rey's car in there and shot a whole sequence in the middle of a traffic jam on the Brooklyn Bridge at rush hour with no permission. The police helicopters started coming over and they were very angry.

To make a picture like *The French Connection* you have to get into a zone where that's all you think about and that's all you care about. You become obsessed with the material and once you're obsessed other factors start to fall away. Then it takes people like assistant directors and stunt coordinators to hold you back, because when you get in that zone you're ready to let anything happen. On *The French Connection* I virtually had total control of New York. I mean, "We're gonna shoot a chase going right through here. Well, does anybody know about it? No. Okay, fine, let's go."

Since then there have been a lot more stringent rules put together where cities don't allow you to do these things without permission and great discomfort to the citizenry. The only consolation is that very often the very citizens who hated the discomfort the most, when they see the picture they love it. They say, "See that? I was there when they did that."

An Academy Award Comes His Way

It was a very strange feeling to win the Academy Award for *The French Connection* because I was really young. Neither was I a member of the Academy at the time. I knew very few people out here because the film was made in New York. But it was a great honor. It's something that you're never prepared for, I guess, unless you've won it once before. But the honor comes from the fact that it's the people in the industry voting for your work above the work of other people that year. And, to be quite honest with you, I love the Academy Awards but I don't really believe that it is an indication of anything measurable. I don't think you can say that one picture is better than another picture, that there are five pictures better than all the rest, or that one is better than those five. It's apples and oranges. If you have five films about Hamlet you could presumably say, well, this one's better than that one. But five films on different subjects, it's impossible. It becomes a popularity contest, ultimately. And the most popular film with the voters wins. The idea that my film was better than anything else that year never entered my mind, not then and not to this day.

I was nominated the following year for *The Exorcist* but we didn't win. I was surprised, frankly, that *The Exorcist* didn't win because *The Exorcist* is the only film I've ever made that I really think is pretty good. I would not have been surprised if *The Exorcist* had won. I was very surprised that *The French Connection* had won because it was so out of the mainstream of the typical Hollywood film.

> *I think a good director is passionate about trying to bring a story about honestly, and Billy is incredibly passionate. He also doesn't like a lull to come down. Sometimes when you are working day in and day out, it gets to be like, "Okay, when's the next shot?" Billy doesn't let that happen.*
>
> Michael Biehn—Actor

The Exorcist (1973)

Ellen Burstyn; Max von Sydow; Lee J. Cobb; Kitty Winn; Jack MacGowran; Jason Miller; Linda Blair; Reverend William O'Malley; Barton Heyman; Peter Masterson; Rudolf Schündler; Gina Petrushka; Robert Symonds; Arthur Storch; Reverend Thomas Bermingham.

I knew Bill Blatty for many years before he wrote *The Exorcist*. I knew him socially around the time I was doing *Good Times*. Blake Edwards invited me to direct a feature-film version of the television series *Peter Gunn*. I met with Blake and I told him I thought his script had an awful lot of problems. Blake said, "You're telling me about scripts?" I told him I didn't think the script worked for me. He said, "Well, how would you like to tell that to the fellow who wrote it?" I said, "Well, if you want me to, I will." Then he brought Bill Blatty into the room and I began to critique Bill's script in no uncertain terms. Of course I never got the job. I think Blake wound up directing the film himself.

Right after that meeting Bill got ahold of me and told me that Blake had a lot of yes-men around him and that I was the only one that had told him the truth. Bill agreed that the script had a lot of problems. Now I don't say this in any way to put down Blake Edwards, who I admire among American directors at the highest level. This was just my opinion and it was Blatty's opinion. But we sort of got together over that and then we'd see each other over the years socially.

One day I was on a tour for *The French Connection* and this manuscript arrived in my hotel room. It was from Bill but I didn't open it. I took it with me from city to city. Finally in San Francisco I was in the hotel alone one evening and I decided to open up this thing and read Bill's novel. I read the first page and I was hooked like a fish. I read the whole book that night in one sitting and I was absolutely terrified by it.

The next day I called Bill and said, "Bill, this is great." And he said, "Well, do you want to make a film of it?" And I said, "I would love to, I think it's a masterpiece. I think it's perhaps as good as anything Edgar Allan Poe ever wrote in the same category." I later found out that about five other directors had been offered the picture, including Stanley Kubrick and Mike Nichols, who had turned it down for one reason or another. There was another director attached to it at the studio but Bill said, "Look, if you want to do it, I don't want this other director, I want you."

Bill went in and he sort of bamboozled Warner Bros. and told them that I had to direct the film. I had just come out with *The French Connection* but nobody knew what the hell that was yet. But by the time I started to get interested in this script and said I would do it, the studio became aware of *The French Connection* and figured I had made a good picture and agreed to my directing *Exorcist*. So they actually paid off the other director and signed me.

Then what happened was that Bill presented me with a script. Now, he had really gone to the mat to get me to direct the film. I read it and I thought it was terrible. I said, "Bill, you are your own worst enemy. Nobody would do what you've done to this great novel." I told Bill that I wanted him to go right back to the novel. I wanted to literally do the novel. I didn't want any outside stuff brought in. I wanted to do the novel from beginning to end, the straight-ahead story with no flashbacks. And he went back and wrote another script over a matter of several months and that's the script that we shot. It's a brilliant script, as it was a great novel, and that's how I got into it.

Finding a Young Girl to Play Regan

I, personally, saw probably a hundred girls between the ages of ten to thirteen. It wasn't looking too good. We had casting agents all over the place looking for young women who could act. One day Linda Blair came in with her mother and I saw Linda and thought she was kind of adorable. I knew that the main quality that this girl had to have was a kind of innocence, and yet a freedom in her own body and a freedom of mind and the ability to deal with all this wild stuff that was gonna happen.

I asked Linda if she knew what the story of *The Exorcist* was and she said she did. So I asked her to tell me what it was about. She says, "Well, it's about a little girl who gets possessed by the devil and she does a lot of bad things." And I said, "What sort of bad things?" And she said, "She pushes a man out a window, and she hits her mother, and she masturbates with a crucifix." I said, "What?" She said, "She masturbates with a crucifix." I said, "Do you know what that means?" She said, "Masturbates?" I said, "Yeah." She said, "That's like jerking off, isn't it?" I said, "Yeah. Have you ever done that?" And she said, "Sure, haven't you?" And at that moment, I knew that I had found Regan. Linda had a complete ease with the language, with the whole idea of it.

I made it all a big game for her from the first day on the set to the last. If anyone had seen the outtakes you'd see this little girl going through the most wild and outrageous things on camera. Then whenever I'd say, "Cut," Linda would turn and laugh and a prop man would hand her a milkshake and she'd be sucking on her milkshake. I often wished that the audience had seen what went on after the take was over, to see how little it actually affected her, because she was so free and innocent.

Those Amazing Special Effects

All the special effects we did were either experimental or they hadn't really been done before. They were all done mechanically. There are no optical effects in *The Exorcist*. If the bed goes off the floor, you see it go off the floor. When the little girl rises off the bed, we had to bring her off the bed, literally, by means of a rather simple set of mechanisms.

The most difficult effect to achieve was the cold room. In the old days, when they wanted to show breath in an inside space or an outside space, they used to film at the Glendale icehouse. Well the icehouse doesn't exist anymore and you can't take a movie set into an icehouse anyway. We had to show breath because Regan's bedroom was supposed to be freezing cold due to the workings of the demon. So we built the set inside a refrigerated cocoon. There were big refrigerator units behind all four walls of the set. We started off with one unit but it didn't get cold enough. Then a second unit and a third and a fourth—gigantic restaurant refrigeration units all around the set. We would bring down the temperature to where it got to be well below freezing. But then the minute we turned on the movie lights, the temperature would come back up inside of an hour. So we had to film for an hour and then shut down and build up the cold again. The crew was wearing overcoats and parkas and snow gear, but the little girl had to be in a nightgown with just an undershirt underneath. We had to put her in at the last minute in below freezing weather for these shots so you'd see her breath when the lights were turned on. We could film for a short time. We were sometimes making two shots a day.

After the first day of shooting, the cameraman and I realized that the breath wasn't photographing on film. The only way breath can be seen on film is if it's side- or backlit. If there's no light hitting the breath itself, it will evaporate on film and you won't see it. We put little lights all over the floor so that the actors would get side-lighted and back-lighted as they were moving to highlight their breath.

The shot I'm most asked about is how we made the little girl's head turn 360 degrees. Makeup artist Dick Smith built a replica of Linda Blair's face that we put on a dummy that was operated on a stick below the dummy's body. Dick would be below frame, turning a stick that would turn the head. Linda's in a big close-up and she turns just so far in the shot and then the dummy head turning does the rest of it. Another amazing fact was that actor Max von Sydow was about forty years old when we made the film and he had to be made up to look like a man in his seventies. His makeup took four hours to put on and then over an hour to remove.

There were a number of actors who wanted to play Father Damien Karras. Among them were Jack Nicholson and Paul Newman, who didn't want to do *The French Connection*, but then wanted to do *The Exorcist*. Nicholson actually came to me and said, "I want do it." But I had this idea that it should be a new face, someone you had never seen before. I felt that the material was so powerful that I really didn't want well-known actors in those roles, with rare exceptions.

One day I went to see a play in New York called *That Championship Season*, which was written by a man called Jason Miller. It was a brilliant play that subsequently went on to win the Pulitzer Prize for playwriting, among other things. The characters were all lapsed Catholics and the whole piece was about Catholic guilt. I said to my casting director, "Who wrote this, who is this guy?" And he said, "He's a young guy trying to get acting jobs. He's acted Off Broadway in small parts and road companies but he's never made a film. He's really a playwright." I said, "I have to meet him."

I was staying up at the Sherry Netherland Hotel in New York and I had bronchitis. Jason Miller comes up to my suite and he was sort of sulky and sullen. I thought he was very short. I just wanted to talk to him about his play but he was very uncommunicative. Later he told me he thought I was a pill freak because he saw all the pills that were really antibiotics and stuff for my bronchitis. I, on the other hand, thought he was either a junkie or very uncommunicative. It was a very bad first meeting.

I went back to Hollywood and signed this other actor to do the part of Father Karras. Then about a week or so later I get a call from Jason. He tells me that he has read *The Exorcist* and that he was Karras, that he was right for that part. He told me that he had studied to be a Jesuit priest and had gone to Catholic University in Washington for three years and then dropped out, but still had all that guilt that Father Karras had. I told him that unfortunately we had already cast the part. He told me I was making a big mistake. He told me I should test him on film. Well, I loved his play and this little voice starts whispering in my ear so I said, "All right, if you can fly out here this week I'll screen test you." He said he didn't fly and couldn't get out there that week but he could be there in a week.

So I get a hold of Ellen Burstyn and I said, "Let's run some scenes with this guy." I got cameraman Bill Fraker and we went into it with the idea of shooting a couple of scenes. Then I said to Ellen, "You interview him, I'll be over you shoulder, and you just sit there and talk to him and get him to talk about himself and we'll see how he comes off, and then I'll get him to say the Mass in a close-up."

So we run a couple of scenes and then Ellen interviewed Jason and he talked about his life very candidly and then I had him say the Mass in a big close-up very quietly, as though he was doing it for himself and not for a congregation. Now, don't forget I've already cast another actor to play the part. When it was over I asked Ellen what she thought. She says, "Please don't cast this guy. First of all he's too short. Father Karras has to be a man of stature and I've got to look up to him and I've got to feel he's so strong and powerful." And I said, "I hear you."

The next day the test comes back. I look at the film of this guy in a close-up and it was incredible. I mean, the camera just loved his features. He was wonderful and I said to the studio and to Ellen and to Bill Blatty, "I'm gonna pay off the other actor and we're gonna go with Jason Miller." They all thought I was nuts. First of all, the head of the studio at that point didn't want Ellen Burstyn in the movie. When she heard I was directing, she called me up and asked if I knew who she was. I told her I did, and she said she was going to play Chris MacNeil in *The Exorcist*. And I said, "Oh, really? The studio wants Audrey Hepburn, Jane Fonda, or Anne Bancroft." She said, "You're gonna wind up with me." I said, "Oh, really?"

In any case, we offered the part to Audrey Hepburn who said she would do it if we would shoot the film in Rome because she was married and lived there. I wasn't going to Rome to make this picture. I needed an American crew that I could communicate with. I loved Italian crews but I wasn't going to make this all-American film in Rome. It made no sense. We then offered it to Anne Bancroft who was pregnant, so she was out. Then Jane Fonda turned it down. At that time her response was, "Why would I want to be seen in a piece of capitalist dribble like this?" Jane was very political at the time. So now all of those choices are gone.

I get another call from Ellen Burstyn and she said, "You want to meet with me yet about this part?" And I said, "All right, come on into the office." She said, "I'm not going to your office because that's not a good place to have a meeting." She told me that she lived on my way home from Warner Bros. and that I should stop by. Now I go up to her house and I know who she is by now and I know she's a wonderful supporting actress but I had never seen her in a lead. At that time she was seventy or so pounds overweight, but she was so interesting and fascinating and she understood the part totally and knew all of the metaphysics surrounding it and everything else. But I didn't really think it was going to happen. She said, "I'm gonna lose the weight, you watch and see." So months go by, she's losing the weight, and she starts to look great.

We still have nobody else for the part. One day I go to the head of the studio, Ted Ashley, and I tell him I'm going to put Ellen Burstyn in the lead. Ashley told me that he had total confidence in me and thought I would make a great picture but Ellen Burstyn would play the lead in that movie over his dead body. Now time goes on and I've seen a lot of other people, but there's nobody else I want. I finally said, "Ted, I hope you're not gonna drop dead on me or something, but I want to go with Ellen." Reluctantly he let me cast her, and it was the god of movies that smiled on that film. We ended up with Ellen Burstyn, who had not really had a lead in a major picture before; Jason Miller, who had never done a picture; and Linda Blair, who had never been in a movie. The god of movies smiled on us and that's the only way I can put it. Ellen was wonderful. She was nominated for an Academy Award that year. Jason was nominated. Linda was nominated. It was very rewarding and I'm really pleased with *The Exorcist*. I have to say the script was so powerful, the story so great. It's about the mystery of faith and the mystery of fate. I think Blatty handled it in a way that obviously scared a lot of people. But there's an awful lot to think about in terms of the nature of good and evil after you've seen the film. That's why I think it's lasted, and I must say I feel that that's the one film that I've worked on that I think is something of a classic. But again, it's because of the story and the way the actors brought it to life. What makes a classic? A great timeless story that has wonderful performances, and that's what *The Exorcist* has.

There are many stories about what went on during the filming of *The Exorcist*. One day at five in the morning I got a call from the production manager. He said, "Don't bother to come to work today because the set burned to the ground." We built a three-story house on a stage and for some reason the set burned to the ground. There was a guard sitting outside who never saw a fire develop. The theory later was that because it was an old stage, there were pigeons flying around, who supposedly flew into a light box and short circuited some electricity and caused a fire, but who knows.

Then there was the first day that Max von Sydow arrived to do his first shot. It's the one where he walks up to the house that became the famous poster shot for the film. Just then a messenger comes up with a telegram that Max's brother died in Sweden. So we film Max walking up to the house and then he has to fly right back to Sweden for the funeral of his brother.

Then there was the time we got word that Jason Miller's youngest son was run down by a motorcycle at Rockaway Beach. There were only three or four people on the beach along with Jason's son and a kid on a motorbike about a mile away. Somehow or another the kid on the motorbike ran down Jason's son, who was near death for a week.

There were all sorts of things like that that went wrong from time to time and every time something would go wrong, I'd have a priest come in and bless the set and literally exorcise the set and then for a while things would go fine again. And then a week or two weeks later some other catastrophe would take place. And we'd bless the set again and then we'd be okay for a while. Any number of things like that that happened, from the grotesque to the near fatal.

Sorcerer (1977)

Roy Scheider; Bruno Cremer; Francisco Rabal; Amidou; Ramon Bieri; Peter Capell; Karl John; Frederick Ledebur; Chico Martinez; Joe Spinell; Rosario Almontes; Richard Holley; Anne-Marie Deschott; Jean-Luc Bideau; Jacques François.

I was a big fan of *Wages of Fear,* the 1953 Henri-Georges Clouzot film. I always thought it was a timeless story and it was really a theme that interested me. The notion of four or five strangers, people who actually hate each other, who are thrown together by circumstance, by fate, and they either have to cooperate or die. It seems to me to be a wonderful metaphor for the world condition. I took a couple of years off and went around the world and then decided to make an adaptation of Clouzot's *Wages of Fear* in an entirely new version that would only draw on the theme of the characters. Originally I was going to do the film with Steve McQueen. Steve wanted to play the part and loved the script, but didn't want to leave the country. He wanted to do the whole film in the United States and at that time I felt I had to go to South America to make it. So I decided to pass on Steve McQueen. As good as I think *Sorcerer* is, it was really written for Steve McQueen and I'll always have a sad spot in my heart that I never made it with him. But I think Roy Scheider did a fine job with it and it's probably the one film of mine I can still watch.

The bridge sequence in *The Sorcerer* is very much like the chase in *French Connection,* one shot at a time. Only in this case, some of it was very dangerous. We had to build a suspension bridge and we were gonna build it in the Dominican Republic over a raging river. And it was a river that in the memory of man had not varied by as much as a foot in the dry season. We go there and we build this bridge at a cost of about a million dollars. It was hydraulically controlled so that we could control the movement of the trucks. What looks to be a wooden bridge was really concealing hydraulics. We built this bridge and every day the river is going down, down, down. Finally the river receded to about one foot and we couldn't shoot there. We had to tear the bridge down and find another location where in the memory of man the water level had not receded so much as six inches.

We found this river in Mexico and rebuilt our bridge there at a cost of a million dollars and sure enough the water receded to about a foot and a half above the ground. It was ridiculous. So we had to manufacture a rainstorm and hide the camera at certain angles so you wouldn't know how high the river really was. We literally had to re-route the river current and invent a current so that things would be racing down that foot-and-a-half river. That one sequence took about three months to film—one shot at a time. Many times when you see the truck seesawing on the bridge, we actually dumped the truck and the stunt men accidentally into the water. We had to fish it out of the water, set it up and do it again. It's the most difficult sequence I've ever filmed; perhaps one of the most difficult sequences ever filmed.

About half the crew on that picture, including myself, got malaria. Many more people on the crew got gangrene and had to leave and go home. I had lost about thirty-five or forty pounds making the film. When I came back to the United States I looked like the survivor of a concentration camp. It had taken a great deal out of everyone that worked on the film.

It was extremely difficult to shoot and the fact that the film was not a success is one of the most disappointing things that's ever happened to me. I thought, after it was finished, that I had finally made a film that really worked for me and I was very pleased with it, but it was really a failure. I have to say it was both a critical and a commercial failure and it hurt me very deeply. There was a deep wound from which I may have only recovered recently. It becomes like losing a person close to you, or a child, when you work that hard on a film and then you think you've achieved something beautiful and the critics and the public tell you that it doesn't work for them. That's the toughest part of directing. The actual work, every part of the process, is a joy. When it doesn't work it hits very hard.

We were shooting a sequence that was nothing more than a simple crossing of a river when a big thunderstorm came up suddenly that made this river rise to overflowing. The crew became stranded and we had to literally pull each other across this raging river to the other side. We had to stop filming and just evacuate everybody from the flood.

When we were shooting in Israel we were doing a terrorist attack right across the street from the mayor of Jerusalem's office. We set this bomb off and actually shattered the windows of the mayor's office. The brigades came out and people knew we were filming, but it was so real. An actual terrorist attack took place two blocks away while we were filming ours, so I pulled the crew away from where we were filming and we went down and shot the aftermath of an actual terrorist bombing that co-incided with the one that I had staged. There's a little bit of both of them in that sequence.

Sorcerer was the film that took the most out of me and it made me doubt my own...I felt that when I made *The French Connection* and *The Exorcist* that I had a real grasp on public taste. Public taste was my taste—I rode the subways, I lived very simply, and I was the audience. And I think that's the best way for an American film director to be working. To be completely in synch with your audience, because we don't make these films to hang in the Louvre, we make them to be seen by as many people as possible. And when the film is not seen and doesn't have a good release it's disappointing. In my case I felt I had lost the magic touch or it had just eluded me. I don't know whether I ever really had it but I felt that I had it and lost it.

The Brink's Job (1978)

Peter Falk; Peter Boyle; Allen Garfield; Warren Oates; Gena Rowlands;
Paul Sorvino; Sheldon Leonard; Gerard Murphy; Kevin O'Connor; Claudia Peluso;
Patrick Hines; Malachy McCourt; Walter Klavun; Randy Jurgensen; John Brandon.

The Brink's robbery was something that I was interested in as a child. They were like Robin Hood—they would rob from the rich and give to the poor. They robbed the Brink's Company, which was a pushover, and they gave the money to friends and relatives to open little garages and grocery stores and gas stations. I met the Brink's robbers who were still alive and I thought they were a real fine bunch of men. It was that thin line between what makes a decent guy and what makes a hardened crim-inal that fascinated me.

I had a wonderful cast that included Peter Falk, Allen Garfield, and Peter Boyle, who had turned down *The French Connection*; and Paul Sorvino, Gena Rowlands, and the late Warren Oates. It was a great ensemble cast and a lot of fun to make. We filmed in the actual place where the robbery had taken place. We had the actual Brink's robbers as technical consultants, so we knew exactly how they did it. I only varied from the facts where I thought the facts weren't interesting enough.

One unusual thing that happened while we were making the film was that some actual robbers in Boston broke into our cutting room and stole the film. They pistol-whipped the editors and stole the work prints, and then they called up and asked for a ransom of six hundred thousand dollars. The police and the FBI got involved. I was on the phone with these robbers, and what they had stolen in their stupidity was the work print, which was totally replaceable. These guys never knew that you needed a negative to make prints from and it would be easy for us to just make another print off the negative. They thought they really had something that they could hold for ransom.

Peter Falk was the only actor I ever thought of to play Tony Pino. Peter has a great range from comedy to drama. He could break your heart or he could make you laugh. He was on-the-nose casting for that role and he was wonderful. I don't know if you can use this, but Peter was very well known for playing *Columbo* on television. One day we were shooting in the heart of the North End of Boston. We had a fellow guarding Peter's trailer, a guy named Mike, a neighborhood guy. This old gentleman came up and he said, "Mikey, my wife made lasagna for Mr. Columbo." Mikey said, "I'll give it to him, don't worry about it." The guy used to come around for days like that. One day he asked if he could meet Mr. Columbo. And Mike said, "Well, Joey, he's busy right now. Come around some other time and he'll give you an autographed picture."

The old man came around five or six times and finally we're about to wrap and leave and Mikey got Peter to sign a picture for this gentleman. The gentleman gets the picture and it says, "To Joey with all my best wishes from Peter Falk." The old gentleman looks at this and he says, "Peter Falk? Peter Falk? Who's that?" And Mikey says, "That's Columbo, that's his real name." The old man says, "His name's not Columbo? He's not Italian?" Mike said no. So the guy ripped the picture up and threw it back. I told that to Peter and Peter laughs every time I tell it in public.

What Does He Think of His Career?

I never think about my career. I really don't. When people ask me about it, I stop and think about it, and if I had to make a comment I'd say that as of yet I haven't fulfilled early promise. I've still fallen far short of *Citizen Kane* and that's what keeps me going. Directing film is a young man's game. You have to have a lot of energy and can't let anything stop you and you've got to believe that the world is your oyster. In other words, you have to have a great deal of self-confidence to go with your energy. That's why it's a young man's game. But frankly, I stay with it and keep at it not only because I love the work but also because I was inspired to do a film as good as *Citizen Kane* and I'm gonna keep trying until I get it right. I haven't done it yet, by any means.

I always feel that the film I'm working on is the best work I've ever done. Often, after it's released, I don't know what the hell I was thinking. I've made a couple of films recently that I don't think work at all, like *The Guardian*. I don't think it works on any level. I say this with no reflection on the people who worked on it, who I think did do terrific work, but I think the filmmaking itself is my fault and doesn't make it. It's as bad as *Good Times* was. It's inept. And yet at the time I was making it, I thought it was going to be brilliant. I had in mind a kind of modern day Grimm's fairy-tale. Again, it just doesn't make it and that's my fault. Failure of will, failure of talent.

Directing films in America is different from most other countries. If you cannot score with the American public, if you can't make contact with them, you're not going to get a second chance. When you work in television, it's different. Television directors can go on and on and have failures and successes. But any time you fail with a major feature motion picture, especially today, you've got a lot of problems because the industry is only really concerned with success. Critical success to some extent, but box office success is what rules. All of the studios are set up only to make hit pictures. They don't want soft hits and they certainly don't want films that fail to return their cost at the box office.

What's interesting is that the films that I admire the most and love the best are usually not films that have done all that well, such as *Citizen Kane*. That was a great critical success but never was a popular success. And yet I'm aware that an American film director's obligation is to connect with the audience. That's what the studios are interested in and that's what the audiences are interested in. As I said before, we don't make these films to hang in the Louvre. You make them to be seen by as many people as possible.

Cruising (1980)

Al Pacino; Paul Sorvino; Karen Allen; Richard Cox; Don Scardino;
Joe Spinell; Jay Acovone; Randy Jurgensen; Barton Heyman; Gene Davis;
Arnaldo Santana; Larry Atlas; Allan Miller; Sonny Grosso; Ed O'Neill.

Cruising was a film that I resisted making. Phil D'Antoni talked to me about it. It was a novel by *New York Times* journalist Gerald Walker, and it had nothing to do with the leather bar scene. It was about a guy who was killing homosexuals because he hated the homosexuality in himself. At one point Steven Spielberg was preparing to make it with Phil but they could never get a script they liked and they abandoned it. So then producer Jerry Weintraub got it and he brought it back to me.

I still wasn't interested, but then certain things began to happen in the gay community in New York that I started to pay attention to. A series of articles appeared in the *Village Voice* describing body parts that were floating in the East River. And I said to Jerry, "If we can make a film about that, take Gerald Walker's premise, and put this character into the leather bar scene, this undercover cop, that's something I'd be interested in doing." We found out that Mafia guys and some ex–New York City police officers owned the hardcore gay bars. We got permissions through various contacts that Jerry and I had to go into the leather bars and to observe firsthand what went on, and for me it was like Sodom and Gomorrah. I mean, I had never seen so much group sex with no limits, no holds barred, and in some of the most incredible and unimaginable situations.

There was a guy in a sling and another man who put his hand up through his anus and went all the way up where you could see a hand in contact with the human heart. And a bathtub full of urine with a man being urinated on by eight other guys. I filmed all of this. Much of it had been cut out of the film but I'm actually planning to do another, uncut version. But I saw this stuff in the leather bars and I found this fascinating, not judgmental of what was going on, but simply as a documentarian coming upon a situation and saying, this is extraordinary, this is unusual, and that's the beginning of a film. This situation, this scene is something that I think the general audience doesn't know a lot about and would be fascinated by it as I was.

So I then set out to make the film in those leather bars with many of those same people doing what they do. It was a story about an obsessive young rookie police officer that goes undercover into the leather bars because he has the same type of features as the victims that have been killed. He set out into this world as a decoy and that seemed to me to be a very interesting situation because one of the *French Connection* cops who worked as a technical advisor on *Cruising* actually had been put in that situation. He was sent into the gay bars as a decoy to trap a killer because he looked like the victim. And this experience really shook him up and changed his life. He contributed a lot of the material that went into Al's character.

To Live and Die in L.A. (1985)

William L. Petersen; Willem Dafoe; John Pankow; Debra Feuer;
John Turturro; Darlanne Fluegel; Dean Stockwell; Steve James;
Robert Downey Sr.; Michael Greene; Christopher Allport;
Jack Hoar; Val DeVargas; Dwier Brown; Michael Chong.

To Live and Die in L.A. was originally a kind of a memoir written as a fiction project by an ex–Secret Service agent named Gerry Petievich. In fact, Gerry was still in the Secret Service when he wrote the book and helped us make the film. He had been a Secret Service man for, I think, nineteen years. I was fascinated by the life of a Secret Service agent, which never received a lot of publicity, obviously because it's the Secret Service.

The idea that a Secret Service agent can one day be in a room with the president of the United States, to protect him, and the next day be assigned to chase a guy in a very bad neighborhood for a fifty dollar forged credit card was what interested me to do that film. I wrote the screenplay from Gerry's novel and I took quite a few liberties with it. I put in a chase scene because I enjoy doing chase scenes. They're something of a challenge. Gerry didn't have one in the book.

A lot of people have told me that they like that chase scene. I frankly don't think it's as good as the one in *The French Connection*. It's hard to go back and do them again. This one was a lot easier to shoot because it all took place on a freeway. The city of Los Angeles dedicated a freeway for our use over in Long Beach every Saturday and Sunday. They closed that freeway from seven in the morning till about five in the afternoon and let us shoot our chase. So everything was confined to that one area, which, frankly, made it a lot less challenging. I think we came up with a few new wrinkles that I now see in almost every chase scene, which is going against traffic. That was something that was new that we invented for that picture. It's very difficult now to think up something to do that's new. I have a chase in my new picture, *Jade*. It's about as contemporary as I can get with a chase because so much has been done since *The French Connection* with high technology, with more money, more of a body count, that it's very difficult now to do a chase scene that an audience feels they haven't seen before.

Blue Chips (1994)

Nick Nolte; Mary McDonnell; J.T. Walsh; Ed O'Neill; Alfre Woodard; Bob Cousy;
Shaquille O'Neal; Anfernee 'Penny' Hardaway; Matt Nover; Cylk Cozart;
Anthony C. Hall; Kevin Benton; Bill Cross; Marques Johnson; Robert Wuhl.

Nick Nolte was my first and only choice to play the part of Pete Bell. I felt that he embodied the very nature of a tough, hard-as-nails coach. I primarily did the film because of my love for basketball, but working with Nick was a fantastic experience and a great challenge. Nick comes in with a carload of ideas every day and the work of a director is largely in helping him to shape his performance. There are some actors that you work with where they'll come in almost virginal and you have to tell them exactly what to do and think and how to approach their character. An actor like Nolte comes in with all of that stuff and then it's a question of, as I say, shaping them, guiding them, setting a tempo for the tone and keeping it in focus.

We agreed early on that we were going to try and portray a character that we both knew. We based Bell on Bobby Knight, the coach of Indiana. The character was not going to be all that sympathetic to the audience. It was going to be difficult for the audience to like this guy, and we knew that, and we relished that challenge. What happens when you make a film is that the studio looks at a script and they generally always say, "Is this character likeable?" They're so afraid that the audience won't like the character. I think that if they did a biography of Hitler today they would want to make him likeable. Their theory is that if the audience doesn't like this guy, they aren't going to follow the story. I think they would try to humanize the worst villains in history out of their fear that the audience might not like the central character.

Make It as Real as You Can

One of the things that I've always felt about sports films is that they usually fall apart for the real sports fan when it comes to depicting the sport itself. It doesn't look like they're really playing. The techniques and the coverage that is required to shoot a sequence and to make sure it's edited into something fluent, that very technique defeats the purpose of a real athletic competition, which is totally spontaneous. A basketball game is spontaneous. That's why you watch it. You don't know what's going to happen from moment to moment, therefore you don't want to put the camera in a position where the camera seems to know what's gonna happen before it does happen. So I decided that if I ever did a sports film I would try and depict— and I would only do a basketball film because it's the only sport that I'm really interested in—but I would try to do it in actual game tension. I would try to do it with all the ebb and flow of an actual game with an actual crowd participating, without cueing the crowd when to cheer or when to boo or when to react at all.

When it came to doing *Blue Chips*, I realized that about the only place on earth where you get anywhere from six to ten thousand people into an arena at the drop of a hat to watch a basketball game was in Indiana, right in the very heartland of the Midwest where basketball is a religion. So I went to a small town in Indiana and we took over a high school gym there. We got some of the best athletes in collegiate basketball and a couple from the pro game who were young enough to appear as college players, and we staged three actual basketball games. I shot them with nine cameras and had Nick Nolte actually coaching his team. He had been trained to such an extent that he could go out and actually coach a basketball team. And he had assistants. I had one of the great minds in basketball sitting on the bench next to him, Keith Newell, who is a strategist and a legend in the game. So Keith was giving Nick a lot of advice and help and he would whisper in his ear during the shooting.

We shot three actual games in front of a live audience where the outcome was completely unknown. This decision was obviously questioned at the studio level—could you get these people and would they react the way you wanted them to? Once again my belief in that came from my documentary background, knowing that there are certain things that will draw people to participate as they would if it were actually happening, and that you could cover such an event realistically. And that's what I was going for in *Blue Chips*. In some of the films I've made I would go for a kind of poetic realism, sometimes surrealism. In *The Exorcist*, there's a bit of surrealism. Also a touch of it in *French Connection*. But in *Blue Chips* I wanted absolute, total realism because I felt the game of basketball was exciting enough to support that.

Casting Shaquille O'Neal

Shaquille O'Neal obviously isn't a trained actor but from about the age of sixteen years old he's had to appear in front of tens of thousands of people and many more millions of people on television. So he's not nervous in front of a camera. The role that Ron Shelton wrote for him was a role that called for a 7'3" black man who was a wizard at basketball. Now, it's very difficult to cast an actor to do that. First of all, you're not gonna find a lot of 7'3" actors who could also be skilled at basketball. It was the kind of a role that Ron wrote that had to be cast with a real player. Before he ever came to do this film Shaquille had done a lot of commercials where he was performing, where he had to act, where he had to pretend. He is very skilled at that.

There are some people who are so gifted that they don't need training to do that, if it's playing something that's close to them. Sometimes playing something that's close to you can be the most difficult thing to do. If a director says to you as an actor, "Just be yourself," that's the worst direction that a director can give to an actor because generally the actor doesn't know really what the director is seeing when he says, "Be yourself." The self is different to the person and to an observer. But in the case of Shaquille I spent several weeks with him, and I rehearsed the script with him and I realized that I could create a reality for him that would allow him to give free rein to his wonderful personality. And in doing that, we were able to bring about something that I'm very pleased with. I think he came off very well. I very often use real cops to play cops, doctors to play doctors, criminals to play criminals. So it wasn't a great leap to get a basketball player to also act those scenes where he's off the basketball court. There are a number of such situations in *Blue Chips*.

How Happy Is He with His Work?

I'm never happy with the result of a film. I've never made a film that is the same as the one that I carry in my head. There is an old joke told by comedian Mort Sahl. He was commenting on a biography that had come out by Wernher von Braun, the German rocket scientist. Von Braun's biography was called *I Aim at the Stars* and Mort Sahl said it should have been called *I Aim at the Stars but Sometimes Hit London*. And that's how I feel about the films that I make. I always aim at the stars but sometimes I hit London. I very often miss the mark—more often than not. I have never made a film that is in anyway satisfying to me and it's probably what keeps me going. It is also a source of frustration. Earlier I spoke to you about how influenced I was by *Citizen Kane*. That is both a blessing and a curse. If *Citizen Kane* or another great film brings you into the profession and inspires you to become a part of it, you spend the rest of your career with the knowledge that you can never come near that kind of achievement. But I always keep try-

ing. I always keep trying to aim at the stars. The difficulty comes at the end
when I've seen it all put together. During the making of any film I always
think, yeah, this is gonna be the one. This is the one that I think I'm really
gonna achieve what I set out to do and I always fall short of that.

> *There are four or five of the great directors left, and Billy's certainly
> one of those. I mean, I'm coming back to zero here, because I believe
> he's taking us all to school. This is the big leagues because of him and
> the tone that he sets and his take on things.*
>
> David Caruso—Actor

Jade (1995)

*David Caruso; Linda Fiorentino; Chazz Palminteri;
Richard Crenna; Michael Biehn; Donna Murphy; Ken King;
Holt McCallany; David Hunt; Angie Everhart; Kevin Tighe;
Robin Thomas; Jay Jacobus; Victoria Smith; Drew Snyder.*

Jade is a marvelous script by Joe Eszterhas. It's an original screenplay not
based on anything else and it's a murder mystery. It's a three-character story,
basically. It's about two idealistic men who went to Stanford Law School together and a woman that they were both in love with. The woman becomes
a clinical psychologist. One of the young men becomes the district attorney
of San Francisco and the other becomes a very prominent criminal and corporate lawyer. In the course of this story a murder takes place that impli-
cates the woman. And so in the course of the film it appears as though the
district attorney, who is investigating the case, may have to bring charges
against this woman that he loves but who is married to the criminal attorney, who may have to defend her.

The film never gets involved with the trial and it never answers all of the
questions, but that's what I like about it. That sort of film has kind of gone
out of vogue. Today, most of the films that are made provide easy answers
to easy questions. But the films that I most love and respect are those films

---

EDITOR'S NOTE: This interview was conducted on a sound stage over a two-day period during the final weeks of production of *Jade*. Friedkin would direct a scene,
then spend time with our crew answering questions while the *Jade* film crew set up
the next scene.

that raise questions and leave the answers with the audience so that when the audience leaves the theater they have something to take with them. They have questions and the questions are not fully resolved. I mean, that, to me, is the greatness of *Citizen Kane*. It's like a chain reaction. Every day for the last thirty years or so since I've seen that film I think about it and discover new things. It doesn't give up all of its answers easily. And that's the attempt with *Jade* as well. But it's a very powerful thriller and I'm getting three really great performances—Linda Fiorentino, who won the New York Film Critic's Award and various international critics awards last year, along with David Caruso and Chazz Palminteri.

On Scripts

My attitude about a script is as follows: A script is a cocoon from which the butterfly emerges. A script is something that will be read by as many as maybe two hundred people at the most. A script is not meant to be literature. It's probably never going to be published. It's only read by the people who are involved with it, and out of what the script gives them comes this butterfly, this film. The script is something that constantly evolves on the set with the actors. Once the script leaves the writer's typewriter it becomes the province of the actor to make it live, to give it flesh and blood, with the help of a director. And so there are constant changes in even the greatest of scripts. Shakespeare's plays were never published in his own lifetime. The first folio of Shakespeare's plays were first published fifty years after his death from the recollections and memories of the actors who had performed them originally. That's why there's such a great question mark about who wrote Shakespeare's plays, because they were reconstructed from the memories of the performers.

My point is that the script is the province of the actors. The actor owns it. The actor embodies the character. So that's how I regard a script. I regard it as something obviously very important. It's much more than a blueprint. It's like a music score, but it's constantly open to interpretation and re-interpretation. If you take fifty directors and fifty actors and give them the same script, you'll get that many interpretations.

What Does a Director Really Do?

A film director's work with an actor is different for motion pictures than it is for theater, and certainly than for opera or any other form where you tend to be working on something from beginning to end. If you're working on a play, you work on the play from its beginning and the actor starts at a certain point and has to reach a certain point by the end of the evening. On a motion picture, all of that is jumbled up. You might work on the last scene first or a couple of shots from a scene in the middle, then jump into some shots from something else.

The difficulty that an actor has is to keep the whole thing in mind—not only his own performance but the shape of the whole film from shot to shot. That's what the director does. The director has to keep in his head the shape of the entire film that may consist of anywhere from one thousand to two thousand different shots or setups. Very often an actor has to come in right off of the street, get on the sound stage, and act scared or act brutal or act powerful or act cowardly from a dead start, without the ability to have performed those moments that lead up to that moment. A film is usually a constant series of emotions being portrayed by the actor. So as a director you have to first gauge how far can this actor go. If this actor, for example, is supposed to be portraying fear, how much can I push the actor to achieve the result without going over the top or without falling short of the actor's potential. That's something that a director is constantly thinking.

When you see a depiction of a director working with an actor and the director says, "All right, cut, let's do it again," very often someone who's not in the business would say, "Why are they doing it again, it seemed okay the first time?" They're doing it again because it's usually the director or the actor who feels they can do a little more, do a little better. It's like trying to catch lightning in a bottle. You're trying to catch something that is effervescent, that is unknown, and it's always the director's feeling about the actor and knowledge of the actor that allows the director to push the actor further and further. I've worked with actors where I knew that they could only go so far, and to take them any further or to even do another take would be a waste of time.

I've worked with actors where occasionally it comes alive on take 15 or take 37. Generally, if the film is cast properly and the actor and director are in synch, you can achieve these results quickly. But even if the actor and director are in synch, the director is still asking the actor to step in front of the camera and act scared, or act powerful, or act courageous, or act frightened, or act sick, or be dying, on a moment's notice from a dead start. And that's what the process consists of. It's shaping a performance. The director is constantly riding with the ebb and flow of what the actor is giving them and making a value judgment each time as to whether or not the actor has given all that they're capable of. Generally even the greatest actors don't know what their potential is. They may have a sense of it, but they're not quite sure how far they can go. So as a director, you're constantly trying to give an actor a surprise within a scene, not let the actor react to the same dialogue he just heard, but I'll give them fresh dialogue or I'll make something happen that surprises the actor just before he has to go into a take. Because it's that act of provocation or surprise that triggers the actor's emotions.

As I always say, a film is made up of a series of emotions. It's a collection of emotions. Just as a book is a collection of words or words and pictures and subsequently thoughts and ideas, a film is first of all a collection of emotions, one tumbling after another.

What Does He Consider the Low Points in His Career?

I've had many low points in my career. I'm wondering about the question, whether you mean in terms of artistic achievement or just in terms... I'll tell you that after I won the Academy Award for *The French Connection* I paid the one and only visit I've ever paid to a psychiatrist. I was in such deep depression after I won because I felt that that award meant a great deal because of the recognition by people in the industry. I knew then that I really had done nothing to achieve it. I consider *The French Connection* a pretty good police thriller. I don't think it's a great film. So when I won this award I was depressed because I felt that I was living a lie. And I went to see a psychiatrist who was running the psychiatric program at USC. He had a full calendar but allowed me to come in as a patient.

What it consisted of was my sitting and talking about myself while he took notes on a yellow pad. He never said anything and never commented and I spent an hour just talking about myself and I figured, well this isn't really very helpful because I have friends I could do this with. I remained depressed for a long time and then I finally gave into the fact that this had happened to me. I had really worked for this and now I had achieved it. That was, strangely enough, a low point.

I always reach a low point when I'm winding up a film. It's always very sad. It's just like leaving a family behind and that's sad. Often the lowest ebb that I reach is after a film comes out and doesn't do well. When a film that you make and you give so much to goes out to the audience for whom it's intended and it doesn't do well, that can be as depressing an experience as you can imagine for a film director. It's what's driven a lot of people out of it. They just can't take it any more. Because every time you make a film and it doesn't work, it's an uphill climb to do your next film. And what you're trying to do as a filmmaker is just keep on making films. But the economics of it are so difficult today.

What Have Been His Career High Points?

Well, personally, the highest point was the birth and the raising of my son. He's now twelve years old. Professionally, to bring it down to earth and try and get with the theme of this show, the film that I am most pleased with, though was one of my least successful, was *Sorcerer.* The film that I think worked best, which we did get as close to the vision as Bill Blatty had when he wrote it and as I had when I directed it, was *The Exorcist.* I mean, the best that I can say about it is that we stayed there, we kept doing it until we got the most out of it that we could, and I'm very pleased with the result. To this day when I see it acting on the emotions of an audience I feel very good. I feel elated.

What Does the Future Hold for Billy Friedkin?

I have no idea what the future holds. The thing that I think about every day and the thing that I look forward to is just doing this. I mean, not this interview but just directing. I love directing films. I love the challenge of it. I find that every day that I'm directing I'm trying to synthesize all of the arts—writing, composition, photography, performance, music, painting, everything. And what I look forward to is doing it again and again and again. I hope that I can keep doing what I'm doing right on into the afterlife, wherever it may be, and I just hope that the studio heads up there will be sympathetic.

What was that great joke I heard that just popped in and out of my head? Oh, yes. There's a wonderful joke about Cecil B. DeMille dying and going to heaven. St. Peter comes to DeMille and says, "Mr. DeMille, don't worry about anything, everything's gonna be great up there. You're gonna direct all the films for God." And DeMille says, "Yes, but down on earth I'm used to having thousands of extras in my films." St. Peter says, "Well, in heaven you can have millions of extras." DeMille says, "What about technicians?" St. Peter says, "You have your choice of the greatest who ever lived." DeMille says, "I've always worked with the finest composers." St. Peter says, "You can have Beethoven or Mozart compose for your films." DeMille says, "Well, I've always worked with the very greatest of actors." St. Peter says,

"Well, you can have Sir Laurence Olivier or Humphrey Bogart or any actor of your choice." DeMille says, "What about actresses?" St. Peter says, "Well, there is this one actress that God would like you to consider."

I really think that that's probably what I have to look forward to if I go up there and make films. Perhaps I can get everything I want but there will be this one actress that God suggests I use.

His Parting Words

Film can move people in ways that make them better than they are or ever thought they could be.

Filmography

Time-Life Specials: The March of Time (TV series, 1965)
Good Times (1967)
The Night They Raided Minsky's (1968)
The Birthday Party (1968)
The Boys in the Band (1970)
The French Connection (1971)
The Exorcist (1973)
Sorcerer (1977)
The Brink's Job (1978)
Cruising (1980)
Deal of the Century (1983)
To Live and Die in L.A. (1985)
The Twilight Zone (TV series, 1985)
C.A.T. Squad (TV, 1986)

EDITOR'S NOTE: After the completion of this interview Friedkin directed a television remake of *12 Angry Men,* with a cast that included Jack Lemmon, George C. Scott, Hume Cronyn, Edward James Olmos, William L. Peterson, and Mary McDonnell. He was then scheduled to shoot the feature film *Rules of Engagement,* with Samuel L. Jackson, Tommy Lee Jones, and Guy Pearce, and *Night Train,* starring Ving Rhames.

C.A.T. Squad: Python Wolf (TV, 1988)
Rampage (1988)
Tales from the Crypt (TV series, 1989)
The Guardian (1990)
Blue Chips (1994)
Jailbreakers (TV, 1994)
Jade (1995)
12 Angry Men (TV, 1997)
Rules of Engagement (2000)
Night Train (2000)

Awards

Academy Awards, USA
The Exorcist, Best Director (nominated), 1974
The French Connection, 1972

Academy of Science Fiction, Horror and Fantasy Films, USA
President's Award, 1999

British Academy Awards
The French Connection, Best Film Direction (nominated) 1973

Cognac Festival du Film Policier
To Live and Die in L.A., Audience Award, 1986

Deauville Film Festival
Rampage, Critics Award (nominated), 1988

Directors Guild of America, USA
12 Angry Men, Outstanding Directorial Achievement in Dramatic Specials (nominated), 1998

The French Connection, Outstanding Directorial Achievement in Motion Pictures (shared with Paul Ganapoler, William C. Gerrity, and Terence A. Donnelly), 1972

Emmy Awards
12 Angry Men, Outstanding Directing for a Miniseries or a Movie (nominated), 1998

Golden Globes, USA
The Exorcist, Best Director—Motion Picture, 1974
The French Connection, Best Director—Motion Picture, 1972

Razzie Awards
Cruising, Worst Director (nominated), 1981
Cruising, Worst Screenplay (nominated), 1981

Walk of Fame
Star on the Walk of Fame, 1997

The Films of Arthur Hiller

Arthur Hiller was born on November 22, 1923, in Edmonton, Alberta, Canada. He completed his education in his native country (earning a master's degree in psychology from the University of Toronto, after a year of heading for a law degree at the University of British Columbia). During his schooling, he realized that his great love of theater was commanding him to make entertainment his life's work.

The Americanization of Emily, Plaza Suite, Love Story, Man of La Mancha, The Man in the Glass Booth, The Out-of-Towners, Hospital, Silver Streak, The In-Laws, Outrageous Fortune, The Babe—film buffs would tell you these movies have one thing in common: Arthur Hiller as director.

Arthur Hiller himself is more likely to say of these films, "They're all relationship movies in which people with whom we are asked to identify undergo a life change, for the better."

Hiller sees the affirmation of the human spirit as the key component of a story which attracts him to a film project, and has maintained that perspective since he began his film career in the 1950s at the Canadian Broadcasting Corporation. He moved steadily up from producer and director for the CBC Radio Network to television when, finally, NBC coaxed him to Hollywood as director of several of their Matinee Theater productions.

He followed with many prestigious *Playhouse 90* dramas, including *Massacre at Sand Creek*. He quickly became a director of choice for some of the industry's best known series including *Naked City, Alfred Hitchcock Presents, Gunsmoke, Ben Casey,* and *Route 66*.

Hollywood's motion picture industry soon beckoned and he began what has become a string of highly successful and critically acclaimed films. He has directed notable screenplays by the likes of Paddy Chayefsky and Neil Simon.

Much to his continued embarrassment, Hiller is known as Mister Nice Guy in Hollywood. He is a gentle and kind man who feels that no one person makes a movie; that it takes the contributions of the entire cast and crew to make a good film.

> *Arthur has a great way of working which is very gentle. He's always taking care of you and always making sure you feel good and that you know that he appreciates what you're doing and that just makes an actor feel good. Yet he gets the job done in a smart, beautiful way. I really enjoyed my time working with Arthur. He's always open and you can talk to him, which I like a lot.*
>
> Steve Martin—Actor

The Conversation

My first interest in theater came when I was about seven or eight years old. My parents started a Yiddish theater up in Edmonton, Alberta, in western Canada. They weren't professional or anything. It was just for the community once or twice a year. I was helping to build and paint the sets and I just loved it all. By the time I was eleven I was acting in Yiddish Theater and I kept on with the acting at school and Little Theater things. In fact, when I finished high school, there was a drama professor from Ohio State University who was teaching drama at the University of Alberta where I lived, and he taught teachers how to teach drama. He taught them by putting on a play. They had to build the sets, paint the sets, create the costumes, find the props, do the set dressing, and they had to act in it. That's how they learned, by doing everything. He was short two actors so he called the high school drama teacher and he said, "Who are the best kid actors?" I ended up playing Donald, the black servant in *You Can't Take It with You*. From that I was offered a drama scholarship to Ohio State, but I turned it down because I thought that's something that you do on the weekends, you don't earn your living in the theater.

I went off to World War II and when I came back took my Arts degree and then studied a year of law. Then I took my masters degree in psychology. I realized it was the communications part of psychology that I like the best. I thought, "Why am I not doing what I really want to do?" So the next day I wandered into the headquarters of the Canadian Broadcasting Corporation, this was in radio days, and went up to the front desk and said, "Whom do I see about a job?" Three weeks later I was directing talk shows.

The first show that I directed was a show called *Pro or Con*. You had to choose a topic with, obviously, a person on either side and the topic. I chose for a topic, "Should Canada Have a National Theater?" So you see my interests were still there. Then, because of my love of drama, I started to direct what you would call radio drama documentaries about a social issue or civic problem. Then I shifted into general directing, which included music, talk, and drama. Then along came live television and I shifted into that. I selected drama, which is my true love. I worked as a director in live television and then NBC offered me a job here in Hollywood.

When I came to Hollywood initially, I worked on *Matinee Theater*. We were doing a drama every day. There were ten directors working on it. Then I got a call to do a *Climax,* which was a CBS show. From that Martin Manulis asked me if I would like to do a *Playhouse 90*. What a question! I'd give anything to do a *Playhouse 90*! I did a few *Playhouse 90*s with Martin, who was just so wonderfully ahead of his time and so into the theatricality of it—the bringing of theater to the audience. You know, I'm just thinking back that I was the only director who directed live and film *Playhouse 90*s.

I can't tell you how much those early days in television prepared me for everything that came later because live television was called organized chaos. You'd have to be so prepared, planning where to put your cameras and how to keep things moving. No matter how prepared you were, when that second hand hit the top, boy, you had to pray because there were eight hundred things that could go wrong. It was live and you had to be able to do something if something went wrong. So your mind was working all the time and it gave you not only excitement but also a creativity to get around problems, both before going on the air and while on the air.

There's nothing more exciting than live television. I think if you ask each of the film directors who came out of live television—John Frankenheimer, Sidney Lumet, and the others—if you ask them what they would rather do, almost all would say if there was still live television, they would rather do that than make films. The excitement of it and how everybody had to work together and had to contribute and it just had to go right. When you finished a show you were floating off the ground. You couldn't just go home.

You had to go and sit in the coffee shop across the street or have a beer for a couple of hours and just sort of settle back down to normal.

The Careless Years (1957)

Dean Stockwell; Natalie Trundy; John Larch; Barbara Billingsley;
John Stephenson; Maureen Cassidy; Alan Dinehart III; Virginia Christine.

I was working on a television film one day and I got a call from my agent and he said, "Arthur, would you be interested in directing a film?" And I said, "What kind of a question is that? Of course I would be interested." I then realized he was sitting in the producer's office and didn't want to give me away at too cheap a price. I, on the other hand, would have happily done it for nothing. That's how I got my start in feature film. It was for Kirk Douglas's company and Eddie Lewis, who was the head of the company, had written a screenplay and he hired me for my first film.

I can't remember my first day on the set of *The Careless Years*. But somewhere in the first week on almost every film I find myself saying to myself, "Arthur, you're not good enough for this, get out of this." If I could get out then it wouldn't hurt anybody and it wouldn't cost the company any money and they could get somebody else. Nowadays I'd say to myself, "Arthur come on, you've been doing this for years." We are all insecure. If you're in a creative work, as we are in the film industry, you can't judge your work. You cannot say, "I built a good table." Or, "Yes, I built this automobile, it's done," and you know right away whether it's good or bad. When you're creating, when you do a painting, when you do a film, you don't know what acceptance the finished piece will receive when it goes out there. When I did *The Careless Years* I thought, "This may be my first and my last film." It didn't take off and it wasn't a big smash and it was a few years before I did another feature film.

The Americanization of Emily (1964)

James Garner; Julie Andrews; Melvyn Douglas; James Coburn; Joyce Grenfell;
Ed Binns; Liz Fraser; Keenan Wynn; William Windom; John Crawford;
Douglas Henderson; Edmon Ryan; Steve Franken; Paul Newlan; Gary Cockrell.

The Americanization of Emily is my favorite film of any that I've directed. I read the script while I was doing another film for Marty Ransohoff, the producer, and I just was bowled over by it. It's the only picture I went after. I told Marty I had to direct it. He said, "No, no kid, you're too young—you're not ready." Then he went through seven or eight directors and finally said, "Okay, kid." So it just worked out. It's still my favorite film and it's still, I think, Marty Ransohoff's, James Garner's, James Coburn's, and Julie Andrews' favorite film.

I felt, when we were filming *The Americanization of Emily,* that we were conveying a wonderful message in a very entertaining way. A lot of people said that it was an anti-war film and I said, "No, it was not anti-war, it was anti- the glorification of war." It said, don't make war and heroes seem so wonderful that kids want to grow up to be heroes. Treat war for what it is. Yes, sometimes you have to go to war, you have to defend yourself, but don't glorify it. To be able to do that in an entertaining, satiric way with reality and a love story and with a D-Day landing where one man is turning away from the beach and the other one is saying, "The beach is the other way." And he says, "I know which way the beach is." You clearly see the effect it has on people.

To work with Julie Andrews on *The Americanization of Emily* was sheer heaven. I guess that would be the best way to say it. You just touch a button and Julie does it. Aside from the fact that she's a dear, charming, wonderful, warm person. I just knew that she would be the perfect one and she was. Wonderful actors make your life so easy because they do things in their acting that you know that the critics are going to call "a nice directorial touch." To that I say thank you. But then you think of all the times you've pulled a performance from the actor and the critics say, "Oh, what a wonderful acting job that person did." What I love about making movies is that it's a group activity. It's the coming together of so many creative juices that you pour into this pot and out comes this little entity—a movie.

Emily was a very difficult film to make, just in physical terms, because of the D-Day landings. I hate to admit it, but we filmed those scenes here at a beach whose name is Hollywood by the Sea. I would go there with the special-effects person and I would show him exactly where I was going to have James Garner running on the beach and where the other people would be so we could prepare the explosions so that everything would be safe. It took us two weeks of careful planning. When we actually filmed the beach sequence and James Garner, the explosions are going off and finally he's hit and he drops to the ground. When we filmed him dropping to the ground he bounced a little. "Oh my God," I thought, "What happened, what happened?" With all the care we took, putting all these explosions in all the right places, he fell on the metal water can on his belt and it cracked a rib.

The Out-of-Towners (1970)

Jack Lemmon; Sandy Dennis; Sandy Baron; Anne Meara; Robert Nichols;
Ann Prentiss; Ron Carey; Philip Bruns; Graham Jarvis; Carlos Montalbán;
Robert King; Johnny Brown; Dolph Sweet; Thalmus Rasulala; Jon Korkes.

To shoot *The Out-of-Towners* in New York was very difficult. When you have
a bus strike, a taxi strike, and a garbage strike in your script, how do you
shoot in midtown and not see a taxi or a bus, and piles of garbage? We were
filming on Second Avenue and we put out our own garbage and the police
film division assisted us. They were just remarkable. They blocked off all
the intersections for about five blocks. It's not easy to do that. When they
called us on the radio and said, "Okay, we're ready," we had to be ready because obviously they could only hold traffic for about ten seconds. I was
fortunate to have Jack Lemmon as the actor because when they called and
said, "Okay, we're ready," I would roll the cameras and I'd give Jack action
and Jack crossed the street playing the scene. I know any number of other
actors who when I said, "Ready, action," would have stepped off the curb
and then turned back and said, "Arthur, should I have stepped off with my
left foot or my right foot?"

To work with Jack Lemmon and Sandy Dennis was so rewarding to me
as a director because they were both so responsive and so eager to do what
was right. In fact, Jack would come over and say, "Arthur, what do you
think if we did such and such?" and I would say, "No, I don't think so."
Then he'd say, "Yeah, that's what I thought" and he'd walk away. And I finally said, "Jack, if you feel strongly, argue with me." They were both wonderful to work with.

Love Story (1970)

Ali MacGraw; Ryan O'Neal; John Marley; Ray Milland; Russell Nype;
Katharine Balfour; Sydney Walker; Robert Modica; Walker Daniels;
Tommy Lee Jones; John Merensky; Andrew Duncan;
Charlotte Ford; Sudie Bond; Julie Garfield.

Love Story was a screenplay before it was a book. Many people think it was
adapted from Erich Segal's book. Not so. Erich wrote the screenplay and it

was submitted to all the studios and everybody turned it down. A meeting was held in the New York office of the William Morris Agency, who represented Erich Segal, and they said, "We're sorry, we can't sell *Love Story*." Then Howard Minsky, who was the head of the motion picture division on the east coast at the William Morris office said, "Yes you can, because I'm going to buy it." He gave up his job and made an arrangement with Erich Segal because he had such faith in that project. He mothered it all the way through. If it hadn't been for him, it would never have been a film. He then got it to Ali McGraw and once he got Ali interested Paramount Pictures said they would do it.

We had no idea when we were making *Love Story* that it was going to be a big blockbuster with people lined up to see it. We thought we were making a nice little movie. Well, all of us thought that except the producer who kept saying, "Arthur, believe me, this will be big." And I said, "Yes Howard, you're the producer, you have to feel that way." But he was totally right.

The message of *Love Story* really is what two people can give to each other for love alone. You know, people made fun of the phrase "Love means never having to say you're sorry." But think about it. All it says is that if you love somebody, you understand they're not perfect and they don't have to apologize for every little thing they do that isn't perfect. It's an affirmation of the human spirit. If we had made that film two years earlier I think it would have been run over by the motorcycles. But we hit at a time when if you disagreed with somebody, you hated them. That was the feeling in 1969 and 1970. Well, people were tired of that and were looking to say, hey, love is okay. You can be mad at somebody and still love them.

We had a lot of problems in casting the role Ryan O'Neal finally played. I think we tested eight or nine different actors and Ryan was the best. He didn't bowl us over at first. Then I saw some footage of a film he was just completing at 20th Century Fox and I thought it would be wonderful. He just had that empathy and feeling that was so necessary. I had worked with Ryan before and I liked him very much, so that helped me too.

Ali McGraw was just a sheer delight to work with. Ali's aware she's not the greatest actress but she's a fine actress and she's a caring person. All that came together and she was very open to any suggestions and tried to do whatever I asked. It was just a lovely, lovely performance that this wonderful lady gave in that film.

When we did *Love Story*, Paramount was going under. They wanted to back out of the production but Robert Evans got in there and he fought for it. Finally I had to literally swear that I would not go over two million dollars. We finished filming here at Newport Beach, which stood in for Cape Cod, and came in twenty-five thousand dollars under budget. Then I went to the executives and I said, "I'd like to go back to Boston." I told them that I had cut some corners because of the budget. And they said, "No, you'll spend too much." I said, "Wait a minute, I just brought the picture in twenty-five thousand dollars under!" They said, "Okay, you can have fifteen thousand dollars and a small crew." I said, "Fine, that's exactly what I'm asking for—fifteen thousand dollars and a small crew." We went back to Boston and bumped into the worst snowstorm in twenty years. I flew out with Erich Segal and finally we got to Boston at two in the morning. I was up all night because I had to make the decision in the morning as to whether they should put Ali McGraw and Ryan O'Neal on a flight out of Los Angeles to do our filming. I decided yes, we should. Now, the virtue in going back was we were able to look at what we had filmed and see that we could enhance it with a couple of additional scenes. Well, the first morning that we went out to film it was snowing and I thought, "Oh," and I was the one who said, "Let's do this." We shot a scene of Ryan coming out of his father's office and I shot a beautiful scene with a Boston background.

Then I thought we could shoot at the airport waiting for the plane. So we go out to the airport and I find a place at American Airlines that I liked and Howard Minsky said, "I'll go get permission from the manager." Needless to say, it was still chaos at the airport because of the storm. Howard came back and said it would be forty-five minutes before he could even talk to the manager. I said, "Let's just go shoot it. It's an airport, what's the worst that can happen? They'll throw us out and we'll find another place." So we shot the scene. Then I went to Howard, who was still standing in line to see the manager, and said, "Forget it, we got the scene."

The actors went to lunch and I told Howard I would think of something else to shoot. After lunch the snow was still falling, so I told Howard we needed the football stadium opened and that I needed a football. I had worked out a scene where Ryan would throw the football and Ali would catch it and he would tackle her. With a hand-held camera we just kept shooting. I said, "Build a snow castle," and they built a snow castle. And the actors contributed too. It was just a lot of ad-libbing. I can remember the producer telling the story on a TV show once. He says he was standing there and remembers me screaming at Ryan and Ali, "Make angels, make angels," and he said to himself, what's "Make angels?" But the actors knew what I meant, so they spread their legs and arms in the snow and they made angels.

I often think if we hadn't done that, the film would not be quite the same. But that's taking away from that beautiful music that Francis Lai wrote for that scene. Actually he contributed an entire score that was unbelievable. Francis does not speak English and I do not speak French. I wrote him a letter explaining the kind of music I wanted along with notes of every little spot I wanted music in and what feeling I was looking for and how long. And when it came back I cried when I heard the tape. He had just given me everything I asked for and better. The two of them playing in the snow just said to me, be joyous. When things like that happen its just part of the excitement of filming.

Plaza Suite (1971)

Walter Matthau; Maureen Stapleton; Barbara Harris; Lee Grant;
Louise Sorel; José Ocasio; Dan Ferrone; Tom Carey;
Jenny Sullivan; Augusta Dabney; Alan North.

Neil Simon and I had a wonderful relationship on *Out-of-Towners*, so it was a pleasure to segue into *Plaza Suite* down the line, particularly when *Plaza Suite* was the roots of *Out-of-Towners*: *Out-of-Towners* was once the fourth act of *Plaza Suite* and then Neil took it out and made a movie out of it because he had the material. As much as *Out-of-Towners* was very much on the streets, *Plaza Suite* was very contained in a suite at the Plaza Hotel. You have to take such a totally different approach to a film that is basically in four walls as opposed to something that is outdoors and in motion and going all the time.

It was interesting to have Walter Matthau in all three acts. Walter is very, very skilled and has a sardonic wit that is, how should I say, untouched by anybody else. He just manages to keep the reality of these characters so well with such depth and yet to put in these funny lines and not make them seem like jokes at all. They come out of the character.

The Hospital (1971)

George C. Scott; Diana Rigg; Richard A. Dysart; Stephen Elliott; Donald Harron;
Andrew Duncan; Nancy Marchand; Jordan Charney; Roberts Blossom;
Lenny Baker; Richard Hamilton; Arthur Junaluska; Kate Harrington;
Katherine Helmond; David Hooks; Barnard Hughes.

When I got a call and Paddy Chayefsky wanted me to direct *Hospital* I was thrilled, because, as I told you, *Americanization of Emily* is my favorite film and Paddy is really the only genius I have ever worked with. There's just nothing he couldn't do. It's funny, you know, that to the day Paddy died, we would sit in the Carnegie Deli in New York and we would still be rewriting the ending. We never got it quite where we thought it should be and we'd say, "What if we had done this or that?" The picture had been out for ten years or so and we were still thinking about it and discussing it.

I decided to film it sort of like a drama/documentary. I wanted to get the feeling that you, the viewer, were peeking around the corner and always sort of on the inside, that you were a part of it. So I did a lot of it hand-held or what I call messy-good. There were situations where cameras moved and bounced around a lot. There's one scene that was five and a half pages and we did it in one shot. It took a few hours to get it ready and people said, "Why are you doing it all in one, it's so much work, blah, blah, blah." At any rate, by noon we had the scene and we had done two days work in a half-day. George C. Scott could have done the whole picture in one day if I could do it in one day, that's how prepared he was.

Harold Gould was to play the administrator of the hospital. He just finished a play in New York and he came over and said, "Arthur, I want to go back home." So I let him out of it and he went back to California. I made Steven Elliott, who was supposed to play a doctor operating on the wrong person, the administrator instead. Then I wondered who would be good to play the doctor that operates on the wrong patient? I thought, ah, Barney Hughes, who was already playing Diana Riggs' father in the film. And everybody said, "Wait a minute, he's playing another role, how can he play the doctor too?" I said, "No, he'll be in a medical outfit and we'll put a moustache and glasses on. Nobody's going to know it's him except his wife." Everybody thought I was crazy. Barney played both roles and nobody ever noticed.

Man of La Mancha (1972)

Peter O'Toole; Sophia Loren; James Coco; Harry Andrews;
John Castle; Brian Blessed; Ian Richardson; Julie Gregg; Rosalie Crutchley;
Gino Conforti; Marne Maitland; Dorothy Sinclair; Miriam Acevedo.

There was another director on *The Man of La Mancha* and the studio was not happy and they asked me to replace him. They were happy with me because I had just done *Hospital* for them and they loved that film. And so I went to Rome and I took over the picture

I thought we were making this wonderful musical and I thought, "Ah, it's so great," and it came out and the audience said, "Yes, that's good; that's very good." But they weren't bowled over. It actually put me into depression for about eight months. I couldn't work because I felt I had this wonderful, world-famous play, and I had this cast that I just loved, and such support from United Artists, and I could only blame myself. Then I realized that the problem was that the film should never have been made. The fantasy element didn't work. When Sophia Loren is standing there thirty feet tall on the screen it's too real, and when Peter O'Toole says, "That's not a kitchen scullery maid, that's a princess," it's hard for the audience to make that change. I thought, "Should I have changed her each time he looked at her, or should I have done the whole picture more as a fantasy?" It's hard to know. It worked and it was very good, and it went into profit, but I felt that it wasn't as good as it should have been.

Silver Streak (1976)

Gene Wilder; Jill Clayburgh; Richard Pryor; Patrick McGoohan; Ned Beatty;
Clifton James; Ray Walston; Stefan Gierasch; Len Birman; Valerie Curtin;
Lucille Benson; Scatman Crothers; Richard Kiel; Fred Willard; Delos V. Smith Jr.

Marty Ransohoff, who I had done *Americanization of Emily* with and *Wheeler Dealers* for, called and said, "Arthur, I've got your next picture. Come over and pick it up and take it home and read it—now! And let me know right away because," he said, "this is for you and this is perfect." When I got to page thirty-two I called and said, "Marty, you're right, I'll do this picture." Many times you read a script and at page thirty-two you think, "I'm loving this, I'm loving this, I hope the writer can keep a grip on it. I hope it's not going to fall apart." But with *Silver Streak* you could feel that Colin Higgins had a hold on it and he knew where he was going and he knew where to take that picture.

When I came onto it none of the actors were attached yet. Alan Ladd, Jr., who was head of Fox at that time, suggested that we use Gene Wilder. We all thought that was a clever idea. I met with Richard Pryor, who liked my work. He had seen *Man in the Glass Booth* fourteen times, so he said. We hit it off very well. Actually we've remained dear friends.

A lot of people always comment on the scene where Richard Pryor was teaching Gene Wilder how to be in black face or how to get away with being black so he could get past the security guard. People thought that was mostly ad libbed, but it wasn't. It's ad libbed to some extent, but if you read Colin Higgins' script, the scene was written beautifully. Then, hopefully, the actors and I contributed to make it work the way it did. But that's what's so wonderful about making films. It is a group activity. It's the coming together of many creative juices.

The In-Laws (1979)

Peter Falk; Alan Arkin; Richard Libertini; Nancy Dussault; Penny Peyser; Arlene Golonka; Michael Lembeck; Paul Smith; Carmine Caridi; Ed Begley Jr.; Sammy Smith; James Hong; Barbara Dana; Rozsika Halmos; Álvaro Carcaño.

That film started out because Alan Arkin and Peter Falk wanted to work together. They went to Warner's and said, "We'd like to do a picture," and Warner's said fine and suggested Andy Bergman to write it and out came *The In-Laws*. Alan Arkin, who was the executive producer, worked with Andy on the story. Then they asked me if I would direct it. It's funny, because of all the films I've done, *The In-Laws* is the one I get the most comments on. You'd think that *Love Story* would be the most, or something like *The Hospital,* but no, that's the one that gets the comments.

When you go on location everybody says, "Oh, you're going to Mexico," or "You're going to New York, isn't that wonderful." And I always say, "No, we are going on location, not vacation." But when we did *The In-Laws*, it was a lot like vacation because it was the one film where just somehow almost everything went right. The New York streets didn't seem to be a problem, things just worked so easily. Everywhere we went everybody was cooperative and if I said, "Gee, I like this bicycle shop, could that be the hotel interior"—boom, it became a hotel interior. And Alan and Peter worked with each other so well, as did the rest of the cast. But the rest of the cast was wonderful too.

There's a sequence in *The In-Laws* where Peter Falk is driving backwards on the freeway and cars are going all around and people say, "My God, how can he drive backwards with all that going on?" There's a stunt driver in the trunk of the car. We had all the gears rebuilt back there and the stunt driver is looking through two little holes so he can see where he is going. Stunt drivers drove all of the other cars and of course it was choreographed. In fact, I remember Jack Roe, my assistant, and I sitting on the floor with miniature cars that we bought, working out the rhythms of the scenes. To audiences it looks like Peter is driving backwards but really it's the stunt driver and Peter looks like he's driving backwards.

Author! Author! (1982)

Al Pacino; Dyan Cannon; Tuesday Weld; Bob Dishy; Bob Elliott;
Ray Goulding; Eric Gurry; Elva Josephson; B.J. Barie; Ari Meyers;
Alan King; Benjamin H. Carlin; Ken Sylk; James Tolkan; Tony Munafo.

You could almost say Al Pacino's a perfectionist. He really can keep going and keep changing and keep doing things differently until it hits. He doesn't realize how good he is. He doesn't realize that he hit the first time too. There's no way you're going to get a bad performance from Al Pacino. He creates characters in a just delicious way with such depth and such interest.

More on Actors in General

The wonderful thing about working with somebody like Al Pacino or John Goodman or Jack Lemmon is that you just have to throw a thought or a word at them and they will give you the whole thing. I know that with John Goodman in *The Babe*, there is a shot where we're on his legs and we follow those legs in a pan across the field and down into the dugout until he sits down and we see his whole body. When I finished take 1 I said, "John, on take 2 I need your legs more dejected," and everybody laughed. But on take 2, those legs were more dejected. He knew what I meant. I didn't have to explain it to him. That's the wonderful thing about working with those kinds of actors.

The Lonely Guy (1984)

Steve Martin; Charles Grodin; Judith Ivey; Steve Lawrence; Robyn Douglass; Merv Griffin; Dr. Joyce Brothers; Candi Brough; Randi Brough; Julie Payne; Madison Arnold; Roger Robinson; David P. Hannafin; Joan Suveny; Nicholas Mele.

In *Lonely Guy* you saw an example of different ways that you work with actors. I'm one for holding very much to the script because that's been developed and it's got its nuances. I'm not resistant to change, but I like to stay close to the script. When you have two actors like Steve Martin and Charles Grodin who can ad lib and create, it's best to engage their full talents. On almost every set or location, when we finished the scene, I would put them together, either on a park bench or sitting across from each other in the kitchen, and just let them do two or three minutes of chit-chat. As a result, a lot of those pieces are in the film because those two guys can do that. With other actors you have to be very specific because they need very specific lines. That doesn't make one better than the other. There are many actors who become that person and place. That is their acting skill. There are other actors who create it all in their mind and act it out. There's not right or wrong. It works either way and you, the audience, feel the performance. You don't know that it's a performance because that person became the character.

Outrageous Fortune (1987)

Shelley Long; Bette Midler; Peter Coyote; Robert Prosky; John Schuck; George Carlin; Anthony Heald; Ji-Tu Cumbuka; Florence Stanley; Jerry Zaks; John DiSanti; Diana Bellamy; Gary Morgan; Christopher McDonald; J.W. Smith.

I was very happy with the results of *Outrageous Fortune*. Shelley Long and Bette Midler were just wonderful in it. Bette went from four to seven months of a real pregnancy in that film. Not an easy transition, particularly with all the action and the climbing of mountains she had to do. Now, you can hide her pregnancy in the wardrobe, we always made sure she had loose fittings, you organize all that ahead of time. But I checked with three different obstetrician/gynecologists, hers and two others, and asked if we were endangering her. They said, no, as long as there isn't a sharp hit of some sort.

When you see the film and you see Bette climbing down something, you often don't see her feet because we created little steps to make it work. Or we created little places where her hand could hold on that you're not aware of. I would shoot in a close and they'd go behind a tree and then in the wide shot the stunt girl would take over. It feels like one shot but there are two different women playing the character—Bette and her double.

There is one scene I have to tell you about that scared us all. Bette and Shelley have become dear friends in the film and they are both mad at the Peter Coyote character. They're out in the middle of nowhere and they're trying to hitchhike and there are no cars. Finally this huge oil truck comes and they rush across the road to flag it down. We're looking straight down the road and the truck is coming and the two of them run across the road and Bette tripped and fell. I almost had a heart attack because I thought, "What have I done? I've killed a child! Oh my God!" I can't tell you the feelings that went through me of having done this to her and to the child. Shelley helped Bette up and they got on with the scene and it was okay. Turns out Bette did it on purpose. It just hit her as a funny thought as she was crossing the road. When she fell she protected herself, but what I went through you'll never know.

See No Evil, Hear No Evil (1989)

Richard Pryor; Gene Wilder; Joan Severance; Kevin Spacey; Alan North; Anthony Zerbe; Louis Giambalvo; Kristen Childs; Hardy Rawls; Audrie J. Neenan; Lauren Tom; John Capodice; George Bartenieff; Alexandra Neil; Tonya Pinkins.

When I was approached to work with Gene Wilder and Richard Pryor again I was thrilled because I had enjoyed them so much and had remained close friends with both of them. I worked with Gene on a rewrite that the script needed and then we proceeded. The most difficult part of directing that film was to get Richard Pryor to believe in himself. The man is such a wonderful talent. It's just amazing what he can do in acting and comedy terms. I think that burning incident that he went through caused him to lose faith, and my big job was to get him to believe in himself. Indeed he did come through again with that wonderful performance.

The Babe (1992)

John Goodman; Kelly McGillis; Trini Alvarado; Bruce Boxleitner; Peter Donat;
James Cromwell; J.C. Quinn; Joe Ragno; Richard Tyson; Ralph Marrero;
Bob Swan; Bernard Kates; Michael McGrady; Stephen Caffrey; Gene Ross.

I was really turned on to *The Babe* by the fact that it was really the story of a boy who was born at age nineteen. It was somebody who had been in a detention home and had not really been outdoors from the time he was seven to the time he was nineteen. Suddenly, through his baseball prowess, a major league ball team adopts him. Can you imagine what happens to a kid like that when the gates open and the world is yours? I thought it was a very interesting story because you understand then why he grabbed at so many things, why he did so many things that people said were terrible. I thought Babe's love for kids and what he did for kids in terms of buying them hot dogs, hamburgers, anything they wanted, was a story worth telling. He hit the two home runs for a little kid and that kid really did bring the baseball back to Babe many years later. The kid said, "You gave me this, I want you to have it now."

John Goodman had to learn to swing a bat right- and left-handed. He had to learn to ride a motorcycle and to run the way Babe would run. Look at the amount of effort that an actor goes through. He was working on the *Roseanne* series at the time. In the morning he would get up and spend two hours of each day working on his baseball practice with a good teacher. John was the only one I thought of to play the Babe. Sometimes a role cries out for this one person and you say that's it. John Goodman made my life easier.

It's very difficult to make a period film. For instance, we had to take three blocks in Chicago and create a totally different period look for the twenties and the thirties. We had to cover the streets with dirt so you wouldn't see pavement, because they were dirt streets back then. Obviously the wardrobe needs to be taken into consideration as well. Each day John went through an hour and a half of makeup to get the cheeks and chin right and also to age him. He played from nineteen till Babe died. With all these changes it took an hour and a half of makeup every day.

Everything that you see in that film really happened. Sometimes we took the liberty of changing the time of it to make the dramatic flow better, but everything that's in there happened. You know, a lot of people say, "Oh, he didn't point to center field when he hit that home run." Well, there is proof that he pointed. The proof is that they found the tapes of the radio announcer saying that he was pointing toward centerfield. Or Karl Malden who said to me, "Arthur, I know it's right, I was at the game." Now the proof is that he was indeed pointing. Whether he was pointing at the pitcher, pointing at the fence, pointing and saying he was putting it over the fence—nobody can be sure. But he did point.

I was very satisfied with *The Babe*. We did not get a very warm response from the critics. There were also many fine reviews but it didn't go across the board and it didn't do great business. I look back and I don't know the answer. I'm not saying we wouldn't make certain changes but basically it's the film we intended to make. People say to me, "You did wonderful but the script wasn't so great." My answer to that is simply that I accepted the script, I worked with the writer. I loved the script or I wouldn't have been doing it. But as I said, I was happy with the film. Yes, I would have made the ending a more little upbeat. We had a version where at the end we cut back to a newsreel and he comes out of the stadium and kids rush over and he's grabbing them and he's playing with them. The music comes up and he carries one of the kids on his shoulder and he's smoking his cigar and we have narration over it. Maybe that would have enhanced it. Who knows?

Carpool (1996)

Tom Arnold; David Paymer; Rhea Perlman; Rod Steiger; Kim Coates; Rachael Leigh Cook; Mikey Kovar; Micah Gardener; Jordan Warkol; Colleen Rennison; Ian Tracey; John Tench; Stellina Rusich; David Kaye; Obba Babatundé.

I'm working on a film now called *Carpool*, which, as you can tell from the title, should be a comedy, and it is. It is a fun story about an uptight advertising executive father (David Paymer) who's going to make the big presentation of his life that day. His wife, who has the carpool that morning, gets sick and he has to do the carpool himself. He and the kids end up being taken hostage by the Tom Arnold character—not really a robber but the police think he is. Of course it's a wonderful chase film. The father, who's very upset and uptight, learns that there is more to life and

EDITOR'S NOTE: This interview was conducted prior to the production of *Carpool.*

learns to pay more attention to his kids and to care for them more. It's a very sweet, warm picture.

How Does He Assess His Work?

I think if I had to find a theme going through my films, it would be an affirmation of the human spirit. I like to see something that says hey, you can be good or you can be better, whether we're saying it in a comedic way, dramatic way, or a musical way—that people can live together. People can work together, people can be friendly, and you can accomplish things. I'm disturbed by what I call fractionalization in society now, where it seems that we're becoming smaller and smaller groups and only my group counts. I say, why can't it all be like it is on a movie set? On a movie set, it's wonderful. There's so much hard work, so many difficulties, and so many people working together all cooperating, all caring about each other, and all pointed towards the same goal and you think, why can't the country be run that way?

I'm a very organized director. I like to be able to answer any question that anybody's going to ask me two weeks before we start filming. I go through it very carefully over and over. I just keep reading the script to work out what it is I'm looking for in the characters. I create background characters for the actors. They don't have to follow it but they get the feel for what I'm looking for in the character. I actually find that the more organized I am, the more flexible I am. If something happens on a set, like snow falling in *Love Story*, I can grab it and do something with it. I'm flexible because I have the security to fall back on, what it is I've prepared so carefully.

The Industry Today

The major studios have gone through some transitions over the years, depending on how far back you go. In the old days there were the moguls. But they had a great love for making films. They loved movies. They would do things that would make money but they would also do films that didn't make money but were worth doing. Today the major studios have boards of directors and the boards of directors want to know what their return will be each quarter.

His Parting Words

I hope that I can just keep directing movies. I could have retired many years ago, but I love making movies. I hope that the community will still like my work and keep offering me jobs. They still are and I'm so happy about that, because many directors, like Frank Capra, couldn't get a film after the age of fifty-six. Can you imagine a man like Capra, who did those wonderful films, not being able to direct because he's considered too old? So I consider myself very fortunate to still be out there and still be making movies.

Filmography

Gunsmoke (TV Series, 1955)
Alfred Hitchcock Presents (TV Series, 1955)
The Careless Years (1957)
Naked City (TV Series, 1958)
Thriller (TV Series, 1960)
The Barbara Stanwyck Show (TV Series, 1960)
The Dick Powell Show (TV Series, 1961)
This Rugged Land (1962)
The Wheeler Dealers (1963)
Miracle of the White Stallions (1963)
The Addams Family (TV Series, 1964)
The Americanization of Emily (1964)
Penelope (1966)
Promise Her Anything (1966)
The Tiger Makes Out (1967)
Tobruk (1967)
Popi (1969)
Love Story (1970)
The Out-of-Towners (1970)

EDITOR'S NOTE: Since this interview was completed, Arthur Hiller has directed *An Alan Smithee Film: Burn Hollywood Burn*. The name "Alan Smithee" is the one designated by the Directors Guild for directors who wish to remove their name from a film for whatever reason. Interestingly enough, Hiller chose to do just that when disagreements arose with the producers of the film.

The Hospital (1971)
Plaza Suite (1971)
Man of La Mancha (1972)
The Crazy World of Julius Vrooder (1974)
The Man in the Glass Booth (1975)
W.C. Fields and Me (1976)
Silver Streak (1976)
Nightwing (1979)
The In-Laws (1979)
Making Love (1982)
Author! Author! (1982)
Romantic Comedy (1983)
Teachers (1984)
The Lonely Guy (1984)
Outrageous Fortune (1987)
See No Evil, Hear No Evil (1989)
Taking Care of Business (1991)
The Babe (1992)
Married To It (1993)
Carpool (1996)
An Alan Smithee Film: Burn Hollywood Burn (as Alan Smithee, 1997)

Awards

Academy Awards, USA
Love Story, Best Director (nominated), 1971

Berlin International Film Festival
The Hospital, Special Jury Prize, 1972

Directors Guild of America, USA
Robert B. Aldrich Achievement Award, 1999

Golden Globes, USA

Love Story, Best Motion Picture Director, 1971

Razzie Awards

An Alan Smithee Film: Burn Hollywood Burn, Worst Director (nominated), 1999

The Films of Terry Gilliam

Terry Gilliam's sense of humor is slightly different from that of the rest of us. If you do not believe that, read his biography as he submitted it:

1940. Born in Minneapolis, Minnesota, on November 22, 1940.

1951. Goes west to Los Angeles. Finds no Indians.

1958–62. Attends Occidental College, Los Angeles. Edits college humor magazine. Eventually majors and graduates in Political Science.

1962–65. In search of the Big Time moves to New York. Becomes associate editor of *Help!* magazine, brainchild of *Mad Magazine's* originator, Harvey Kurtzman. Also does freelance illustrating for a variety of publications. Decided film schools are a waste of time.

1965–66. Lost somewhere in Europe.

1966. Back in Los Angeles fails as a freelance illustrator. Tries advertising as a copywriter and art director. Gets bored.

1967. Moves to London, England. Does freelance illustration for *Sunday Times, Nova, Queen,* etc. Pretentiously becomes the artistic director of the *Londoner Magazine,* which soon ceases publications.

1968. Sells two short sketches to *Do Not Adjust Your Set.* Is ignored by Mike Palin and Terry Jones. Befriended by Eric Idle, buys first round of drinks (The last time he did. You thought Jack Benny was tight, eh?—J.C.). Becomes resident cartoonist on *We Have Ways of Making You Laugh* TV series. Does first animated cartoon to help the show out of a nasty spot. Strangely enough, is asked to do a second animation. Does full-color animation section on *Marty* (BBC-2 series). Makes three animated films for second series of *Do Not Adjust Your Set.*

1969. *Monty Python* begins. Doesn't think it will be successful.

Terry Gilliam is one of those people that everybody wants to please because he has such a great sense of humor and he cares so much about his work that it makes everyone else care. I mean, Terry is a true artist. In every way, he lives and breathes his work and he enjoys the hell out of it.

Shelly Duvall—Actress

The Conversation

I think I'm the black sheep of our family. I don't know where I got this brain that's sort of floating around in this skull. I think I'm just one of nature's mutants. I've got a cousin who's an artist, a painter, but other than that, I am the black sheep.

The first eleven or twelve years of my life was spent running around on dirt roads playing in swamps, swimming in rivers, having a fairly Tom Sawyer-esque childhood, which was great. I've always loved the country. It stays with me, I think. A lot of what I do comes from this problem of being a country boy living in cities. From Minnesota we moved to Los Angeles. We moved to a place called Panorama City that is one of those tracts that were built in the San Fernando Valley just after the period of the Valley that you see in *Chinatown*. I liked seeing *Chinatown* because that was just before we destroyed that part of the world.

After college I went off to New York and was the assistant editor on a magazine called *Help!*, working with Harvey Kurtzman, who was one of my great idols as a kid. He was the guy that began *Mad* comics. I think I learned most everything I know from that period. My films are like some of those comic books. They're just full of details. Willie Elder, who is one of the cartoonists of *Mad*, filled his world with gags and things.

New York led to a couple of things. I met John Cleese there, which ultimately led to *Python*. He appeared in one of the photo stories we did for the magazine. We would write these satirical, silly stories, then go out and film them with a still camera. I met John on one of those. Then I went off to Europe; hitchhiked around for six months and fell in love with it because the castles were real. I came back to America and worked in advertising for about a year. In fact, it was with the people who invented the Happy Face, things like that, that went on to plague us in later years. I was out here in L.A. wanting to be a filmmaker but didn't like the system. Couldn't work my way up through a system. I've never been able to do that. Eventually, I went off to England and that was the end of my career.

I went to London two or three years later. I was a cartoonist and an illustrator making my living doing cartoons for magazines back in L.A. and magazines in France, plus doing illustrations for color supplements in London. I was also the art director for a magazine called *The Londoner.* I was getting more and more frustrated because I wanted to do something beside magazines.

I knew John Cleese from our period back in New York. At that point he was on the David Frost program and was becoming quite well known in television. And I approached him and asked him, "How do I get into television?" John introduced me to a producer who was producing a television show called *Do Not Adjust Your Set* which was a kids' show, written and performed by Mike Palin, Terry Jones, and Eric Idle. They didn't like me at all because I was a foreigner invading their turf, and especially an American! But we became friends eventually and went on to another show called *We Have Ways of Making You Laugh.* I was the guest cartoonist on the show and I would draw caricatures of whoever was coming on. I was doing this week after week.

One day they approached me and said they had this material and didn't know what to do with it. I suggested we make an animated film of it. I'd never done one but I knew how these things were done. I had two weeks and four hundred pounds and the only way I could do it was with cutouts. So I made photographs, cut them up, and moved them around very quickly and it went on the television, and literally overnight I was an animator. Millions of people saw it and nobody had ever seen anything quite like this. So now I was an animator.

When *Do Not Adjust Your Set* began its second series I was an animator on that. John had a standing offer from the BBC to do a program. John was keen to work with Mike Palin and he was also writing and performing with Graham Chapman. So this brought us all together. We took up BBC's offer and became *Monty Python's Flying Circus* and my career finished again.

Working on *Python* doing all this animation became a rather lonely job. I was on my own day after day, night after night, talking to pieces of paper. That was my relationship with humanity at that point. I would always turn up the day of the show with my little can of film and I'd have to sit around all day and I got terribly bored. So I thought I'd start putting on some of the funny clothes that nobody else wants to wear. I'd do the grotesque parts that nobody else wanted to do. And little by little I started doing more and more characters in the show. Most of the others didn't like wearing makeup and I just felt one could add visually to the show by having strange characters, creatures. I was always happier hiding behind a lot of disguise and so I would start putting on weirder and weirder makeup.

And Now for Something Completely Different (1971)

Graham Chapman; John Cleese; Eric Idle; Terry Jones; Michael Palin;
Terry Gilliam; Carol Cleveland; Connie Booth.

I didn't direct this. You have your notes all wrong. Erase them immediately. Ian McNaughton, who had been directing the television show, directed this first film. It was really a series of the sketches from the first series and some of the second. Terry Jones and I had always been frustrated film directors. We knew better, of course, than Ian. We would sit there and try to tell him where to place the camera. And so when the offer came to do another Python film, *Monty Python and The Holy Grail,* Terry and I took the opportunity to offer to anybody in the group named Terry the opportunity to direct. And since there were two of us, we got the job.

Monty Python and The Holy Grail (1975)

Graham Chapman; John Cleese; Eric Idle; Terry Gilliam; Terry Jones;
Michael Palin; Connie Booth; Carol Cleveland; Neil Innes; Bee Duffell;
John Young; Rita Davies; Avril Stewart; Sally Kinghorne; Mark Zycon.

We actually learned on the job. We shot *Holy Grail* in five weeks and we were up in the highlands of Scotland. The very first day of the very first film that we ever directed we carried all the gear out of the vans and cars, down a mountainside, across the river, up another mountainside, to the famous Bridge of Death scene in the Seven Sisters Peaks of Scotland. We'd built this bridge across this chasm and we turn over in the very first shot and the camera breaks. That was our introduction to filmmaking. We did everything wrong we could possibly do at that point. We panicked and shot closeups. We had the most gorgeous scenery and we're shooting closeups, something that could be shot in anybody's garden. But we somehow survived.

We had chosen about four or five castles to shoot at. Unfortunately the National Trust, which is in charge of the historical buildings in England, deemed Python would not respect the dignity of the fabric of the buildings. So, with a couple of weeks to go, we were thrown out of all of these castles, places where the most awful tortures had taken place, awful behavior by the real people who'd built them, but comedy was not allowed. So we had to fake it really quickly. We built castles as cutouts, fifty-foot high painted cutouts, and we'd stick them on hills. It was a very fast and furious way of learning how to fake filmmaking.

When we were doing television, we always had big ideas. We did a lot of parodies of films and film directors. I think we were all frustrated by the limitations of that little screen. So, when we set out to do an epic we wanted to have scale, we wanted to have horses. Of course we didn't get horses, we got coconuts. The success of *The Holy Grail* is due to the fact that we didn't have the money to make a mediocre epic. Because given the time and the money we would have been mediocre. But because we didn't we had to come up with silly ideas, which in the end, proved to be much more interesting.

Terry Jones and I, who had been very close during the television shows, felt we had the same view of the film. What we discovered very soon was we seemed to have slightly divergent views. So for the crew there were two voices, two directors directing. We got the assistant director to try to be the common voice. Well, it turned out he had film directing aspirations as well, so he was directing a third film which Terry and I didn't want to make. So we solved the problem by letting Terry work with the actors and I would stay back behind the camera because the guys didn't behave like pieces of paper.

I would sit and draw the storyboard out, especially on the special-effects shots where we needed a matte shot because we were throwing animals over the embattlement. We didn't have real animals, of course. Months later we would throw little toy animals up in the air in somebody's back garden. But the day we were shooting it required the guys to keep their heads below the parapet of the castle in the foreground. The only way to do that was to dig a hole and put the camera in it. But the guys were still too tall. Then we had them kneeling down but the guys didn't like kneeling down in armor. They felt it was a very silly way of acting. At that time I didn't have many social skills because I had been in my garret lo those many years. So I would just walk off in a huff and say, "You wrote the scene, you wanted me to direct it for you, but you're not taking my orders. Good-bye!" And I'd go off and lie down in the grass and Terry would then take over. It was an interesting way of learning to make films.

I think *Holy Grail* is a great film. I think it's wonderful. We somehow managed to do in four and half weeks things that I could never even think of doing now. There was something about our naiveté and our ambition that got us through these nightmares. It really was a series of sketches. We kept thinking we wanted to make a film that was more dramatic, that was more integrated, in a more normal, narrative sense. But it doesn't matter when you look at it. It's funny. Also, we managed to achieve visuals that were as rich as you'd find in a proper epic. We made it dirty. We made it feel like you could smell the times despite the fact the people were running around banging coconuts together. We approached it very seriously.

If You Like Us, Fine. If You Don't, That's Fine Too!

One of the things about Python is that we never set out to please everybody. That's one of the things we were rebelling against. We were rebelling against the TV network, rebelling against film studios that were trying to reach the biggest possible audience at the expense of the quality of the film. We said, we're going to make stuff that makes us laugh. We're going to make six people laugh and that's good enough for us. It was very unique. We weren't in a situation where we had producers, managers, or directors telling us what we had to do. We were spared all of that advice. We did things to please ourselves. I don't think that's been the case with many groups or individuals in film or in television. It was a very special time and we were allowed to get away with murder. And the fact that it translates and other people like it is partly due to the fact that it is so unique and special and not trying to please anybody but us. And so, a lot of people don't get it and they never will and we don't care. The people who do get it, love it. I'd always rather go for people being passionate about what we do as opposed to saying, "Oh, that was okay." I'd rather they say, "That's rubbish. That's a piece of shit!" Or, "That's wonderful. It's the best thing I've ever seen." The middle ground I don't want to know about.

Jabberwocky (1977)

Michael Palin; Harry H. Corbett; John Le Mesurier; Warren Mitchell; Max Wall; Rodney Bewes; John Bird; Bernard Bresslaw; Anthony Carrick; Peter Cellier; Deborah Fallender; Derek Francis; Terry Gilliam; Neil Innes; Terry Jones.

Jabberwocky was born out of frustration and the fact that I didn't get to do all the things I wanted to do in *Holy Grail*. I felt limited by the fact that we had to always be funny. I wanted to escape from that trap. I wanted to be adventurous, suspenseful, and romantic, and a lot of other things. I felt we had failed on certain levels in *Grail*. So I set out to do my medieval film.

Jabberwocky, the Lewis Carroll poem, has always been a favorite of mine. The madness of his world is the sanest thing I've ever read. The idea of taking this poem, this nonsensical poem, and turning it into a film was just a starting point. I'm not sure what the film has to do with the poem other than we have a monster and somebody kills him with a sword. So that's where we started.

You have a character, Dennis Cooper, played by Michael Palin, who's got very small dreams. He just wants to open a little shop. I like the fact he wants to marry the big fat girl and not a beautiful, obvious, Doris Day type. He's fallen in love with someone who's not attractive. And yet he ends up winning half the kingdom and the hand of the princess. So it's a terrible irony. He gets the happy ending, but it's the wrong happy ending.

That started me on my way. I really don't like the character, except he gets caught up in this situation where he becomes a hero, unwittingly, and gets everything he ever wanted by terms of the way the media works, or the way fairy tales work. These are the things you're supposed to want and he gets them all but it's not what he wanted.

It's placed in a medieval setting because I like the Middle Ages. We're able to deal with kings and princesses. We're able to deal with things that everybody understands. They're archetypes. Once you've got the archetype you can twist and turn it upside down and everybody knows what you're doing.

Time Bandits (1981)

John Cleese; Sean Connery; Shelley Duvall; Katherine Helmond; Ian Holm; Michael Palin; Ralph Richardson; Peter Vaughan; David Warner; David Rappaport; Kenny Baker; Malcolm Dixon; Mike Edmonds; Jack Purvis; Tiny Ross.

I had been working on a script that eventually was going to become *Brazil*, but nobody wanted to know about that. I was getting more and more frustrated. We had made Python's *Life of Brian* and George Harrison and his manager, Denis O'Brien, had basically come to the rescue and with Python we started a company called Handmade Films. Because of that and because of my frustration of not getting *Brazil* off the ground I sat down one afternoon and said, "Let's take advantage of the situation. Let's write a film that would appeal to everybody in the family. A film that would be exciting enough for adults and intelligent enough for children."

I wanted the film to be from a kid's point of view. I wanted the camera to be low but I was worried that a kid couldn't sustain it. So I thought, let's put a gang around him, but they've got to be his height. So we ended up with a group of little people who become the *Time Bandits*. Then we set this adventure in a time when these people were part of heaven, part of creation, they were God's helpers. But that wasn't good enough for them. They wanted money, like most people in the world. Again, low ambition. And so they set out to rob time and space.

Once I got into this way of thinking, that you could commit a robbery and escape back before that time was even invented, it was wonderful. So they were criminals, always moving back in time, escaping their pursuers who were going in the other direction. I love the idea that time and space is not perfect. God got distracted, was not perfect, he made mistakes. So it's all about flawed creation, and about greed, and about things being seen from a child's point of view. That's where it started. I basically scribbled this down over a weekend and off we went.

I called Mike Palin up and said, "Hey, come on. Do you want to do this?" There's a great relationship between Mike and I. Mike is so funny. He's so prolific. Ideas and words just flow from him. I'm not nearly as prolific as that but I'm much more focused and I can set a course and steer it pretty severely, while Mike can do a dance all over the place and keep going. And that's how we work. In a very short while we did a script. We then went to Denis and George and said, "Let's do this film." Denis loved it because he somehow saw George writing music for *Snow White and the Seven Dwarfs*. Hi, ho, it's off to work we go.

It went out to all the world for consideration but the world didn't want films for all the family at that particular juncture in the history of Hollywood. The studios did not understand that you could actually make something that kids would like and adults would like. We got turned down by everybody!

Sean Connery appearing in *Time Bandits* started out as a joke, basically. Mike and I wrote in the script *"The Greek warrior removed his helmet revealing himself to be Sean Connery or an actor of equal but cheaper stature."* We never dreamed that we could actually get Sean, but he turned out to be a golfer playing with Denis O'Brien one day and the idea came up. It came up at a point when Sean's career was, I think, in its low years, pretty low at that point. And he said yes, he was interested. I also think at the time he felt something about parenthood and fatherhood and here was a chance to be a surrogate father in this thing.

We finally met and he had wonderful ideas, all of which I ignored. And then we went out to shoot the film. We were shooting in Morocco in 130-degree heat on the top of the mountain. And there was Sean with the rest of us sitting there with his cardboard box eating lunch. He was wonderful. There were no problems. He saved me, basically, because the fight with the Minotaur was on the very first day of the shoot and I hadn't shot anything for a couple of years. I had this elaborate storyboard worked out with about twenty-five set-ups. It was madness. And Craig Warnock, the boy, had never been in a film before and suddenly he's on top of a mountain in Morocco with Sean Connery. I was crazed because I knew I couldn't get all these shots and Sean said, "All right, let's just stop. Here's what you've got to do. Shoot my stuff. Shoot it simply. Let me get out of here. Then you can concentrate on the boy. Forget about this storyboard, let's just get on and do it."

It was great. No nonsense. We got through it. He's an interesting man because he's not the most trusting man and he doesn't suffer fools and he wasn't sure who he was dealing with. He said, "I'm not going to let you see me get on the horse because I won't look good. So what I'll do is just rise up in the stirrups and you can film me sitting down. That's all you get. You've got to work your way around that one, kid." But it was fantastic because it got us through it.

We had Sean contracted for fourteen days. But the part was actually much more complicated than that because at the big battle at the end, when the archers appear, Sean was to be leading the charge and he was going to be killed in the battle. So we never got any of that material because we didn't have him anymore. We changed the battle so that Fidgit got killed instead. I thought, "Oh, it's better one of the *Time Bandits* gets killed, anyway." We still didn't have an ending to the film.

But I remembered a conversation I had with Sean when we first met. He had said, "Wouldn't it be great if I was the fireman at the end of the film?" I remembered that conversation and said, "Let's get Sean as the fireman." We got him literally the day he had come over to England to see his accountant. It was between lunch and the appointment. We put him in a fireman's outfit. I did two shots with him, one putting the boy down with Sean delivering a line, and another one getting into the truck and winking. That's all we did. Two months later we wrote a scene incorporating that.

That's what intrigues me about making films. You've got to listen to the people who are there. You're getting all this information. You're getting clues to the puzzle. And even though everything's scripted there's a puzzle beyond the script and it's the film itself. And if you listen to all these things somehow they're going to come in and save your ass somewhere in the process. And that was my lesson on *Time Bandits*.

A Beatle! Wow!

When Eric Idle and I came out to L.A. for the promotion of *Monty Python and the Holy Grail*, we met George Harrison at a party. A Beatle! Wow! It turned out this Beatle was the number one Python fan on the planet. He knew every sketch. It used to be embarrassing because George would do a feed line from a Python sketch and I would just look blankly at him because I didn't know what he was talking about because I couldn't remember what we had done. He seems to have remembered everything we had done. Anyway, we all became friends. In fact, Eric became a very close friend of George.

EMI had put up the money for *Life of Brian* and we got a call from them because the boss of EMI had finally gotten around to reading the script and decided it was blasphemous and they pulled the money. We were in major trouble. We didn't know what to do. Eric had been talking to George and George said, "Why don't I help finance it." And he got together with his manager Denis O'Brien and they managed to raise money. They mortgaged buildings and everything else they had and we made *Life of Brian*. That's how that relationship began. And because of that we formed Handmade Films. Monty Python, George, and Denis became Handmade Films. We were very successful with *Life of Brian* and it was great to have some payback for all the Beatles albums I'd bought.

Monty Python's The Meaning of Life (1983)

Graham Chapman; John Cleese; Terry Gilliam; Eric Idle; Terry Jones; Michael Palin; Carol Cleveland; Simon Jones; Patricia Quinn; Judy Loe; Andrew MacLachlan; Mark Holmes; Valerie Whittington; Jennifer Franks; Imogen Bickford-Smith; Myrtle Devenish; Matt Frewer.

The Meaning of Life, I think, was a tired attempt to keep the group together. We had stopped doing television but we still wanted to work together in some way. Movies take up a lot less time than a television series so we agreed to make a movie. We all went off and wrote something called *Monty Python's World War III* and then we re-wrote it and it became *Monty Python's The Meaning of Life*.

The group wasn't really working together as well as we'd worked on *Life of Brian*. We'd all gone our separate ways, our work habits were different, and so *The Meaning of Life* ended up being much more about sketches. It was a series of independently written things and I think it's an uneven film. But the good bits are very good, as good if not better than anything we've done.

It was still considered my job to do the animation in the group but I didn't want to be an animator anymore. I had directed a couple of my own films and enjoyed that freedom. I had an idea that had been originally an animation idea about this group of old accountants who set off on the high seas of finance and become pirates. Out of my frustration of being trapped as an animator I said, "Why don't you let me make it as a live action piece?" It was called *The Crimson Permanent Assurance*.

So basically I made my own little film, had my own set, my own crew, and we made this short film which was originally supposed to appear about two-thirds of the way into the movie. But in the end it didn't fit like it was supposed to. I realized that my rhythm had become different from the group's rhythms, with the expectations of laugh, laugh, laugh. My piece didn't work that way. It worked on a different level and we kept cutting it shorter and shorter, and it reached a point where I said, "Well, we can't cut it any shorter. Let's just pull it out of the film." So we pulled it out and put it on as a feature-ette before the film. So you have this short film, *The Crimson Permanent Assurance*, that goes on before the main film and it's a treat.

The Pythons Worked Well Together

Python work was interesting because we were a group of six people who chose each other and respected and liked each other. We would work in different groups. John and Graham Chapman wrote together. Mike Palin and Terry Jones wrote together. Eric wrote on his own and I did my animations on my own.

When it came time to doing something new, a new series for example, we would set a few months aside and everybody would go away and start writing separately. Then we would have a group meeting and start weeding the stuff out. Ideas would spring from that. Some sketches would be half a good sketch and then the other half fell apart. One of the other guys would take it, rewrite it and carry on. And eventually we would put things in piles. Ones we all agreed on, ones we were mixed on and so on. We would start assembling shows out of those stacks of ideas.

There was one thing within Python that was very important. Back then television shows all tended to be based on sketches. You'd do a very funny sketch but you'd have to end it with a punch line and invariably the punch lines weren't as good as the sketch. You'd end up with a very sour taste in your mouth. So we said, okay, let's get rid of the punch lines. I had done a cartoon for *Do Not Adjust Your Set* that was a stream of consciousness cartoon. It was about elephants and other things and things flowed one into the other. Terry Jones got very excited about it and thought that's the way the show ought to work. When things reach their peak, let's move on to something else. We'd make connections in strange, different, and odd ways. We could reconstruct the scene and rearrange it any way we wanted. And it just generally worked.

I was the lucky one because the others had to submit their material to the group to be voted on. Because my animation was never completed until the last moment I got more freedom than the others did. I would just turn up at the end of the day and say, "Here." They didn't know how to react to my stuff. It just had to go in. It was fortunate, or lucky, that we were all on the same wavelength and it seemed to work. What I enjoyed as the series went on is how some of the sketches became like the cartoons and some of the cartoons became like the sketches. And Eric's stuff seemed to be like Mike's stuff. You didn't know after a while who was creating what because we were all working so well together. In many instances it is very hard to know who wrote what.

> *What I think about Terry, besides being a genius and the visual artist that he is, is that the man has no ego. He really doesn't, and he's so aware of what he knows and he's so aware of what he doesn't know.*
> Brad Pitt—Actor

Brazil (1985)

Jonathan Pryce; Robert De Niro; Katherine Helmond; Ian Holm; Bob Hoskins; Michael Palin; Ian Richardson; Peter Vaughan; Kim Greist; Jim Broadbent; Barbara Hicks; Charles McKeown; Derrick O'Connor; Kathryn Pogson; Bryan Pringle.

Brazil was the result of years of anger and frustration at the way things worked and the way the system and the world worked. I first called it *The Ministry*. At one time I called it *1984½*. I felt that we had to do a modern version of *1984* and try to deal with society the way that it really was. I wanted to have some kind of catharsis. I had all this bile building up in me about the way things were.

I had written about a hundred pages of stuff but it wasn't necessarily in the right order. I couldn't quite get the thing in shape. At one point somebody suggested I work with Tom Stoppard because verbally he was as pyrotechnical as I was visual. So Tom and I got involved. It was quite wonderful. He took the stuff and rearranged it in the right order and he made wonderful leaps. Tom had been contracted for three drafts and we reached a point where I still wasn't happy.

Then I got involved with Charles McKeown. We talked about the ideas where I thought we were right and where we were wrong. We ended up with this massive script that was twice as long as the film would be. It was even more complicated than the film itself because the dream sequence was an entire story all on its own. It involved extraordinary sets, huge numbers of people, and ideas that in the end never made it into the film. Like most of my projects I ended up wanting to do more than I was capable of doing.

I had met producer Arnon Milchan. At that point he was really just beginning in Hollywood. I liked him because he was a pirate and because I didn't like Hollywood and I didn't want to deal with that system. We became a couple of buccaneers, raping and pillaging our way through Hollywood.

For the longest time we tried to get the money for the film but nobody was interested. Then we went to the Cannes Film Festival and we started running around the corridors there. Somehow in a couple of days we got a feeding frenzy going between Universal and 20th Century Fox.

Now listen carefully, because these are important things to know about how films get made. We initially had a twelve million-dollar budget and nobody was taking us seriously. We then raised it to fifteen. Suddenly we were in a new league.

There was another thing that became important. *Time Bandits* had become very successful in America. It made about fifty million dollars, which would be over a hundred now in today's dollars. So I had been elevated to hot director status. Now, there was a big film some people were trying to get made and they clearly had gone through Spielberg and Lucas and all the other directors and finally got down to my name. There's a mentality at work here.

It was a number one project and as they went down the list of directors, rather than going lower, they were elevating each director up. So, suddenly I became the hot director that they wanted to do this hot project with. When I turned it down, they said, "What? How could you?" I said, "Because

I have something better called *Brazil.*" And *Brazil,* which had been rejected by them all, suddenly had been elevated to be a hot property because the hot director had turned down the number one hot property for another hot property. Complex, but true. For the record that other hot property was *Enemy Mine* which nobody went to see, but that's another story.

So now we are running around Cannes telling our tale to people at Universal. The nice thing about Cannes is that the sun is shining and you're in France. The food is good, the wine is flowing, and people are away from their desks in Hollywood. They're relaxed for a moment. They're vulnerable. Then parasites like Arnon and myself can come in and take advantage of these people. So we lulled them into a false sense of security with this complicated story that they didn't quite understand but since somebody else wanted it they had to have it. We ended up with two studios giving us the money to make *Brazil.*

Then we went off and made it and everything went wrong. Within twelve weeks we knew we were going to be two or three times over budget. The film was going to be about five hours long, so we actually stopped production for two weeks. I started tearing pages out of the script. We started up again. We somehow finished the film.

It was a strange experience because we were scheduled for a twenty-one week shoot. In the end we shot for nine months and came in under budget by about a million dollars.

Arnon was a good buddy of Robert De Niro's. Bob had just done *Once Upon a Time in America,* and I think he was a Python fan as well. I offered him any part in the script he wanted and he chose the role I had already given to Mike Palin. It took a month or two to convince him to play Harry Tuttle, the freelance engineer, the man who makes things work, the real hero of the film as far as I was concerned. It was interesting because Bob thought it was too simplistic a character. I thought it would be wonderful for him to play a hero. I told him he was a hero to us in real life. So it's simple, you just go in there and you do it, and he did. What was extraordinary was that even though he's only on film for a few minutes, he spent months preparing for it. I told him he was a plumber, but really more like a brain surgeon. So he went to brain surgery operations. He had doctors showing him. He worked and worked and trained. It was pretty amazing because even for a small part he's got to put everything into it. That's impressive.

I think a lot of people aren't trained to watch a dense, visual film because most films put the key thing right there in front of you and it lingers. I clutter the thing up. So a lot of people weren't sure what was the most interesting thing they were suppose to be watching. They get lost in it. They didn't know if they were supposed to laugh or cry. I just remember people getting edgy watching that film.

There was a lawyer in New York who saw it and went back to his office and apparently closed the door and sat in that office for three days without taking any calls. There was a lady at Universal in the publicity department who said she saw it and later that night she was taking a shower and just started sobbing uncontrollably in the shower because of the film. And I thought, "God, I've done something really well here."

The first inkling I got of having done something special was in Paris while promoting the film. The journalists were coming and asking me if I read poetry. And I said, "Not much, why?" "Because," they said, "this film is a poem, it's poetic, it's symphonic." I said, "What?" I didn't know what they were talking about. But I sensed what they were talking about. The French got it immediately. They were the first to get it. They understood it. The American audiences took a while.

The Adventures of Baron Munchausen (1988)

John Neville; Eric Idle; Sarah Polley; Oliver Reed; Charles McKeown;
Winston Dennis; Jack Purvis; Valentina Cortese; Jonathan Pryce; Bill Paterson;
Peter Jeffrey; Uma Thurman; Alison Steadman; Ray Cooper; Robin Williams.

The first time I was aware of Baron Munchausen was in a catalog at the British Film Institute. There was an amazing picture that was a combination of live actors and what looked like engraved backgrounds. It was a film made by Karel Zeman, a Czech filmmaker. He was using these engravings as backgrounds for this tale of Baron Munchausen. It was fantastic! It really excited me!

Then George Harrison started talking to me about doing Munchausen. It turned out he was a big fan. Up through the fifties Munchausen was hugely popular all around the world. I think the book was translated into as many languages as the Bible. There had even been a radio show in America. But somehow it had disappeared. It was gone. And I thought, let's bring it back. I loved the idea of a man who was the biggest liar in the world. He tells phenomenal tales but they're also wonderful stories. But if anyone else tells his stories and alters the details in any way, he goes crazy. They become the liars. And I like playing with the idea that a good lie is better than the truth any day and maybe closer to reality. It was a product of the Thatcher years in England where Thatcher had changed things. She knew the cost of every-thing and the value of nothing. Everything was being measured in economic terms. Its financial worth; its cost, as opposed to its real value. This was ob-sessing me and Munchausen was my way of dealing with that.

Everything about *Munchausen*—the movie—was a lie, you've got to un-derstand, from the beginning. There are so many lies told about the mak-ing of *Munchausen* that I hesitate to correct because they're always more interesting than the truth. I read it's one of the most expensive films of all time. That's not true. I read that it cost fifty or sixty million to make. That's not true. I'm not going to tell you the truth about these things because that's not why I'm here. But in a way those lies have created a film that is bigger than it really was. What it was, though, was a nightmare.

David Putnam was running Columbia Pictures at the time. We raised twenty-three and a half million dollars and we set off on this little project. I think we went through four accountants. The accountant would come in and say, "This is going to cost sixty million." He was fired. The next ac-countant would come in and say, "It's going to cost forty million." He was fired. One came in and said thirty million. He was fired. One came in and said twenty-three and a half and that's what we had. He was hired! That's what was going on with the film. It was a very bizarre experience.

Just before we started shooting, David Putnam was fired from Columbia. The dogs that we had on the picture developed a sickness. There was an outbreak of horse fever in Spain, so the horse that we had trained for sev-eral months to do the tricks couldn't be brought to Spain. Everything that could go wrong did go wrong. It was like reality trying to prove to me that dreamers don't win. That fantasy is a lie. This is reality.

There's no stopping certain kinds of films once you set off and the train leaves the station, and this was one of them. It's the one experience I find hardest to talk about because it is so painful. It went out of control. It wasn't that anything had been hidden because I storyboarded everything. There were no secrets. The variety of people and events created a situation that was unstoppable. I was the one person who knew we couldn't finish the film, but it was my secret that I had to carry every day, knowing there was no way the film would ever be finished. I was like the black mulch, that filthy, dark stuff that beautiful flowers grow out of.

We were threatened with misrepresentation because they thought I lied to them about what the film was. It was perfect for a film about a liar. I was being threatened with a lawsuit and they said they would seize all of my assets. My wife was pregnant at the time, trying to get the house out of my name, while we were shooting every day. The film was eventually stopped in the sixth week of shooting in Spain. They charged that we were two million dollars over budget on the first day. Eventually they said it would be ten million.

So they pulled us off and cut the cord and we all went back to Rome. Charles McKeown and I had this choice of going home but Charles said that I couldn't do this to them. He said, "You brought us all here and we're stuck here in Rome and we're never going to get out of here unless we finish this film. You have to sit down and work on this thing." So Charles and I started cutting the script. It had worked on *Brazil* and we were going to do it again. And so the movie sequence, which was written with two thousand people all losing their heads, with huge, spectacular Cecil B. DeMille sets and with Sean Connery as the king, was pulled out. It ended up with two people in the movie rather than two thousand.

What was interesting about this situation is that we found solutions which were slightly more interesting than what we originally set out to do. This whole idea of this body/mind duality being what the king is suffering from is a much simpler idea, a funnier idea, and we ended up getting Robin Williams to come in and play the king. Again, Eric Idle to the rescue. Eric was trapped in Rome wanting to go home too, so he called Robin. "You want to do it?" he asked Robin. Yes, was the answer, as long as his name wasn't associated with the film in any way.

Eventually we got through the film but it was an extraordinarily difficult experience. But what I like is when you look at the film you don't see any of that. You don't see the pain, the blood, and the awfulness. What you see is something beautiful and funny and sad and exhilarating.

The Fisher King (1991)

Jeff Bridges; Robin Williams; Adam Bryant; Mercedes Ruehl; Paul J. Lombardi; Amanda Plummer; David Hyde Pierce; Ted Ross; Lara Harris; Warren Olney; Frazer Smith; Kathy Najimy; Harry Shearer; Melinda Culea; James Remini.

After *Munchausen* I was really fed up and I didn't think I'd ever make a movie again. I was just tired. I didn't want to make big special-effects films anymore. They were just too taxing. Then this script arrived. My agent sent it to me and I said I didn't want to read anybody else's script. He said, "It's interesting, read

it." I opened it and read until three o'clock in the morning. I just kept reading it because from the very first page I thought, wow, what wonderful dialogue, what really good characters. It was like I wished I had written it. I felt
as though I could have written this, except I'm not that talented.

I think one of the reasons they offered the film to me was that they
wanted Robin to play Perry, and I think they sat down and had gone
through the list of directors he had worked with that he liked and discovered they were all working except for me. And so one of my jobs was to
convince Robin to do it so that was the first thing I did. I thought he was
fantastic and he was a friend. Then I felt I really wanted an actor that would
ground him because I was frightened that Robin and me together would
just fly off into madness and silliness. Basically I was looking for a young
Jack Nicholson, because the character really had to be fast talking and
snappy and cynical and sharp, and the last person I was thinking of was Jeff
Bridges because Jeff was laconic.

I was on a plane and *The Fabulous Baker Boys* was on and I saw him and
said, "Oh, he can do it, he'd be fantastic." So Jeff and I got together and
liked each other right away. He's such a solid and brilliant actor and every
woman I know finds him the sexiest man on the screen. And every guy
likes him. He's intelligent. When he does a character, he's totally, totally
convincing, totally believable. I was working hard to try to ground myself,
to not do my cheap tricks. I wanted to be grounded in reality and Jeff
helped me do that. What I think was important was that Robin and Jeff got
on so well. They both sort of watched each other and learned from each
other and they were a perfect balance for each other.

Robin is so generous with his talent but he's sometimes his own worst
enemy on a film because he's funny all the time. The crew loves him. And
when it gets on film, it's often not as funny, somehow. It was interesting working with him. He makes me laugh so much and if I laughed that encouraged
him. So we agreed that we would be doing the script. Stay on the script. But
within any number of scenes Robin wanted to explode. He had ideas, he
wanted to try things out and he'd ad lib it. And so I let him go and we'd do
it for a couple of takes and then we'd go back to the script. You have to provide a safety valve for him because there's so much waiting to come out. And
rather than repress it and say don't do it, we worked out this arrangement.

It was an interesting exercise making *Fisher King* because I was trying not
to make a Terry Gilliam film. I was trying to make that script. I was always
sort of nervous about putting too many of my fantastical ideas on the script.

There was a scene in Grand Central Station that Rich LaGravenese had written about a poor black woman singing. People would stop by and give her money and a little by little a crowd grew and it was kind of a beautiful moment. But it was basically a realistic, naturalistic moment in the film. I was in Grand Central trying to get a sense of the rhythm of the place and I was watching all these commuters rushing back and forth. And as rush hour developed they got faster and faster, it was like a swarm, building, building, and building. I thought, wouldn't it be wonderful as this thing builds and builds and builds and then breaks out into a waltz.

I said, "Nah, that's a silly idea." But the producers said, "No, you've got to use it." And I said, "No, no, no, that would be a Terry Gilliam film. This is Richard LaGravenese's film." And everybody kept pestering me until finally I agreed to do it. We basically had one night to pull that thing off. Supposedly we cast people from dance schools who already knew how to waltz so we wouldn't have to teach them. The terrible thing was the sound system boomed so much in Grand Central Station you couldn't hear the Strauss waltz, you couldn't hear the beat. So we had the choreographers up on ladders with megaphones going one two three, one one-three. Then we discovered half these people couldn't dance the waltz. So we had to wait several hours while dance school was set up in Grand Central Station. "And it goes like this, one two three, one one-three."

It was about three in the morning before we started to shoot. We needed more rehearsal, but it was getting really late and we had to start. We ran like mad, cameras everywhere pushing and shooting. And we managed to get it. We were supposed to be out of there by six o'clock in the morning when rush hour commuters started coming in. And we weren't finished. Real people began to appear on the scene. A lot of the extras had been sent off. I had to get more shots. I said, "Robin, run in there, just get in there." And the cameras started turning and the real commuters were walking by. I would send in anybody who was standing around and tell them to walk through the shot. "Keep shooting," I shouted, "keep shooting." I don't know what time we got out of there, but we finally did. And it turned out to be a nice shot.

> *Terry has a huge sense of time and place and history. I'm not talking about his own place in history, because there will be a place for that, but a love for the ages. And I think he responds to texture and architecture and permanence.*
>
> Madeleine Stowe—Actress

Twelve Monkeys (1995)

Bruce Willis; Joseph Melito; Joey Perillo; Brad Pitt; Christopher Plummer;
Michael Chance; Vernon Campbell; David Morse; H. Michael Walls;
Bob Adrian; Christopher Meloni; Simon Jones; Carol Florence;
Bill Raymond; Ernest Abuba; Madeleine Stowe; Frank Gorshin.

After *Fisher King* I became a victim of success. I had made my first film in Hollywood, actually, and I think I succumbed to the seduction of the system because I was suddenly offered a lot of projects. My problem is I can only concentrate on one thing at a time. I simply willed all my films into existence. I now started diffusing my focus and nothing happened. I was running in many directions at once, going nowhere. It's very dangerous to be appreciated and encouraged. I lose focus.

I was also working on my own project with Richard LaGravenese, who wrote *Fisher King*. It was called *The Defective Detective,* a very complicated and expensive film to get off the ground. I spent a year and a half on it and couldn't get it going. Producer Chuck Roven kept coming around with this other script that I didn't want to focus on called *Twelve Monkeys*. Eventually *Defective Detective* looked like it was dead and I took the nearest thing. The nearest thing was *Twelve Monkeys.*

A mole within Universal Studios sent me the script and told me not to tell anyone they had sent it. I read it and it was extraordinary. It was such a complex story to tell. It was such an unlikely tale to get through the studio system. David and Janet Peoples' writing was wonderful. Clint Eastwood's *Unforgiven* was really one of the great films of the last ten years and David had written that, so I was a big fan. To read something as intelligent as this about a kid with a dream, with an image, and as you discover in the film, it's a dream of his own death, was extraordinary. Add to that the fact that it was a studio picture and not just any studio, but a Universal picture, the very studio I had a battle with over *Brazil*. And I thought this ultimately too ironic to pass up.

The studio was happy with the original actors we were talking about. I kept walking away from this project because they kept offering up the big names and they were all the wrong names. Then one day I got a call from my agent saying Bruce Willis was interested. I had met Bruce on *Fisher King* because he was interested in the part that Jeff ultimately played. We had spent an afternoon together and I really liked him. He was a really different guy than I expected. Much smarter, much more interesting. When his name came up on this one, I thought, "That's a good idea." I went to New York and we met and we talked about it. I told him that this was a serious acting job and I didn't want him to bring the Bruce Willis baggage along. I told him he had to approach this one totally different. He'd have to really expose himself. To his credit he agreed. I think it's the best performance he's ever given. I'm actually very sad he wasn't nominated for something because I think it's a really fine performance, and the more I watch the film, the more I appreciate it.

Brad Pitt was apparently interested in the part Bruce was playing. We'd get these messages via agents and messengers in the night. And I told them that part was taken. And then Brad turned up in London and we had dinner. He said he was interested in the other part. Brad's slow-speaking. He's not the kind of guy you would normally cast for a fast, manic kind of character. I'm a real sucker for enthusiasm and Brad was incredibly enthusiastic and determined to prove something to the world. And I said, "Let's go for it."

When we were working with Brad he was supposed to be sending me tapes of his progress which he determinedly refused to do and I was getting very nervous as we were approaching shooting days. "Oh, it's not going to work; it's going to be a disaster. He's conned me. I made a major mistake here." And then he turns up a couple of days in advance and we started talking and he said he was ready. And Steven called up and said he can do it, he's hot. And then on the first day of shooting he just got on the set and he exploded. Whoa! Jesus! This is fantastic. And we just shot and shot and shot, and by the end of the day he was like a wet dishrag, he was just drained. He could barely stand up.

Those ticks and twitches and leaps and things were just extraordinary. It was this weird mixture of hypnotic and charming and funny and dangerous. It was great watching Bruce and him working together. Again, Bruce was the old gun fighter and the new kid on the block was there and rather than being threatened by that, Bruce became almost father-like to him. It was great to watch the two.

I remember when we were casting for Dr. Railly's part, and we went down the list of names of actresses and we came to Madeleine Stowe and I said, "That's it. Done. End of conversation." Not only is she this incredible ethereal beauty, but she's intelligent and funny. I said, "Okay, if we have to have a woman psychiatrist, who better than Madeleine?" She's the anchor for the film; she's the audience. And in many ways she was the anchor for me when we were shooting. She was the one person that I could always rely on, because Bruce and Brad were out there on the edge, dangerous, sometimes maybe, sometimes not, and she was the center. She was the one person I could always talk to about whatever was going right or wrong.

Twelve Monkeys Sent a Message

I don't send my messages via Western Union; I send them by cinema. *Twelve Monkeys* is kind of a warning shot across the bow of humanity. It's the ever-presence of nature and nature taking its revenge. As the millennium approaches, we should consider where we're going. In the fifties the atomic bomb was a threat to mankind. Now we've moved into viruses, which is nature fighting back. The thing that was intriguing about *Twelve Monkeys* is how it appealed to young people. I think young people have a better sense of the doomsday scenario. They can see things are not going well and yet nobody seems to be able to stop it. They expect adults to behave like adults and take responsibility to stop or control what mankind does to the world. But adults are the least responsible people on the planet.

I've got the ability to wipe out the making of the films because I find filmmaking incredibly difficult and painful and dispiriting. You start a film with this picture in your head, this great monument, this great thing. And as you're making it, it's all falling apart. Every day, you're getting more and more dispirited and depressed because I failed again in not achieving what we set out to achieve. To me, it's always a difficult process and that's why I take a fair time between films. It's time to forget the whole thing. Which is what I do. So memories of filmmaking, it's really hard for me to remember. If I can forget how difficult it is, I can convince myself it's worth making another one and I can begin the process once more.

Fear and Loathing in Las Vegas (1998)

Johnny Depp; Benicio Del Toro; Tobey Maguire; Michael Lee Gogin; Larry Cedar;
Brian Le Baron; Katherine Helmond; Michael Warwick; Craig Bierko; Tyde Kierney;
Mark Harmon; Tim Thomerson; Richard Riehle; Frank Romano; Ransom Gates.

Fear and Loathing in Las Vegas was one of the great books of the seventies. It defined the attitude of a time and an explosion of frustration and freedom

---

EDITOR'S NOTE: At the time of this interview Terry was preparing to shoot *Fear and Loathing in Las Vegas*.

at the same time. And it's a book that's been strangely pursuing me for many years. I thought it would be a very useful film to make in the beginning of the nineties because the eighties to me had been such a closing-in, selfish kind of time. I thought it would be a kind of cinematic enema for the nineties to start the new decade off. Well, it's now the latter part of the nineties. I feel I'm always ahead of my time.

One of the reasons I'm doing *Fear and Loathing* is to work with Johnny Depp. To me he's one of the best actors of his generation. He's the most wide-ranging, versatile actor going. Not only do I get to work with Johnny, but also then I get this bonus of working with Benicio Del Toro. I only knew him from his role in *The Usual Suspects*. I discovered he's the second best actor. He's brilliant. The two of them are going to be extraordinary. I don't know yet what they're going to do. I've only got hints of it so far. We'll discover once we hit the sets exactly how far we're going. We've also got a lot of fine actors in cameo parts. A lot of people are coming forward just to be a part of it.

His Thoughts on Acting and Actors

I think, having been in Python movies and other things, I realize how painful acting can be and how exposed a good actor can be. I think that I've learned that. To give a good performance the actor has got to trust me. They have to trust the camera. They have to expose themselves. They have to take down all the barriers. And I think, having done it myself in some small and mediocre way, I can understand how painful it can be.

Actors are very delicate creatures, I find. I want to make it as enjoyable—not enjoyable—but as safe as it can be. My job is to build a really good perimeter wall around the sandbox, because we've got to be children again and be able to play, to feel safe. The real world and all that nonsense has to be put out of the way. And that's what I hope I do.

I build a really defensive wall. And then we go in there and we make fools of ourselves and we fumble around in the dark and we don't know where we're going and then we get the stuff on film. Then I build another wall around the editing room and then we hopefully put the pieces together in the right order in ways that don't embarrass anybody.

His Thoughts on the Industry

I think we're living in disturbing times because we've managed to uneducate the cinema public. Films are being released on five thousand screens at once. There's a kind of "dumbing down" process that's going on. I think the public enjoys "e" rides. That's fine, but there's also intelligence that needs to be pushed back into their expectations. Their expectations are lower and lower because of the nature of it.

There are several things that are happening. In a sense it goes back to George Lucas and Steven Spielberg's success with *Star Wars* and *Jaws* and films like that which received huge releases. It started changing the way exhibition worked. Then we went to multiplex theaters and we thought we'd get more choice, but in fact we find the theaters just want the big money-making films. And so the films that aren't making immediate big money are getting pushed out more quickly than ever. Films don't have as long to linger to find an audience because they're up against these huge block-busters with these huge campaigns that dominate your thinking.

There's a weird thing happening in America. It's all about immediate reaction and immediate gratification. It's the infantilization of America. It's like feeding babies. You put something in front of them; they see it and grab for it. Put something else in front of them, they grab for that. What seems to be happening in America is that each time they grab, they get disappointed, and yet they're told their lives should have changed having seen *Batman 10* or *Jaws 900,* or whatever. But their lives haven't changed so they become more frustrated and then they wait for the next movie to come out to give them that satisfaction and make it all worthwhile. And they're disappointed again.

The view of the world just gets smaller and smaller in America and it's processed in Hollywood, which is dictating everything. Hollywood's a very small village. It's a very small number of people here. We all go to the same restaurants. We're all fighting for the same jobs. We're all basically middle management, because big corporations own it all. Most of the really good people, the really talented, the really energetic people don't want to be studio executives. This is not a good job. So you end up with mediocre people sitting in these positions and the talent has to somehow get through this.

The choices start closing in because only certain kinds of films are going to be made because we need our big blockbusters. We need to spend eighty million. So if you're going to spend eighty million you've got to have safe subject matter. You can't do demanding subject matter. You simplify your subject matter. You put your big stars in there. So you have these huge packages going out and everybody is concentrating on them. The only good side to all of this, it seems to me, is that there's so much money floating around that occasionally little films fall through the cracks. The studios were too busy working on the big one and a little film gets done and it gets out there. It may only have been seen by a small number of people, but it's out there. At least it'll turn up in your video shop and it will be around on laser disk and DVD and somehow it may have an effect.

I would say that less than a hundred nervous people are deciding what gets made and they're not the best or the brightest. They are the most mediocre and the most nervous. So films aren't made from a position of confidence and bravery, they're made out of fear and the pressure of the bottom line. And that's the gantlet that talent runs through. The thing that bothers me is working with writers and seeing them censoring themselves because they know if they're going to spend several months writing a script they want it to get made. So you start writing the things that are going to get made, not the things you should be writing, not the dangerous one, not the idea you really want to share with the world. It's a vicious cycle.

Will There Be More Python Films?

A Monty Python movie would always have to have Graham Chapman in it if we were ever to do one again.* We decided to fuel rumors that the possibilities had now improved. But what we can guarantee is if we ever do, Graham will be in the film, but only bits of him will, and not all of him. It's going to be very interesting to see if we can pull it off. We've talked about it. Within some of the living Pythons there's enthusiasm. We've all become so different it would be very difficult to get us all together again. But for a brief moment a couple of months ago we all got excited about it. Eric Idle had a good idea. And Terry and Mike got excited. John announced he wouldn't do it. And I don't know what I'd do. But it's something to keep people talking about.

How Does He Want to Be Remembered?

Oh, no, no, no! Not that question! Whoa, how does history remember me? I don't know. I do know what I want on my gravestone. I was in Texas promoting *Munchausen* and I was on a radio talk show, and some guy called and said he saw *Baron Munchausen* and he giggled in awe. And that's what I want on my tombstone. *Terry Gilliam—R.I.P.—"He giggled in awe."*

And that's about it. The films will be what they are, and they'll be around for a while. They'll be around long after I am. And no matter how old they become I hope they continue to surprise people and make them look at the world through different eyes. That's all I care about.

---

* Graham Chapman died of throat cancer in 1989.

Filmography

Monty Python and the Holy Grail (1975)
Jabberwocky (1977)
Time Bandits (1981)
Monty Python's The Meaning of Life (*The Crimson Permanent Assurance*, 1983)
Brazil (1985)
The Adventures of Baron Munchausen (1988)
The Fisher King (1991)
Twelve Monkeys (1995)
Monty Python & the Quest for the Holy Grail (Video Game, 1996)
Fear and Loathing in Las Vegas (1998)

Awards

Academy Awards, USA
Brazil, Best Writing, Screenplay Written Directly for the Screen (nominated, shared with Tom Stoppard and Charles McKeown), 1986

Berlin International Film Festival
Twelve Monkeys, Reader Jury of the *Berliner Morgenpost,* 3rd place, 1996

British Academy Awards
The Crimson Permanent Assurance, Best Short Film (nominated), 1984

Cannes Film Festival
Fear and Loathing in Las Vegas, Golden Palm (nominated), 1998

Golden Globes, USA

The Fisher King, Best Director—Motion Picture (nominated), 1992

Los Angeles Film Critics Association Awards

Brazil, Best Director, 1985

Brazil, Best Screenplay (shared with Charles McKeown and Tom Stoppard), 1985

Venice Film Festival

The Fisher King, Silver Lion, 1991

The Films of John Badham

John Badham was born on August 25, 1939, in Luton, Bedfordshire, England. He is the son of English actress Mary Hewitt and the stepson of an American army colonel. Raised in Alabama and schooled at Yale, he cut his teeth producing and directing TV before making his feature debut with *The Bingo Long Traveling All-Stars & Motor Kings*. His breakthrough credit was the box office smash *Saturday Night Fever.*

Badham has drawn critical praise and box office success during a career distinguished by its range and diversity. His career began with a job in the mailroom at Universal Studios, where he moved up through the ranks and eventually began directing such television shows as *The Senator, Night Gallery, Kung Fu,* and *The Streets of San Francisco,* as well as a number of movies-of-the-week.

As fate would have it, the original director of *Saturday Night Fever* left the project before filming began and gave Badham the biggest break of his budding career.

> *He knows how to run the ship and he doesn't show fear, doesn't lose his temper or get mean, and he's very straight-forward. Most directors will give in sooner or later to some kind of anxiety and nail-biting and stuff like that. I don't think I can remember a time when he'd do that.*
>
> Richard Dreyfuss—Actor

The Conversation

I started as an actor. I enjoyed acting in grammar school and high school and college and had this fantasy that I would like to go into acting. But I realized in college that I was going to be left behind, that everybody else was getting all the good parts and I was getting little tiny parts. And I thought that maybe I should look around for something else to do. I was enjoying the stage-managing side of it, the back-stage side of it, and had noticed that there were these men walking around the Yale Drama School who had all of these people following them and writing down everything they said. I said, "Who are these guys?" They said, "Those are the directors." I said, "Oh, that sounds like something I want to do."

I became interested in directing while I was a student at Yale and began with theater and went to the drama school as a director. But, of course, not studying film at all. I became interested in film along the way. It seemed like an interesting different path to take than just theater. So when I left the Yale drama school I came to California with not much more preparation than I told you. Time at the Yale drama school in theater and that's it. The only job, with that kind of preparation, I could get was delivering mail at the Universal Studio's mailroom. And it took a lot of months before I could find that job. I spent a lot of weeks in the mailroom with people like Walter Hill and other people who said they wanted to be producers and directors and so on. It seemed very unrealistic that we would actually achieve that kind of a goal doing even local television. But we persevered. Eventually I left the mailroom and was a tour guide.

My first real job in the movie business was as a trainee casting director at Universal Television. I cast episodes of television shows for two or three years, still thinking of trying to work toward directing. One day a television producer asked me if I would come and be his assistant. That was a lot closer to my goal than being a casting director, which was interesting, but kind of limited. So as a producer's assistant I got to get much more closely involved with the production of television episodes.

Finally this producer let me start shooting little inserts and the close-ups that they didn't have time to shoot on the television episodes. He eventually allowed me to shoot the whole episode of a television show all by myself. This was a series with Hal Holbrook called *The Senator.* It was part of another series called *The Bold Ones.* I did two episodes of that show and from there went on to direct a lot of different television series like *The Streets of San Francisco, Kung Fu, Night Gallery,* and more of *The Bold Ones.* That was very good training for a director because you were doing these hour shows in six days and having to shoot a lot of material very quickly and on schedule and yet try to find interesting things to do with them.

Dick Donner and I used to shoot episodes of *The Bold Ones* and *The Doctors* with E. G. Marshall and David Hartman. He and I would alternate episodes. We always had a little competition going as to who could do the most interesting things with what was basically a doctor show, other than just shoot the dialogue scenes of the doctors and the patients and so on. All during that time I was hoping to move into feature films. Eventually the film scripts started to arrive. I think I must have read scripts for three years before I found something that I felt was interesting enough to do. Usually the only reason someone would send a film script to a television director was because they couldn't get any decent film directors to do it. So they would start looking around for who was in television that they could sort of put up with and give a break to. So most of the scripts I got were pretty dreadful.

The Bingo Long Traveling All-Stars & Motor Kings (1976)

Billy Dee Williams; James Earl Jones; Richard Pryor; Rico Dawson;
Sam "Birmingham" Briston; Jophery C. Brown; DeWayne Jessie; Tony Burton.

One day a young producer named Rob Cohen called me and asked me to look at a screenplay based on a novel called *The Bingo Long Traveling All-Stars & Motor Kings.* It was to be produced by Motown for Universal. Originally Steven Spielberg was going to direct it, but he had to withdraw from the film because he was very much involved with a picture called *Jaws.* They had already cast James Earl Jones, Richard Pryor, and Billy Dee Williams.

Bingo was a wonderful, very funny, very sad look at the history of the Negro baseball leagues and it was done in a rather sweet and fanciful manner. So I was very excited to get involved with this project and also because director George Roy Hill was helping us as an advisor. I was making trips all over the country looking at old baseball parks. We finally settled on

Macon, Georgia, because within an hour and a half of Macon there was every kind of baseball park you could want. You could have something as fancy and brand new as the Atlanta Braves ballpark, or you could have a rundown, ramshackle old stadium, and everything in between. Of course the older ones were the ones we wanted because we were talking about a period in the late 1930s, early 1940s, when these leagues were at their peak and also coming to an end at the same time.

During that period there were no African-American ballplayers in the National or American Leagues. They weren't allowed, so they had formed their own leagues. It wasn't until 1947 that the owner of the Brooklyn Dodgers saw a young player named Jackie Robinson and decided he was going put him on the Dodgers team come hell or high water. There was a lot of screaming and fussing and also a lot of encouragement from people saying, yes, this is the right thing to do.

The day that Jackie Robinson joined the Brooklyn Dodgers was probably the end of the Negro leagues. Then, one after another, there was a flood of black ballplayers coming into the National and American Leagues and the old Negro leagues sort of faded away.

We were not only trying to find good actors but also good ballplayers who could express the spirit and the style of baseball that was played in the Negro leagues. That style was very playful, so to speak. They loved to goof around. If there was ever baseball with a great sense of humor these teams had it and it was very entertaining to watch them. They didn't take it all as seriously as we sometimes see nowadays. There was always a great deal of fun being had even under the grimmest of circumstances, because these guys weren't flying from one ballgame to another in jet airplanes. They were traveling in broken-down buses. They were not allowed to sleep in hotels that only catered to whites. They often could not find hotels to sleep in at all. They often could not find places to serve them food. Rather than be all down about it, they chose to deal with it in a humorous way. That's part of the charm of this film.

My first day on *Bingo* wasn't unlike what I had been doing in television. I had done a lot of movies-of-the-week with relatively big budgets. It was just more complicated and you're always nervous the night before you start shooting a movie. As many as I've done, I still get nervous. It takes me a good week or ten days before I calm down enough that I'm able to sleep at night. I suppose this movie was no exception.

We had taken a large group of actors and ballplayers into the heart of Dixie, into the South, into an area that still had segregation and there was still prejudice. We were all nervous about how that was going to work. I was nervous about what I should do differently in shooting a movie than I did in shooting a television show. How do I cover it differently, get the big expanse and go for the big screen versus the little tiny television box? I don't think I've answered that question yet. I've now been shooting movies for twenty years and I still don't know the answer to that question. I hope I figure it out before I quit.

I never feel that my future as a film director is secure. I feel it could vanish at any minute. This is too good of a job to feel secure about. You always feel this is the last movie you're going to do, that they're going to find out that you're really a fraud and that you don't know what you're doing. With *Bingo Long* we had a movie that played brilliantly to audiences. I mean, to watch a performance of this movie being screened for an audience was like dying and going to heaven. People cheered and hollered and clapped and laughed. It was everything that you could want. When it got to the movie theaters, that was another matter. Where were all those people? They didn't show up. They didn't seem to be interested in it. We knew for sure if we could get them in the theaters they would love the movie, but getting them there seemed to be another matter. I didn't know if anyone was ever going to let me do another movie.

Saturday Night Fever (1977)

John Travolta; Karen Lynn Gorney; Barry Miller; Joseph Cali; Paul Pape; Donna Pescow; Bruce Ornstein; Julie Bovasso; Martin Shakar; Sam Coppola; Nina Hansen; Lisa Peluso; Denny Dillon; Bert Michaels; Robert Costanzo.

I had actually been involved in the preparation of another movie called *The Wiz*, which was a black musical version of *The Wizard of Oz*. It enjoyed a very successful run on Broadway. Rob Cohen, who had worked with me on *Bingo Long*, had written the script, and here I was preparing to do a big musical. One day Universal and Motown came to me and said we have a star for you. It's going to be Diana Ross. I said, "Well, I think Diana Ross is a wonderful singer. She's a terrific actress and she's a great dancer, but she's not this character. She's not the little six-year-old girl Dorothy in *The Wizard of Oz*." They said, "Oh, it will be fine. It's all make believe and magic and movies and you'll make it work." I said, "Well, I actually don't know what to say to her."

One thing led to another and I said, "I think the best thing that you can do is to find another director. Find one that will know what to say to her because I don't." Everybody told me I was a fool for pulling out on this great big musical. So now I was sitting there with nothing to do, until this script arrived called *Tribal Rights of the New Saturday Night*. It arrived in a panic because the original director (John Avildsen) was no longer connected with it and they needed to get going right away and they needed to have me fly to New York the next day.

My agent called me and said, "Do not read this script. You don't want to read it until we have negotiated some kind of a deal. Wait until I call you." I said, "Yes, absolutely, I won't read it." I hung up the phone, picked up the script, and I started to read it. About an hour and a half later when I was done I was running around the room going, "Yeah, this is a great, great movie." What I read was a beautiful story of a young man in Brooklyn who had much more potential than his little community was offering him. He was straining to get out of there. All of his friends were telling him to get out of there, to go to another place, to go someplace where he could use more of his potential, but he wouldn't. He was afraid to. Finally, it takes the death of one of his closest friends to sort of eject him from this community, to start exploring his real potential.

It was told with great humor. There was brilliant character writing. One of the best scripts I had ever read. Now I'm calling my agent back and saying, "I know you told me not to read this but I read it anyway. It's great! I want to do it." He negotiates a deal. The next morning at eight o'clock I get to meet John Travolta who is going to decide whether or not he can put up with me. Then at four o'clock that afternoon I get on a plane to New York and on the way I have a big job to do. The script is extremely long. It's a hundred and sixty pages long. Normally, a hundred and twenty pages is plenty. I've got to figure out how to cut forty pages out of it. So I'm reading on the plane and I suddenly had this horrible realization that this was a major musical. I had not realized that in my first rapid reading of it because it seemed to be all about this young man. It was not about music. I mean, there were lines in the script that would say "and he goes into the disco and he dances." Suddenly you realize that one little line on the page is three minutes of film. You've got a whole piece of music to play. You've got a whole dance to film. Suddenly it becomes a major musical. I think that's when I started to get scared.

When I got to New York the producer, Robert Stigwood, handed me a little cassette and said, "Here's five songs from the Bee Gees." And if you could see behind my eyes I was going, "Who are they? Who are those guys?" I mean, I remembered the Bee Gees from a long time ago, but I hadn't heard of them in a long time. He said, "These songs are really great. In fact, there are probably three number-one hits here." I thought that was probably one of the most arrogant things I had ever heard in my life. How do you know if the song is going to be a hit or not? You don't know. Of course, I was right. I mean, Robert Stigwood was dead wrong. There were not three number-one hits on cassette. There were four number-one hits and the fifth one was an almost. There was no map that came with these songs. I didn't know where they went in the script. It was up to me to place them wherever I thought was appropriate. The Bee Gees had never read the script. They were told the story and they wrote these brilliant songs.

I knew from the very first day that we had a major undiscovered movie star in John Travolta. On the first morning we were shooting in Brooklyn on 86th Street where there is a big elevated train. As I'm lining up the first shot there are students going up the steps to the elevated train and they look down and they start talking to John. The girls are calling him by his character name from the television series he was in, *Welcome Back Kotter.* They are saying, "Hey, Barbarino." There are seven or eight girls up there. Ten minutes later there were sixty. Five minutes later there were three hundred. By eleven o'clock in the morning we had fifteen thousand people gathered around this little intersection, all screaming and hollering and trying to see Travolta. It got so bad that about twelve o'clock we had to wrap the company and go home. We couldn't do the rest of our work because there was no place we could turn the camera. The only shot I could get was to literally put Travolta up against a wall and shoot into the wall. Even if I shot up to the sky, there were people hanging over buildings screaming at him.

It was a very low-budget movie, which meant that Paramount Studios had no confidence in it. They said, "If you can make this movie for two million dollars, go ahead. But this isn't really going to be a big success like *Grease* is going to be a big success." Now, the reason we had to start *Saturday Night Fever* so quickly was because John Travolta was committed to do *Grease.* So this was just a little movie to sort of get out of the way.

When we previewed the film it went badly. The audience didn't seem to respond to it at all. Michael Eisner and Barry Diller, who were the heads of Paramount at the time, kept begging me to take out all the profanity. Robert Stigwood, who had final cut, said, "Do not take out any profanity." So now I've got these people on either side of me telling me conflicting things. I would tell Robert that we weren't taking out any profanity. I would tell Eisner that I was. In fact, I was. There was so much in there that it didn't matter how much you took out, it still sounded pretty rough. I would tell Michael we had deleted fifty of this kind of word and seventy-five of this kind of word and he would feel much better. But when Robert would come to see the movie, it sounded the same to him.

John and I had good days and bad days. We had wonderful days where we got along very well. Then there were days when we would have a big knock down, drag out fight over something that was probably as petty as most fights are. He was always very nervous about looking his best. I was very nervous about making the film work.

One day he had a terrible tragedy in his life. A girlfriend of his died. He went to California to go to the funeral and be with her family. He was terribly upset. We, on the other hand, had nothing to shoot. He was in every scene in the movie. So I said to the crew, "You know that shot of the feet that I want to have in the beginning of the movie? Well, at least we can shoot that."

We went out to the street in Brooklyn and we took the playback of "Staying Alive," because we decided that was going to open the movie. We did this with John's stand-in and he's walking down the street like he thinks John would walk and he's walking to the beat of "Staying Alive." We spent a good half-day shooting this footage. When John comes back we go out to get the parts of that scene where we actually see him. I showed him the footage and I said, "What do you think?" He said, "There's only one problem. I don't walk like that." I said, "But John, this is what we shot. If you could find it in your heart to walk like that it will cut together." He said, "No, I'm not doing that. I'll walk the way I walk. If you shot something wrong that's your fault." So we shot his scenes the way he walks.

I then started to think; well maybe this isn't a big problem after all. We'll cut it together and maybe no one will notice that these two men walk totally differently. In the dailies the next day I said to the editor, "How does this film look to you?" He said, "Well, it's okay, but you know, these two guys don't walk at all alike and I'll never be able to cut from one to the other." But he said he could fix it. He took the cuts that we had made with the stand-in and he cut them directly into a shot that comes up from John Travolta's body to his face. Now this is one of those big no-no's in editing. You never cut from "A" to "A." You're supposed to cut from "A" to "C" or "A" to "Z," anything other than "A." You don't cut from the same thing to the same thing.

During this sequence we were running the titles of the movie, so he put the titles over the cuts. The title comes up, "music by the BeeGees," at that certain point and it covers it. His philosophy was that when a credit comes on it makes your eye blink so you don't notice that we've actually done this cut. So there it sits in the movie all this time and people don't know that those feet aren't John's.

Dracula (1979)

Frank Langella; Laurence Olivier; Donald Pleasence; Kate Nelligan; Trevor Eve; Jan Francis; Janine Duvitski; Tony Haygarth; Teddy Turner; Sylvester McCoy; Kristine Howarth; Joe Belcher; Ted Carroll; Frank Birch; Gabor Vernon.

Dracula was a play that had been around since, oh, the 1920s, and Frank Langella had starred in a revival of it that was done with a great deal of humor on Broadway. I thought that it would make a wonderful movie with Frank, who is a very elegant leading man and has a very romantic quality to him. We could do it in England in interesting locations. W.D. Richter and I worked on a fresh adaptation of the novel. Richter went back to the novel and tried to adapt it for Frank's particular talents.

We were very lucky to get Laurence Olivier to do it with us. He had been quite ill for many years but was recovering. Even though he was now seventy-one or seventy-two years old, he was in better health than he had been in a decade. He was quite interested in working with us on this film.

Laurence Olivier was not only one of the greatest English actors of our time but also a great athletic actor as well. On stage he always did very daring things physically. If the part called for falling down stairs, falling off stages, doing sword fights, doing battles, doing anything physical, Olivier was the best at it. But I was now working with a man who had trouble walking around—who had trouble walking fifty feet in any direction. We always kept a big armchair and ottoman on the set for him to keep his feet up. In the mornings we wondered if we would make it through the day with him. What was interesting, however, was whenever we said we were ready to go he would slowly rise from his chair and you would be worrying about him. Then the slate would come down and this other person would emerge. There was energy. I don't know where it came from. He must have been saving it in reserve for the takes. He was bringing a wonderful quality to the film, with great simplicity, yet with great energy and vitality.

The character that Olivier played was a Dutchman named Dr. Van Helsing, and he said that he would do the part with a Dutch accent. At one point in the movie he opens up Dracula's coffin and prays. He takes a host, the holy wafer, and breaks it in half and then says in English "In the name of the Father, the Son and the Holy Ghost, I bless this earth." He's referring to the earth in the coffin. So he said to me, "I think I'm going to do this prayer in Dutch," and he now learns it in the Dutch language. The night before shooting I thought, "What if nobody understands what he's saying? Maybe we should have him do it in English as well." We get through the takes in Dutch and it's about five minutes before lunch and lunch in the movie business is quite sacred. If you don't stop for lunch there are all these penalties; otherwise nobody would ever get to eat.

So I said to Olivier, "Sir, in these last few minutes, let's do one more take and would you say this prayer in English?" He looked at me and he said no. I explained to him that I thought no one would understand it and so if that were the case we would be covered and at least have the English version. And he said, "No; it's heretical to pray in a language other than your own. My character is Dutch. So I will only pray in Dutch." I went through it again with him. Now we're down to about two minutes before lunch. And the production manager is starting to turn a little white and Olivier is standing his ground. I explained it to him a third time. And after the third time, he looked at me and said, "Oh, all right, let's do it."

I thought to myself, well, all right, he'll do it, but he'll do it badly. He'll do it once to get it out of the way and that will be it. Well, let me tell you, he did it brilliantly. It was wonderful. You couldn't have asked for a better version. I said, "Cut, print, thank you; we're all going to lunch." Everybody piles out the door. We just made it. Lord Olivier turns to me and says, "Young man, I just want you to know you are never going to use that take. I only did it because I did not want to embarrass you in front of the crew." I said, "Yes, sir, thank you very much. I appreciate your consideration." Well, he never would allow me to use that take. He said to me, "If you use that take I will call a press conference and tell everyone in the English-speaking world that you have lied to me."

What I admired about him was that he was a gentleman and that he would do it to save my face in front of everyone else. Many people would have said no and let me just hang there with egg on my face.

Whose Life Is It Anyway? (1981)

*Richard Dreyfuss; John Cassavetes; Christine Lahti; Bob Balaban;
Kaki Hunter; Kenneth McMillan; Thomas Carter; Juli Andelman; Steven Bourne.*

While I was in England working on *Dracula* I went to see Tom Conti in *Whose Life Is It Anyway?* at the Savoy Theatre. I loved this play a lot but I was kind of dubious about whether or not anyone would ever come to see a movie based on it. I thought it was a very powerful piece about our ability to control our own destiny. I worked on it for about a year trying to get someone to make the movie. Universal said they didn't want to make it but finally MGM said they were very interested.

Our first choice for the lead was Richard Dreyfuss, who agreed to do it because he had the same feelings about the play that I did. Dreyfuss is one of the most intelligent actors on the planet, and to work with him is a great joy. He always has very, very sharp insights into whatever the character is, and he brings such great humor and energy to everything that he does.

How do you shoot a movie where someone is paralyzed and stuck in a bed for the whole film? In the stage version, the character was in the middle of the stage the entire time and the hospital staff would circulate around him. I realized that this was symbolic of the physical jail that he was in. But in the film we could move the bed and we could move him and put him in a wheelchair, so we decided to use the entire hospital as the jail. Even though he was being moved from his hospital room to an examining room, to a dialysis center, or to a patient sunroom, he was still in that basic jail. He was trapped inside his own body and could not get out and only went where people took him. While he was in these various locations he was always being monitored on television, being spied upon by people who were making decisions for him that he didn't agree with.

I wanted to shoot the film in black and white. In fact, I have a beautiful 35 mm black-and-white print of it. MGM, on the other hand, did not believe in black and white the way I believed in black and white. They said, "You can shoot it in black and white but you have to shoot it on color film and then we'll make a black and white print from that." I knew they probably were going to release it in color but I was naïve enough to think that I might convince them how wonderful it would be in black and white. When we went to preview the film we took a color print and a black and white. One night we ran the color, the next night we ran the black and white. The audience responded much better to the black and white than the color print. Who knows why? But MGM released it in color anyway. The one thing I did get out of it is that I have the black and white print. The cameraman had done a brilliant job lighting it for black and white.

Blue Thunder (1983)

Roy Scheider; Warren Oates; Candy Clark; Daniel Stern;
Paul Roebling; David Sheiner; Joe Santos; Malcolm McDowell;
Ed Bernard; Jason Bernard; Mario Machado; James Murtaugh;
Pat McNamara; Jack Murdock; Clifford A. Pellow.

Blue Thunder is a script that I was attracted to because of two things. One, it had a very dark story reminiscent of George Orwell's novel *1984*—people being spied upon by the government. *Blue Thunder* was a story of a helicopter that had the capability of spying on people through the walls of their houses. I felt with the coming age of computers and with the advancements being made in technology, *1984* was becoming more of a reality.

I was very attracted by the idea of the character that Roy Scheider played, a Vietnam Vet suffering from post-traumatic stress syndrome, which was not very well known in 1981 when we started working on the movie. I was also attracted because it had more action and more excitement than any other picture I had done up to that point. I had always wanted to do action pictures and had never been able to do one because I had developed a reputation as a director who worked with the actors. But here was *Blue Thunder* that was just filled with near-impossible action demands like helicopters flying through Los Angeles fifty feet above the ground. It was an amazing challenge and quite exciting.

The decision was made early on to do it with real helicopters, not models, and to actually do the filming in the style that was written in the script. Our chief pilot, Jim Gavin, said there nothing that was not achievable in reality except for one particular stunt at the end of the movie where the helicopter is supposed to make a 360-degree loop in the air. So that one particular shot we did with a miniature helicopter that was about six feet long. But other than that everything was done real, including the close-ups.

We flew the actors through the streets of Los Angeles fifty feet above the ground and in between all those buildings. It was quite exciting and a bit terrifying at the same time. Malcolm McDowell was absolutely terrified. He hates flying. He doesn't like to be in a big 747, much less a helicopter. In fact, part of his deal was that he would not have to get into a helicopter. Obviously the person representing Malcolm had not read our script, because that's the only place he is. He's in a helicopter, flying! So when Malcolm McDowell showed up on the set the first thing I did was put him in a helicopter.

The helicopter took off and flew around the block then came back, set down, and the door opened. Malcolm McDowell leaned out and threw up all over the heli-pad. That was our first day with him. When we got to shooting the close-ups at the very end Jim Gavin was actually flying the helicopter and Malcolm was simulating flying with the camera trained on him. There was no room for me to go along so when they would come back I'd ask how it was going. Malcolm would say, "Oh, you'd be so proud of me. I just looked very stern and mean and I really was gunning in on Roy Scheider."

When I saw the dailies the next day, I saw what a big fibber he was. He just didn't know what he was doing. His eyes were as big as saucers. I said, "Malcolm, I hate to tell you this, but we have to do this again. We can't put this in the movie. You look terrified." So we went out to do it a second time. In the movie you see him looking very stern, but the minute Jim Gavin would say "Cut," he would fall apart.

Thank goodness the only close call that we had was when we were flying beside another helicopter one Sunday afternoon to line up a shot on a skyscraper that was under construction. We were sixty stories up, shooting through the steel girders. We had the *Blue Thunder* helicopter on one side of the building and Malcolm McDowell's helicopter close to us. They were supposed to be stalking one another. Then all of a sudden, from Malcolm McDowell's helicopter, a little puff of smoke came out and it plunged sixty stories to the ground in six seconds.

What had happened was the engine had exploded sixty stories up, and he auto-rotated the helicopter to the ground. The worst that happened was there was a bent skid, but it terrified everybody so much and got everybody so upset that we all went home at two o'clock in the afternoon to pull ourselves together and start again. Thank goodness that was the worst accident that we had on the movie.

WarGames (1983)

Matthew Broderick; Dabney Coleman; John Wood; Ally Sheedy;
Barry Corbin; Juanin Clay; Kent Williams; Dennis Lipscomb;
Joe Dorsey; Irving Metzman; Michael Ensign; William Bogert;
Susan Davis; James Tolkan; David Clover.

I picked up the phone one day and my famous agent said to me, "There's this movie that they want a director for, but I don't think you want to read it because they're replacing the original director and you don't want to get involved because that's nothing but trouble." I said, "Have you read the script?" He said no. I said, "It could be good." He said, "Oh, I never thought of that. Well, I'll send it over to you."

It's very seldom that you have a really powerful, positive response to a script. I read a lot of material and to get one that excites you on the first read is wonderful. *WarGames* was that kind of a screenplay. I knew what to do with it and I knew how to approach the material. Interestingly enough, I knew nothing about computers except the most rudimentary, layman sort of knowledge. But I knew that the story had a lot to say about the way that governments deal with defense systems and the kind of crazy situations we get ourselves into with our defense networks, and how we deal with other countries in the world. So it was about many things. The fact that it was a very young man that gets involved was a very smart, clever approach. There'd been a lot of movies done about computers before, but they were always much more science fiction in nature. This smacked of truth, like it could really happen.

Actor Dabney Coleman was already involved in the movie when I came aboard. I had liked Dabney Coleman ever since seeing him in Michael Ritchie's movie *Downhill Racer.* I thought, he has not only a great sense of humor but also a tremendous reality about him. There's something slightly sleazy about Dabney that we love to hate.

No one really knew the young stars of the film, Matthew Broderick and Ally Sheedy. They were just beginning their careers. The minute I saw them on film, however, I knew they were very, very talented. The movie was being well served by having them in it.

WarGames was one of the first movies to work extensively with computers. It was difficult on several levels. We had to make a computer that

Matthew could work, because he was not highly computer literate. The script called for him to do very complicated things so we had to devise methods to have that happen and be believable. But even more difficult than that was the war room. The war room was a very complicated concept because there were going to be eighty-five screens in there displaying information. There were ten motion picture screens and seventy-five video screens, and sometimes the information on all eighty-five of them had to be exactly the same. No one had ever tried lumping that amount of information and have it all come out together at the same time and be photographed by a motion picture camera at twenty-four frames per second. The fact that we had ten rear projection screens going at once with screens all in dead synch with one another was an audacious concept.

The experts who do all the rear projection work in Hollywood said, "We don't know how we're going to make this work. No one has ever put ten screens together. We don't even know how we're going to deal with the video." Then, there was a question of what to put on it. All of the films that are up there—the maps of the world that show missiles leaving Russia and then coming to the United States, and leaving the submarines and so on—all of those things had to be hand-animated. It took them months and months to get it right. The computer was doing some of this but computers weren't set up to do these kinds of things like they are now. Sometimes it took eighteen minutes to do one single frame of film. Multiply eighteen minutes times twenty-four and that's how long it would take to get one second of film and we would often have the film running for four and five minutes at a time.

You know, as interesting as all the computers are in *WarGames*, and I think they are quite fascinating, I think my favorite mechanical objects in there are the flying birds, the pterodactyls. A man who makes miniature airplanes constructed them. If you ever meet this man he will start pulling out of his pockets little airplanes that are run with things as silly as rubber bands. But they fly. He had made a pterodactyl that he would literally launch with a giant rubber band. For its navigation while in flight it was controlled by remote control. So when we flew this pterodactyl up at Big Bear Lake we had police coming to see what we were doing. Archeologists were showing up thinking they had sighted a pterodactyl. It was a lot of fun. This guy was so good at flying it he could bring it down in a shot so precisely he could actually hit Matthew Broderick in the middle of the back and knock him to the ground.

No Time to Think about His Career

I quite honestly wasn't thinking about my career in 1983. I had *Blue Thunder* on the dubbing stages, getting the soundtrack put together, and I was trying to get *WarGames* finished at the same time, so I don't think I slept for all of 1983. I was going from one place to another. *Blue Thunder* was released in May of that year, and six weeks later *WarGames* came out. I was so busy I had no time to be thinking about it. These are problems that everybody should have.

American Flyers (1985)

Kevin Costner; David Marshall Grant; Rae Dawn Chong;
Alexandra Paul; Janice Rule; Luca Bercovici; Robert Townsend;
John Amos; Doi Johnson; John Garber; Jennifer Grey; James Terry;
Jessica Nelson; Tom Lawrence; Brian Drebber.

American Flyers came about because Steve Tesich is a writer that I have admired for a long time. He had wanted to do a film about a bicycle race that goes all across the western United States every summer that was sponsored at the time by the Coors Beer Company. It was an exciting concept about a group of bicycle riders, a sub-cult, if you will, of avid bike riders. They would ride every day for eighty to a hundred miles. It's the American version of the *Tour de France*. I was very interested with the characters and in the phenomenon of bicycle riding as a group sport.

Kevin Costner was a young actor who had starred in one picture for Warner Bros. called *Fandango*. Warner Bros. was smart enough to see that here was a major motion picture star. They came to me and said, "We think you ought to use this young man, but you decide for yourself." But you could tell right away that there was a great charm and sense of humor. What we didn't know was that he had tremendous athletic ability.

We trained every morning. At seven o'clock we would meet at Griffith Park in Hollywood and we would ride for about two and a half hours through the mountains, past the observatory in Griffith Park, and up steep hills to strengthen these guys up. The first day we took them out for their training they rode for about one mile. They fell to the side of the road panting and said they could never do it. About five weeks later they were riding fifty and sixty miles at a time and saying, "Let's do more, let's do more." Kevin Costner had tremendous cycling abilities in addition to his acting.

One day they were coming down a complicated mountain where they were switching back and forth and doing turns and they go through a tunnel. As they came out of the tunnel someone crashed right in front of Kevin and his bike went down. Kevin was basically going to be wiped out. The other cyclist said that Kevin levitated his bike off the ground and went over the cyclist who was directly in front of him and never crashed at all. We thought we were going to have a hospitalized Costner on our hands, but he had that great physical ability.

It's a movie that is very much about what you can do if you want to do it and what you can do if you don't allow a lot of negative thinking to get in your way. A lot of the characters in the movie are stymied in their athletic performance by negative thinking. Things like: I could have done better if I had a better bicycle; I could have done better if only I didn't have a twisted ankle. That's all excuses and bullshit. You can do whatever you set your mind to and put your heart into. A lot of the movie is about that. A lot of it is about the love between two brothers and the kind of inspiration it can bring to people to perform way beyond the abilities they thought they had.

Short Circuit (1986)

Ally Sheedy; Steve Guttenberg; Fisher Stevens; Austin Pendleton; G.W. Bailey; Brian McNamara; Tim Blaney; Marvin J. McIntyre; John Garber; Penny Santon; Vernon Weddle; Barbara Tarbuck; Tom Lawrence; Fred Slyter; Billy Ray Sharkey.

My friend David Foster and his partner Larry Turman came to me with a script that I thought was extremely special. Its lead character was a robot that believed it was alive. It was so charming and sweet and funny that I knew I had to do this movie. I picked up the phone and said, "This is a major hit. It was so wonderful. Won't this be fun to devise a robot that can go up and down steps and wave his arms and talk and create a character? We won't have Eddie Murphy in the movie. We won't have Richard Dreyfuss and we won't have Tom Cruise. We'll just have this robot."

There was only one technical difficulty in *Short Circuit,* and that was how to make the robot work. I mean, the robot is not a real robot. It's a movie prop. It's not able to think on its own. Eight or ten people ran it. If you saw behind the robot you would have seen all kind of wires coming out of it. You would have seen special-effects men with radio controls. You would have seen three and sometimes four puppeteers who were operating his eyes and his mouth and his arms. All of these men had to work in great synchronization with one another to make it appear to be alive and be animated. This was extremely difficult.

I insisted that we treat this robot as a human being. The first thing in the morning, when I would come on the set, I would go over to the robot and hug him and talk to him. The puppeteers, who were used to dealing with creatures like this, they would talk right back to me. He had his own motor home—a forty-foot van. There were actually about twenty versions of him. There were half-size versions we could throw off bridges. There were ones that would go left, ones that would go right, and they all had to be kept working. Eric Allard was the real mechanical genius who was able to figure out how to assemble this for a reasonable price. He was a lot cheaper than Eddie Murphy, but we still had a million dollars in this robot.

Stakeout (1987)

Richard Dreyfuss; Emilio Estevez; Madeleine Stowe; Aidan Quinn; Dan Lauria; Forest Whitaker; Ian Tracey; Earl Billings; Jackson Davies; J.J. Makaro; Scott Andersen; Tony Pantages; Beatrice Boepple; Kyle Wodia; Jan Speck.

If there's a knack to finding good scripts it's about being patient. If you are patient enough to read, eventually you'll find something you like enough to give your passion to. If you do a movie you don't have passion for it probably won't turn out very well. *Stakeout* is a movie that I felt had a wonderful love story, a very funny relationship between two men that was quite amusing, and a kind of wry, realistic look at something that maybe we thought was kind of romantic, being on a stakeout, which is probably one of the dullest, most horrible things that you could ever be subjected to. I've never had any policeman ever have kind words for a stakeout. You're cramped in awful places. You can't eat and you can't go to the bathroom. You're in a car, if you're lucky. But sometimes you're stuffed in a locker or in some awful hallway that's just nasty smelling for days, sometimes weeks.

Jim Kouf is a writer who managed to find humor in this.

Richard Dreyfuss was our first choice for the character of Chris Lecce.

I've always gotten along beautifully with Dreyfuss. I so respect his talent and his intelligence and we get along extremely well. He has very bright things to say about the material. I believe that when you have talented actors you should take every idea they have and try to use it when it makes sense for the movie.

Emilio Estevez's character was actually supposed to be a much older man. Every actor we thought of that would be good Disney said no to. They kept saying we needed a bigger star. We finally realized there probably was no such person who would do it. But if we went for a younger actor we could probably find a lot of actors that Disney would think were stars that would also be good. So Emilio Estevez became this other character, Bill Reimers. Thank goodness Emilio was a writer. He worked with Jim Kouf and rewrote the part to suit his age and his relationship with Richard.

I got to see some dailies on Madeleine Stowe that were from a South American film. She had a truly magical quality. She had a great beauty to her and a kind of devilish quality in her eyes. She is a very good actress with a lovely, intriguing quality. Dreyfuss asked if he could consult with us on this role because he wanted to make sure we had somebody that he liked and could work with. He also thought that this woman was terrific and he was right. She was just really a magical choice. I think it's nice to be able to present a new person to the audience. If they come because of someone they know, that's great. When they get there if they discover somebody new, it's wonderful. They audience thinks at that point they have discovered Madeleine Stowe.

I remember we had Richard Dreyfuss and Madeleine Stowe in bed doing love scenes. After we had worked for about half a day Richard Dreyfuss said, "You know those interviews where actors say that doing love scenes are very hard work and it may look glamorous on film, but there is nothing magical about it? That's what I always hear actors saying. Let me say that I just got to do my first love scene and I want to tell you that they are all liars. It's great! Let's do some more of this!"

Point of No Return (1993)

Bridget Fonda; Gabriel Byrne; Dermot Mulroney; Miguel Ferrer; Anne Bancroft; Olivia d'Abo; Richard Romanus; Harvey Keitel; Lorraine Toussaint; Geoffrey Lewis; Mic Rodgers; Michael Rapaport; Ray Oriel; Spike McClure; Lieux Dressler.

I saw Luc Besson's film in Los Angeles one day, and my first response to it was that it was a very exciting and a different, dark look at the world. I realized also that because it was in French and I was seeing it subtitled that it probably would not be seen very much in the United States. In the United States, sad to say, people will not go to see movies in another language. Some people will go to see French films or Spanish films, but basically, most of the movie public won't, and they miss some wonderful movies because they refuse to sit through subtitles. I thought that it would be nice to see if we could make an English-language version of it. But I thought, if I'm seeing this in the movie theater somebody else might get the same idea. Sure enough, Warner Bros. had already gone to Besson and he agreed to make an English version of it. About the time I went to them, Besson said, "You know, I already made this movie and I don't think I want to do it a second time." So they were ready to listen to me.

Bridget Fonda is the first person to tell you that she hates to exercise. She hates physical activity. She came to me and said, "I don't like to do any of this but I know I need to do it for this character so you're going to have to work with me." I got her together with our stunt people and a very good stuntwoman who exercised with her on a daily basis and taught her how to do high kicks and how to fight and how to fire guns. She overcame her natural resistance to physical activity for the part. You'll find actors do this a lot. They are some of the best students in the world. Do not ever get into an argument with Bridget Fonda because she can shoot you right between the eyes. She's really quite good.

Another Stakeout (1993)

Richard Dreyfuss; Emilio Estevez; Rosie O'Donnell; Dennis Farina;
Marcia Strassman; Cathy Moriarty; John Rubinstein; Miguel Ferrer;
Sharon Mughan; Christopher Doyle; Sharon Schaffer; Rick Seaman;
Jan Speck; Gene Ellison; Frank DeAngelo.

I'm basically opposed to doing sequels, but I liked the characters in *Stakeout* so much and I found the script so funny that I couldn't resist it. The thought of being able to work with Richard and Emilio again and to go back to one of my favorite cities in the world, Vancouver, was irresistible. I could not say no to this. We had a great time because we also added Rosie O'Donnell, who is a very funny woman. With Rosie O'Donnell and Richard Dreyfuss together you don't need any entertainment. You don't need movies. You don't need to go out to dinner. You just sit and watch them. They will keep you entertained for days at a time.

Drop Zone (1994)

Wesley Snipes; Gary Busey; Yancy Butler; Michael Jeter; Corin Nemec;
Kyle Secor; Luca Bercovici; Malcolm-Jamal Warner; Grace Zabriskie; Rex Linn;
Robert LaSardo; Sam Hennings; Claire Stansfield; Mickey Jones; Andy Romano.

Drop Zone is a really fascinating movie about skydiving. It was conceived by skydivers who had always wanted to have a movie made about their sport. All of the stunts in the film were actually thought up by the skydivers. I said to them, "I don't know if this can be done." They said, "Oh, absolutely, it can be done and we know exactly how to do it. We know how to throw a guy out of a plane with no parachute, have another guy go after him, put a parachute on him and land safely on the ground." It was just mind-boggling.

Their whole goal in skydiving is to see how much activity they can pack into the sixty seconds between the time they jump out of the plane and the time they have to open their parachute. I mean, they only have sixty seconds! At first they learn how to do simple flying and simple little tricks. Then they just say, "Well, let's do something else. Let's see if we can take all our clothes off. Let's see if we can make love up in the air. Let's see if we can change parachutes!" If you can think of anything nutty, I'll find a skydiver for you who will try it.

We're trying to photograph all of this with cameramen who are wearing 35 mm cameras on their helmets. They not only have a 35 mm camera, but they also have a video camera on this side of their helmet and a Nikon still camera on this side because they are doing a coffee-table book at the same time. All of the shots are quite magical. There were two cameramen up in the air for most of the sequences. Thank goodness we didn't have any disasters. Nobody broke anything. But I was terrified every day that I was going to get a phone call that something awful had happened, because it was so dangerous.

Skydiving into Miami at night is one of the most difficult things I think I have ever seen them try. They skydived between the buildings, just like we were doing with the helicopters in *Blue Thunder,* only the sky divers only had their parachutes to maneuver with, no motor power.

I think what's interesting in that picture, as death-defying and frightening as skydiving is, is that every actor in the movie wanted to do it. I would have to say to them, "No, you cannot skydive, because if anything happens to you we will be in terrible trouble. Even if you just twist your ankle, we could be out of business. We will just have to do it with doubles." Then I go to see the dailies from the second unit and I started seeing my actors showing up in the scenes. I see the real Michael Jeter jumping out of the plane. He had sneaked out with the second unit, got on the plane, and parachuted out himself. So, much to my surprise, we have the actual actors in a lot of the shots. The studio had a heart attack when they saw the footage. They said, "You can't do this!" I said, "I know that, but I'm shooting the first unit. The second unit is out there and I don't know what they are doing."

I think *Drop Zone* is a very exciting movie and the visuals of the skydiving are quite special. I don't think anybody has ever really achieved on film what we were able to achieve. The movie worked very well for audiences. I mean, they were really quite taken with the visuals.

Nick of Time (1995)

Johnny Depp; Courtney Chase; Charles Dutton; Christopher Walken; Roma Maffia; Marsha Mason; Peter Strauss; Gloria Reuben; Bill Smitrovich; G.D. Spradlin; Yul Vazquez; Edith Diaz; Armando Ortega; C.J. Bau; Cynthena Sanders.

Nick of Time was sort of a thriller like Hitchcock would make thrillers, only instead of having Jimmy Stewart or Cary Grant, we've got Johnny Depp. Johnny Depp is really a very special actor. He has so much honesty in his acting. He is able to make you believe almost anything. He does it with such conviction.

The movie is about a young man visiting Los Angeles and he has his little daughter with him. He's told that he somehow has to murder the governor of California in the next ninety minutes or his daughter will be killed. We follow him through the course of this movie as he tries to get out of it and to save his daughter. But at every turn he's confounded by how clever this plot is and how devious these men are willing to be in order to achieve their goal of assassinating the governor. It's a wonderful thriller. I think that if Mr. Hitchcock were still with us he would be dying to make it. Christopher Walken is in it along with Marsha Mason and Peter Strauss and Charles Dutton. It's an excellent cast, which speaks to the excellence of the material.

EDITOR'S NOTE: This interview took place during the filming of *Nick of Time*.

How He Chooses and Prepares His Scripts

When I read scripts I'm looking for something that entertains me. I have to be interested in it, excited about it, and challenged by it in some way. If that doesn't happen, it's not something I will do a very good job with. Sometimes I will read a script and think it's very entertaining and interesting but I don't want to do this because I don't want to shoot in the Arctic or I don't want to be in the desert. I think I'm at a point where I will avoid going to places or doing things that are going to wind up being painful. But other than that, my real goal is to find characters that I like and characters in an intriguing situation.

It's very hard to see what goes on inside a director's head. Often it seems that the director isn't doing anything to prepare for a movie. And yet, hopefully, inside their head, they're turning things around. You're looking at the movie from different aspects. What's the tone of the move? Whose point of view is driving the story? What's the most exciting way to tell the story? A lot of these ideas may develop over a period of months as you continue to think about it or when you're preparing with your crew. During this period you're doing very concrete things. You're picking a cameraman; you're picking a location, wardrobe, and actors. All those decisions have to be based on what's going on inside your head. Sometimes you're not really ready to make those choices, but you have to. You just hope you're making the right choices.

There are movies of mine that people liked a lot and that's always gratifying. But often there are moments that only I appreciated that are very quiet and private to me. Things that I think worked very well. When I see a first cut of a movie, and it works very well, that's always very satisfying to me. I don't get particularly excited if it does great business or depressed if it does bad business. If I know that it satisfied me and it played well to the audience, that's what's important to me. I'm doing it for the audience to enjoy it and for me to enjoy it.

The Studios of Today

The major studios have become much more like independent filmmakers used to be in the sense that they don't control the making of the movie as much. People now bring them packages. I will come to them with a star and a script and say, "Would you like to make this movie?" They will put up the money. In olden days, they would be developing all the scripts and have the stars under contract as well as the directors. Now you will find that none of that goes on. They will do a little bit of development. Warner Bros.

may have Clint Eastwood or Dick Donner under a long-term arrangement, but that's it. But other than that, they treat everything very independently.

It was always difficult to break into doing movies or television or directing. I've always believed that talent will find its way somehow. It's not organized like becoming a doctor or lawyer. If you graduate from law school and you have done a good job, the law firms are trying to get you to come to them. If you graduate from a film school and you've done a good job, it's much harder. People may not pay any attention to you. You're out there on your own, like a businessman trying to get his business started. You're trying to get your film off the ground, trying to get someone to give you some money. It's a very expensive business. It requires a lot of hard work and I think there's a lot of survival of the fittest that goes on here.

I think the people who are willing to work the hardest and fight against all of the difficulties, the people who just keep coming back for more, are the ones that come through. It's not necessarily the people who have the best talent. Sometimes it's just the people who are most persistent that break through. Often people with the most talent may give up and go home. When you have someone like Jim Cameron who has great talent and great persistence at the same time, who made the first *Terminator* for twenty-five cents and it looks terrific, you're talking about somebody who's going to have major importance in the movie business.

When I was first getting started I received a great deal of encouragement from directors who were doing television and movies, directors like Michael Ritchie and Lamont Johnson. They're the kinds of directors who are willing to answer questions and listen to you and put up with whatever notions you have about how to direct movies.

I would like to be able to tell you that the movie I'm going to make next has a story and the script. But I always feel faintly embarrassed when people ask what I'm going to do next and I don't really know. I always feel like maybe I won't get a job and nobody will ever hire me again and that will be the end of me. What I'm doing next is completing *Nick of Time*. I have a lot of work to do on it. We're four weeks into shooting. We have about seven weeks to go. I'll spend the next six months doing all the editing and scoring and finally getting it set. And maybe by then I will have bamboozled somebody into letting me do some other piece of material.

EDITOR'S NOTE: After this interview was completed Badham directed the HBO feature *The Jack Bull* with John Cusack.

Filmography

The Bingo Long Traveling All-Stars & Motor Kings (1976)
Saturday Night Fever (1977)
Dracula (1979)
Whose Life Is It Anyway? (1981)
Blue Thunder (1983)
WarGames (1983)
American Flyers (1985)
Short Circuit (1986)
Stakeout (1987)
Bird on a Wire (1990)
The Hard Way (1991)
Point of No Return (1993)
Another Stakeout (1993)
Drop Zone (1994)
Nick of Time (1995)
Incognito (1997)
Floating Away (1998)
The Jack Bull (TV, 1999)

Index

368

Index

About the Author

President and CEO of Media Entertainment Inc., **Robert J. Emery** has been a writer-producer-director for thirty-five years. He has written and produced a wide variety of screenplays and television shows, has taught film production, and has been the recipient of over seventy industry awards for his work. Mr. Emery is a member of the Directors Guild of America.